ISBN: 9781314756852

Published by:
HardPress Publishing
8345 NW 66TH ST #2561
MIAMI FL 33166-2626

Email: info@hardpress.net
Web: http://www.hardpress.net

REPORT

OF THE

CITY COUNCIL

COMMITTEE ON CRIME

OF THE

CITY OF CHICAGO

ALDERMAN CHARLES E. MERRIAM, *Chairman*

MARCH 22, 1915

PRESS OF H. G. ADAIR
107-111 N. MARKET ST.
CHICAGO, ILLINOIS
20

Members of Committee

ALD. CHARLES E. MERRIAM, Chairman

ALD. THEODORE K. LONG   ALD. S. S. WALKOWIAK

ALD. THOMAS D. NASH

ALD. OTTO KERNER, Secretary

Table of Contents

i

Table of Contents—Continued

Table of Contents—Continued

List of Tables

Statistics of Crime in Chicago

List of Tables—Continued

Introduction
and
Summary

INTRODUCTION

The Council Committee on Crime was created by resolution of the City Council, introduced by Alderman Charles E. Merriam, May 18, 1914. The resolution was as follows:

"Ordered that the Mayor be and is hereby authorized and directed to appoint a committee of five aldermen for the purpose of investigating and reporting to this Council upon the frequency of murder, assault, burglary, robbery, theft and like crimes in Chicago; upon the official disposition of such cases; upon the causes of the prevalence of such crimes; and upon the best practical methods of preventing these crimes."

In accordance with the terms of the foregoing order the following committee was appointed:

Alderman Merriam,
Alderman Nash,
Alderman Long,
Alderman Walkowiak,
Alderman Kerner.

Alderman Merriam was chosen as Chairman of the Committee and Alderman Kerner was made the Secretary.

Morgan L. Davies was made the Attorney for the Commission, and was assisted in the investigation by Mr. James McKeag. Mr. Fletcher Dobyns acted as Associate Counsel and was in personal charge of the work regarding pickpockets, fences, gambling and police inefficiency. The statistical work of the Commission was conducted by Miss Edith Abbott of the Chicago School of Civics and Philanthrophy. The criminological side of the inquiry was carried on by Robert H. Gault, Professor of Psychology at Northwestern University and editor of the Journal of Criminal Law and Criminology. He was assisted in this work by Dr. H. C. Stevens, of the Psychopathic Laboratory of the University of Chicago.

Detailed reports were presented to the Committee by the experts employed and hearings were held at which the subjects discussed in these reports were considered. At the sessions of the Committee extended testimony was given by judges, members of the police force, experts on charitable and correctional work, police work and others.

This report embodies the reports made to the Commission by experts in charge of special investigations, the findings of the Commission, and the recommendations for action, based upon the investigation. The general outline of the report is as follows:

I. Summary of findings of the Commission.

II. Summary of the recommendations of the Commission.

III. Report of Miss Edith Abbott, on criminal statistics.

IV. Report of Professor Robert H. Gault on the underlying causes of crime, and the practical methods of preventing crime.

V. Report of Messrs. Davies and Dobyns, giving a description and anaylsis of criminal conditions.

SUMMARY OF FINDINGS

The treatment of crime in Chicago is wholly inadequate in that:

1. Many professional criminals escape the penalties of the law and prey at will upon society.

2. Poor and petty criminals are often punished more heavily than is just.

3. The treatment of those sentenced to penal institutions is pitifully ineffective.

4. Practical methods of preventing crime are not applied as extensively as experience warrants and demands.

The technique of man-hunting, the process of prosecuting, the care of the "caged man," and the means of preventing the creation of criminals are far below standards already in practical operation elsewhere.

I.

1. The police and criminal judicial statistics in Chicago are wholly incomplete and are not even assembled or published by any authority.

2. The list of "criminal complaints," complaints of crimes to the police, has not been open to the public, but regarded as a private police affair. (Publicity has recently been given to certain of these complaints as a result of the work of this Committee.)

3. The amount of crime in Chicago is rapidly increasing. Total number of arrests:

1905	82,472
1909	70,375
1913	109,764

The total number of criminal complaints (felonies) in

1905	11,732
1909	10,697
1913	14,340

Arrests or arraignments for murder, burglary and robbery:

	Murder	Robbery	Burglary
Chicago, 1913	262	1,022	1,041
New York, 1913	131	928	1,755
London, 1913	36	78	1,129

4. There were in 1913, 14,340 criminal complaints, as follows: (From police classification.)

Robbery	1,389
Larceny	5,375
Burglary	6,534
Other	1,042

5. Fifty-seven and seven-tenths per cent of the men arrested and 61.5% of all women arrested are under thirty years of age.

6. Of those arrested 64.7% are native Americans, and 35.3 % foreign born, the relative percentage of population being 53.2% and 46.8%. (Population over 15 years of age taken as basis.)

7. Thousands of innocent persons are annually imprisoned in the County Jail, many of them under disgraceful conditions, tending to create criminals.

8. The present machinery catches poor, petty and occasional criminals, and punishes them severely, but fails signally to suppress the professional criminal.

9. There were in 1913, 109,764 arrests and 58,532 persons discharged, on first hearing. Of 121,333 cases disposed of in the Municipal Court, 57.5% were discharged.

10. Of 7,342 felony "cases," in 1913, there were 932 convictions, 773 given a term, of which 208 were penitentiary or reformatory sentences.

11. Of the 14,709 persons sentenced to the House of Correction, 5,214 or 35.4% admitted having served a previous term, 1,545 or 10.5% five terms, 453 or 3.1% ten terms, 18 fifty terms, six 101 terms or over, and one 301 terms.

12. Nine-tenths of those arrested in Chicago are men.

13. Over 80% of those committed to the Bridewell are sent for non-payment of fines. Thirty-five per cent are sent for the non-payment of fines of less than $15, and 19% for fines of $15 to $20—a total of 56% for fines of less than $20.

II.

1. There are in Chicago a large number of "hang-outs" which are the meeting places of well-known professional criminals. The Committee found 100 of these, most of which were saloons and pool rooms, without exhausting the list of them. In a number of instances these hang-outs are conducted by men with criminal records.

2. There were in Chicago at the time of the investigation a large number of professional criminals, of whom the Committee has located about five hundred. This list includes pickpockets, burglars, holdup men, confidence men, gamblers, pimps, safe-blowers, shoplifters, and all around crooks. Most of the burglary, robbery and larceny is committed by them.

3. Professional criminals have built up a system which may be called a "crime trust," with roots running through the police force, the bar, the bondsmen, the prosecutor's office, and political officials.

4. We find the business of theft in Chicago highly organized. There is a large number of "fences" where stolen goods may be readily sold. Of these, the Committee has located thirty-nine. The burglars' trust has its wholesalers, its jobbers, and its retailers, its interurban and interstate branches. Six thousand five hundred and thirty-four burglaries were reported for 1913, and five thousand three hundred and seventy-five cases of larceny. The value of property stolen reaches millions of dollars. The greater part of the stealing in Chicago is done by organized thieves.

5. We find collusion between members of the detective force and professional criminals. Graft, favoritism, and political influence tend strongly toward a demoralization of the police force, and particularly the detective branch of the service.

6. We find a close connection between alcoholism, "dope," prostitution, gambling, and crime.

7. Certain professional bondsmen not only supply a bond, but serve as general "fixers."

8. There is a group of criminal lawyers whose work includes dealing with the police, furnishing professional alibis and professional witnesses, jury fixing, spiriting away of witnesses, exhaustive continuances, and all the underground activtity of all around "fixers".

9. Appointments in the office of City Prosecutor and State's Attorney are made on a political basis; hence the permanent employment of expert prosecutors is made impossible.

III.

Police organization and methods are wholly inadequate to deal with the crime situation in Chicago, assuming the integrity of all members of the force. Incompetence, lack of discipline, and aggressiveness are noticeable on a large scale. These may be summed up under the following heads:

    a. Lack of adequate publicity regarding police statistics.
    b. Lack of follow-up system for criminal complaints.
    c. Lack of effective supervision of patrolmen.
    d. Lack of effective direction of detective work.
    e. Lack of discipline and aggressiveness.

1. Failure of patrolmen to cover night beats seriously cripples the protection of persons and property.

2. Detective sergeants are not required to make adequate and detailed reports of their work.

3. The first need of the force is the more effective use of those now available rather than an increase of the force.

4. Sanitary conditions in many of the police stations are intolerable.

5. No adequate provision is made for the defense of poor persons, charged with crime, and as a result, serious injustice is often done.

6. No provision is made for official interpreters, and consequently, the guilty sometimes escape and the innocent are punished because of ignorance of the language.

IV.

1. Many criminals suffer from serious physical and mental disorders, and require hospital treatment rather than ordinary imprisonment.

2. Examination of Juvenile delinquents at John Worthy School shows many suffer from profound disorders of the nervous system, and cannot be reclaimed under methods now in vogue. 41% of the boys examined were mentally retarded, and many others suffer from grave physical defects.

3. Study of delinquents in Juvenile Court shows that cause of delinquency, in many "normal" cases, was environmental; 47% of this group "making good." Of "subnormal" cases under present methods, relatively few are reclaimed.

4. No adequate provision is made for assistance of boys from St. Charles School. Hence many boys are re-arrested and brought back.

5. St. Charles School, with one thousand boys on parole, one-half from Chicago, has one parole officer to care for them.

6. The Psychopathic Laboratory renders indispensible service in diagnosing cases and indicating treatment of defective delinquents.

7. Many insane persons are committed to and serve sentences in the House of Correction. 132 such cases were discovered between January 1, 1914, and August 20, 1914.

8. Of 126 women examined in the House of Correction there were found:

Number.	Mental Age.
1	between 5 and 6 years
1	between 6 and 7 years
5	between 7 and 8 years
8	between 8 and 9 years
32	between 9 and 10 years
29	between 10 and 11 years
36	between 11 and 12 years
12	between 12 and 13 years
2	between 13 and 14 years

9. The working of the adult probation law is seriously hindered by the legal limitation of the number of probation officers to 20, who have charge of about 5,000 cases arising annually. The inevitable result is failure to investigate thoroughly and to provide proper supervision for those paroled. With adequate facilities for supervision, the work of this office would be of immense value in preventing first offenders from becoming professional criminals.

10. Of 700 boys sent to the Boys' Court and examined in the Psychopathic Laboratory during the first six weeks, 84% were found mentally deficient. No adequate provision is made for the care of such cases.

11. Adequate facilities for vocational guidance and training would prevent much delinquency, and vocational guidance with employment would reclaim much more.

12. Professional criminals are recruited from the ranks of the delinquent boy, but no adequate means of treatment for such boys is available.

13. The chief causes of crime are:

(a) The defective physical and mental (psychological) condition of the individual, as nervous disorders, infection, psychosis, and feeble-mindedness.

(b) Defective environment: the home, the school, regularity of employment, and poverty.

14. The pressure of economic conditions has an enormous influence in producing certain types of crime. Unsanitary housing and working conditions, unemployment, wages inadequate to maintain a human standard of living, inevitably produce the crushed or distorted bodies and minds from which the army of crime is recruited. The crime problem is not merely a question of police and courts, it leads to the broader problems of public sanitation, education, home care, a living wage, and industrial democracy.

SUMMARY OF RECOMMENDATIONS

I.

1. That the licenses of known criminal "hangouts" be revoked and that they should not be restored either to the same person or the same place.

2. That professional criminals be arrested and convicted under the state vagrancy law in accordance with the plan submitted by this Committee.

3. That the record of all applicants for saloon and pool room licenses in precincts where the crime rate is unusually high be scrutinized with extreme care in order to prevent the issuance of a license to a person with a criminal record. On the petition of six citizens it should be the duty of the Second Deputy Superintendent of Police to make an investigation and report.

4. That lists of criminal complaints, including robbery, burglary and larceny, be reported monthly to the City Council, classified according to the character of the complaint and the police precinct; that the total number of all criminal complaints be likewise reported, and that these facts be published in pamphlet form; and that the disposition of cases be likewise reported monthly and published.

5. That the General Superintendent of Police, the Civil Service Commission and the State's Attorney co-operate in a persistent and systematic effort to eliminate collusion between police officials and criminals.

6. That the Civil Service Commission report to the City Council at once and thereafter annually a list of police officers discharged and reinstated, with the cause of discharge and the reason for reinstatement.

7. That a systematic method be made to locate "fences," in the manner employed by the Committee, or other adequate method.

8. That an efficiency system for police officials be installed to the end that promotions may be made on the basis of definite ascertained merit.

9. That present police methods be thoroughly overhauled and improved types be adopted and installed under expert supervision, with especial attention to records and filing systems, detective work, training and supervision of officers and the best type of patrol system.

10. That crime maps be prepared by the police department showing the various classes of crime by precincts and kept up in such a way that any increase in crime may be immediately indicated and that prompt investigation may be made and action taken.

11. That adequate daily reports of work be made by detective sergeants in the manner outlined before this Committee.

12. That measures be taken to prevent "friendly pulls" by local operators either by providing that patrolmen's pulls be made directly to a central bureau or by other adequate means.

13. That the vice reports made to the General Superintendent by the Second Deputy's office be made public monthly, as a check on the local commanding officers.

14. That police officers be given instruction in the nature and value of evidence, and that evidence be reviewed by the commanding officer before presentation.

15. That captains should make written reports to the chief in all cases where warrants are refused by the court.

16. That the Municipal Court and the Criminal Court investigate the activities of professional bondsmen with special reference to:

1. The number of times any person appears on bonds within a period of six months.
2. The character of the charge and the record of the defendant.
3. The amount of bond already given by the bondsman.
4. The political connections, if any, of the bondsman; and that lists of bondsmen appearing more than once during a six-month period be published every six months.

17. That the Bar Association of Chicago investigate the disreputable practices of certain criminal lawyers and secure their disbarment, if possible.

18. That the State's Attorney endeavor to secure the evidence of and conviction for conspiracy to obstruct the administration of justice on the part of certain attorneys and certain groups of pickpockets and other criminals.

19. That the State's Attorney and the Municipal Court co-operate more closely in dealing with cases held to the Grand Jury after preliminary hearing in the Municipal Court.

20. That a joint commission be appointed by the Chief Justice of the Municipal Court and the presiding judge of the Criminal Court for the purpose of studying the criminal practice and procedure in the courts of Chicago and recommending necessary changes in methods or in law for the better administration of justice; that such an inquiry should include among other things the study of:

1. An improved system of criminal statistics.
2. Actual methods and practices in police courts.
3. Actual methods and practices in Criminal Courts.
4. Methods in office of City Prosecutor and State's Attorney.
5. Necessary changes in criminal law and procedure and drafts of the same.
6. Operation of the parole and probation systems.
7. Creation of a consolidated court of Chicago.
8. Improved methods of electing judges.

21. That the bond issue of $1,199,000 for the construction of additional police stations be ratified in the interest of the health and well-being of the police force and of those detained in the stations.

22. That the state law be amended to provide that the minor positions in the State's Attorney's office be placed under the merit system.

23. That a central bureau of official interpreters be established for use in stations where there is greatest need for such an agency.

24. That provision be made for a police attorney not active in any political party or faction, and that he should not engage in outside practice.

25. That the general fining system be so modified either by legislation or court rule as to provide for:

1. Payment of fines on the installment plan.
2. Committment to an appropriate institution in place of fine where where such committment is necessary.

26. That payment be made out of earnings of prisoners to their families.

27. That the state law be so amended as to change the fining system for prostitutes to a sentence of committment to an appropriate institution.

II.

1. That a farm colony be established by the city in connection with the work of the House of Correction; and that necessary funds for that purpose be voted.

2. That the facilities of the Psychopathic Laboratory be increased.

3. That a House of Shelter be constructed in connection with the present Bridewell, to be located outside the city; and that necessary funds for that purpose be voted.

4. That the present inadequate County Jail be replaced by an institution corresponding to modern ideas of the humane treatment of criminals.

5. That the office of Public Defender be established in connection with the Criminal Court of Cook County as a means of securing justice to those unable to secure adequate counsel.

6. That a physician be employed permanently at the House of Correction to carry on medical work of the character performed for this Committee by Dr. Stevens.

7. That prisoners who are addicted to the drug habit and now sent to the House of Correction be segregated in farm colonies or treated in hospitals until cured.

8. That an amendment to Chapter 85, Section 32, of the Illinois Revised Statutes (1913) be enacted so that the medical staff at the House of Correction would have the same authority as the state penitentiary physicians now have in regard to committing insane persons to an insane asylum.

9. That a farm colony be established by the state for the care of insane prisoners.

10. That the following criteria of fitness be employed in selecting subjects for adult probation:

(1) Habits of industry; (2) abstention from alcohol and drugs, or at least habitual temperance; (3) mental normality; (4) physical health of a sufficient degree to enable the probationer to engage successfully in his occupation; (a) negative Wasserman reaction and other evidence of freedom from all dangerous infections; (5) proof of employment which can be undertaken at once at a living wage; (6) possession of friends of good character who will co-operate with the officer in keeping in touch with the probationer; (7) proof of first offense, unless on the other points the offender has exceptionally strong recommendations; and that a psychopathic and medical laboratory be employed to assist the court in making the selection of probationers.

11. That those denied probation because of physical and mental defects be given institutional care until cured.

12. That the state law limiting the number of probation officers to 20 be so amended as to remove this limit; and that a preliminary investigation be made by the probation officer of each applicant for probation, and that probation officers be selected on a civil service basis.

13. That the state authorities take steps to provide suitable institutions for the segregation of feeble-minded children in addition to that at Lincoln.

14. That a new institution on the farm colony plan, which will provide a permanent home and suitable industrial training and occupation for feeble-minded persons of all ages, be established; that the present state law be so amended as to remove the age limit for admission to institutions for the feeble-minded; and that it be further amended so as to provide for the committment

of defective delinquents both to the Lincoln State School and Colony and to the proposed new institution.

15. That farm colonies and hospitals recommended in this report relating to the treatment of mentally alienated and otherwise abnormal adult prisoners, be supplemented by places of detention for repeated juvenile delinquents. Such places of detention should be farm colonies, maintained by the State of Illinois.

16. That the Juvenile Court made definite provision for following up and assisting Chicago boys subsequent to their parole from St. Charles; and to this end that the number of parole officers be increased.

17. That the Board of Education enlarge its facilities (a) for vocational education; and (b) for vocational guidance; and that the system of part time and night schools in the city be extended, and that juvenile probationers be required to attend such school during the period of probation.

18. That further investigation be made of (a) the 1,200 or more prisoners in the House of Correction who have been committed to such an institution either in this city or elsewhere, more than three times; (b) the history of 500 or more Chicago boys during the period subsequent to the date of their parole from St. Charles; and (c) the history of Chicago men and women during the period subsequent to the date of their parole from the penal institutions of the state.

Statistics Relating to Crime in Chicago

by

MISS EDITH ABBOTT, Ph. D., CHICAGO SCHOOL OF CIVICS
AND PHILANTHROPY

Part I
ARREST AND TRIAL OF OFFENDERS

In the following report an attempt is made to bring together from various sources the available statistics,* published or unpublished, relating to the subject of crime in Chicago, that is, statistics of complaints and arrests, trial and disposition, together with the statistics relating to the social status—age, sex, nationality and occupation—of the persons arrested. Unfortunately, there is in Illinois no central bureau of criminal statistics through which statistics from the police department, the courts, the jails, prisons, and the probation department are collected and correlated. A state bureau of criminal statistics does exist on our statute books, for, by a law approved June 11, 1912, the State Charities Commission was directed to establish such a bureau with the secretary of the Commission as director in charge. This proposed bureau was charged with the duty of collecting and publishing annually the statistics of Illinois relating to crime, and all courts of Illinois, police magistrates, justices of the peace, clerks of all courts of record, sheriffs, keepers of all places of detention for crime or misdemeanors or violations of the criminal statutes are to "furnish said bureau annually such information on request as it may require in compiling such statistics." Up to the present time, however, owing chiefly to the fact that no appropriation has been made to cover the expenses of this work, no steps have been taken by the executive secretary of the Commission towards putting this law into effect. Moreover, there has never been in Chicago any attempt at an annual "stock-taking' in which the statistics furnished by the various departments and agencies dealing with the problem of crime might be brought together and examined with the hope of determining how far the problem is being adequately met.

In the following report, statistics of criminal complaints and arrests that are furnished by the police department will be first dealt with, since questions relating to the extent or quantity of crime and the number of persons apprehended are usually first raised in any discussion of the subject.

Following this, there will be presented statistics from the courts relating to the disposition of offenders who have been arrested, statistics from the Adult Probation Office, and, finally, statistics relating to the "social status" of those arrested.

Sec. 1. Extent of Crime: Criminal Complaints and Arrests on Felony Charges.

The amount of crime in any community is a subject about which definite information is anxiously sought. Since, however, much crime is undetected, it is not to be expected that statistics should furnish exact information on this point. There should be available, however, statistics showing the number of crimes known to the authorities. In Chicago the number of serious crimes is probably best indicated by the number of "criminal complaints" received by the police. Criminal complaints for the years 1905 to 1910, inclusive, were published in the **Annual Report of the General Superintendent of Police for the year ending December 31, 1910.** Since 1910, no statistics of criminal complaints have been published, but unpublished statistics for the

---

*There were available at the time this report was prepared (autumn of 1914) the following published reports containing statistics relating to crime in Chicago.

1. Annual Report of the Police Department, City of Chicago. (Last published report, for the year ending December 31, 1913.)

2. Annual Report of the Municipal Court of Chicago. (Last published report, for the year ending November 30, 1913.)

3. Annual Report of the Adult Probation Office, Cook County. (Last published report, for the year ending September 30, 1913.)

4. Annual Report of the Superintendent of the House of Correction, City of Chicago. (Last published report, for the year ending December 31, 1910.)

5. There were also available the Report of the Commissioners of the Illinois State Penitentiary at Joliet, and the Biennial Report of the Board of Managers of the Illinois State Reformatory at Pontiac. These reports, however, give statistics only for Illinois and not for Chicago or for Cook County.

years 1910 to 1913 were furnished by the police department. These statistics of criminal complaints should, of course, be published each year; they are the only statistics that correspond to the statistics of "Crimes Known to the Police" that are, for example, published each year as part of the English Criminal Judicial Statistics.*

The following table shows the number of criminal complaints in Chicago for a series of years together with the number of arrests on felony charges:

TABLE 1.   CRIMINAL COMPLAINTS AND ARRESTS (FELONY CHARGES): 1905-1913.**

Date.	Criminal Complaints. Number.	Increase or Decrease.	Arrests (Felony Charges). Number.	Increase or Decrease.	Per Cent Increase or Decrease. Complaints.	Arrests.
1905	11,732		12,144			
1906	10,754	— 978	12,376	+ 232	— 8.3	+ 1.9
1907	11,292	+ 538	10,653	—1,723	+ 5.0	—13.9
1908	11,034	— 258	10,551	— 102	— 2.3	— .9
1909	10,697	— 337	9,656	— 895	— 3.1	— 8.5
1910	10,718	+ 21	9,376	— 280	+ .2	— 2.9
1911	11,730	+1,012	9,881	+ 505	+ 9.4	+ 5.4
1912	13,032	+1,302	10,276	+ 395	+11.1	+ 3.9
1913	14,340	+1,308	11,203	+ 927	+10.0	+ 9.0

This table shows that the number of complaints has fluctuated, decreasing in 1906, increasing in 1907, decreasing again in 1908 and 1909, remaining almost stationary in 1910, and increasing noticeably in the last three years. The number of arrests in 1913 represented an increase of 927, or 9 per cent, over 1912, a larger increase than has occurred in any other year during the period. It is interesting to note that there does not seem to be any consistent relation between the number of complaints and the number of arrests. In the year 1906, for example, the number of complaints **decreased** by nearly a thousand and the arrests during the same year **increased** by 232. In the following year the complaints increased by more than five hundred and the arrests decreased by more than seventeen hundred. Both complaints and arrests have increased in the last three years, although until 1913 the percentage increase was considerably greater for complaints than for arrests.

Sec. 2.   Increase and Decrease in Number of Arrests, 1900-1913.

Not only the arrests for felonies but the arrests on all charges should be examined. Moreover, while the number of arrests in any one year is significant, it is also important to note the changes in the number of arrests from year to year. The next table shows the number of arrests on felony and misdemeanor charges from 1900 to 1913 and the increase or decrease each year:

TABLE 2.   TOTAL NUMBER OF ARRESTS (FELONIES AND MISDEMEANORS): 1900-1913.

(From Annual Reports of the Police Department.)

Year.	Felonies.	Misdemeanors.	Total.	Increase or Decrease in Total Number.	Per Cent.
1900	10,838	58,251	69,089		
1901	11,383	56,641	68,024	— 1,065	— 1.5
1902	10,495	58,363	68,858	+ 834	+ 1.2
1903	12,550	65,123	77,673	+ 8,815	+12.8
1904	11,116	67,890	79,006	+ 1,323	+ 1.7
1905	12,144	70,328	82,472	+ 3,466	+ 4.4
1906	12,376	79,177	91,553	+ 9,081	+11.0
1907	10,653	52,479	63,132	—28,421	—31.0

Statistics for arrests are from the published annual report of the General Superintendent of Police. It should be explained that the number of arrests simply means the number of charges. That is, one person may be charged with several different offenses, e. g., burglary, assault, receiving stolen property, etc. In 1913 there were 109,764 offenses charged against 107,257 persons arraigned in the Municipal Court. (See **Annual Report of the Department of Police, 1913, pp. 11 and 8.)

*For a discussion of the value of these statistics of criminal complaints and their lack of availability for comparative purposes, see Appendix C.

Year.	Felonies.	Misdemeanors.	Total.	Increase or Decrease in Total Number.	Per Cent.
1908	10,551	57,669	68,220	+ 5,088	+ 8.1
1909	9,656	60,719	70,375	+ 2,155	+ 3.2
1910	·9,376	71,893	81,269	+10,894	+15.5
1911	9,881	74,959	84,840	+ 3,571	+ 4.4
1912	10,276	76,674	86,950	+ 2,110	+ 2.4
1913	11,203	98,561	109,764	+22,814	+26.2

This table shows a very uneven series of increases and decreases, chiefly increases, in the total number of arrests. The number decreased slightly in 1901, increased slightly in 1902, increased very greatly the next year, increased slightly the two following years (1904 and 1905), increased substantially in 1906, and then decreased greatly in 1907.

The year 1907 was the first year following the establishment of the new Municipal Court, and there may be some relation between the work of the court and the marked decline in the total number of arrests, which fell from 91,553 to 63,132, or 31 per cent, in a single year. This decrease occurred both in the number of arrests for felonies and arrests for misdemeanors, though the decline in the number of arrests for felonies was not so great, as for misdemeanors.* However, the decrease in charges did not continue. There has been an increase each year from 1907 to 1913, the rate of increase varying from 2.4 per cent to 26.2 per cent.

Sec. 3. Increase in Arrests in 1913.

Finally, a most significant fact in this table is that there was in 1913 the greatest increase in arrests that has occurred in any single year in the entire period from 1900 to 1913.

There was in the year 1913 an increase over the year 1912 of 9.0 per cent in arrests for felonies, an increase of 28.5 per cent in arrests for misdemeanors and an increase of 26.2 per cent in the total number of arrests.

Over the year 1911 the arrests for 1913 represent an increase of 13.4 per cent in arrests for felonies, of 31.5 per cent in arrests for misdemeanors, and 29.4 per cent in the total numbers of arrests.

Over the year 1910, the arrests for 1913 represent an increase of 19.5 per cent in arrests for felonies, 37.1 per cent in arrests for misdemeanors, and 35.1 per cent in total number of arrests. The table below summarizes these percentages.

TABLE 3. PERCENTAGE INCREASE OF ARRESTS IN 1913 OVER 1912, 1911, 1910.

	Percentage increase in number of arrests in 1913 over 1910.	over 1911.	over 1912.
Felonies	19.5	13.4	9.0
Misdemeanors	37.1	31.5	28.5
All offenses	35.1	29.4	26.2

Sec. 4. Increase in Arrests Compared with Increase in Population.

An increase in the number of arrests should, of course, be considered in relation to the increase in population during the corresponding period. The following table shows the number of arrests to every 10,000 people in the population during the years 1880 and 1890, and the period 1900 to 1913.

TABLE 4. ARRESTS PER 10,000 POPULATION.**

Year.	Felonies.	Misdemeanors.	All Offenses.
1880	....	....	486.4
1890	....	....	565.8
1900	63.8	342.9	406.7
1901	64.9	323.3	388.2
1902	58.3	324.0	382.3
1903	67.8	351.9	419.7
1904	58.5	357.3	.415.8

*It is important to note, however, that in the preceding year (1906) there had been an increase of 11 per cent, compared with 2 and 4 per cent for the two years immediately preceding 1906.

**The population for 1890, 1900 and 1910 is taken from the Federal Census. For the other years, Chicago population estimates, computed as of July 1, have been furnished by the Director of the United States Bureau of the Census.

Year.	Felonies.	Misdemeanors.	All Offenses.
1905	62.3	360.8	423.1
1906	61.9	396.2	458.1
1907	52.0	256.3	308.5
1908	50.3	275.0	325.3
1909	45.0	282.9	327.9
1910	42.9	329.0	371.9
1911	44.0	333.8	377.8
1912	44.8	334.1	378.9
1913	47.8	420.5	468.3

According to this table there were in 1880, 486.4 arrests in Chicago for every 10,000 persons in the population; in 1890 this had increased to 565.8 and in 1900 had fallen to 406.7 arrests for every 10,000 population; in 1910 the number of arrests had fallen still more to 371.9 for every 10,000 population. Since 1910, however, there has been a steady increase in the number of arrests per 10,000 population and this increase in 1913 was so substantial that the number of arrests per 10,000 population in that year was greater not only than the corresponding number for 1910, but greater than the corresponding number for 1900.

Sec. 5. Relation Between Number of Arrests and Number of Crimes.

From the statistics that have been given, it appears that there was in the year 1913 not only an increase in the number of criminal complaints per 10,000 of the population, but there was also in this year an unmistakably large increase in the number of arrests. If the number of arrests indicates the extent of crime, then there was obviously a very marked increase in crime in the year 1913. If the figures as to the relation between arrests and population are to be trusted, the year 1913 would popularly be called a serious "crime year" that put our crime-rate back more than a decade. It is very important therefore to note that the number of arrests is not synonymous with number of crimes, among other reasons because (1) a large number of persons may be arrested for complicity in a single crime; (2) many innocent persons are arrested through misapprehension and later discharged; and (3) the vast majority of arrests are for petty offenses that are not serious enough to be called "crimes" at all. Some consideration should be given to the question of "new crimes." When laws are passed creating new offenses, there may be an increase in arrests without any corresponding increase in criminality. As a matter of fact, however, the new offenses are chiefly those involving misdemeanors and violations of ordinances. New felonies are rarely created. In Chicago the police classification does, however, include two new offenses improperly classed as felonies, "contributing to delinquency," and "pandering.* The latter is so unimportant numerically that it may be disregarded. Offenses involving violations of laws relating to motor vehicles might be considered "new offenses" in comparing 1890 and 1900 with 1910, but they are not new offenses in comparing 1910 with 1913. Violations of the factory laws, violations of the compulsory education laws, and some similar offenses are not important enough numerically to have much weight in the total of nearly 110,000 offenses.

Sec. 6. Small Per Cent of Arrests for Serious Offenses.

The most important point, however, regarding the relation between "arrests" and "crimes" is the fact that the great majority of arrests are not for "crimes" at all in the sense that most people understand the word "crime;" on the contrary, the great majority of offenses are for violations of city ordinances and for misdemeanors, and many, if not most, of them are for relatively petty offenses. The following table, for example, shows for a series of years the percentage of the total number of arrests that were made on felony charges.

*These offenses are not classified as "felonies" in the Municipal Court report. An attempt was made to ascertain why the police department classed them as felonies, but no explanation was given except that "they had been started that way."

TABLE 5. ARRESTS FOR FELONIES IN RELATION TO TOTAL NUMBER OF ARRESTS.

	Arrests (All Offenses).	Arrests for Felonies. Number.	Per Cent of Total.
1900	69,089	10,838	15.7
1901	68,024	11,383	16.7
1902	68,858	10.495	15.2
1903	77,673	12,550	16.2
1904	79,006	11,116	14.1
1905	82,472	12,144	14.7
1906	91,553	12,376	13.5
1907	63,132	10,653	16.9
1908	68,220	10,551	15.5
1909	70,375	9,656	13.7
1910	81,269	9,376	11.5
1911	84,840	9,881	11.6
1912	86,950	10,276	11.8
1913	109,764	11,203	10.2

In 1900, 15.7 per cent of all the arrests were for felonies, and from 1900 through the year 1908, the per cent of felonies ranged from 13.5 per cent to 16.9 per cent. In the last four years, however, the per cent of arrests on felony charges has shown a decrease over the earlier years, and in 1913 the arrests for felonies were only 10.2 per cent of the total.

It seems important to emphasize the fact that the table of arrests shows that out of the 109,764 offenses charged against persons arrested in 1913, only 11,203 or 10.2 per cent were really for "crimes," if we use the word crime to mean felony. Another point that should not be overlooked with regard to the relation between number of arrests and number of crimes is the fact that an increase in the number of arrests may indicate merely a change in policy on the part of the state's attorney or of the police department and a sudden decision to arrest for certain types of offenses that had hitherto been overlooked. Or the increase in arrests may be due to changes in the police force leading to greater success in the apprehension of offenders. That is, instead of an increase in crime the increase in arrests may merely indicate greater activity on the part of the police, due to whatever cause; or as has been pointed out, this may, of course, be merely pseudo-activity resulting in the arrest of large numbers of innocent persons.

Sec. 7. Relation Between Arrests and Convictions, 1900-1913.

Statistics are available, however, showing that there was in 1913 not only a very substantial increase in the number of those arrested but that there was also a noticeable increase in the number of persons convicted and held to the Criminal Court. In the annual report of the Chief of Police the disposition of cases in the Municipal Court is given each year. The followng table shows the total number of cases disposed of, the total number discharged each year, and those held to the Criminal Court, fined, sentenced and otherwise disposed of. The number convicted per 10,000 population has been computed, but it should be emphasized that grouped together as "convicted" are all cases that are not discharged. Some of these are only held for trial in the Criminal Court and a few are disposed of in other ways.

TABLE 6. DISPOSITION OF CASES IN MUNICIPAL COURT, 1900-1913.*

Year	Total No. Cases Disposed Of	Discharged	Convicted Etc.	†Per Cent of Total No. of Cases Convicted, Etc.	Number Convicted, "Held" and Otherwise Disposed of Per 10,000 Population
1900	69,124	45,247	23,877	34.5	140.6
1901	67,452	40,318	27,134	40.2	154.9
1902	68,530	41,693	26,837	39.2	148.9

---

* Statistics compiled from the annual reports of the police department. Juvenile cases have been excluded. In a few of the annual reports the total number of cases disposed of did not agree with the total number of charges. This discrepancy, however, was slight in every case.

†Includes all those convicted, held to the Criminal Court, and "otherwise disposed of."

Year	Total No. Cases Disposed Of	Discharged	Convicted Etc.	Per Cent of Total No. of Cases Convicted, Etc.	Number Convicted, "Held" and Otherwise Disposed of Per 10,000 Population
1903	75,121	46,597	28,524	37.9	154.1
1904	77,468	43.045	34,423	44.4	181.2
1905	78,662	50,436	28,226	35.9	144.8
1906	87,369	59,706	27,663	31.7	138.4
1907	60,181	29,867	30,314	50.4	148.0
1908	67,431	35,593	31,838	47.2	151.8
1909	70,809	39,000	31,809	44.9	148.2
1910	80,238	44,286	35,952	44.8	164.5
1911	84,537	49,034	35,503	41.9	158.1
1912	85,357	51,978	33,379	39.1	145.5
1913	109,711	58,532	51,179	46.6	218.3

This table shows that along with the increase in arrests there was in 1913 a very substantial increase in the number of convictions. Of the total number of cases disposed of in 1913, 46.6 per cent were convicted and held for trial, in contrast to 39.1 per cent in 1912, and 41.9 per cent in 1911. In 1912, 33,379 persons were convicted or held for trial, but in 1913 the number of convictions had risen from 33,379 to 51,179, an increase of 53.3 per cent, in contrast to a decrease of 5.9 per cent from 1911 to 1912 and of 1.2 per cent between 1910 and 1911. There was a marked increase in the number of persons convicted and held for trial out of every 10,000 persons in the population. The number of convictions rose from 158.1 per 10,000 population in 1911 and 145.5 per 10,000 population in 1912 to 218.3 per 10,000 population in 1913.

There are, moreover, other statistics available showing that along with the increase in the number of arrests there has been an increase in cases held and convicted. In the first place there are published reports of the Municipal Court, which show (1) the largest number of cases held to the Grand Jury in any year since 1908; (2) an increase in the number of convictions for misdemeanors (criminal cases) and for violations of ordinances (quasi-criminal cases) in 1913; and (3) an increase during the year in the number of persons sentenced to imprisonment by the Municipal Court.

There are also available some unpublished statistics from the Criminal Court that indicate that the increase in arrests probably had a legitimate basis. These are: (1) Statistics showing an increase in the number of cases heard by the Grand Jury in the year 1913 over the preceding four years (but not over the preceding eight years save for the single year 1907); (2) an increase in the number of true bills found, which was again an increase over the preceding four years only, for the number of true bills in 1913 was smaller than in any one of the years from 1901 to 1909. In order to avoid duplication, these statistics will not be presented here, but will be discussed in connection with the tables in the following section dealing with statistics relating to the disposition of cases in the Municipal and Criminal Courts.

Sec. 8. Statistics Relating to the Disposition of Cases in the Municipal and Criminal Courts.

In the preceding section statistics of arrests and their possible value as indicating the extent of crime have been discussed. Statistics have also been given showing the number of convictions together with the number of cases held to the Criminal Court and their relation to the number of arrests. The statistics that have been given were all compiled from the annual reports of the General Superintendent of Police. Since the establishment in 1906 of the Municipal Court, there has been published each year an admirable report of the work of the various branches of that court, so that we have for the period 1907-1913 statistics showing the disposition of each class of cases heard in the Municipal Court. There will follow, then, tables showing separately for felonies, misdemeanors and violations of ordinances the disposition of the cases heard in the Municipal Court since its establishment, the number of cases fined, sentenced, and held to the Grand Jury, together with the number of cases discharged.

Sec. 9. Disposition of All Cases in the Municipal Court of Chicago, 1908 -1913. Total Number Discharged and Convicted.

The following tables show the disposition of all cases heard in the Muni-

cipal Court from 1908 * to 1913. The statistics in this table must not be compared with the police statistics for the same year, since the police reports are
for the calendar year from January 1 to December 31, and the Municipal Court
reports are for the year from December 1 to November 30. Percentages
would, of course, be fairly comparable, but numbers cannot be compared.

TABLE 7. DISPOSITION OF ALL CASES IN THE MUNICIPAL
COURT.

(From Annual Reports of the Municipal Court of Chicago, 1908-1913.)

Numbers.

Disposition	1913	1912	1911	1910	*1909	*1908
Defendant not apprehended......	3,586	5,413	5,965	4,080	.....	.....
Dismissed, want of prosecution..	6,593	5,048	3,225	2,519	.....	.....
Non-suits	5,340	11,186	6,505	6,290	.....	.....
Nolle pros.	2,433	4,238	4,322	2,981	.....	.....
Discharged	51,797	42,101	37,408	34,746	.....	.....
Total discharged	69,749	67,986	57,425	50,616	46,905	41,487
Fined	34,086	24,006	19,312	20,633	16,559	16,785
Committed to County Jail and House of Correction...........	14,463	11,764	13,047	13,790	12,479	13,325
Held to Grand Jury...........	3,035	2,613	2,946	2,883	2,428	†3,333
Total convicted and "held"..	51,584	38,383	35,305	37,306	31,466	33,443
Total cases disposed of....	121,333	106,369	92,730	87,922	78,371	74,930

Percentages.

	1913	1912	1911	1910	*1909	*1908
Defendant not apprehended.......	3.0	5.1	6.4	4.7	....	....
Dismissed, want of prosecution...	5.4	4.7	3.5	2.9	....	....
Non-suits and nolle pros.........	6.4	14.5	11.8	10.5	....	....
Discharged	42.7	39.6	40.3	39.5	....	....
Total discharged	57.5	63.9	62.0	57.6	59.9	55.4
Fined	28.1	22.6	20.8	23.5	21.2	22.4
Committed to County Jail and House of Correction............	11.9	11.1	14.0	15.7	15.8	17.8
Held to Grand Jury.............	2.5	2.4	3.2	3.2	3.1	†4.4
Total convicted and "held"...	42.5	36.1	38.0	42.4	40.1	44.6
Total cases disposed of....	100.0	100.0	100.0	100.0	100.0	100.0

*No statistics available except for total number discharged in 1908 and 1909.
†Includes 182, or .2 per cent, held to the Juvenile Court.

The outstanding fact in this table is that the number of those discharged
each year is greater than the number convicted, even when all of those held
to the Grand Jury are counted as convicted. The total per cent discharged
ranges from 55.4 per cent in 1908 to as high as 63.9 per cent in 1912. The
cases convicted and held to the Grand Jury have not only been less than
half, they have been less than 45.0 per cent of the total number of cases

*1908 was not the first but the second year of the court. Statistics for the
first year are not given because comparable statistics of disposition are not
available for 1907. The first annual report of the court was a very slight
report and was largely devoted to comparisons between the work of the court
and the work accomplished under the former Justice of the Peace regime.
This first report shows that the total number of cases disposed of was 58,227,
and that the number committed to the County Jail and House of Correction
was 10,783, but no statistics are available showing the number of persons
fined, although the total amount of fines assessed is given. Since no statistics
are given showing the number discharged, it is impossible to ascertain the
total number convicted.

disposed of each year since the establishment of the Municipal Court, and fell one year to 36.1 per cent of the total number of cases disposed of.*

It is important to note the reasons for the discharge of this large per-centage of cases. In the year 1913, 3,586, or 3 per cent, were discharged be-cause the defendant was "not apprehended;" 6,593, or 5.4 per cent, because of "want of prosecution;" 2,433, or 2 per cent, because the state's attorney had "nolle prossed;" 5,340, or 4.4 per cent, because the corporation counsel had "non-suited," and 51,797, or 42.7 per cent, were discharged by the court after trial. These methods of discharge should, however, be considered with refer-ence to the separate groups of cases heard, that is, felonies, misdemeanors, and "violations," or quasi-criminal cases. In the sections following, statistics relating to each of these groups of cases will be considered separately.

Sec. 10. Disposition of Preliminary Hearings in Municipal Court, 1908-1913.

The question of the number of persons discharged is, of course, most important in the cases of serious crimes. The following table shows the dis-position of all felony cases on preliminary hearings in the Municipal Court for the period 1908-1913. Similar statistics for 1907, the first year of the court, are not available.

TABLE 8. DISPOSITION OF FELONY CASES ON PRELIMINARY HEARINGS.

Municipal Court Statistics, 1908-1913.

Numbers.

Disposition	1913	1912	1911	1910	1909	1908
Defendant not apprehended	948	1,051	1,882	835		
Discharged, want of prosecution	742	501	390	243	4,032	4,388
Nolle pros.	1,298	1,746	2,178	1,429		
Discharged	2,079	1,451	2,130	2,228		
Held to Grand Jury	3,035	2,613	2,946	2,883	2,428	*3,333
Total preliminary hearings	8,102	7,362	9,526	7,618	6,460	7,721

Percentages.

	1913	1912	1911	1910	1909	1908
Defendant not apprehended	11.7	14.2	19.8	11.0	....	....
Discharged, want of prosecution	9.1	6.8	4.1	3.2	....	....
Nolle pros.	16.0	23.7	22.8	18.7	....	....
Discharged	25.7	19.8	22.4	29.2	....	....
Total discharged	62.5	64.5	69.1	62.1	62.3	56.0
Held to Grand Jury	37.5	35.5	30.9	37.9	37.7	*44.0
Total preliminary hearings	100.0	100.0	100.0	100.0	100.0	100.0

*Includes 182, or 3 per cent, transferred to the Juvenile Court.

This table shows that in 1913 only 3,035, or 37.5 per cent, of the felony cases were held to the Grand Jury after preliminary hearings in the Municipal Court. The remaining 5,067 cases, or 62.5 per cent of the total number, "got off" in the following way: 948, or 11.7 per cent, were discharged because the defendant was not apprehended; 742, or 9.1 per cent, were dropped for want of prosecution; 1,298, or 16 per cent, were nolle prossed, and 2,079, or 25.7 per cent, were discharged by the various judges after preliminary hear-ings in court, leaving in round numbers only 3,000 cases to be heard by the Grand Jury. In comparing statistics for the preceding years, it appears that the percentage held to the Grand Jury in 1913 was slightly larger than the percentage held in 1912 or 1911, but smaller than the percentage held in 1910, 1909, or 1908. Some interesting changes are to be noticed in connection with the method of discharge. The per cent of cases in which the defendant was "not apprehended" increased in 1911 and decreased in 1912 and 1913, the per

*The percentages convicted and "held" in this table do not agree with the percentages given in **Table 6**, which shows the disposition of cases in the Municipal Court based on statistics compiled from the annual reports of the General Superintendent of Police. The police statistics do not include some of the violations of ordinances that are heard in the Municipal Court on summons, and the number of "non-suits" would therefore be smaller. A further difference is that the police statistics do not include in their classifica-tion any group of persons "not apprehended." Still another difference results from the group "otherwise disposed of" in the police classification.

cent "nolle prossed" increased in 1911 and 1912 and decreased in 1913, the per cent "discharged for want of prosecution" has steadily increased, and the per cent discharged by the judges decreased in 1911 and 1912 and increased in 1913.

By way of summary it may be said that in the six years for which statistics are available, there have been altogether *46,607 preliminary hearings and *17,056 cases held to the Grand Jury, an average for the six years of 36.6 per cent of the cases held and 63.4 per cent discharged.

Going back to the table of arrests (Table 2, p. 20) it will be remembered that only about one-tenth of those arrested last year were arrested on serious charges. Now it becomes necessary to add the further fact that, although only a small number of felony cases are brought into the Municipal Court, about two-thirds of these are discharged without ever being held to the Grand Jury.

Sec. 11. Disposition of Cases Held to the Grand Jury, 1901-1913.

The next stage in the progress towards a trial in the Criminal Court is the hearing before the Grand Jury, where the number of cases held for trial is still further reduced. The following table shows the number of cases heard by the Grand Jury each year from 1901 to 1913, and the number of "true bills" and "no bills."

TABLE 9. NUMBER OF TRUE BILLS AND NO BILLS RETURNED BY GRAND JURY OF COOK COUNTY: 1901-1913.

Year Ending November 30.	True Bills.	No Bills.	Total.**	Per Cent of True Bills.
1901	2,932	989	3,921	74.8
1902†	3,038	837	3,875	78.4
1903	3,596	917	4,513	79.7
1904†	3,650	1,053	4,703	77.6
1905†	3,345	827	4,172	80.2
1906†	3,469	852	4,321	80.3
1907	2,644	336	2,980	88.7
1908	3,064	405	3,469	88.3
1909	1,551	575	2,126	73.0
1910	2,144	713	2,857	75.0
1911	2,326	806	3,132	74.3
1912	1,874	783	2,657	70.5
1913	2,468	857	3,325	74.2
Total for the period......	36,101	9,950	46,051	78.4

This table shows that during the period for which Grand Jury statistics are available—from 1901 to 1913—the percentages of true bills ranged from 70.5 per cent to 88.7 per cent of all cases heard, and averaged for the whole period 78.4 per cent. The percentage of cases discharged by the Grand Jury varied, therefore, from 11.3 per cent to 29.5 per cent of all cases heard, and averaged 21.6 per cent for the whole period. The total number of cases heard by the Grand Jury does not correspond exactly with the total number of cases held from the Municipal Court. It is not possible to say, therefore

*The 182 cases transferred to the Juvenile Court have been excluded from these totals.

**It is assumed that the total number of cases before the Grand Jury is equal to the sum of true bills and no bills. There are, however, a few cases "passed" each month that are heard at the next session. The total for any one year, therefore, would include a few cases held over from the preceding year and would not include a few of the cases brought in during the current year and "passed" at the last session. The "left-over" cases heard and the "passed" cases would be approximately the same. The point is, however, that the totals do not represent the precise number of cases brought before the Grand Jury during any one year.

†The figures were lacking for the months of April and September in 1902, November in 1904, February, May and October in 1905, and September in 1906. The number of cases for each of these months was estimated on the basis of the relative number of cases during the same month of the preceding year. The figures for September, 1906, however, were estimated on the basis of September, 1907, because the reports for that year were more complete.

as a result of these statistics precisely how many of the cases held by the
Municipal Court in any one year "got off" after the Grand Jury hearing, but
it is fair to assume that the per cent of no bills was the same for the Municipal Court cases as for the total number of cases heard. On this assumption,
the total number of felony cases discharged up to this point would have
increased from the 62.5 per cent for 1913 indicated in Table 8 to 72.2 per cent,
from 64.5 per cent to 75.0 per cent for 1912, from 69.1 per cent to 77.0 per cent
for 1911, and so on.*

Returning to the question of the per cent of discharged cases, it may be
said that, in round numbers, slightly more than one-third of all the felony
cases heard in the Municipal Court are held over to the Grand Jury and that
about one-fourth of these "get-off" because the Grand Jury returns "no bills."

Sec. 12.   Final Disposition of Felony Cases.

Even after leaving the Grand Jury there are other chances of escape from
trial, by having the case "nolle prossed" or "stricken off" by the State's Attorney. Moreover, a considerable number of cases are of course discharged as
"not guilty" after trial in the Criminal Court. Unfortunately, statistics showing the number of cases which are discharged in this way are available only
for a single year, that ending November 30, 1912. The following table shows
for that year the total number of discharges from the time of preliminary
hearing to trial in the Criminal Court together with the number discharged
as not guilty after trial.

TABLE 10.   DISPOSITION OF ALL FELONY CASES GIVEN PRE-
LIMINARY HEARINGS IN THE MUNICIPAL
COURT OF CHICAGO: 1912.

Disposition.	Number.	Per cent.	
Discharged in Municipal Court.			
Defendant not apprehended....	1,051	14.3	Discharged in Muni-
Discharged: want of prosecution	501	6.8	cipal Court: 4,749
Discharged	1,451	19.7	(64.5 per cent).
Nolle Pros	1,746	23.7	Total discharged be-
Discharged by Grand Jury, etc.			fore trial: 5,959
"No bills" Grand Jury**.......	783	10.6	(80.9 per cent).
Nolle Pros.	89	5.8	Total discharged:
Stricken off	338		6,199 (84.2 per
Discharged by Criminal Court.			cent).
(Tried and found "not guilty")..	240	3.3	
Sentenced to imprisonment........	773	10.5	
County Jail and House of Cor-			
rection 565			Found guilty: 1,932.
Joliet, Pontiac, etc......... 208			(12.7 per cent.)
Fined	25	.4	
Probation	134	1.8	
Pending and transferred and not re-			
ported	231	3.1	
Total preliminary hearings.	7,362	100.0	

*Table 9 is of further interest since it affords an interesting contrast be-
tween the work of the Grand Jury under four different State's Attorneys.
During the period of 1901 to 1904, when Mr. Deneen was State's Attorney,
the average number of cases heard per year was 4,253 and the average number
of true bills was 77.7 per cent of all cases heard. In the four-year period,
1905-1908, when Mr. Healey was State's Attorney, the average number of
cases heard per year was 3,735 and the average number of true bills was 83.8
per cent of all cases heard. During Mr. Wayman's State's Attorneyship, 1909-
1912, the average number of cases heard fell to 2,693, and the average number
of true bills fell also to 73.3 per cent of all cases heard. Mr. Hoyne's first year
shows a total number of cases heard and a percentage of true bills which is
above Mr. Wayman's average, but considerably below the average of Mr.
Healey's term and slightly below the average of Mr. Deneen's term.

**These statistics were obtained from some unpublished material collected
by the Clerk of Criminal Records in the Municipal Court, with the exception
of the number of "no bills" from the Grand Jury. Since he had not collected

This table may be briefly summarized as follows: In 1912, 4,749 felony cases, or 64.5 per cent of the total number, were discharged in the Municipal Court; 783, or 10.6 per cent, were discharged by the Grand Jury; 427, or 5.8 per cent, were "nolle prossed" or "stricken out" before trial. That is, out of 7,362 felony cases, 5,959, or 80.9 per cent, were discharged without ever being tried, leaving 19.1 per cent for trial in the Criminal Court. That is, a man arrested for a serious crime stands only about one chance out of five of ever getting to the Criminal Court for trial. Of those tried in the Criminal Court in 1912, 240 were found not guilty and 932 were convicted, but of the convicted only 773 were sentenced, while the others were fined or released on probation. Moreover, of those sentenced only 208 were given penitentiary or reformatory sentences. That is, a criminal in Chicago who has been arrested on a felony charge and comes before the Municipal Court, stands about one chance in thirty of going to the penitentiary or reformatory.

Sec. 13. Per Cent of Convictions for Different Crimes.

The per cent of convictions is, however, much higher for some crimes than for others, and, fortunately, statistics are available for the year 1912 showing for the different crimes the number of convictions of the cases that were actually tried in the Criminal Court. Table 11 gives therefore by crimes the number of convictions in the Criminal Court, together with the number of preliminary hearings. It should be noted that in the table below the 231 pending and transferred cases have been subtracted, which raises the per cent of convictions from 12.7 per cent to 13.1 per cent.

TABLE 11.   NUMBER OF PRELIMINARY HEARINGS AND CONVICTIONS IN FELONY CASES, BY CRIMES: 1912.

(Statistics from Municipal and Criminal Courts.)

Charge	* Preliminary Hearings Municipal Court.	Convictions in Criminal Court Number.	Per Cent of Preliminary Hearings.
Arson	98	2	2.0
Assault to kill	301	34	11.3
Burglary	1,125	335	29.8
Confidence game	900	85	9.4
Embezzlement	188	26	13.8
Larceny	2,203	171	7.8
Manslaughter	40	...	0.0
Murder	87	2	2.3
Rape	326	32	9.8
Robbery	987	197	19.9
Receiving stolen property	183	6	3.3
Other felonies	693	42	6.1
Total	7,131	932	13.1

* From this column have been subtracted 211 cases pending, 3 transferred, and 17 unaccounted for.

According to this table there was a higher per cent of convictions for burglary (29.8 per cent) than for any other crime. This is probably to be explained by the fact that many of these cases were not very serious and that a large proportion of those convicted received House of Correction sentences; for the Illinois Criminal Code gives a definition of burglary so broad that it includes almost every kind of stealing.* The crimes in which the number of convictions did not equal 5 per cent of the number of preliminary hearings were arson, murder, and receiving stolen property. Other crimes for which less than 10 per cent of convictions were secured were larceny (grand), "running a confidence game," and "rape." In the cases of "assault with intent to kill," 11.3 per cent of convictions were secured, 13.8 per cent in the cases of embezzlement, and 19.9 per cent in the cases of robbery. In the cases of robbery and burglary alone did the per cent of convictions run above the average.

the number of no bills or true bills, the number from the Grand Jury reports (see Table 9) was used, since in this year, 1912, the total number of cases heard by the Grand Jury (2,657) and the total number held by the Municipal Court (2,613) were approximately the same.

* See Appendix C.

Sec. 14. Other Statistics of Felony Convictions.

Statistics of convictions by crimes are available also for the year 1913, but these statistics are from the police report for that year, and are for several reasons not properly comparable with the Municipal Court statistics.

The following table presents a summary from the police statistics of the convictions for the various kinds of felonies, together with the number of arrests for each of these offenses, the per cent of convictions for each offense, and the percentage of convictions for the same offenses from the Municipal Court statistics for 1912. The percentages of convictions based on the two sets of statistics are thus given in parallel columns so that they may be easily compared. The statistics are, of course, not only from different sources, but for different years, and therefore the numbers are not comparable, but the percentages may be legitimately compared. Only those offenses are included that are classified as felonies in the Municipal Court reports.* Larceny is also excluded because the police statistics are for both grand and petit larceny, and since the court statistics include only grand larceny, the two are not properly comparable.

TABLE 12. CONVICTIONS AND ARRESTS FOR FELONIES (EXCEPT GRAND LARCENY): 1913.

(Statistics from Police Report, 1913, using the Municipal Court Classification of Felonies.)

Charge	Arrests	Convictions Number	Convictions Per cent of Arrests	Convictions *Per cent of arrests from court statistics, 1912
†Arson	85	3	3.5	2.0
Assault to kill	246	49	19.9	11.3
‡Burglary	1,053	289	27.4	29.8
Confidence game	681	110	16.2	9.4
Embezzlement	199	29	14.6	13.8
Manslaughter	43	2	4.7	0.0
Murder	219	31	14.2 }	2.3
Murder, accessory to.......	33	1	3.0 }	
§Rape	258	16	6.2	9.8
Receiving stolen property....	451	96	21.3	3.3
‖Robbery	1,022	171	16.7	19.9
Threats to kidnap or murder.	68	25	36.8	**....
Other felonies	438	38	8.7	6.1
Total	4,796	860	17.9	¶15.4

*See Table 11.

**Included under other felonies.

†Includes 1 case of "attempted arson."

‡Includes 56 cases of "attempted burglary" and 12 cases of "having burglar's tools."

§Includes 54 cases of "assault to commit rape."

‖Includes 7 cases of "accessory to robbery" and 180 cases of "assault to commit robbery."

¶The percentage is changed because larceny has been omitted in order to make the two columns comparable. If larceny is included in the two columns the per cent of convictions from the police columns is 32.7 per cent, from the Municipal Court column, 13.1 per cent.

---

*Attention has already been called to some differences between the statistics from the police reports and from the Municipal Court reports. For the year 1913, the police report gives statistics of convictions in felony cases, but there are included some offenses that are not felonies: e. g., "larceny" includes petit as well as grand larceny; "contributing to delinquency" and "pandering" are included, although neither of these last offenses is a felony. It should also be noted that statistics showing convictions by crimes are furnished only in the police report for 1913.

Unfortunately the result of preliminary hearing and the disposition of the cases on which convictions were not secured, that is, the number rejected by the Grand Jury, the number "nolle prossed," "stricken off," or tried and found not guilty, are not published.

Comparing the two columns of percentages, it appears that although the percentage of convictions according to the police statistics is slightly higher than the percentage based on the court statistics (17.9 per cent compared with 13.1 per cent), on the whole, the police statistics for 1913 confirm the court statistics for 1912 in showing a very low percentage of convictions.

The police statistics show a slightly smaller per cent of convictions than the Municipal Court statistics for three offenses, burglary, rape and robbery, and a higher percentage of convictions than the court statistics for the offenses of assault to kill, "confidence game," embezzlement, murder and receiving stolen property.

In discussing statistics of arrests and convictions on felony charges, the fact should not be overlooked that persons charged with felonies are sometimes convicted of less serious crimes. This is probably true especially of burglary and robbery. The Illinois Criminal Code gives a definition of burglary so broad that it might include almost any kind of stealing,* and convictions for larceny sometimes follow arrests for burglary. For example, two boys were brought into the "Boys' Court" recently on charges of burglary. Their actual offense was stealing a small basket of eggs from the basement of a store where they had recently worked. The charge was very properly changed to petit larceny and the boys released on probation. The police are undoubtedly very careless and indifferent in deciding upon what charge an arrested person is to be "booked." Their mistakes may be readjusted in the courts, but they are disastrous to statistical comparisons.

In the case of robbery, as in burglary, persons are arrested, and charged with robbery** by the police when they should be charged with larceny. For example, five boys, ranging in ages from eighteen to twenty-two years, were recently brought into court charged with **robbery**. But their actual offense had been teasing a peddler on the street and finally taking from him five small brooms valued at 75 cents. They were finally discharged upon making restitution. These five arrests may or may not have been necessary, but it was clearly wrong for the police to charge the boys with **robbery**, for which the minimum sentence is one year in the penitentiary, instead of charging them with disorderly conduct or at most petit larceny.

A further statistical difficulty should be noted with regard to the police statistics, and that is that the arrests and convictions may not cover precisely the same period. That is, arrests of one year may result in convictions the following year. Arrests for burglary in December would probably not be disposed of during that year. It may, of course, be assumed that the proportions will be very much the same from year to year, and that the margin of error here is not a very large one.

Sec. 15. The Significance of Unnecessary Arrests

The outstanding fact about the statistics of convictions on felony charges is that, even if large allowances be made for possible statistical errors, there will still remain a very low percentage of convictions. Police and court statistics alike show a per cent of convictions on felony cases ranging from 13.1 to 17.9 per cent of arrests for all felonies and in the case of specific crimes, from 2.0 per cent to 29.8 per cent. Back of this lie two possible explanations: (1) A large number of innocent persons are arrested and are in consequence discharged without conviction; or (2) a large number of persons who are legitimately arrested and who should be convicted are being released because of some defect in our prosecuting machinery. Whether this defect is to be attributed to the police, the courts, the Grand Jury, or the State's Attorney's office, is not within the province of this discussion.

---

*The Revised Statutes give the following definition of **burglary**: "Whoever wilfully, and maliciously and forcibly breaks and enters, or **wilfully and maliciously, without force** (the doors and windows being open), enters into any dwelling-house, kitchen, office, shop, store-house, etc., or other building with intent to commit murder, robbery, rape, mayhem, or **other felony or larceny**, shall be deemed guilty of burglary and be imprisoned in the penitentiary for a term not less than one year nor more than twenty years." **Illinois Revised Statutes**, 1909, p. 750.

According to the Revised Statutes **robbery is "the felonious and violent taking of money, goods, or other valuable thing from the person of another by force or intimidation" and the penalty is from one to ten years in the penitentiary. **Ibid**, p. 779.

One important fact, however, should not be overlooked in connection with the discussion concerning the per cent of those held for felony charges who are discharged and sentenced. All of those who are held from the Municipal Court to the Grand Jury, 3,035 persons in 1913 and 2,613 in 1912, must stay in the County Jail until their case has been heard by the Grand Jury unless they are able to secure bail. If they are held by the Grand Jury for trial in the Criminal Court, they must continue to lie in jail until their case comes to trial. The report of the jailer for 1913 showed that nearly 700 persons were kept in jail for varying periods of time and then discharged without conviction as follows:

TABLE 13.. PERSONS RELEASED FROM COOK COUNTY JAIL IN 1913 WITHOUT CONVICTION.

Reason for Release	Number
Released without trial—	
No bill Grand Jury	290
Stricken off	117
Nolle pros	39
	446
Tried and found not guilty	245
Total	691

It is certainly a fact of great importance that nearly 450 persons were held in the County Jail last year and then released either because the Grand Jury or the State's Attorney thought there was not sufficient evidence against them to justify their being tried, or because upon trial they were found not guilty, and that 250 more were released who had been tried and found "not guilty" by the Criminal Court. These 691 persons were presumably innocent and suffered the degradation and discomforts of imprisonment without cause. Even for those who are able to obtain release on bond, the burdens and humiliation of arrest, preliminary hearing, Grand Jury hearing, and in many cases Criminal Court trial are very great, and if these are due to unjust arrests, some remedy should be available.*

Sec. 16. Disposition of Criminal (Misdemeanor) Cases in the Municipal Court, 1908-1913.

So far only the disposition of felony cases has been discussed. Equally important is the question of the number of misdemeanors and of quasi-criminal cases (violations of ordinances) and the disposition of these cases. There were, in the year 1913, nearly 20,000 misdemeanor cases disposed of in the Municipal Court. The largest single group of misdemeanors were automobile offenses, and following these in order of numerical importance were the cases of assault (including "assault with a deadly weapon" and "assault and battery"), petit larceny, contributing to delinquency, abandonment, violations of the state factory law, adultery and similar offenses, obtaining money on false pretenses, vagrancy, receiving stolen property, malicious mischief and other offenses** of minor importance numerically.

The disposition of these cases in the Municipal Court from 1908 to 1913 is shown in the following table:

TABLE 14. DISPOSITION OF CRIMINAL CASES (MISDEMEANORS) IN THE MUNICIPAL COURT: 1908-1913.

Disposition	Numbers.					
	1913	1912	1911	1910	1909	1908
Defendant not apprehended	849	1,731	1,376	1,275	.....	.....
Dismissed: want of prosecution	1,709	1,403	762	615	2,181	6,253
Nolle pros.	1,135	2,492	2,144	1,552		
Discharged	5,616	3,748	2,616	2,381	4,284	
Total discharged	9,309	9,374	6,898	5,823	6,465	6,253

* Thousands of other persons whose cases are postponed and continued in the Municipal Court are also held in the County Jail awaiting trial, and of course a very large percentage of these persons are also discharged without conviction. The total number of innocent persons therefore who suffer imprisonment in the County Jail is much greater than the 691 shown in Table 13. Unfortunately, the jailer's report merely shows that their cases are "disposed of in the Municipal Court," and it is not possible to determine how large a percentage of them were discharged. See Appendix B for the jailer's report for the year 1913 and for further statistics relating to the County Jail.
**Appendix G contains table showing number of cases of each charge.

Fined	7,808	4,439	3,355	2,310	1,380	1,990
Committed to County Jail or House of Correction	2,403	2,075	1,517	1,692	2,285	2,224
Total convicted	10,211	6,514	4,872	4,002	3,665	4,214
Total cases disposed of	19,520	15,888	11,770	9,825	10,130	10,467

Percentages.

Defendant not apprehended	4.3	10.9	11.7	12.9	...	...
Dismissed: want of prosecution	8.8	8.8	6.5	6.3	...	...
Nolle pros.	5.8	15.7	18.2	15.8	...	...
Discharged	28.8	23.6	22.2	24.3	...	...
Total discharged	47.7	59.0	58.6	59.3	63.8	59.7
Fined	40.0	28.0	28.5	23.5	13.6	19.0
Committed to County Jail or House of Correction	12.3	13.0	12.9	17.2	22.6	21.3
Total convicted	52.3	41.0	41.4	40.7	36.2	40.3
Total cases disposed of	100.0	100.0	100.0	100.0	100.0	100.0

This table shows that in 1913 nearly one-half, or 47.7 per cent, of all misdemeanor cases were discharged; that the 52.3 per cent convicted were divided into 40 per cent fined and only 12.3 per cent sentenced to imprisonment in the County Jail or House of Correction. Moreover, the per cent of cases discharged was lower and the per cent of cases convicted was higher than in any preceding year since the establishment of the Municipal Court, with the possible exception, of course, of the year 1907, for which statistics are not available. But when the disposition of the convicted cases is examined it appears that the increase in the number of convictions was an increase in the number fined alone, which rose from 28.0 per cent in 1912 to 40.0 per cent in 1913, a larger percentage of persons fined than had occurred in the five years preceding. As a matter of fact, the percentage committed to the County Jail and the House of Correction actually decreased. The percentage committed in 1913 was 12.3 per cent in comparison with 13.0 per cent in 1912, 12.9 per cent in 1911, 17.2 per cent in 1910, 22.6 per cent in 1909, and 21.3 per cent in 1908.

Sec. 17. Disposition of Quasi-Criminal Cases (Violations of Ordinances) in the Municipal Court, 1908-1913.

Statistics showing the disposition of quasi-criminal cases, tell much the same story regarding discharges and convictions. Quasi-criminal cases are those involving the violations of city ordinances. There were in 1913, more than 93,000 of such cases disposed of * and 60 per cent of these were cases that may be classified as "disorderly" including cases of disorderly conduct, violating park ordinances and vagrancy ("vagabonds"). The following table shows the disposition of all quasi-criminal cases from 1908 to 1913:

TABLE 15. DISPOSITION OF QUASI-CRIMINAL CASES (VIOLATIONS OF ORDINANCES) IN THE MUNICIPAL COURT: 1908-1913.

Numbers.

Disposition.	1913.	1912.	1911.	1910.	1909.	1908.
Defendant not apprehended	1,789	2,631	2,707	1,970	....	....
Dismissed: want of prosecution	4,142	3,144	2,073	1,661	....	....
Non-suits	5,340	11,186	6,505	6,290	9,749 }	30,846
Discharged	44,102	36,902	32,662	30,137	26,659 }	
Total discharged	55,373	53,863	43,947	40,058	36,408	30,846
Fined	26,278	19,567	15,957	18,323	15,179	14,795
Committed to County Jail	43	58	74 }			
Committed to House of Correction	12,017	9,631	11,456 }	12,098	10,194	11,101
Total convicted	38,338	29,256	27,487	30,421	25,373	25,896
Total cases disposed of	93,711	83,119	71,434	70,479	61,781	56,742

*Appendix H contains tables giving complete lists of all cases disposed of.

Percentages.

Defendant not apprehended......	1.9	3.2	3.7	2.9	....	....
Dismissed: want of prosecution..	4.4	3.8	2.9	2.3	....	....
Non-suits	5.7	13.4	9.1	9.0	15.8 }	54.5
Discharged	47.1	44.5	45.7	42.7	43.1 }	
Total discharged	59.1	64.9	61.4	56.9	58.9	54.5
Fined	28.0	23.5	22.3	26.0	24.6	26.0
Committed to County Jail or House of Correction.........	12.9	11.6	16.3	17.1	16.5	19.5
Total convicted	40.9	35.1	38.6	43.1	41.1	45.5
Total cases disposed of.......	100.0	100.0	100.0	100.0	100.0	100.0

This table shows that in 1913 more than 55,000 of the quasi-criminal cases were discharged; that is, 59.1 per cent were discharged, compared with 40.9 per cent convicted. This table shows also the method of discharge and the kind of sentence imposed. Thus it appears 44,102, or 47.1 per cent, were discharged in court, and the 12.0 per cent never reached the court; of the latter, 5.7 per cent were non-suited by the City Prosecutor's office, 4.4 per cent were dismissed for want of prosecution, and 1.9 per cent of the offenders were discharged because they could not be apprehended. The 40.9 per cent convicted were divided into 28.0 per cent fined and 12.9 per cent committed to the County Jail or House of Correction, including those committed for non-payment of fines. Looking over the statistics for the series of six years, it appears that the year 1912 showed the largest per cent of discharged cases and the year 1908 the smallest per cent discharged. In comparison with the earlier years, the year 1913 shows a larger per cent of convictions than the three earlier years. The statistics indicate that the tendency is towards fining rather than imprisoning those convicted.

Sec. 18. Statistics from Reports of Police Department Relating to Disposition of Cases in the Municipal Court, 1913.

Statistics of disposition published in the annual reports of the police department show not the number of persons committed, but only the number sentenced, exclusive of those committed for non-payment of fines. These statistics show that less than 2 per cent of those arrested in 1913 were actually sentenced to imprisonment. The following table shows the total number of persons arrested last year, the number sentenced, the number fined, and the number placed on probation:

TABLE 16.　DISPOSITION OF ALL CASES IN THE MUNICIPAL COURT AS PUBLISHED IN THE REPORT OF THE POLICE DEPARTMENT: 1913.

Disposition	Number	Per cent
Held to Grand Jury..................................	2,182	2.0
Sentenced to County Jail	141	.1
Sentenced to House of Correction...................	*1,935	1.8
Fined	43,690	39.8
Probation, peace bonds, and weekly payments........	2,899	2.6
Discharged	56,529	51.5
Nolle pros. and stricken off.......................	2,003	1.8
Otherwise disposed of..............................	385	.4
	109,764	100.0

*Includes 2 cases sentenced to other correctional institutions.

This table shows again very clearly that the machinery of our court and police system exists chiefly for the petty offender. Out of 109,764 cases, only 2,182, or 2 per cent, are serious enough to be held to the Grand Jury; 141, or one-tenth of 1 per cent, are serious enough to be sentenced to the County Jail, and 1,935, or 1.8 per cent, are serious enough to be sentenced to the House of Correction; that is, out of 109,764 cases, 56,529 are discharged, 2,076 sentenced, 2,182 held to the Grand Jury, and 43,690 fined. It will be noted that the Municipal Court statistics (Table 7) showed that 11.9 per cent of all cases disposed of were committed to the County Jail or House of Correction, in contrast to the 1.9 per cent in Table 16 committed to these institutions. This difference is due to the fact that the Municipal Court statistics include those committed for non-payment of fine.

Sec. 19.   Statistics from the Boys' Court.

The establishment in March, 1914, of a special branch court to hear cases of boys under twenty-one makes possible a separate examination of arrests and discharges of these boys' cases.   Table 17 therefore presents the statistics showing the disposition of cases brought into the Boys' Court from its establishment in March, 1914, to the end of September, 1914, a period of slightly more than six months.

TABLE 17.   DISPOSITION OF CASES: VIOLATIONS, MISDEMEANORS, FELONIES.

Disposition	Violations of city ordinances (Quasi-Criminal) No.	Per cent	Misdemeanors (Criminal) No.	Per cent	Felonies (Preliminary Hearings) No.	Per cent	Total No.	Per cent
Discharged	3,140	79.7	287	40.7	456	47.2	3,883	69.2
Nolle pros. or non-suit	19 ⎤		1 ⎤		26 ⎤		46	0.8
Discharged for want of prosecution....	123 ⎦	3.6	39 ⎦	5.7	49 ⎦	7.7	211	3.8
Total discharged	3,282	83.3	327	46.4	531	54.9	4,140	73.8
Fined	309	7.9	19	2.7	....	....	328	5.8
Committed to House of Correction or County Jail	312	7.9	182	25.9	....	....	494	8.8
Probation	36	0.9	176	25.0	....	....	212	3.8
Total convicted.	657	16.7	377	53.6	....	....	1,034	18.4
Held to Criminal Court	....	....	....	....	436	45.1	436	7.8
Total	3,939	100.0	704	100.0	967	100.0	5,610	100.0

This table shows that of the most numerous group of cases, that is, the "quasi-criminal," 3,282, or 83 per cent, were discharged; that 46 per cent of the criminal (misdemeanor) cases were discharged and nearly half of those convicted were released on probation; of the felony cases, only 45 per cent were even held to the Grand Jury.

Sec. 20.   Large Percentage of Petty Offenders in the Boys' Court.

To understand why so large a percentage of the persons arrested are discharged, it is necessary to examine the precise charges on which the cases are brought into court.   Fortunately, it is possible to present, for the Boys' Court,* a list of typically trival offenses for which persons have been arrested. For example, J— T— is arrested because he "made a loud noise at 21st and Dearborn and threw a dog out in the street by the leg." H— S— is arrested for "standing on street corner at 8:50 p. m," A— D— for sleeping in a barn, and F— W— for sleeping on the prairie because he had just got a job and had no other place to go that night. S— T—, first offender, seventeen years, "found in poolroom, under age to be allowed there, first time even in this poolroom, no evidence of gambling, several boys arrested." D— S—, nineteen years, "playing cards in a vacant store, several boys arrested and discharged." E— H— "did not move when officer spoke; going into dance hall 1 a. m., no evidence of disorder." E— S— "was with a man who had a stolen bicycle." M— S— "with sixteen boys over eighteen years, in poolroom raid; only one gambling; others orderly and of good character." E— E— "playing ball on street." G— S— "with two men sleeping in wagon at 2 a. m. at Liberty and Halsted streets;" all arrested. A— F— "sleeping in barn."

---

* See an article by Miss Evelina Belden on the Boys' Court of Chicago, with statistics covering the first six months of the court's work; to be published in the **American Journal of Sociology**, May, 1915.   The material for Table 17 was kindly furnished by Miss Belden.

C— T— "flipping trains into town." W— G— "singing in Lincoln Park at the High Bridge." A— U—, "girl said some remarks were made to her on street by defendant; defendant cannot speak English nor she his language." G— K— "fight in saloon at Wells and Fugel streets; defendant had a lemon squeezer." G— H— "1:45 a. m., Western avenue, coming home from a party." A— D— "5 a. m. refused to move on 'quickly.'" O— M—, son and father arrested together, "driving a horse which ran away in their possession." A— F— "complainant says defendant throws a dog over the fence." L— J— "in crowd near fight." M— K— "fighting with man who refused to leave the hallway where defendant was working." H— U— "in freight yards of railroad." F— W— "sleeping outside Polk Street Depot." F— L— "2:15 a. m. on street at 44th and Montrose," three boys arrested.

Sometimes the same boy is arrested and rearrested on trivial charges several times within a few months. The following cases are those of typical "repeaters":

S— E—, nineteen years, "no license, father had applied for license"; five times in Boys' Court. L— S— "4:30 a. m. on street," has been arrested for disorderly conduct numerous times before and since. E— N— "ran away from home; not working"; arrested three times for similar offenses. J— G— "drinking beer on prairie on way from party," arrested following month for similar offense. J— L— "sleeping in barn"; two weeks later, "rushing the can with a crowd." J— B— "two boys sleeping in hallway," both boys arrested again within a few weeks for similar offense and discharged.

Sec. 21.   The Waste of Needless Arrests.

Judges are not going to sentence or even fine people for trivial offenses, and the question must surely be raised as to whether the costly machinery of the courts, police and jails were devised and are to be supported by the taxpayers for the purpose of dealing with petty offenders. The expense of this machinery in Chicago and Cook County is, in round numbers, something like eight millions of dollars a year.* It is certainly large enough to demand some analysis of the relation between cost and results.

By way of summary it might be repeated with regard to the statistics of arrests and "cases disposed of" that all available statistics show that more than 50 per cent of all the persons arrested and tried are discharged, and for the more serious crimes the percentage discharged runs very much higher. Following the assumption that those discharged are innocent, or at most are guilty of such small offenses that no penalty can be imposed, then more than half of all the 121,333 persons† who were brought into the Municipal Court for felonies, for misdemeanors, or for violations of ordinances should not have been brought into court at all; that is, that more than 60,000 persons were brought into court needlessly. Most of these persons had been arrested, many thousands of them had spent twenty-four hours at least in the police stations,‡ many hundreds had spent weeks or months in the County Jail.§ They had had all the humiliation of being arrested and tried, and the taxpayers had borne the cost of the police who arrested them, of the police stations or jail that had detained them, of the courts and judges and other court officials who had been part of the machinery that tried them. There is more than this to be considered. Unjustified arrests and imprisonment create a disrespect for the law that in turn breeds lawlessness.

---

*This estimate is based on the Comptroller's report for 1913, which showed the following expenditures: For Police Department, $6,622,654.90; for County Jail, Criminal Court, etc., $959,080.51; for the criminal branches of the Municipal Court, $346,714.67; for the City Prosecutor's Office, $54,169.40; for the House of Correction, $226,668.29. Total, $8,209,287.77.

†In 1913, 8,102 felony cases, 19,520 misdemeanors, and 93,711 violations (quasi-criminal) were disposed of; a total of 121,333.

‡It is unfortunately not possible to ascertain precisely how many arrested persons were held over night in the various police stations. But statistics have been obtained showing that 47,862 bail-bonds were accepted by the judges of the Municipal Court during the year 1913. The number granted each month was as follows: January, 3,793; February, 3,801; March, 3,761; April, 3,644; May, 3,467; June, 3,648; July, 4,147; August, 4,522; September, 4,508; October, 4,058; November, 4,502; December, 4,011; total, 47,862.

§See Appendix B of this report.

Sec. 22. Imprisonment for Non-Payment of Fines.

The report of the Department of Police for 1913 shows 1,933 persons sentenced to the House of Correction, and the report of the Municipal Court shows 14,274 persons sentenced during the same year to the same institution. The difference between these two numbers is undoubtedly due to the fact that the number given in the Municipal Court report includes those committed for the non-payment of fine in addition to those who were sentenced as a penalty for the offenses they had committed.* Statistics from the House of Correction confirm the fact that the great majority of the persons committed there are committed for the non-payment of fines.

The following table, which has been compiled from statistics furnished by the Superintendent of the House of Correction, shows the number of persons committed to that institution from 1910 to 1913 and the reason for commitment; i. e., how many and what per cent of those committed were sentenced, committed for non-payment of fines, or both.

TABLE 18. COMMITMENTS TO HOUSE OF CORRECTION: 1910-1913.

Order.	1913.	1912.	1911.	1910.
Numbers.				
Sentenced	895	857	1,097	910
Committed for non-payment of fines..	12,124	9,317	10,987	11,111
Fined and sentenced	1,690	1,108	715	707
Total	14,709	11,282	12,799	12,728
Percentages.				
Order				
Sentenced	6.1	7.6	8.6	7.1
Committed for non-payment of fines..	82.4	82.6	85.8	87.3
Fined and sentenced	11.5	9.8	5.6	5.6
Total	100.0	100.0	100.0	100.0

This table shows that in the year 1913 there were 14,709 persons committed to the House of Correction, but only a very small proportion of these fourteen thousand men and women were committed because they had been sentenced to imprisonment. There were 12,124 persons, or 82.4 per cent of the total number committed, who were sent to the House of Correction solely because of the non-payment of fines. The percentage of commitments for the non-payment of fines was much the same in the three preceding years. In 1910, 87.3 per cent of all persons committed; in 1911, 85.8 per cent; and in 1912, 82.6 per cent were committed for non-payment of fines. During these years the percentage sentenced has slightly decreased, and the percentage of persons who were both fined and sentenced has slightly increased. It should be noted that there were in 1913, 1,690 persons who were both sentenced and fined. The terms of many of these prisoners are extended after sentence of imprisonment has been served because they cannot pay fines. The total number of persons, therefore, whose "board and keep" are being paid by the taxpayers because of non-payment of fines is considerably more than the 12,124 persons who were committed only for this purpose.

It has already been said that most of the commitments for non-payment of fines were for small fines. The following table shows the number of persons committed for fines of specified amounts in the years 1910-1913.

TABLE 19. NUMBER OF PERSONS COMMITTED FOR NON-PAYMENT OF FINES OF SPECIFIED AMOUNTS: 1910-1913.

	1913.	1912.	1911.	1910.
Less than $5	622	257	484	373
$5 and less than $10	1,476	981	1,398	2,050
$10 and less than $15	2,375	1,796	1,905	2,570
$15 and less than $20	2,305	1,900	2,309	2,287
$20 and less than $30	616	746	816	745
$30 and less than $40	2,050	1,694	1,931	1,555
$40 and less than $50	67	110	118	176

*The numbers given are from p. 14, **Annual Report of the Department of Police, 1913**, and from p. 129, **Annual Report of the Municipal Court of Chicago, 1913**. It should be noted that the former report is from the year ending December 30, 1913, and the latter for the year ending November 30, 1913, so that they do not cover exactly the same period.

	1913.	1912.	1911.	1910.
$50 and less than $100	1,346	965	1,238	902
$100 or more	1,267	868	788	453
Total	12,124	9,317	10,987	11,111

According to this table in 1913, 4,473 persons, or more than one-third of those committed for non-payment of fines were committed because they were unable to pay fines of less than $15; 2,305 more could not pay fines ranging from $15 to $20, so that more than one-half of all the 12,124 persons committed for non-payment of fines were serving terms at the House of Correction because they could not pay fines of less than $20. Fines are "laid out" at the rate of 50 cents per day, and these fines are, therefore, paid in two ways: (1) by the taxpayers, for the expense of maintenance at the Bridewell is 46.2 cents per man per day and the total cost of maintenance in 1913 was $290,814.78;* and (2) by the men and their families in privation and deep humiliation. Many states and cities are now substituting the more enlightened system of payment of fines in installments, under probation, with very satisfactory results. The old theory was, of course, that fines were "worked out" in prison, but the recent report of the Civil Service Commission on **Prison Labor and Management House of Correction** shows how far, in practice, we have departed from that theory.

The following tables show the terms for which prisoners were sentenced when they were sentenced only and not fined, and the terms when both sentenced and fined.

TABLE 20. TERMS OF THOSE COMMITTED TO SERVE SENTENCES IN THE HOUSE OF CORRECTION. (NOT INCLUDING THOSE SENTENCED AND FINED): 1913.

Term.	Number.
Less than 10 days	8
10 days and less than 1 month	14
1 and less than 2 months	60
2 and less than 3 months	47
3 and less than 4 months	60
4 and less than 5 months	18
5 and less than 6 months	4
6 and less than 7 months	469
7 and less than 8 months	...
8 and less than 9 months	8
9 and less than 10 months	10
10 and less than 11 months	5
11 months to 1 year (inclusive)	192
Total	895

TABLE 21. TERMS OF THOSE COMMITTED TO SERVE SENTENCES IN THE HOUSE OF CORRECTION IN ADDITION TO PAYING FINES: 1913.

Term.	Number.
Less than 10 days	281
10 days and less than 1 month	149
1 and less than 2 months	346
2 and less than 3 months	116
3 and less than 4 months	208
4 and less than 5 months	28
5 and less than 6 months	6
6 and less than 7 months	260
7 and less than 8 months	6
8 and less than 9 months	5
9 and less than 10 months	31
10 and less than 11 months	13
11 months and over	241
Total	1,690

*This is not the net cost, because the labor of prisoners earned $64,190.51 in the contract industries. The net cost was, therefore, $226,624.27 or 36.05 cents per man per day. See Report by the Civil Service Commission, City of Chicago, 1914, on **Prison Labor and Management House of Correction**, pp. 15-16; and p. 60.

All those committed, however, do not pay off their whole fine by imprisonment, and some of those sentenced do not serve out the whole of their terms. The following table shows how the prisoners convicted from 1908-1913 obtained their release.

TABLE 22. METHOD OF RELEASE OF PRISONERS COMMITTED TO HOUSE OF CORRECTION: 1908-1913.

How Released.	1908.	1909.	1910.	1911.	1912.	1913.
Expiration of sentence.............	8,156	7,940	8,280	7,934	7,045	8,584
Paid fine to House of Correction....	2,224	2,540	2,760	2,632	2,570	3,172
Pardoned by Mayor.................	1,145	852	904	720	443	523
Pardoned by Governor.............	4	2	4	3	1	6
Pardoned by President of the U. S..	....	2	....	....	....	....
Paroled by U. S. Board of Parole....	....	....	....	1	....	....
Court Orders	725	750	844	1,102	1,280	1,781
Order Other Municipal Authorities..	17	13	34	43	44	65
Transferred Detention Hospital, etc..	26	35	30	49	42	69
Deaths	34	43	50	48	51	46
Escapes ....√.................	2	4	7	1	4	6
Total	12,333	12,181	12,913	12,533	11,480	14,252
Circuit Court (Juvenile Branch)......	456	347	343	....	....	....
Total	12,789	12,528	13,256	12,533	11,480	14,252

According to this table, 3,172 of the prisoners who were convicted in 1913 because they could not pay their fine, managed in some way to get enough money to pay some part of it at least. Five hundred and twenty-three, or 3.7 per cent, were released by Mayor's pardons, but the statistics do not show how many of those pardoned were sentenced and how many were merely serving out fines.

To summarize: There were 14,709 persons committed to the House of Correction in 1913. Only 2,585, or 17.6 per cent of this number, were committed because they had been sentenced to imprisonment, and of this 2,585 who were sentenced, 2,074, or 80.2 per cent, were sentenced for short terms varying from one day to six months. Of all the 14,709 persons committed only 511 had committed offenses serious enough to earn them a prison term of as long a period as seven months. The great majority, more than 80 per cent of these 14,709 persons who were committed were not imprisoned because of their offenses but because of their poverty. That is, 12,124 of the 14,709 men and women in the House of Correction were there only because they were too poor to pay the small fines assessed against them.

Sec. 23. Habitual Criminals.

The publication of statistics showing the number of previous convictions of those who were adjudged guilty is a matter of great importance. It is necessary that the judge should know before passing sentence on a prisoner exactly what the man's record has been. Statistics showing the proportion of convicted criminals who have been convicted before have long been available in the official statistics of England, France and Germany. Very recently New York has inaugurated a most admirable system of finger printing, which is used at present for all persons convicted of certain offenses. The person is finger-printed immediately after conviction, his finger print can be quickly identified, and his record is placed before the judge who is then able to pronounce sentence intelligently on the basis of the man's actual record.*

---

*See the **Annual Report of the Board of City Magistrates of the City of New York (First Division),** 1913; the report of the Chief Magistrate says: "The right to finger-print defendants after conviction, in such cases as the Board of Magistrates may determine upon, was put in force early in the year and is now in successful operation. * * * Under a resolution of the Board, we first began with those convicted of intoxication, which resulted in a very short time in detecting repeated offenders, men and women, as chronic drunkards. These prints will be invaluable when the Inebriate Home, which the city is about to construct, is completed. * * * Later the Board extended the system to those convicted of "jostling" (professional pickpockets), "mashers" (insulters of women) and "rowdies." (Pp. 30-35. See also pp. 61-62.)

For Chicago no statistics are available either in the police or court reports showing the previous convictions or sentences of those arrested and sentenced. No records are kept anywhere from which such statistics can be compiled. The Department of Police maintains a Bureau of Identification with a system of photographing and finger-printing, but it is largely a matter of chance as to who is photographed and as to whether the record of a criminal is asked for before he is sentenced, the judge relying largely on the statement of the prisoner and the memory of the officer.* In general, all persons who are held to the Grand Jury and are **not released on bail** are taken to the Bureau, photographed and finger-printed. This seems a very unfair

---

*The recent reports of the Department of Police publish statistics from the Bureau of Identification with little or no comment or explanations. In one of the earlier reports (1907), however, there is the following statement in the report on the Bureau of Identification made by Captain Evans, its superintendent: "Many of our Municipal Judges desire records of persons brought before them, and during the past year I have supplied a large number of such records to our Judges. In fact, some of the Judges send prisoners to the Bureau to find out if they have criminal records, before passing sentence; and they show excellent judgement in the subjects selected, as in the majority of cases, upon being checked up, it is found that they have previously passed through the Bureau on criminal charges. All subjects are measured and checked up by the Bertillon system, and also the Finger Print system, to ascertain if they have previously passed through this Bureau or other similar Bureaus throughout this country and Europe. If there is no record found against them, then, from a police standpoint, it is a recommendation of good character; but we find a great many of such suspects are ex-convicts and ex-reformatories, wanted for violation of parole in this and other states or wanted for forfeiting their bonds in Chicago, or elsewhere. All such persons are held by us to be returned where they are wanted; this also includes the professional thieves arrested and photographed in other cities or penitentiaries. The fact that out of 1,660 suspects brought to this Bureau, 655 of them, or over 39 per cent, were identified, shows conclusively that this system should be followed up. Some of our stations are very efficient in doing so, while others are not. While the identification of persons arrested may mean little or nothing to the average citizen, to the experienced officer it means a great deal. In the majority of cases where said identifications show the persons to have a previous criminal record, it means the breaking down of the prisoner; this is followed by a confession which ultimately means the recovery of stolen property, information in regard to other thieves, and best of all, the location of 'Fences,' where stolen property is disposed of, and which are schools for the education of young criminals."

In the 1909 report, there is further explanation of the work of the Bureau by Captain Evans: "In relation to photographing persons brought to the Bureau, I regret to state that comments have recently been made by officials and others, that photographs have been taken of persons who have been simply charged and found guilty of violating City Ordinances. This is not so, unless we are sure that the persons had previous criminal record here or elsewhere. A very large number of people and some officials believe that all persons brought to this Bureau are photographed. The following statement shows conclusively that this is not so: For instance, out of the 8,282 brought to the Bureau last year, only 3,175 were photographed. In regard to suspects, these are persons brought to the Bureau to be checked up to see if they had previous criminal records here or elsewhere; these persons are never photographed unless we find that they had a previous criminal record, and among this class are the persons who are fined $50.00 or more by the Municipal Courts and by general order are brought to the Bureau to be checked up to see if they have previous criminal records. I am pleased to state that the number of suspects brought to the Bureau during the past year, and the following results shown in connection with them, is very creditable to the Department. Of the 3,258 suspects brought to the Bureau, 1,397 were identified as having previously been here or had records elsewhere, and as I stated in my last annual report, there is no class of work performed by the Department which tends to keep professional criminals away from our city as this does, especially those wanted for violation of parole, forfeiture of bond, etc."

and illogical arrangement. If there is a reason for photographing a man before he is tried and while he is still only a suspect, the reason should apply equally to those in jail and on bail. A practice of finger-printing and photo-graphing only the men and women who cannot afford bail seems hard to justify.

Last year (1913), 3,272 persons, including 157 women, were photographed and 2,383, including 136 women, were finger-printed. There were, however, 7 476 persons (7,222 men and 254 women) taken to the bureau during that year. Of these, 3,460 were "suspects" and the others were those brought to be registered. The following table shows the previous records of 2,575 men and women who had "criminal records."

TABLE 23. NUMBER BROUGHT TO THE BUREAU OF IDENTIFI-CATION WHO HAD CRIMINAL RECORDS IN THE FOLLOW-ING INSTITUTIONS:

Record in Joliet	540
Record in Pontiac	288
Record in County Jail	116
Record in House of Correction	1,041
"Local identification"*	590
Total	2,575

This table is not very valuable since it does not tell us why these 2,575 persons were brought to the Bureau of Identification. Were they "suspects" only or were they being held for some new crime? If the latter, what was done with them?

The following table shows the total number of persons brought to the bureau.

TABLE 24. NUMBER OF PERSONS BROUGHT TO THE BUREAU OF IDENTIFICATION.

Brought to the Bureau	7,476
N. G. cases*	744
Photographs taken	3,272
Finger-prints taken	2,383
Number identified	3,874

A table is given showing the disposition of the cases that passed through the bureau as follows:

TABLE 25. DISPOSITION OF CASES WHICH PASSED THROUGH THE BUREAU.

Guilty	1,862
Not guilty	1,001
Nolle pros.	131
Stricken off	288
Own recognizances	56
No bills	532
Pending	146
Total criminal cases	4,016
"Suspects"	3,460
Total	7,476

This table is not very enlightening. It does not show us whether those found guilty were those who were found to have had previous records; or were they the first offenders and were those who "got off" the habituals?

It seems clear, however, that such system as exists of photographing and finger-printing is primarily, if not exclusively, for those arrested on felony charges. No records are kept of the number of times those guilty of misde-meanors or violations reappear and are resentenced or let off, as the case may be. Some interesting statistics are kept, however, at the House of Cor-rection. There an attempt is made to ascertain from those committed the number of previous commitments. The following table shows the number of first offenders and habitual offenders in 1913.

*These terms "Local identification" and "N. G. cases" are used in the tables in the police report without explanation. The latter seems to mean "unidentified."

TABLE 26. NUMBER OF TIMES PERSONS OVER 16 YEARS OF AGE
ADMIT HAVING BEEN COMMITTED TO THE HOUSE
OF CORRECTION: 1913.

Number of Times.	Men.	Women.
1 time	7,815	679
2 times	2,557	254
3 times	1,106	126
4 times	539	88
5 times	308	72
6 times	178	52
7 times	225	51
8 times	87	20
9 times	73	26
10 and less than 12 times	81	44
12 and less than 15 times	96	46
15 and less than 20 times	36	29
20 and less than 30 times	34	47
30 and less than 50 times	4	16
50 and less than 70 times	....	12
70 and less than 100 times	....	1
100 times and over *	2	5
Total	13,141	1,568

*One man and five women said they had been there 101 times or more,
and one man said this was his 301st time.

Sec. 24. General Summary.

To summarize the statistical material relating to arrest and trial, the following points should, perhaps, be emphasized:

1. A very small percentage of the large number of persons arrested are charged with serious offenses. Last, year, the number of arrests (charges) all came to the large total of 109,764, but only 11,203 of these were felony charges, even according to the police classification, which includes some offenses, e. g., petit larceny and "contributing to delinquency," that are not felonies. That is, according to the police classification only about 10 per cent of all offenses were felony charges. The Municipal Court statistics show even a smaller percentage of serious offenses. Out of 121,333 cases disposed of in the criminal branches, including all preliminary hearings. criminal and quasi-criminal cases only 8,102, or 7 per cent, were preliminary hearings on felony charges. The vast majority of persons arrested and the vast majority of persons tried in the criminal branches of our Municipal Court are petty offenders.

2. The next point of importance is the fact that the majority of the thousands of persons who are brought into our courts are discharged without conviction. The statistics of the criminal branches of the Municipal Court show that out of the 121,333 cases disposed of in 1913, 57.5 per cent were discharged and that for the more serious crimes the percentage of discharges was very much higher. More than 60 per cent of all felony cases were discharged on preliminary hearings alone and many others were discharged by the Grand Jury and by the Criminal Court without conviction. In 1912, the only year for which statistics of final disposition in the Criminal Court were available, the number of convictions was only 13 per cent of the number of preliminary hearings, making a total of 87 per cent of discharged felony cases.

The hardships and waste of this system are obvious. Following the assumption that those discharged are innocent, then 57 per cent of all the 121,333 persons who were brought into the Municipal Court for felonies, for misdemeanors, or for violations of ordinances were innocent and should not have been brought into court at all; that is, more than 60,000 persons were brought into court needlessly. Nearly all of these persons had been arrested, many thousands of them had spent hours at the police stations, many hundreds had spent weeks or months in the County Jail. They had all had the humiliation and expense of being arrested and tried, and the taxpayers had borne the cost of the police who arrested them, of the police stations or jails that had detained them, of the courts and judges and other court officials who

*In 1913, 8,102 felony cases, 19,520 misdemeanors and 93,711 violations (quasi-criminal) were disposed of; a total of 121,333.

had been part of the machinery that tried them. There is more than this to be considered. Unjustified arrests and imprisonment create a disrespect for the law that in turn breeds lawlessness.

In New York, a marked decrease in the number of unnecessary arrests has been brought about by the increased use of the "summons" in the last few years. The last report (1913) of the Board of City Magistrates of New York publishes statistics showing that the percentage convicted or held has increased from 54.5 per cent in 1910 to 72.8 per cent in 1913. In Chicago the percentage convicted or held was 42.4 per cent in 1910 and 42.5 per cent in 1913. In the New York Magistrates' report the following statement is made with regard to the results of the new system: "The use of the summons was very widely extended by the Inferior Courts Act in 1910 in order to avoid taking citizens needlessly into custody * * * in former years about half of those arrested were adjudged not guilty, and were, therefore, discharged. Since 1910 the percentage discharged has much decreased, indicating great diminution in the number of needless arrests."*

3. The next point of interest is that the percentage of those sentenced to imprisonment is about 3 per cent of the total number charged. This again emphasizes the fact that the machinery of courts and police are maintained largely for those who are discharged as innocent or for those whose offenses are not serious enough to deserve more than a fine. Out of 109,711 persons arrested in 1913, only 141 were sentenced to the County Jail, 1,935 were sentenced to the House of Correction and 2,182 were held to the Grand Jury, altogether 3 per cent of the total, and of those held to the Grand Jury (2.0 per cent) the proportion given prison sentences is about one-half. It seems beyond question, therefore, that not more than three out of every hundred cases brought before the Municipal Courts by the police department are considered serious enough to be given sentences of imprisonment.

4. Another important and closely related point is the fact that more than 80 per cent of the persons committed to the House of Correction are there for the non-payment of fines. The Municipal Court statistics show that although only about two thousand persons were sentenced to imprisonment, more than twelve thousand others were committed to the House of Correction for the non-payment of fines. The statistics furnished by the House of Correction show that 82.4 per cent of the persons committed in 1913 were committed only for the non-payment of fines. In 1912, 82.6 per cent were committed for the non-payment of fines; in 1911, 85.8 per cent and in 1910, 87.3 per cent were committed for this reason.

That this system which virtually sends men to jail because of their poverty is not only unjust but demoralizing to the individual and costly to the state is now becoming widely recognized. In many places the more enlightened system has been adopted of suspending sentence and sending the man back to his family and his "job," and allowing him to pay back his fine in small installments. This installment-fine system was adopted in Massachusetts in 1909, and has been more widely used each year in that state. It is also used at the present time in New York, in Indianapolis, in Kansas City and in Cleveland. Chicago would not be making a hazardous experiment if she released the 85 per cent of offenders in the House of Correction who are

---

*See discussion of "The Summons" and "Needless Arrests," **Annual Report of the Board of City Magistrates of the City of New York (First Division)**, 1913, p. 97. The Report of New York Criminal Courts Committee contains the following paragraph regarding the success of the new system: "The use of the summons, which has proved so beneficial in practice, has been extended by providing that the summons may be used in cases of violations of the Sanitary Code or failure to observe regulations of the various City Departments, thus permitting such cases as spitting on the sidewalk and smoking in the subway to be brought to court by summons and not subject offenders, who in such case generally err through thoughtlessness or ignorance, to the ignominy of arrest."

there for the non-payment of fines to go back to work under the supervision of probation officers.*

5. This summary is not complete without noting the fact that there are no available statistics either in the police reports or the Municipal Court reports showing the number of previous convictions of persons sentenced. If the work of the courts and penal institutions is for the reformation rather than the punishment of those arrested and convicted, it is of the first importance that the first offenders be distinguished from the habitual criminal. The official reports of England, France and Germany furnish statistics showing the number of habitual criminals among those convicted, and, more recently, New York has taken a step in advance of Chicago by inaugurating an excellent system of finger-printing all convicted persons of certain classes and placing the record of each person before the judge in order that sentence may be pronounced that is in some measure likely to be the treatment needed and merited.

6. In conclusion, the importance of collecting and publishing adequate statistics relating to crime in a great city like Chicago may be emphasized. In this part of the report, it has been pointed out, for example, that there are no published statistics available for Chicago showing the number of "crimes known to the police," the number of habitual offenders, the number of persons discharged by the Grand Jury and the Criminal Court, the number of discharged persons who have not only been arrested and tried but who have been imprisoned one or more days in a police station or for a longer

---

*This system has been recommended by the Chief Probation Officer of the Adult Probation Office of Cook County in his two annual reports. In Massachusetts during the year 1913, $49,304.09 of fines imposed was collected by probation officers from persons on probation. The last report of the New York State Probation Association contains the following statement regarding the practice of collecting fines in installments from persons on probation in that state: "Never was there a wider recognition than at present of the injustice and social short-sightedness of the prevailing fine system, whereby defendants unable to pay their fines in full at the time of conviction are ordinarily obliged to suffer imprisonment at the rate (in this State) of one day for each unpaid dollar of the fine. As has repeatedly been pointed out, this equivalent to imprisonment for debt, and the persons thereby made to suffer the most are often the innocent wives and children.

"Although the actual amount of the fines reported above as collected by probation officers in installments from persons permitted to earn and pay their fines while on probation looks small, it is very gratifying (in view of the humanitarian benefits of this means of collecting fines) to know that the collections nearly doubled during the past year. In cases where the requiring of large installments would inflict hardship upon the probationer or his family, the court usually allows the installments to be small, often not more than fifty or twenty-five cents a week, or even less. While the ordinary fine system may be said to place a price upon the commission of offenses, the collection of fines from probationers, in installments has as it object, in most cases, not so much the enacting of a money penalty as the exerting of a disciplinary and reformatory influence." **Sixth Annual Report of the New York State Probation Commission** (1912), pp. 27-28, "Installment Fines."

In the Municipal Court of Kansas City, the system of installment fines was instituted in 1912 and the last (1913) report of the Court says: "The installment fine plan has continued to work out in the manner described in the last report. It is no longer in an experimental stage and has become a permanent institution in the work of this Court. * * * Up to this date, of all those who have been given the chance to pay in installments only 2 per cent have come back on second offenses, while at least 25 per cent of all those brought into court are "repeaters." **Annual Report of Division No. 2 of the Municipal Court of Kansas City, Missouri, 1913.**

In the City Court of Indianapolis, the system of installment fines was established in 1910, and the last (1912) report of the Court reported that "The payment of money fines on installments is a most important feature of the work of the Court. * * * During the 36 months that this plan has been in operation these probationers have paid into the Court the sum of $27,410.00." Out of 1,211 persons placed on probation in 1912, 69 had failed to keep their agreement with the Court and had been ordered re-arrested.

period in the County Jail, the length of term of persons sentenced, the amount of fine assessed * —to mention only some of the most significant omissions in our Chicago crime statistics.†

Chicago has been making satisfactory progress towards the proper collection of vital statistics. We are included in the "registration area" for mortality statistics under the supervision of the Federal Census Bureau, and there is reason to hope that before the close of the next session of the Legislature we shall become part of the federal birth-registration area. It is to be hoped that progress will also be made towards the proper collection of statistics of crime, so that when the federal census is ready to do for criminal statistics what it has done for vital statistics we shall be prepared to co-operate without delay.

Criminal statistics show us where we are going in the treatment of persons convicted and accused of crime. Lives are really destroyed, not only by death but whenever the efficiency of men or women is so impaired that they are thrown on the human scrap-heap. It is, therefore, no exaggeration to say that the importance to human welfare of a careful examination by the community of its statistics of crime is scarcely less than the study of statistics of mortality and morbidity. It is hardly necessary to point out the importance of knowing the number and the percentage of needless and unjust arrests, and arrests for trifling offenses, the number and the percentage of persons imprisoned for the non-payment of fines, the prevalence of small fines and short sentences. The arrest in a single year of 110,000 persons in a city with an adult population of about a million and a half persons is a matter of grave importance, and it is the duty of the community to inquire why these persons were arrested, and what has been done with them and for them.

---

*Statistics are always given showing the total number of persons fined and total amount of fines assessed, but what is wanted, of course, is not the "average fine," which can be computed from these data, but a table showing the number of persons assessed fines of varying amounts.

†See the report of John Koren, chairman of the Committee on Statistics, American Institute of Criminal Law and Criminology, in the **Journal of Criminal Law and Criminology,** Vol. II: 569 (Nov., 1911), for a list of items relating to the judicial process on which it is suggested statistics should be furnished by the courts.

Part II

STATISTICS RELATING TO SOCIAL STATUS OF OFFENDERS

The Committee on Statistics of the American Institute of Criminal Law and Criminology in its statement of the minimum requirements of Criminal Court records reported that court statistics should furnish information not only regarding the criminal process but should furnish also the following data regarding the social status of the defendants:* Age, sex, color, race, birthplace of parents, conjugal condition, education, occupation, citizenship and previous convictions. It is important to note that the reports of the Municipal Court of Chicago, excellent as they are on the whole, do not contain information on one of these points. The reports of the police department, however, furnish some of the information. Statistics showing age, sex, conjugal condition, color, nationality, and occupations are given in the police reports. Statistics regarding education, citizenship and previous convictions are not furnished in Chicago either in the police or court reports. Moreover, it should be noted that the police statistics relating to nationality and occupation are far from satisfactory. The table of occupations is not very dependable since the occupations of more than 10 per cent are not given at all. The statistics for "nativity" are not at all equivalent to the more accurate data regarding "race, birthplace and birthplace of parents" recommended by the Committee on Criminal Statistics.

In the following pages, then, such statistics as are available regarding the social status of those arrested in Chicago are presented. It should be explained that in all the tables that follow, the statistics relate to "persons arrested" and not to "charges." Since nearly all the tables in Part I dealt with "charges" instead of with "persons arrested," the 1913 total in the two parts will be different.†

Sec. 1. Age and Sex of Chicago Offenders.

In the following table are presented statistics from the **Annual Report of the Police Department, 1913,** showing the age and sex of the persons arrested in 1913:

TABLE 27. NUMBER OF MEN AND WOMEN ARRESTED BY AGE GROUPS.

	Male			Female			Total		
Age	No.	Per cent		No.	Per cent		No.	Per cent	
Under 16 yrs of age	40	*		6	.1		46	*	
From 16 to 19 yrs.	12,151	12.7		817	6.9		12,968	12.1	
From 20 to 24 yrs.	23,433	24.6	69.2	3,639	30.9	85.0	27,072	25.3	82.3
From 25 to 29 yrs.	19,500	20.4		2,776	23.6		22,276	20.8	
From 30 to 39 yrs.	23,093	24.2		2,767	23.5		25,860	24.1	
From 40 to 49 yrs.	11,478	12.0		1,307	11.1		12,785	11.9	
From 50 to 59 yrs.	4,401	4.6		355	3.0		4,756	4.4	
60 years and over..	1,390	1.5		105	.9		1,494	1.4	
Total	95,486	100.0		11,771	100.0		107,257	100.0	
Per cent	89.0	....		11.0	....		100.0	....	

*Less than 1 per cent.

---

*See Journal of Criminal Law and Criminology, Vol. I: 426 (Sept., 1910).

†See Table 1, note, in Part I of this report. In 1913 there were 107,257 "persons arraigned" and 109,764 "charges," so that there were 2,507 cases of more than one charge against the same person. It should, however, be explained further that if the same person is arrested at different times, this is, of course, counted as two arrests since there is in Chicago no method of counting repeaters.

For this reason, our statistics showing "number of persons arrested," do not bear comparison in any exact way with English statistics, since the English method is to count each person arrested only once, and if anyone is arrested more than once, this fact appears in the statistics of previous convictions.

This table shows that in Chicago, as in all other parts of this and other countries, the great majority of the persons charged with crimes or misdemeanors are adult males between twenty and forty years of age. Thus, in Chicago, 89 per cent of those arrested were males, and 69.2 per cent of the total number of males arrested were between the ages of twenty and forty. It is important to note, however, that in Chicago a large number of boys under twenty are among those arrested. Last year more than 12,000 boys between the ages of sixteen and twenty were arrested. Looking at the table of percentages carefully, it is clear that youth is an important factor in crime and disorder. Thus 12.1 per cent were under twenty years of age, 57.7 per cent were under thirty, and 81.9 per cent were under forty years of age.

Sec. 2. Chicago's Women Offenders.

Table 27, which shows that only 11 per cent of the persons arrested in Chicago in 1913 were women and girls, should be compared with the following table from the most recent United States Census Report on Prisoners. This report, published in 1910, gives the following statistics regarding the sex of prisoners committed during 1910 to the two state penitentiaries of Illinois, the Cook County Jail, and the Chicago House of Correction.

TABLE 28. SEX OF PERSONS COMMITTED TO ILLINOIS STATE PENITENTIARIES, COOK COUNTY JAIL, AND HOUSE OF CORRECTION.

	Male		Female		Total	
Committed to	No.	Per cent	No.	Per cent	No.	Per cent
State penitentiaries (Joliet and Menard)	821	97.3	23	2.7	844	100.0
Cook County Jail	595	90.2	65	9.8	660	100.0
Chicago House of Correction.	11,410	89.3	1,379	10.7	12,789	100.0

This table is of interest in showing that the percentage of women prisoners is greatest in the House of Correction and smallest in the penitentiary, where only 2.7 per cent of the prisoners are women.

Examining the statistics in Table 27 relating to the age of the women arrested, it appears that a large proportion of the women are, like the men, under forty years of age. Seven per cent were young girls between the ages of sixteen and twenty, 61.5 per cent were under thirty, and 85 per cent were under forty years of age.

With more than eleven thousand* women and girls arrested in a single year, it seems important to bring together such other statistics as are available relating to Chicago's women offenders. The question of greatest interest is probably the reason for their arrest.

The following tables show the number of charges against the women arrested, the character of the charges, i. e., whether they were felonies or misdemeanors, and the disposition of the cases in the Municipal or Criminal Court.

TABLE 29. CHARGES: MEN AND WOMEN OFFENDERS, 1913.

	Men.		Women.	
Offenses.	Number.	Per Cent.	Number.	Per Cent.
Felonies	10,237	10.5	966	7.8
Misdemeanors	87,156	89.5	11,405	92.2
Total	97,393	100.0	12,371	100.0

*The police report shows 11,771 women arraigned, but it should be pointed out that the number of women arrested was probably considerably larger than this. In the year 1912, for example, there were 9,561 women arraigned, but the police matron's report, published in the General Superintendent's report for that year, showed 12,631 women and 1,851 young girls arrested and brought to the different police stations in the same year. Unfortunately, the chief matron's report is not included in the report for 1913: The following table showing the number brought to the different precinct stations is taken therefore from the report for 1912:

Women arrested 12,631
Young girls arrested................. 1,851

Total 14,482

As a matter of fact even this total of 14,482 women and girls arrested is very far still from the total number of wretched, degraded, criminal, or

Table 29 shows that less than 8 per cent of the women arrested were charged with felonies and that 92.2 per cent were charged only with misdemeanors. Corresponding statistics for the men arrested are presented in the same table, and show that 10.5 per cent of the men were arrested on felony charges and 89.5 per cent for misdemeanors; that is, a slightly larger percentage of the men than of the women are charged with serious offenses. A comparison between the percentages of men and women convicted and discharged, which is also important, is presented in Table 30.

TABLE 30. NUMBER AND PER CENT OF MEN AND WOMEN CONVICTED AND DISCHARGED.

Disposition	Men.		Women.	
	Number.	Per Cent.	Number.	Per Cent.
Convicted and held..........	43,629	44.8	5,946	48.1
Discharged	53,764	55.2	6,425	51.9
Total number arrested...	97,393	100.0	12,371	100.0

Although the total number of men arrested is almost eight times the number of women arrested, this table shows that the percentage of convictions is slightly higher among women than among men. This may be due to the fact, shown in the next table, that a larger percentage of the women who are convicted are fined and that convictions are more easily secured for that reason.

TABLE 31. DISPOSITION OF CASES OF MEN AND WOMEN CONVICTED.

Disposition	Men.		Women.	
	Number.	Per Cent.	Number.	Per Cent.
Sentenced	2,379	5.4	163	2.8
Fined	38,697	88.7	5,437	91.4
Paroled	1,597	3.7	321	5.4

dependent women who passed through the police stations during the year. The following table, taken from the chief matron's report, is important enough to be included:

Disposition of Women Brought to Police Stations, 1912.
(FROM CHIEF MATRON'S REPORT.)

Sent to House of Correction..............................	1,032
Sent to House of Good Shepherd..........................	82
State Home for Female Juvenile Court....................	577
Sent to Erring Woman's Refuge...........................	17
Sent to Martha Washington Home.........................	21
Held to Criminal Court...................................	144
Sent to County Jail.......................................	12
Fined	2,908
Released on Peace Bonds..................................	121
Discharged by the Court..................................	5.371
Held as Witnesses..	2,318
Insane Women Sent Home.................................	88
Insane Women Sent to Detention Hospital................	205
Runaway Girls Returned to their Parents..................	300
Runaway Girls Returned to Institutions...................	24
Destitute Women Sent to County Agent...................	37
Destitute Women Sent to Home for the Friendless.........	50
Destitute Women Sent to Aid Societies....................	26
Destitute Women, Employment Found.....................	73
Sick Women Sent Home...................................	127
Sick Women Sent to Hospital.............................	135
Women Lodgers	1,617
Lost Women Returned to their Homes.....................	161
Children Lodgers	1,255
Destitute Children Sent to Home for the Friendless........	20
Destitute Children Handed over to Humane Society........	2
Lost Children Sent Home..................................	2,731
Foundlings Sent to St. Vincent's Infant Asylum...........	34
Foundlings Sent to Foundlings' Home.....................	3
Boys	1,521
Returned to Courts.......................................	3,459
Total	24,471

| | Men. | | Women. | |
Disposition.	Number.	Per Cent.	Number.	Per Cent.
Weekly payments or peace bonds	956	2.2	25	.4
Total convicted	43,629	100.0	5,946	100.0

From the statistics of disposition presented in Table 31, it is evident that a very small per cent of the men and women convicted, only 5.4 per cent of the men and 2.8 per cent of the women, were sentenced to imprisonment of any kind. The great majority of those convicted, 88.7 per cent of the men and 91.4 per cent of the women, were fined. But although only 163 women were sentenced in 1913, a large number were committed for the non-payment of fines, and the records of the House of Correction show 1,568 women were committed there in 1913. The large proportion of women fined and the large proportion committed for the non-payment of fines is explained by an examination of the offenses for which they are arrested. Table 32 shows the specific offenses, both felonies and misdemeanors, for which women were arrested and convicted in 1913.

TABLE 32. OFFENSES FOR WHICH WOMEN WERE ARRESTED IN 1913.

I. Felonies (including all larcenies.)

Offenses.	Arrests.	Convictions.
Abduction and kidnaping............	8	...
Abortion	5	...
Arson	7	...
Burglary	21	2
Confidence game	35	6
Contributing to delinquency	80	43
Embezzlement and forgery..........	11	...
Larceny	639	254
Malicious mischief	13	3
Murder and manslaughter..........	58	3
Receiving stolen property...........	44	7
Robbery	24	6
Threats to kidnap or murder........	5	3
Other felonies	16	...
Total Felonies	966	327

Burglary includes Accessory and Attempted and Having Burglar's Tools; Larceny includes Accessory and Attempted; Murder includes Accessory and Assault to Commit; Robbery includes Accessory and Assault to Commit; Conspiracy, Counterfeiting, Incest, Perjury, Abandonment of child under one year old (1 case), Pandering (1 case), and Bigamy (3 cases) are included under Other Felonies.

II. Misdemeanors.

		—Convictions—	
			Per cent
		Num-	of
	Arrests.	ber,	Arrests
"Disorderly Cases" (including vice)...............	10,849	5,326	49.1
Adultery, etc.	210	64	...
Disorderly conduct	6,229	1,993	...
Inmates of disorderly houses and houses of ill fame	2,254	1,644	...
Keepers of houses of ill fame.....................	418	315	...
Inmates or keepers of opium dens................	22	15	...
Street walkers	1,645	1,273	...
Vagrancy	71	22	...
Miscellaneous	556	293	52.7
Assault	86	37	...
Carrying concealed weapons......................	16	13	...
Inmates of gambling houses......................	10	5	...

	Arrests.	—Convictions— Number.	Per Cent of Arrests.
Keepers of gambling houses......................	31	3	...
Motor vehicle violations........................	17	13	...
Obtaining money or goods by false pretenses.....	29	9	...
Resisting an officer............................	7	3	...
Selling liquor to minors or drunks..............	9	5	...
Other misdemeanors	351	205	...
Total misdemeanors	11,405	5,619	49.3
Total felonies	966	327	33.9
Total all offenses........................	12,371	5,946	48.1

This table shows that the different forms of disorderly conduct, including under this classification the various offenses against public morals, were charged against 95 per cent of the women arrested for misdemeanors in 1913. The percentage of convictions was very much higher for these cases than for the offenses classified as felonies; that is, 33.9 per cent of those arrested on felony and larceny charges were convicted, whereas ·49.1 per cent of those arrested for the "disorderly" offenses were convicted. It is also of special importance to note that more than one-third (34.2 per cent) of all the women arrested for misdemeanors were charged with the specific offenses of street-soliciting or being inmates of houses of ill-fame. According to the Illinois Statutes women cannot be sentenced for these offenses, they can only be fined. All of those interested in the proper care and treatment of women of this group unite in condemning the system of fining. The Chicago Vice Commission recommended the abolition of fines for this offense, and it is safe to say that little can be done for the women of this group until the present method of treatment is radically changed.

Other statistics of importance concerning the women offenders of Chicago are those showing color and nationality. The following table presents the statistics given in the police report concerning general nativity of the women arrested in 1913. For purposes of comparison statistics from the federal census are given showing the general nativity of the female population over fifteen years of age:

TABLE 33.   GENERAL NATIVITY OF WOMEN OFFENDERS: CHICAGO POLICE REPORT: 1913.

Nativity.	Arrests. Number.	Per Cent.	Convictions. Number.	Per Cent.	Female Population 15 Years and Over, 1910. Number.	Per Cent.
American—						
White	6,823	55.1	3,532	59.4	410,034	53.9
Colored	1,827	14.8	1,019	17.1	17,962	2.4
Foreign	3,721	30.1	1,395	23.5	332,267	43.7
Total	12,371	100.0	5,946	100.0	760,263	100.0

According to this table * the foreign-born women form a very small percentage of the women arrested in 1913 in comparison with their percentage of the population. That is, although 43.7 per cent of the total female population fifteen years of age and over were foreign born, only 30.1 per cent of the women arrested and only 23.5 per cent of the women convicted were foreign born. The percentage of white American women arrested is slightly in excess of their share of the population and the per cent of white Americans among those convicted is still higher, 59.4 per cent of those convicted and 55.1 per cent of those arrested, in comparison with 53.9 per cent of the female population over fifteen years of age.† It is the colored women, however, who

*For discussion of the value of these statistics, see the section on "Crime and Immigration."

†The following table shows the number of women belonging to the various nationalities together with the percentage distribution of the population by nationalities. Unfortunately it is not possible to obtain comparable statistics of the female population by nationalities. So the percentage distribution of the total population of both sexes is given. It is pointed out in the section dealing with Immigration and Crime that this results in a comparison unfair

make the most unfavorable showing in this table. Although the colored women form only 2.4 per cent of the total female population over fifteen years of age, 14.8 per cent of the women arrested are colored and 17.1 per cent of the women convicted are colored. This disproportionately large share of colored women offenders may be attributed largely to the generally unfortunate position in which the whole colored race finds itself, the difficulty of securing and holding employment, the difficulty of finding suitable places to live, the proximity of segregated vice districts to colored residence districts, and the fact that because of the assumption that they belong to an inferior race, young colored women find themselves in a peculiarly defenseless and unprotected position.

Sec. 3.   Statistics Relating to Crime and Immigration in Chicago.

The next item of importance relating to the social status of offenders for which statistics are available is that of nativity. It has already been pointed out that none of the Chicago reports furnishes information regarding "birthplace" or "birthplace of parents" of offenders, the items included in the minimum requirements as laid down by the Committee on Statistics. The "nativity" of persons arrested and convicted is, however, given in the annual report of the Superintendent of Police. The question as to how far these statistics of "nativity" are trustworthy must, of course, be considered. In general, the method of having information about country of birth hurriedly entered by a police officer at the time of an arrest or an arraignment would undoubtedly result in many errors. It is quite probable, however, that the errors would be, on the whole, "unbiased"; that is, some English-speaking immigrants, whose foreign birth was not easily indicated by their speech, would probably be called "American"; but, on the other hand, quite as many American-born citizens who had loyally kept their foreign names or who spoke with a foreign accent would undoubtedly be called Italian, Polish or Russian. It should be noted that the number and the per cent of colored persons arrested would probably be correct.

The following table shows the general nativity of those charged and convicted in 1913, together with the general nativity of the population fifteen years of age and over; that is, the population subject to arrest.*

---

to the immigrant, particularly to those belonging to the races of the "recent immigration"; this fact is less important here, however, since every foreign group, except the French, shows a smaller proportion of women offenders than their share of the population entitles them to have.

NATIVITY OF WOMEN OFFENDERS: ALL OFFENSES.   POLICE REPORTS, 1913.

Nativity.	Arrests. Number.	Per Cent.	Convictions. Number.	Per Cent.	Per Cent Distribution, Chicago Population.
American—					
White	6,823	55.1	3,532	59.4	62.2
Colored	1,827	14.8	1,019	17.1	2.1
Foreign	3,621	30.1	1,395	23.5	35.7
Austrian	414	3.3	168	2.8	6.0
English	242	2.0	104	1.8	3.2
French	59	.5	40	.7	.1
German	1,052	8.5	364	6.1	8.3
Greek	17	.1	4	.1	.3
Hollanders	4	...	2	...	.4
Irish	448	3.6	159	2.7	3.0
Italian	183	1.5	92	1.6	2.1
Russian	924	7.5	304	5.1	5.6
Scandinavian	208	1.7	96	1.6	4.5
Other	170	1.4	62	1.0	2.2
Total...............	12,371	100.0	5,946	100.0	100.0

* The population above the Juvenile Court age, that is 17 years for boys and 18 years for girls should be taken, but general nativity is given in the census only by age groups, and 15 to 20 is the nearest age group. This method of comparing the general nativity of those arrested or convicted with

TABLE 34. TOTAL ARRESTS AND CONVICTIONS BY GENERAL NATIVITY. (COMPILED FROM POLICE REPORT, 1913.)

Nativity.	Arrests. Number.	Per Cent.	Convictions. Number.	Per Cent.	Population Over 15 Years Per Cent Distribution.
American—					
White	63,578	57.9	29,429	59.4	50.9
Colored	7,450	6.8	3,552	7.2	2.4
Foreign	38,736	35.3	16,594	33.4	46.7
Total	109,764	100.0	49,575	100.0	100.0

Comparing first the distribution of arrests with the distribution of the population over fifteen years of age, it appears that the Americans, both white and colored, have a larger percentage of arrests than their proportion of population entitles them to have, while the immigrant, who forms 46.7 per cent of the population, furnishes only 35.3 per cent of the arrests. Comparing the convictions with population, the American, both white and colored, makes a still more unfavorable showing; that is, 59.4 per cent of the convictions were Americans (white), while their percentage of the population was only 50.9 per cent, whereas the immigrants, who formed 46.7 per cent of the population, were only 33.4 per cent of those convicted.

It is important to note that these statistics agree with the results of other investigations bearing on the relation between crime and immigration. The federal Immigration Commission, for example, although notoriously in favor of a restrictive policy, said quite emphatically:

"No satisfactory evidence has yet been produced to show that immigration has resulted in an increase in crime disproportionate to the increase in adult population. Such comparable statistics of crime and population as it has been possible to obtain indicate that immigrants are less prone to commit crime than are native Americans.*

In the special report of the United States Census on Prisoners in Institutions, the statement is made, after an analysis of the statistics presented, that "The figures . . . give little support to the popular belief that the foreign born contribute to the prison class greatly in excess of their representation in the general population"; and, again, it is said: "It is evident that the popular belief that the foreign born are filling the prisons has little foundation in fact. It would seem, however, that they are slightly more prone than the native whites to commit minor offenses. Probably to some degree

the population 15 years and over is that used in the United States Census of Prisoners, 1904. In the introduction to that volume, the following explanation is given: "If the general population of all ages be taken, the basis for the comparison will not be equitable for several reasons. Inmates of the general prisons are all at least 10 years of age and nearly all over 15. For the most part the immigrants are between 15 and 40 years of age. The number of children under 10 years of age is extremely small among the white immigrants as compared with the native whites. In view of these facts a comparison of the proportions of each nativity class in the white prison population with the corresponding proportions of the general population of all ages would clearly be unfair, for the inclusion of children under 10 years of age would so increase the proportion of native in the general population that it would seem as if crime were more prevalent among the foreign born as compared with the native white than is actually the case. * * * In some respects, however, a comparison with the total white population 10 years of age and over is hardly fair to the foreign born. Very few prisoners are under the age of 15, and the great majority of prisoners, 94.5 per cent of the whole number, are males. Therefore, it is perhaps more significant when the percentage of foreign born among white prisoners is compared with the percentage of foreign born in the white population 15 years of age and over, classified by sex." (From **Special Report of the Census Office: Prisoners and Juvenile Delinquents in Institutions,** 1904, pp. 18-19.)

*See **Reports of the U. S. Immigration Commission, Vol. 36, Immigration and Crime,** page 1.

this is attributable to the fact that the foreign born whites are more highly concentrated in urban communities." *

The question as to whether the percentage of offenses committed by immigrants is greater for the more serious crimes than for the lesser ones is of interest. The Chicago police statistics show that there is no appreciable difference in the proportion of immigrant offenders when the statistics for felonies and for misdemeanors are considered separately. The following tables show the number of arrests and convictions for felonies and for misdemeanors instead of for "all offenses."

TABLE 35. GENERAL NATIVITY OF PERSONS ARRESTED AND CONVICTED: 1913.

I. Persons Arrested.

Nativity.	Felonies. Number.	Per Cent.	Misdemeanors. Number.	Per Cent.	Total. Number.	Per Cent.	Population Over 15 Yrs.
American—							
White	6,200	55.4	57,378	58.2	63,578	57.9	50.9
Colored	1,055	9.4	6,395	6.5	7,450	6.8	2.4
Foreign	3,948	35.2	34,788	35.3	38,736	35.3	46.7
Total ..	11,203	100.0	98,561	100.0	109,764	100.0	100.0

II. Persons Convicted.

Nativity.	Felonies. Number.	Per Cent.	Misdemeanors. Number.	Per Cent.	Total. Number.	Per Cent.	Population Over 15 Yrs.
American—							
White	2,389	56.0	27,040	59.7	29,429	59.4	50.9
Colored	400	9.4	3,152	6.9	3,552	7.2	2.4
Foreign	1,477	34.6	15,117	33.4	16,594	33.4	46.7
Total ..	4,266	100.0	45,309	100.0	49,575	100.0	100.0

These tables show no difference between the percentage of immigrants among those arrested for felonies and for misdemeanors; in each group of offenses only 35.3 per cent were foreign born in comparison with 46.7 per cent which is the immigrant or "foreign born" percentage of the population over fifteen years of age. The percentage of immigrants convicted of felonies is, however, 1.2 per cent greater than the percentage convicted for misdemeanors, though in both cases the percentage of immigrants convicted is less than the percentage of immigrants arrested, and very much less than the per cent of immigrants in the Chicago population.

These statistics seem at first sight not to agree wholly with the United States Special Census Report on Prisoners. In the census report statistics seemed to establish the theory that the native American was more prone to commit serious crimes than the immigrant. But the offenses included in the Chicago police statistics under "felonies" and the offenses included in the census classification under "major offenses" are not the same. It must, in the first place, be remembered that the Chicago police statistics classify as felonies some offenses that are only misdemeanors, and that some of these are important numerically. Furthermore, it is important to note that in the census classification the terms "felony" and "misdemeanor" were discarded and a new classification into "major and minor offenses" substituted. The most important change involved in the new classification was that larceny of all

*From **Special Report of the Census Office: Prisoners and Juvenile Delinquents in Institutions,** 1904, pp. 18-19, 40-41. The comparison presented for the United States, as a whole, was as follows:

Among white prisoners of known nativity enumerated June 30, 1904, per cent of foreign born, 23.7.

In the general white population 15 years of age and over, per cent of foreign born, 1900— total, 21.9; male, 23.0; female, 20.7.

See also p. 273, **Statistics and Sociology,** by the late Professor Mayo-Smith, of Columbia University: "Care must be taken to consider the greater proportion of adults among the foreign born. Even then the amount of criminality may be due to the strange environment in which these foreigners find themselves, rather than to any influence of nationality."

kinds, grand or petit, was included among the minor offenses.* In the Chicago police reports a precisely opposite method of classification is used. All cases of larceny are classified as felonies. Such offenses as taking a piece of fruit from a peddler's pushcart, or grain or coal from a neighboring railway elevation are classed as "felonies," according to the police method. These statistics cannot, therefore, be said to disprove the conclusions drawn in the special census report regarding the tendency on the part of the native American to commit more serious crimes than the foreign born. This fact, that the native American commits the more serious crimes, undoubtedly explains why the percentage of foreign born in the state penitentiary is proportionately much less than the percentage of foreign born convicted. For this certainly cannot be explained by an undue leniency on the part of our courts to the immigrant. The table that follows presents the statistics given in the 1910 Census Report on Prisoners showing the general nativity of the prisoners in the state penal institutions, in the Cook County Jail, and in the Chicago House of Correction.

TABLE 36. GENERAL NATIVITY OF PRISONERS.

A. In State Penal Institutions of Illinois
(Joliet, Menard, and Pontiac.)

Nativity	Number.	Per Cent.	Distribution of population over 15 years of age in Illinois, Chicago, and Cook County*
American—			
White	1,998	59.2	69.1
Colored	873	25.9	2.1
Foreign born	502	14.9	28.8
Total	3,373	100.0	100.0

B. In the Chicago House of Correction.

American—			
White	894	55.1	50.9
Colored	150	9.2	2.4
Foreign born	580	35.7	46.7
Total	1,624	100.0	100.0

C. In the Cook County Jail.

American—			
White	60	63.8	43.9
Colored	13	13.8	2.4
Foreign born	21	22.4	53.7
Total	94	100.0	100.0

*The per cent distribution of the population over fifteen years of age is available only for the State of Illinois and for Chicago. In the corresponding column for Cook County the per cent distribution of the male population over twenty-one years of age was substituted.

It seems clear, therefore, that the statistics show beyond any question that a larger proportion of crime is committed by the native American,

---

*Except, however, when the term of imprisonment was for more than a year. The new classification was explained as follows: "The terms 'felony' and 'misdemeanor' do not afford a proper means of differentiating the more serious crimes from the lesser ones. . . . To avoid the confusing use of such terms this report distinguishes between major and minor offenses. All crimes that are universally held to be of a grave nature, regardless of how they happen to be punished in individual instances have invariably been classed as major offenses. Among them are the most aggravated forms of offenses against chastity . . . perjury, counterfeiting, and various violations of the United States laws; all the specified crimes against the person; and arson, burglary, forgery, and embezzlement among the specified crimes against property. The rule has been followed of classifying larceny and a number of other offenses, which may or may not be of a serious nature as minor offenses when the term of imprisonment was not for more than one year." (From **Special Report of the Census Office: Prisoners and Juvenile Delinquents in Institutions,** 1904, pp. 28-29.)

whether white or colored, than by the immigrant. That our immigrants form the criminal element of our population today is clearly a myth which has had a hardy survival owing to our desire to shift responsibility for our own faults. No facts have ever been found to substantiate it.

The record of the immigrant is in fact very much better than the statistics show. The great majority of all those arrested are poor people, and the poorer they are the more liable they are to conviction, since they have neither the money to employ able counsel nor intelligence enough to understand how to present their own defense. The immigrant is engaged in occupations that easily involve violations of the laws. The peddling and junk business, for example, is largely in the hands of immigrants, and undesigned violations of ordinances (petty misdemeanors) are common. Moreover, the immigrant stands a chance that the American does not of failing to understand our laws or the methods of our police or our courts. We have no system in Chicago of official interpreters, and the immigrant, particularly the immigrant from southeastern Europe, is certainly at a disadvantage in a court where he understands no one and no one, except possibly an incompetent interpreter, understands him. Keeping in mind these facts, it is indeed remarkable that all statistics relating to this subject show that in spite of all handicaps the immigrant has a better crime record than the rest of us.

Statistics are also available showing arrests and convictions by specific nationalities, but these statistics are likely to be even more inaccurate than those of general nativity.* Moreover, the census does not give the population of Chicago classified by age and country of birth. There are given statistics showing the male population over twenty-one years by nationalities, and as the great majority of arrests are of this part of the population and as tables have already been given showing the nationality of women †offenders, the tables that follow deal with the nationality of male offenders, and in these tables the per cent distribution of male offenders by nationality is compared with the per cent distribution of the male population over twenty-one years of age. The following table shows, therefore, the arrests and convictions of male offenders together with the per cent distribution of the male population over twenty-one years of age:

TABLE 37. NATIONALITY OF MALE PERSONS ARRESTED AND CONVICTED COMPARED WITH NATIONALITY OF MALE POPULATION OVER TWENTY-ONE YEARS OF AGE.

Nativity	Arrests		Convictions		Male population over 21 years of age, 1910	
	No.	Per cent	No.	Per cent	No.	Per cent
American—						
White	56,755	58.3	25,897	59.4	301,100	43.1
Colored	5,623	5.8	2,533	5.8	17,845	2.6
Foreign	35,015	35.9	15,199	34.8	379,850	34.3
Austrian	3,683	3.8	1,650	3.8	78,545	11.2
English	1,406	1.4	616	1.4	35,818	5.2
French	203	.2	100	.2	....	....
German	7,757	7.9	3,343	7.7	88,176	12.6
Greek	1,731	1.8	976	2.2	4,496	.6
Hollanders	228	.2	123	.3	4,623	.7
Irish	2,540	2.6	999	2.3	30,793	4.4
Italian	3,364	3.5	1,441	3.3	22,668	3.2
Russian	8,546	8.8	3,645	8.4	59,664	8.5
Scandinavian	3,071	3.2	1,423	3.2	46,755	6.7
Other	2,486	2.5	883	2.0	8,312	1.2
Total	97,393	100.0	43,629	100.0	698,795	100.0

†See p. 51.

*The Immigrants' Protective League, for example, reports that it is not uncommon for the police department to report that an immigrant has been arrested and that, for some reason, the services of the league are required. When the police are asked, "What nationality is the prisoner?" in order that

(In this table Bohemian and Slavonian are included in Austrian; Danish, Norwegian, and Swedish are classed together as Scandinavian; Scotch and Canadian are included under English, Lithuanian under Russian, and Chinese and Swiss under others. Polish were divided among German, Russian, and Austrian according to the method of distribution adopted by the 1910 census, Population, vol. 1, p. 879. The same classification is used in the tables in the footnotes on pages 51 and 57.)

This table shows that the Americans, white and colored both, show a percentage of arrests and convictions considerably greater than their percentage of population. On the other hand, the various foreign groups show almost uniformly a smaller percentage of convictions than their proportion of the population entitles them to have.*

Sec. 4. Occupations: Conjugal Condition.

Data regarding occupations and conjugal condition are next in the list of minimum requirements regarding social status of offenders. The **Annual Report of the Police Department** for 1913 gives a list of 76 different occupations, in which 80,605 of the 107,257 persons arrested were engaged. The occupations of 14,795 other persons were not specified, but were grouped together as "other occupations;" and 11,831 persons were returned as having "no occupations." It is probable that a majority of women offenders would have no occupation reported, although 4,789 were reported as "housekeepers," 288 as prostitutes, and 3 as midwives. It is not clear, of course, whether "housekeeper" means more than "housewife" or not. Since the statistics regarding the employment of women are obviously not satisfactory, it seemed well to exclude the women's occupations mentioned above along with the group of "no occupations." The remaining 90,346 persons whose occupations were returned were classified in the police court into 74 occupations, including the miscellaneous group of "other occupations." These 74 groups have been reclassified in thirteen groups. It was first planned to classify all of them into large occupational groups such as "professional men," "merchants and tradesmen," "clerks and salesmen," and "skilled" and "unskilled laborers." There were, however, a few occupations that were so important numerically that it seemed best to leave them as independent groups. These were, in order of numerical importance: chauffeurs and liverymen, peddlers, saloon and bar keepers, city and government employes, students, soldiers and sailors, and farmers. The following table shows, therefore, the occupations of persons arrested in 1913 reclassified from the table of occupations in the police report.

---

the right kind of interpreter may be sent, the answer is likely to be, "We don't know what nationality he is. He can't speak anything that anyone here can understand." It is safe to say that in such cases the "nationality" of the immigrant is not likely to get into the record correctly.

*The Italians show an excess of one-tenth of 1 per cent in convictions, and this is surely so small as to be negligible! And the Greeks, who form .6 per cent of the population, form 1.8 per cent of the arrests and 2.2 per cent of the convictions. That is, the Greeks have 1.2 per cent of the arrests and 1.6 per cent of the convictions in excess of the percentage justified by their proportion of the population. In the following tables, which have been compiled separately for felonies and misdemeanors, it appears that the offenses of the Greeks are largely misdemeanors. That is, .7 per cent of the felony convictions were Greek, while 2.4 per cent of the misdemeanor convictions were Greek. This apparent excess of "crime" among the Greeks is undoubtedly due to the fact that the Greeks are largely engaged in the peddling business, and violations of ordinances would undoubtedly bring them to court often.

A. Nativity of Male Persons Arrested and Convicted for Felonies, 1913.

Nativity	Arrests (Offenses) No.	Per cent	Convictions No.	Per cent	Per cent distribution of male population of Chicago 21 years and over
American—					
White	5,756	56.3	2,241	56.9	43.1
Colored	882	8.6	354	9.0	2.6
Foreign	3,599	35.1	1,344	34.1	54.3
Austrian	401	3.9	158	4.0	11.2
English	166	1.6	79	2.0	5.2
French	22	.2	10	.3	....

TABLE 38. OCCUPATIONS OF PERSONS ARRESTED DURING 1913.

*Occupations	Number	Per cent
Professional men	1,321	1.5
Merchants and tradesmen	3,790	4.2
Clerks, salesmen, etc.	9,445	10.4
Skilled laborers	13,317	14.7
"Laborers" and other unskilled workers	34,331	38.0
Specified occupations—		
Chauffeurs and liverymen	7,668	8.5
Peddlers	2,041	2.3
Saloon and bar keepers	1,871	2.1
City and government employes	790	.9
Students	494	.5
Soldiers and sailors	255	.3
Farmers	202	.2
Other occupations	14,821	16.4
Total	90,346	100.0
†Women's occupations—		
Housekeepers	4,789	
Prostitutes	288	
Midwives	3	
No occupation	11,831	
Total	107,257	

German	815	8.0	366	9.3	12.6
Greek	139	1.4	29	.7	.6
Hollanders	19	.2	8	.2	.7
Irish	186	1.8	98	2.5	4.4
Italian	392	3.8	108	2.7	3.2
Russian	1,027	10.0	331	8.4	8.5
Scandinavian	214	2.1	93	2.4	6.7
Other	218	2.1	64	1.6	1.2
Total	10,237	100.0	3,939	100.0	100.0

B. Nativity of Male Persons Arrested and Convicted for Misdemeanor, 1913.

Nativity	Arrests (Offenses) No.	Per cent	Convictions No.	Per cent	Per cent distribution of male population of Chicago 21 years and over
American—					
White	50,999	58.5	23,656	59.6	43.1
Colored	4,741	5.4	2,179	5.5	2.6
Foreign	31,416	36.1	13,855	34.9	54.3
Austrian	3,282	3.8	1,492	3.8	11.2
English	1,240	1.4	537	1.3	5.2
French	181	.2	90	.2	....
German	6,942	8.0	2,977	7.5	12.6
Greek	1,592	1.8	947	2.4	.6
Hollanders	209	.3	115	.3	.7
Irish	2,354	2.7	901	2.3	4.4
Italian	2,972	3.4	1,333	3.4	3.2
Russian	7,519	8.6	3,314	8.3	8.5
Scandinavian	2,857	3.3	1,330	3.3	6.7
Other	2,268	2.6	819	2.1	1.2
Total	87,156	100.0	39,690	100.0	100.0

†These figures are in accord with other inquiries, e. g., U. S. Bureau of Labor, Report on the Condition of Woman and Child Wage-Earners, Vol. XV, in their evidence showing that the newer industrial and commercial occupations into which women are now going make substantially no contribution to the criminality of women.

*In reclassifying the list of occupations given in the police report the new

This table shows that a very small minority of those arrested are from the well-to-do groups. Only 1.5 per cent are in the group called professional, 4.2 per cent were classed as merchants and tradesmen, 10.4 per cent were clerks, salesmen, etc., while 38.0 per cent were laborers, teamsters, and other unskilled workers and 14.7 per cent were skilled workingmen. Going back to the tables of arrests, it will be remembered that the great majority of those arrests are for petty offenses; and since the rich are seldom arrested on petty charges, it would be expected that the great majority of the arrests would be arrests of people who were poor, or at any rate not well-to-do.

Statistics of conjugal condition are also furnished in the police report and are given below. These statistics are not very valuable because they are probably not accurate. Married men will sometimes report themselves single when they are arrested for petty offenses, and it would seem, too, from the fact that all persons are reported to be either married or single and no persons are reported with their marital state unknown, that the police statistician may have counted as "single" those for whom no report was given. The following table contains such statistics as are furnished, and it is important to note, even if the "single" group is artificially increased, that 40 per cent of the men arrested are married. This means, of course, that the humiliation and expense of an arrest and trial are shared in a large number of cases by others than those arrested.

TABLE 39. CONJUGAL CONDITION OF PERSONS ARRESTED IN 1913.

Conjugal Condition.	Male. Number.	Per Cent.	Female. Number.	Per Cent.	Total. Number.	Per Cent.
Married	38,351	40.2	5,163	43.9	43,514	40.6
Single	57,135	59.8	6,608	56.1	63,743	59.4
Total	95,486	100.0	11,771	100.0	107,257	100.0

Sec. 5. General Summary.

In summarizing the most important points relating to the social status of those arrested in Chicago, the following points should be enumerated:

1. In Chicago, as in all other places for which statistics are available, the great majority of those arrested are men. In 1913 nearly nine-tenths of those arrested were men. The number of women arrested was not only very much smaller than the number of men, but the women were arrested for less serious offenses.

2. In Chicago, again, as in all other places for which statistics are available, the great majority of those arrested are young persons; 57.7 per cent of all the men and 61.5 per cent of all the women arrested were under thirty years of age, and 81.9 per cent of the men and 85 per cent of the women were under forty.

3. The problem of the woman offender appears from the statistics of charges to be the problem of vice. In 1913, 95 per cent of all the women arrested were charged with the different forms of disorderly conduct, including under this classification the various offenses against public morals. More than one-third of all the women arrested were charged with the specific offenses of street soliciting or of occupying a house of ill-fame. According

groups were made up as follows: Under professional men were included 173 actors, 71 artists, 176 attorneys, 17 clergymen, 89 dentists, 205 musicians, 590 physicians; under tradesmen 440 bakers, 653 butchers, 82 confectioners, 145 druggists, 81 florists, 255 grocers, 152 jewelers, 185 junk dealers, 1,605 merchants, 136 milkmen, 8 stock dealers, 48 undertakers; under skilled laborers, 689 barbers, 222 blacksmiths, 226 boilermakers, 1,324 carpenters, 249 cigarmakers, 738 cooks, 111 draughtsmen, 802 electricians, 609 engineers, 33 harness makers, 105 horseshoers, 28 lathers, 2,069 machinists, 491 masons, 338 moulders, 1,382 painters, 21 pattern makers, 214 plasterers, 485 plumbers, 840 printers, 128 roofers, 276 shoemakers, 451 steam fitters, 40 stone cutters, 1,227 tailors, 133 tinsmiths, 69 upholsterers, 17 wagon makers; under clerks, 1,381 agents, 157 brokers, 5,187 clerks, 2,720 salesmen; under city and government employes, 562 firemen, 23 letter carriers, 25 policemen, 180 street car employes; under laborers, 35 bill posters, 734 janitors, 24,004 laborers, 37 miners, 1,236 porters, 611 servants, 7,385 teamsters, 289 watchmen; under other occupations, in addition to the group so designated in the report, are included 26 detectives.

to the Illinois Statutes women can only be fined, they cannot be sentenced for these offenses. In 1911 the Vice Commission recommended the abolition of the system of fining for such offenses, but their recommendation has never been carried out.

4. Another point of importance is the fact that the statistics of nativity show that the native American has a larger proportion of arrests than the immigrant. (See Tables 33-37.) Statistics furnished in the police report show that the native Americans, white and colored both, have a percentage of arrests and convictions considerably greater than their percentage of population. On the other hand, the various foreign groups show a smaller per cent of convictions than their proportion of the population entitles them to have. It is, of course, popularly believed that immigration is a cause of crime. This belief has largely been due to a comfortable theory that we are superior to the people of Europe, and to a desire to shift the responsibility for our shortcomings onto other people. No facts have ever been found to support this belief. The Chicago statistics in this respect agree with the statistics furnished by the United States census and the Federal Commission on Immigration. The report of the commission states emphatically that "no satisfactory evidence has yet been produced to show that immigration has resulted in an increase in crime disproportionate to the increase in adult population. Such comparable statistics of crime and population as it has been possible to obtain indicate that immigrants are less prone to commit crime than are native Americans." The special census report on prisoners after analyzing the statistics of nativity for the whole country said that it was "evident that the popular belief that the foreign born are filling the prisons has little foundation in fact." Chicago statistics furnish further confirmation of this statement.

5. The statistics relating to conjugal condition and occupation are not very satisfactory. Insofar as they are to be trusted, they seem to indicate that a majority of the persons arrested, both men and women, are unmarried, and that the great majority are poor persons. The table of occupations indicates that a very small per cent of those arrested are from the well-to-do groups, 38 per cent were laborers and other unskilled workers, and the majority of the others were workingmen from other groups, clerks, salesmen, etc. Since the great majority of the arrests are for petty offenses and since the rich are seldom arrested on petty charges, it would be expected that the great majority of arrests would be arrests of people who were not well-to-do. It is not that the poor are more criminal than the rich, but that their offenses bring them so easily within the reach of the law.

APPENDIX A
STATISTICS RELATING TO ADULT PROBATION

Two annual reports have been published by the Adult Probation Office since the Adult Probation Law went into effect (July 1, 1911), and a typewritten report has been available for the first six months of 1913-1914. These reports show the number of persons admitted to probation each month, the total number admitted to probation by each judge for the period of a year, the offenses of which the probationers were convicted, and some other data regarding the probationers, such as age, sex, marital condition, color and nationality.

Sec. 1. Number of Persons on Probation.

The following table shows the number of persons admitted to probation during the years 1911-12, 1912-13, and the first six months of the year 1913-14:

TABLE I. NUMBER OF PERSONS ADMITTED TO PROBATION DURING TWO AND ONE-HALF YEARS.

Year.	Number of persons admitted to probation.
1911-12	1,074
1912-13	2,874
1913-14 (6 mos.)	2,422

This table shows that the number of persons admitted to probation has been increasing very steadily. The year 1912-13 showed an increase of more than 150 per cent over the preceding year, and the number admitted during the first six months of the year 1913-14 indicates that there will be an increase of nearly 100 per cent over the year 1912-13. It is, of course, important to know whether or not there was a proportionate increase in the number of probation officers during this period. It appears from the first annual report that there were, in addition to the chief probation officer, 11 adult probation officers in 1911-12, 16 in 1912-13, and 20 in 1913-14. That is, there were 97.6 cases to every officer in the first year, 179.6 in the second year, and 242.2 during the last year. It should be pointed out, however, that these figures do not accurately represent the average number of cases cared for by the different officers because (1) many cases are admitted to probation for shorter terms than one year, and (2) some of the officers are obliged to spend all or a considerable part of their time in court so that they are available for probation work only a portion of their time. The Chief Probation Officer explained that two officers spent all their time in court, that nine spent half a day each at court, and that four others were in court "part of the time." Thus the staff of twenty officers is only a staff of twelve or thirteen officers for active service. (3) The number of cases actually on probation includes a large number of old cases as well as new cases. Thus the total number of persons on probation September 30, 1913, was 2,316; the total number of persons on probation April 1, 1914, was 3,428. It would seem, therefore, as if the number of persons on probation averaged something more than 250 persons to an officer.* Good probationary care under such circumstances is, of course, impossible. In the Juvenile Court, it may be noted, the probation officers have under their care an average of between fifty and sixty cases.

Sec. 2. Offenses of which Probationers were Convicted.

The reports also show the offenses for which the probationers were convicted. The following table shows the offenses of which persons placed on probation in 1912-13 and 1913-14 had been found guilty.

The point of special interest with regard to these lists of offenses is whether or not persons are placed on probation after being convicted of offenses for which the law does not allow probation. Unfortunately, such statistics as are available do not throw much light on this point. It appears that a considerable number of persons who have been convicted of the serious crimes of robbery, burglary, embezzlement, obtaining money under false pretenses, carrying concealed weapons, and receiving stolen property have been placed on probation, but the Adult Probation Law permits probation for all of

*The Chief Probation Officer could, of course, furnish a statement showing the exact number of cases at present under the care of each officer.

these offenses except robbery, provided the value of the property stolen is
not more than $200 or in the case of burglary provided "the place burglarized
was a place other than a business house, dwelling or other habitation." *
There were altogether 167 persons placed on probation for these serious
offenses during the first six months of 1913-14, and, while it is not probable
that all of these 167 cases fell within the very narrow limits prescribed by the
law, the exact offenses can be learned only by a study of the case records of
the Adult Probation Office and these have not been examined. With regard
to the cases of robbery, however, it should be noted that probation is not
allowed by the statute under any circumstances.

TABLE II. OFFENSES OF WHICH PROBATIONERS HAD BEEN
CONVICTED, YEAR ENDING SEPTEMBER 30, 1913.

Larceny	802	Receiving stolen property	20
Disorderly conduct	703	Vagrancy	19
Contributing to dependency	499	Keeping disorderly house	14
Abandonment	287	Confidence game	9
Assault	93	Violation 2844 Chicago Code	9
Soliciting	57	Malicious mischief	8
False Pretenses	54	Inmates disorderly house	6
Burglary	37	Violation park ordinance	5
Contributing to delinquency	34	Attempted burglary	4
Embezzlement	31	Patrons house of ill fame	4
Carrying concealed weapons	28	Violation Chap. 38, Sec. 204, R. S.	4
Fornication	25	Violation Chap. 38, Sec. 167, R. S.	2
Gambling	23	Other causes	54
Violation motor law (not speeding)	22	Total	2,874
Adultery	21		

TABLE III. OFFENSES OF WHICH PROBATIONERS HAD BEEN
CONVICTED DURING SIX MONTHS ENDING MARCH 30, 1914.

Disorderly conduct	598	Violating Chicago Code	20
Larceny	562	Embezzlement	13
Contributing to dependency	474	Confidence game	12
Abandonment	196	Malicious mischief	12
Assault	88	Patrons, disorderly house	5
Soliciting	74	Violating Motor Vehicle Law	5
False pretenses	54	Robbery	4
Burglary	39	Keepers, disorderly house	3
Carrying concealed weapons	36	Blackmail	1
Vagrancy	32	Selling cocaine	1
Adultery	30	Unlicensed employment agency	1
Fornication	29	Other	64
Contributing to delinquency	28		
Receiving stolen property	21	Total	2,422
Inmates disorderly house	20		

That the tendency to place persons convicted of serious offenses on probation is not decreasing is indicated by the large number of such persons
placed on probation during the first six months of the year 1913-14, and this
is confirmed by a mimeographed report of the work of the Adult Probation
Office for the month of April, 1914, which contains the latest figures available.

---

*The Adult Probation Law (Revised Statutes, 1913, Chap. 38) provides
that "Power to release on probation, shall, however, be limited to the following offenses" (509b): 1. All violations of municipal ordinances where the
offense is also a violation, in whole or in part, of a statute. 2. All misdemeanors, except as hereinafter limited. 3. The obtaining of money or property
by false pretenses, where the value thereof does not exceed $200. 4. Larceny,
embezzlement, and malicious mischief where the property taken or converted
or the injury done does not exceed $200 in value and the place burgarlized was
a place other than a business house, dwelling or other habitation. 6. Burglary,
when the burglar is found in a building other than a business house, dwelling
house, or other habitation. "Carrying concealed weapons" is a misdemeanor
and probation is therefore legal in the case of this offense, but so much public
apprehension regarding "gunmen" exists in Chicago that it seems proper to
classify them as a serious offense for which probation is of doubtful expediency
even if legal.

These figures show that in this one month persons admitted to probation had been convicted of the following serious crimes:

Robbery 6, carrying concealed weapons 12, false pretenses 7, embezzlement 3, forgery 2, burglary 5, receiving stolen property 5, threat to kill 1, attempted rape 1.

This is a total of 42 serious crimes out of a total of 415 for the month. The explanation given for this is that persons charged with serious crimes are convicted of lesser offenses, but through carelessness the charge against them is not changed, and although they are quite properly released on probation, the record still shows them to be guilty of serious crimes. The only way the facts can really be ascertained is to have presented the record of the exact offense actually committed by each person.

Sec. 3. Results of Probation.

The next point of importance is the question of whether statistics throw any light on the results of probation. The Adult Probation Office classifies all persons discharged as "improved" or "unimproved," and the following table presents the statistics of discharges for the last two and one-half years.

TABLE IV. NUMBER OF DISCHARGED PROBATIONERS WHO WERE FOUND IMPROVED OR UNIMPROVED DURING 2½ YEARS ENDING MARCH 30, 1914.

	Improved.	Unimproved.	Died.	Total Discharged.	Total Placed on Probation.	Per Cent Discharged.	Per Cent of Discharged Who Were Improved.
First year, 1911-12	171	63	1	235	1,074	21.9	72.8
Second year, 1912-13	1,167	239	8	1,414	2,874	49.2	82.5
Third year, 1913-14 (6 months.)	987	316	5	1,308	2,422	54.0	75.5
Total 2½ years	2,325	618	14	2,957	6,370	46.4	78.6

After a careful examination of this table, it appears fair to say that, in round numbers, the discharges are equal to slightly less than one-half of the new cases placed on probation during the same period and the number discharged improved is slightly more than three-fourths of the total number discharged.*

Sec. 4. The Questionable Value of such Terms as "Improved" and "Unimproved."

It is obvious, however, that the value of these statistics as to the outcome of probation depends on two points: (1) What precisely is meant by the terms "improved" and "unimproved"; and (2) whether the "unimproved" probationers were proportionately distributed among all classes of offenders or whether they were largely those who had committed the most serious offenses. With regard to the first point, the printed reports show that in 1911-12 the unimproved group included 21 "committed" probationers and 42 others, and in 1912-13 the unimproved group included 4 "committed or vacated" and 239 others. The reports do not show the number of probationers who have been lost track of or the number absconded and the number committed for violation of probation with the institutions to which the probationers have been committed. With regard to the other point, the reports offer no information. The tables of "improved," "unimproved," etc., are for all probationers and are not given as they should be for the different offenses separately. In fairness to the Adult Probation Office, it should be pointed out that they have had very little clerical assistance, and that the absence of more elaborate statistics should probably be excused on this ground. Some light on the point

*The Chief Probation Officer in some way draws a different conclusion with regard to the per cent discharged. In his report for six months, after presenting the figures (without percentages) he says: "The general averages of those improved by probation since the law has been in force is about eighty per cent, but during the last six months the percentage is only about seventy-five. The cause is not hard to locate. The domestic cases are by far the most difficult to get good results from, and the officer does not feel like discharging the probationer improved when he knows he is behind in his payments to his wife, does not treat her kindly, drinks or is otherwise bad. We did not commence to get domestic cases till a little over a year ago; and, therefore, are only just commencing to record the results, and this is the first report where any amount of discharges in that class of cases is made."

of the effect of probation on those guilty of serious crimes was obtained from some unpublished material in the Adult Probation Office. This material was the result of an attempt to follow up 148 felony cases that had been placed on probation, including 32 convicted of embezzlement, 34 of robbery, 111 of burglary, and 2 of forgery. As a result of this attempt to check up the records of these 148 cases, 89 were classed as "O. K.," 13 as "fair," 7 as "doubtful," 4 "no good," 3 "not working," 4 "lost," 2 "skipped," 8 "in jail or warrant out," 9 "permitted to go out of town," 9 "no report." This record is, of course, much more illuminating than a mere "improved" and "unimproved" tabulation. Translating "O. K." to mean "doing well," it appears that only 60 per cent were reported in this group, and of the remainder, who it will be noted were considerably more than one-third of the total, some were lost, the inevitable result of having probation officers overburdened with work, others had been committed to jail, and the cases of others were marked, uncertainly, as fair or doubtful or no report. Since these specific terms are so unlike the vague terms "improved" and "unimproved," it is not possible to compare this set of cases with the reports for all offenses. Such a comparison can, in fairness, hardly be attempted since the records of these cases were so much more carefully scrutinized, that this might account for a difference in returns.

Sec. 5. A Comparison with the Statistics Relating to Probation in New York City.

A comparison between our probation statistics and similar statistics for New York City is of interest. The **Seventh Annual Report of the New York State Probation Commission** (1913) gives the following statistics relating to adult probation in New York City.

TABLE V. NUMBER OF PERSONS PLACED ON PROBATION IN THE DIFFERENT COURTS IN NEW YORK CITY, YEAR END-ING SEPT. 30, 1913, TOGETHER WITH NUMBER OF PROBATION OFFICERS.

Court.	Persons Placed on Probation.			No. Probation Officers.
	Men.	Women.	Both.	
Magistrates Courts—				
1st Division	1,302	563	1,865	21
2nd Division	2,891	612	3,503	29
Special Sessions	785	105	890	16
Total	4,978	1,280	6,258	66

If we compare these with our Chicago figures, it appears that the number of cases placed on probation in New York City is greater; 6,258 cases compared with 2,874 cases in Chicago. That the number should be greater is to be expected because the population of New York is greater and also because the adult probation system there is very much older than in Chicago. Thus, the year for which statistics have been quoted was only the second year of the adult probation system in Chicago, whereas it was the sixth year of the corresponding system in New York. Of very great interest, therefore, is the fact that the last year (1913-14), which has seen a great increase in the number of persons placed on probation in Chicago, has witnessed a decrease in the number of persons placed on probation in New York. This has been due to the change in method of work and organization in New York, which will be noticed later.

TABLE VI. OFFENSES OF WHICH MEN AND WOMEN HAD BEEN CONVICTED BEFORE THEY WERE PLACED ON PROBATION IN NEW YORK CITY DURING THE YEAR ENDING SEPTEMBER 30, 1913.

Offenses.	Men.	Women.	Total.
Assault (3rd degree).........................	155	7	162
Disorderly conduct	2,153	365	2,518
Non-support	1,426	6	1,432
Petit larceny	532	83	615
Prostitution, etc..........................	....	412	412
Public intoxication	500	312	812
Violation local ordinances....................	67	58	125
Other misdemeanors	127	37	164
Total	4,960	1,280	6,240

This table is of interest because it seems to make clear the fact that New York, unlike Chicago, does not place on probation persons who are guilty of such offenses as robbery, burglary, and the other serious offenses which appeared in the Chicago list. (See pages ......)

It is important to note too that the New York reports show much more definitely than do our Chicago reports the effect of probation in the cases of persons discharged from probationary care. The following table shows the information given regarding discharged probationers.

TABLE VII. RESULTS OF PROBATION IN CASES OF PERSONS PASSED FROM PROBATION DURING THE YEAR ENDING SEPT. 30, 1914. (COMPILED FROM SEVENTH ANNUAL REPORT OF THE NEW YORK STATE PROBATION ASSOCIATION.)

Completed probationary period and discharged with improvement	4,753
Completed probationary period and discharged without improvement	562
Rearrested and committed	505
Removed to other locality with permission of court or probation officer	8
Absconded or lost from oversight	418
Unstated and other results	22
Total	6,268

This table is of interest because, although it uses also the somewhat vague term "improvement," it does show specifically the number of persons rearrested, the number absconded, the number removed, and the number for whom the results could not be stated, so that these facts at least are available.

The point of greatest importance, however, that appears in studying New York probation statistics is that the Chief Probation Officer's report to the Chief Magistrate in New York shows the number of cases investigated by the probation officers before being placed on probation and the number placed on probation without such a preliminary investigation. No statistics of this sort are furnished in Chicago, for it appears to be the rule here for the judge to overlook entirely the necessity of preliminary investigations by probation officers, and it is the exceptional cases only for which an investigation is asked. That such a system is now being adopted in the New York courts explains, of course, the decreasing number of probationers there, and the absence of such investigations in Chicago explains also the increasingly large number of cases placed on probation in Chicago. It explains also the cases reported by social workers in Chicago of the placing on probation of persons who are not first offenders, of persons who can never be located by the probation department because they have given false names and addresses in court, and of persons who are utterly unfit for probationary care, and also the cases in which one person is, almost simultaneously, placed on probation for different offenses and by different judges who do not know, of course, that the person asking for probation is already a probationer, and should be sentenced for violation of probation if for no other offense.

In contrast to the New York system, judges in Cook County appear to place on probation at random, and the probation department is obliged to accept all who are sent, although the persons released may be unfit for probation and the probation officers already have more cases than they can possibly look after. It should be noted, however, that even with the present small staff of officers allowed by law better service could be rendered:*

---

*It should be pointed out that adult probation work must necessarily be unsatisfactory in Chicago, not only for the reasons given above but also fundamentally: 1. Because of the relatively small number of officers. The law limits the number in any one county to twenty, and in Chicago the majority of these officers give all or a considerable part of their time to court work. Very little time is left for supervision of probationers. For this small number of officers there are more than 2,500 persons on probation. 2. The probation officers are not chosen through civil service examinations but are appointed by the judges. This, of course, has the doubly disastrous effect of not getting the most suitable persons for officers and in making those who are appointed feel that they do not need to maintain a high standard of work.

The Adult Probation Law went into effect July 1, 1911. In September, 1911, the chief probation officer was appointed by the Circuit and Municipal

1. If the amount of clerical and court attendance work required of them could be decreased.

2. If the officers spent a large part of time investigating cases prior to release on probation. This would certainly greatly reduce the number of persons placed on probation and eliminate the second offenders and others unsuitable for probation.

Cases are added at the close of this appendix showing that a probationer can, by giving a false address, escape probation entirely and be placed on probation a second time without being identified; that the same person may be placed on probation two or three times without its being discovered that he is already on probation.* Investigation prior to release on probation is necessary if probation is to be more than a discharge. Moreover, it should be pointed out that the Illinois Adult Probation Law clearly expects the probation officer to investigate upon the judges' request before release.†

The last (1912) report of the New York State Probation Commission says, with regard to **Preliminary Investigations:**

"When so directed by a court or magistrate, probation officers are expected to investigate the surroundings, history, reputation and characteristics of defendants awaiting sentence. These investigations are of great service to the courts in determining whether the defendants will make fit subjects for probationary treatment. It is found that in a large proportion of the cases of probationers who have absconded or otherwise failed to satisfy the probationary requirements, such investigations have been neglected. The number of cases so investigated during the past year was 19,311, an increase of 22 per cent." (Sixth Report, p. 25.)

In Massachusetts preliminary investigations are absolutely insisted upon as a prerequisite for release on probation. The last report of the Massachusetts Commission on Probation (1913) discusses their method: "The standard of probation cases can only be improved by the closest co-operation of judges and probation officers. The probation officer should recommend

---

Courts. At the close of the first year there were eleven other probation officers, four appointed by the Circuit Court judges and seven appointed by the Municipal Court judges. The law provides for not more than twenty officers in any one county. By the close of the second year, sixteen officers had been appointed, six by the Circuit Court judges and ten by the Municipal Court judges. During the past year the number of officers has reached the full quota of twenty. Only three clerks are provided for the Adult **Probation** Office. If it is not constitutional to require the probation officers to be chosen through civil service, it should be possible to induce the judges to do what Judge Pinckney has done in the Juvenile Court, i. e., to establish a voluntary or extra-legal civil service of their own.

*It is also apparent that investigation would prevent the release on probation of those who are not first offenders. The law provides for the release only of first offenders, but when no preliminary investigations are made, second offenders will inevitably be able to escape in this way.

† See **Revised Statutes,** chap. 38, 5091, Duties of Probation Officers. Sec. 12. The duties of probation officers shall be: 1. To investigate, when required by rule of court or by specific order, the case of any person who has invoked the provisions of this act, and as accurately and as fully as diligence will enable to ascertain (a) the personal characteristics, habits, associations and previous conduct of such persons, (b) the names, relationship, ages and conditions of those dependent upon him for support, maintenance and education, and (c) such other and further facts as may aid the court as well in determining the propriety of probation as in fixing the conditions thereof. To the end that such investigation may be properly made, a probation officer commissioned to investigate shall be afforded full opportunity to confer with the person to be investigated when such person is in custody. 2. To report in writing the result of such investigation. 3. To preserve complete and accurate records of cases investigated, including a description of the person investigated, the action of the court with respect to his case and his probation, the subsequent history of such person if he becomes a probationer during the continuance of his probation, which records shall be open to inspection by any judge or by any probation officer pursuant to order of court, but shall not be a public record, and its contents shall not be divulged otherwise than as above provided, except upon order of court.

after a most careful study of the case, and the court should never place on probation any person unfitted for probationary treatment." (Fifth Annual Report, p. 7.) Probation is recommended only when "the past history and present disposition of the person investigated indicate that he may reasonably be expected to reform without punishment."

The Chief Probation Officer's Report in the **Annual Report of the Board of City Magistrates of the City of New York, 1913,** shows the results of the new method, i. e., preliminary investigation before probation, in New York City.

"Under the old method of placing on probation without preliminary investigation (with some exceptions) probation officers received many more cases than they could properly look after, but since last April, when only about 20 per cent of those investigated were placed on probation, the number of cases have materially decreased. During the last eight months of 1912, 1,691 defendants were placed on probation, while during the same period in 1913, under the new system, but 974 were placed on probation. Of that number 369 were disorderly persons and only two had been investigated by probation officers. Under the present system the probation officers have been enabled to devote more time to individual cases, with the result that there have been fewer revocations for violation of probation, and the accounts of the disorderly (non-support) at the Department of Charities are in much better shape than ever before" (p. 73).

The Chief Magistrate reports, for the year ending December 31, 1913, the following results from the change in probation methods in New York City:

"The new probation system has worked admirably in every way. The probation officers, men and women, are now engaged actively in investigating cases, or, as is part of their duty, in seeing that the defendants obey the terms of probation by frequent visits, careful inspection, and active personal interest in those concerned. This they can do, as they do not now have to waste a whole lot of time sitting in the court rooms waiting for possible cases; then to be hurriedly considered as an emergency and disposed of more or less unsatisfactorily. . . .

"One fault of the old system was that cases were carelessly put on probation. Men and women with prison records, who deserved no consideration, and whose cases were hopeless, were turned over to the probation officers, instead of being punished, as they should be, at once. This clogged the probation system. The officers carried long lists of these perfectly impossible people, so far as reformation was concerned, on their hands. These scamps, as soon as they got on probation, either ran away or disappeared, and often turned up again in prison; or they kept the probation officer chasing all over the city and state looking after them, disappearing from one locality to turn up to the annoyance and danger of some other place. The same was true of the women.

"Now, under the new system, we have reduced the number of cases some 60 per cent, which means that probation, which is a favor to the defendant, and based on the hope of the magistrate that he can be reformed without being sent to prison, and this hope in turn founded upon the written report and investigation made by the probation officer, is not misused. Then, too, the probation officer is not laden down with all that waste and rotten material, and gives the cases the real sort of inspection to which they are entitled, looking after the defendant and encouraging him or her to a better life. The removal of this incubus of perfectly useless material gives the probation system a chance to prove what it can do; makes the defendant feel that he is put on his honor and highly favored by the court in an effort to improve himself and retrace his or her steps in a criminal career away from a disorderly way of living" (pp. 29-30).

Sec. 6. Statistics Relating to Restitution and Earnings of Probationers.

Further information regarding the results of probation is furnished by the statistics relating to restitution and the earnings of probationers. A very good summary of these results is included in the typewritten report of the Chief Probation Officer for the first six months of 1913-14, and this is quoted in full below:

"The first year the amount of restitution was not kept, but the second year we find the total amount to be $21,790.28. The first half of the third year we find the total amount to be $8,211.57. I am satisfied that the officers have not kept an account of all restitution, so that I can only give results as they are reported to the office.

"With reference to the earnings of probationers, I find that the first year we only kept the earnings during September, and thought it a great thing that the probationers earned $30,905.50 in that month, and figured that if that good showing continued every month for a year the total would be $360,000.00, but the actual result during the second year was more than $548,000.00. During the first half of the third year the earnings exceeded that sum more than $20,000.00. The amount being $570,127.64, which, if continued at the same rate for the rest of the year, will show more than a million dollars earned in one year. This, indeed, is a large sum of money for people to earn, who, under the old law, might have been in jail at the expense of the county."

This statement alone is a more than sufficient justification of the cost of probation service to the county and to the city, and it is also a more than sufficient justification for a demand for a change in the law that so inadequately limits the number of probation officers for a great city like Chicago.

Sec. 7. Further Reasons for Increasing the Number of Adult Probation Officers.

A further reason for a considerable increase in the number of adult probation officers is that much of the so-called social work in the courts, which is done by a large number of volunteer organizations, should be done by the Adult Probation Office. At present, for example, the following organizations have representatives giving all or a large part of their time to social work in the Boys' Court and the Criminal Court: Legal Aid Society, the Juvenile Protective Association, the Bureau of Personal Service, the Catholic Women's League. In addition to these private organizations, both the Adult Probation Office and the County Welfare Bureau have representatives in the courts. These groups of workers are all unrelated. No one has any authority or control over anyone else. They are responsible only to the heads of their organizations in four different parts of the city. The situation is saved, in part, by the fine spirit of co-operation among the workers, and they believe that they have the field of work so carefully apportioned that the work is co-operating and not duplicating. This can, however, scarcely be possible, and in any event, if the work is worth doing, it should all be concentrated in the hands of one public authority; and there can be no question that the one absolutely essential public authority in the field is the Adult Probation Office.* This office should have an adequate staff on a civil service basis, which alone insures competency, and should have full control of all social work in the courts, as the Probation Department of the Juvenile Court does of similar work in that court.

Sec. 8. Summary.

1. The reports of the Adult Probation Office show a marked increase in the number of persons placed on probation during the three years since the

---

* The one social worker who does not seem to be related to this office is a representative of the Juvenile Protective Association in the Criminal Court, who, in her own words, "investigates all of the sex cases that are held to the Grand Jury." She considers her work as supplementary to the work of the State's Attorney's office. The complainants or witnesses in these cases are chiefly young girls, and she is there in order that their stories may be told to a woman instead of to one of the lawyers in the State's Attorney's office.

There appears to be no reason, in this case, why the State's Attorney should not appoint one woman lawyer as a regular member of his staff who could hear such cases. There can be no question but that a woman lawyer can do such work far more effectively than a man. There seems to have been a bad precedent set in the Court of Domestic Relations when the State's Attorney was given an additional appropriation by the County Board to employ a woman investigator for the bastardy cases. Here again a woman lawyer, appointed as a regular member of the State's Attorney's staff, should have been appointed for such work. A woman assistant State's Attorney would be more satisfactory in many ways than an "investigator." The "investigator" cannot appear before the Grand Jury, whereas an assistant State's Attorney could, and her position in the court would be one of great influence. Moreover, no additional appropriation would be needed for such work, since the State's Attorney could at any time assign one of his assistantships to a woman instead of to a man.

Adult Probation Law was passed. Unfortunately the number of probation officers has not increased proportionately. That is, there appears to have been in round numbers about 100 cases per officer during the first year of the court, about 180 the second, and about 245 during the year just passed. Good probationary care under such circumstances is obviously impossible. In New York, the average number of cases per officer is about 95.* In the Juvenile Court of Cook County, the average number of cases per officer is about 50 to 60.

2. The reports also show the offenses of which probationers are convicted. The question is raised as to whether or not the Adult Probation Law is being violated by the placing on probation persons convicted of offenses for which probation is not legal. The list of persons convicted of serious offenses and placed on probation during the first six months of the year 1913-14 is as follows: False pretenses, 54; burglary, 39; carrying concealed weapons, 36; receiving stolen property, 21; embezzlement, 13; robbery, 4. Whether or not the offenses of these 167 persons entitled them to be placed on probation can only be determined by ascertaining the exact offenses committed.

3. With regard to the results of probation, statistics as to whether discharged probationers are "improved" or "unimproved" are of little value since the standard of what constitutes "improvement" is probably a variable one. It is suggested that statistics could show each time the number of probationers who had absconded, the number who had moved out of the city by permission, and the number who had been re-arrested or for whom warrants had been issued, and the number for whom no report had been recently obtained.

4. In comparing Chicago and New York statistics, one very important point appears: that in New York it is not customary to place persons on probation until a preliminary investigation has been made by probation officers. The convicted person for whom probation appears to be desirable is not hastily released as in Chicago, but is remanded until a thorough investigation has been made. If it does not appear that the prisoner is likely to improve under probationary care, he is not released and the time of the probation officer is conserved for more hopeful cases. A system of preliminary investigation in Chicago would greatly reduce the number of persons placed on probation, and would make possible more successful work with the smaller number of probationers who would be under care. At present the Chicago system makes it possible for second offenders to escape on probation, for persons to give false addresses and thus to escape any supervision by probation officers, or for a person to be placed on probation almost simultaneously by several different judges. Investigation by probation officers is absolutely essential if probation is to be more than a discharge.

5. The valuable results of probation are more tangibly presented in the statistics relating to restitution and earnings of probationers. The earnings of probationers during the past year may be said to be, in round numbers, more than a million dollars, and the amount of money paid back in restitution during the year is between $15,000 and $20,000 (estimating for the whole year on the basis of statistics for six months.) There can be no question as to the success of a system that not only relieves the taxpayers of the heavy burden of supporting thousands of persons in jail for minor offenses and at the same time saves the men and women from the demoralization of a prison term and makes it possible for them to earn large sums in independent employment and to pay back the money they have stolen.

6. At the present time, the Adult Probation Department is not the only organization doing social work in the courts. The County Welfare Bureau and three private societies have representatives giving all or a large part of their time to some form of social service work in the courts. There can be no question but that the work which is now being done by the representatives of these different organizations is socially useful and should not be given up. All such work, however, should be unified and centralized under some controlling authority. Since the Adult Probation Department is the social service agency of first importance in the courts, it would seem to be

---

*This is obtained in the same rough way as the Chicago figures, by dividing the total number of cases placed on probation within the year last past by the number of officers. It is explained elsewhere that the resulting averages are not accurate, but they are perfectly valid for purposes of comparison.

most advantageous to have all the social service work done by this department. This is, of course, another urgent reason why the Adult Probation Law should be so amended as to make possible a very great increase in the number of adult probation officers, and the placing of the department on a civil service basis.

Sec. 9. Illustrations of the Results of the Failure to Investigate Cases Before Placing them on Probation.

S——— W———

August 19, 1913—Placed on probation for one year by Judge Brentano in the Criminal Court on three charges of burglary and was warned that he would be arrested the first time he was caught loafing.

May 26, 1914—In Boys' Court under the name of W——— on disorderly charge (joy riding in stolen auto). Claimed he did not know it was stolen. Case postponed to June 3d then to 30th, when the defendant was not in court. Officer asked to have him discharged, which was done.

M——— C———

July 1, 1914—Placed on probation in Morals Court by Judge Goodnow on adultery charge.

August 9, 1914—Arrested on disorderly charge under another name. Discharged.

J——— B———

Put on probation on larceny charge by Judge Goodnow. Ten days later placed on probation again by Judge Dolan, not knowing of former probation. Arrested again—case continued for several months by Judge Burke in the Criminal Court to give boy a chance to make good by working steadily, etc. J——— was out an bond at this time. If his conduct had been good during this time, case would probably have been disposed of in some way without inflicting further punishment. However, at final hearing his conduct had been so unsatisfactory that he was sentenced to Pontiac.

H——— M———

July 10, 1914—Placed on probation by Judge Brentano on larceny charge. Amount involved, $95. Preliminary hearing June 8, 1914. At time of offense was on probation, which did not expire until June 29, 1914. (An immoral woman.)

H——— S———

December 5, 1913—Placed on probation for six months on burglary charge by Judge Brentano. Felony waived. Charge changed to petit larceny. Boy had already served 30 days in House of Correction on disorderly charge. In less than week stole $20 from fellow employe and left town. At end of six months was discharged improved, though at the time in the County Jail, held to Grand Jury on three carges of burglary—came into jail April 13, 1914. Case still pending. Relatives can do nothing with him.

J——— T———

Placed on probation under another name. April 4, 1914—Probation Department never could locate. May 21, 1914—Held to Grand Jury on burglary charge under name of J——— T———. Through guard at jail discovered his identity. Notified Probation Department and he is now in Pontiac.

T——— J———

April 2, 1914—Placed on probation by Judge McDonald—held on robbery charge. One and one-half years before had been placed on probation (sleeping in empty cars) and later, about one year before, spent three months in the House of Correction for stealing.

H——— S———

On probation three times. Twice at the same time under different names. Was just about to be placed on probation again (robbery charge) when it was discovered that another judge had sentenced him to one year in the House of Correction for violation of probation. Now in House of Correction serving this sentence.

TABLE VIII.

OFFENSES OF MEN, WOMEN AND BOYS PLACED ON PROBATION
BY THE VARIOUS JUDGES DURING THE SIX MONTHS
FROM JANUARY 1 TO JUNE 30, 1914.

(From records of the Adult Probation Office.)

A.—MEN.

Judge.	Abandonment.	Adultery and Fornication.	Assault.	Burglary.	Confidence Game.	Contributing to Delinquency.	Contributing to Dependency.	Embezzlement.	Larceny.	False Pretenses.	Malicious Mischief.	Receiving Stolen Property.	Violating Miscellaneous Ord'nces.	Disorderly.	Other.	Total.
Bowles	..	..	4	..	..	..	..	..	4	1	..	..	1	18	..	28
Brentano	1	..	..	..	2	..	..	1	1	..	..	..	..	..	..	5
Burke	..	..	..	3	..	..	..	..	8	..	..	..	..	..	..	11
Caverly	..	..	2	4	..	..	..	..	8	1	..	..	1	28	..	44
Dever	..	..	..	..	..	1	..	..	..	..	..	..	..	..	..	1
Dolan	..	..	1	..	..	..	..	1	17	..	2	2	1	4	..	28
Fake	..	2	7	..	..	..	..	..	19	1	..	5	10	72	8	124
Fisher	..	..	..	..	..	..	..	..	2	..	..	..	1	2	..	5
Fry	22	..	1	..	..	1	88	..	12	..	..	..	..	65	1	190
Gemmill	1	..	..	..	..	1	2	..	..	..	..	..	..	..	..	4
Goodnow	..	5	..	..	..	..	..	1	8	1	..	..	1	6	1	23
Graham	..	..	..	..	..	..	..	..	34	1	1	3	..	8	..	47
Hill	1	..	..	..	..	..	..	..	3	..	..	..	..	2	..	6
Hopkins	..	10	..	..	..	..	..	..	..	..	..	..	..	2	1	13
Jarecki	..	..	..	..	..	..	..	..	..	1	..	..	..	..	..	1
Kearns	7	..	..	..	..	1	11	..	..	..	..	..	..	..	..	19
Kerstens	..	..	2	4	3	..	..	2	13	..	..	..	..	..	1	25
Mahoney	..	..	1	..	..	..	..	..	11	..	1	..	1	..	1	15
McDonald	..	..	9	8	7	..	..	1	19	2	..	..	..	1	4	51
McKinley	..	..	1	..	4	..	..	1	14	..	..	..	..	..	1	21
Moran	3	..	..	..	..	..	17	..	..	..	..	..	..	..	..	20
Pettit	..	..	1	2	1	..	..	1	6	..	..	..	..	..	..	11
Rafferty	..	..	..	..	..	..	..	..	5	..	..	..	2	6	4	17
Robinson	..	..	..	..	..	..	..	..	1	1	..	..	..	1	..	3
Rooney	..	..	..	..	..	..	..	..	1	..	..	..	1	..	..	2
Ryan	..	..	..	..	..	..	..	..	23	6	..	1	2	20	..	52
Sabath	..	1	19	..	..	..	..	1	17	5	2	7	11	22	3	88
Scott	1	..	..	..	..	..	..	..	4	..	..	..	..	..	..	5
Scully	..	..	3	..	..	5	4	..	12	..	1	1	2	28	1	57
D. Sullivan	..	..	..	..	..	..	..	..	5	..	..	..	..	..	..	5
J. Sullivan	..	..	1	..	..	..	..	1	6	..	..	..	..	4	..	12
Torrison	2	..	..	..	..	1	12	..	..	..	..	..	..	..	..	15
Turnbaugh	..	..	..	..	..	..	..	..	..	..	..	..	1	18	..	19
Uhlir	124	..	6	..	..	8	300	..	6	..	1	..	2	19	..	466
Wade	..	..	1	..	..	..	..	..	1	..	..	1	..	4	..	7
Walker	..	..	2	2	2	..	..	3	24	1	..	1	..	..	..	35
Wells	..	..	2	..	..	..	..	1	35	4	2	..	2	10	1	57
Williams	..	..	..	..	..	..	..	..	1	..	..	..	..	..	..	1
Stewart	..	..	..	..	..	..	..	..	9	..	..	..	..	1	..	10
Newcomer	..	..	1	..	..	..	..	..	..	..	..	..	..	..	..	1
Levy	..	..	..	..	..	..	..	..	..	..	..	..	..	1	..	1
Total	162	18	64	23	19	18	434	14	329	25	10	21	39	342	27	1545

TABLE VIII—Continued.

B.—WOMEN AND GIRLS.

Judge.	Adultery.	Assault.	Contributing to Dependency.	Disorderly.	Fornication.	Larceny.	False Pretenses.	Soliciting.	V. S. 2807.	V. S. 2014-19.	Other.	Total.
·aham	..	..	..	1	..	4	..	..	..	..	1	6
)wles	..	..	..	2	..	1	..	..	..	1	..	4
iverly	..	..	..	2	..	1	..	..	..	..	..	3
)lan	..	1	..	1	..	2	..	..	..	..	..	4
·y	..	..	3	8	..	3	..	..	..	..	..	14
.ke	..	1	..	1	1	2	1	..	..	..	..	6
)odnow	6	1	..	7	4	2	..	15	..	50	1	86
ill	..	..	..	1	..	..	..	..	..	..	..	1
)pkins	9	..	..	22	16	..	..	9	..	32	..	88
recki	..	..	..	..	..	1	1	..	..	..	..	2
:arns	..	1	..	..	..	..	..	..	..	..	..	1
:rstens	..	1	..	..	..	..	..	..	..	..	..	1
ahoney	..	..	..	..	..	3	..	..	..	..	1	4
cDonald	..	..	..	..	..	3	..	..	..	..	2	5
cKinley	..	..	..	..	..	..	..	..	..	..	1	1
)ran	..	..	2	..	..	..	..	..	..	..	..	2
:wcomer	..	1	..	..	..	..	..	..	..	..	..	1
.fferty	..	..	..	..	..	..	..	..	..	..	1	1
)binson	..	..	..	..	..	2	..	..	..	..	..	2
)oney	..	..	..	..	..	1	..	..	..	..	..	1
·an	..	1	..	2	..	10	1	..	..	..	..	14
bath	..	..	..	3	1	4	1	..	3	..	..	12
ott	..	..	..	..	..	1	..	..	..	..	..	1
ully	..	..	1	2	..	..	..	..	..	..	..	3
:wart	..	..	..	..	..	13	..	..	..	..	..	13
Sullivan	..	..	..	..	..	1	..	..	..	..	..	1
irnbaugh	..	..	..	..	..	2	..	..	..	..	..	2
ilir	..	1	20	3	..	1	..	..	..	..	2	27
ade	..	..	..	2	..	3	..	..	..	..	..	5
ells	..	..	..	..	..	26	..	..	..	..	1	27
illiams	..	..	..	..	..	2	..	..	..	..	..	2
Total	15	8	26	57	22	88	4	24	3	83	10	340

TABLE VIII—Continued.

C.—BOYS.

Judge.	Abandonment.	Assault.	Burglary.	Contributing to Delinquency.	Contributing to Dependency.	Disorderly.	Embezzlement.	Larceny.	Malicious Mischief.	False Pretenses.	Receiving Stolen Property.	Robbery.	Vagrancy.	Violating Miscellaneous Ord'nces.	Other.	Total.
Bowles	..	..	..	..	..	3	..	..	..	..	..	..	..	..	..	3
Brentano	..	..	2	..	..	..	1	1	1	..	..	..	..	..	..	5
Burke	..	..	2	..	..	..	..	3	..	..	..	2	..	..	..	7
Courtney	..	..	..	..	..	1	..	..	..	..	..	..	..	..	..	1
Dolan	..	1	..	..	..	6	..	10	3	..	..	..	..	1	..	21
Fake	..	4	..	..	..	6	..	6	1	..	..	..	1	3	..	21
Fisher	..	..	..	..	..	1	..	..	..	..	..	..	..	..	..	1
Fry	..	2	..	2	..	13	..	8	..	..	..	..	2	..	..	27
Goodnow	..	..	..	..	..	2	..	5	..	2	..	..	..	..	..	9
Graham	..	3	..	..	..	1	..	1	..	..	..	..	..	2	..	7
Hill	..	..	..	..	..	..	..	2	..	..	..	..	..	..	..	2
Hopkins	..	..	..	..	..	..	..	..	..	..	..	..	..	1	..	1
Kerstens	..	..	7	..	..	..	..	5	..	..	..	..	..	..	..	12
Mahoney	..	..	..	..	..	..	..	5	..	..	1	..	..	..	..	6
McDonald	..	4	8	..	..	..	..	7	..	..	1	4	..	..	..	24
McKinley	..	..	2	..	..	..	1	2	..	..	..	1	..	..	1	7
Moran	..	..	..	..	1	..	..	..	..	..	..	..	..	..	..	1
Pettit	..	..	..	..	..	..	..	1	..	..	..	..	..	..	..	1
Rafferty	..	..	..	..	..	1	..	4	..	..	..	..	..	..	..	5
Ryan	..	2	..	..	..	4	..	7	..	..	..	..	..	4	1	18
Sabath	..	1	..	..	..	8	..	9	..	..	..	..	..	4	..	22
Scott	..	..	..	1	..	..	..	2	..	1	..	..	..	..	..	4
Scully	..	5	..	4	..	48	..	84	1	5	3	..	..	12	..	162
D. Sullivan	..	..	1	..	..	3	..	2	..	..	..	..	..	..	..	6
Torrison	..	..	..	4	..	..	..	..	..	..	..	..	..	..	..	4
Uhlir	5	1	..	8	3	..	..	1	..	..	..	..	..	..	..	18
Wade	..	1	..	..	..	5	..	5	..	..	..	..	1	..	..	12
Walker	..	..	3	..	..	..	..	16	..	..	..	..	..	..	1	20
Wells	..	..	..	..	..	..	1	6	..	2	..	..	..	3	..	12
Total	5	24	25	19	4	102	3	192	6	10	5	7	4	30	3	439

APPENDIX B
NOTE ON THE COUNTY JAIL AND THE
HOUSE OF CORRECTION

In discussing the costs of a system that involves the arrest and the trial of large numbers of innocent persons, it was pointed out (Text p. 36) that not the least of these costs was the imprisonment of many people who were later released without conviction. Statistics were given showing that in 1913, 691 persons suffered the really terrible experience of imprisonment in the County Jail, and were then released either because they were tried and found not guilty or because the Grand Jury or State's Attorney did not think the evidence against them warranted their being tried.

The report of the jailer, from which these statistics were taken, shows the disposition of the cases of all the persons imprisoned during the past year as follows:

TABLE I. DISPOSITION OF CASES COMMITTED TO COOK
COUNTY JAIL DURING THE YEAR ENDING
DECEMBER 30, 1913.

Disposed of in Municipal Court	3,783
Bail given in Municipal Court	1,151
Sent to penitentiary	260
Sent to reformatory	78
Sent to House of Correction	764
Committed to State Insane Asylum	7
Jail sentence expired	283
Released on probation	298
Stricken off Criminal Court	117
Own recognizance Criminal Court	26
No bill Grand Jury	290
Nolle pros.	39
Not guilty	245
Bail given Criminal Court	865
Order of Circuit Court	127
Order of County Court	11
Order of U. S. Court	214
Habeas Corpus	5
Died	3
Supersedeas bonds	15
Miscellaneous	12
Total	8,593

This report shows that of the 8,593 persons who were held in the County Jail last year, only 283 were there serving sentences, but 338 others were later committed to Joliet or Pontiac so that they were judged to merit imprisonment. Seven hundred and sixty-four others were sent to the House of Correction, but how many of them were sent because of their inability to pay fines and how many were actually committed, the statistics, of course, do not indicate. It is not possible to ascertain whether the 3,783 whose cases were "disposed of in the Municipal Court" were discharged, or fined, or whether they reappear among those sentenced. The great majority are undoubtedly discharged or fined. Certainly an examination of this table makes it clear that not only hundreds, but probably thousands of innocent persons are imprisoned for longer or shorter terms in the County Jail. The question of the length of time they are imprisoned there is a matter of great interest and the following table shows the time spent there by the different classes of prisoners:

TABLE II. NUMBER OF PERSONS COMMITTED TO COOK
COUNTY JAIL, 1913, WITH REASONS FOR COMMIT-
MENT TO JAIL AND NUMBER OF DAYS
SPENT IN JAIL

(Data from County Jail Records.)

Time spent in County Jail	Cases continued	Held to Grand Jury	*No billed	Awaiting trial after indictment	†Pending after commitment	Sentenced to jail term	‡Miscellaneous	Total
Less than 1 week	3,303	276	2	245	74	175	147	4,222
1 week and less than 2	1,090	119	27	75	..	48	42	1,401
2 weeks and less than 3	331	52	67	66	..	18	20	554
3 weeks and less than 4	145	30	55	65	..	12	38	345
4 weeks and less than 8	103	9	109	406	..	58	26	711
8 weeks and less than 12	5	1	17	389	..	29	13	454
12 weeks and less than 16	2	...	3	321	..	30	6	362
16 weeks and less than 20	...	1	...	154	..	20	7	182
20 weeks and less than 24	1	...	...	65	..	12	5	83
24 weeks and less than 28	...	...	...	35	..	19	1	55
28 weeks and less than 32	...	...	...	12	..	7	1	20
32 weeks and over	...	...	...	§27	..	||27	2	56
Total	4,980	488	280	1,860	74	455	308	8,445

*This does not include all "no-billed" cases, for many of the others who
gave bail and left the jail probably failed of indictment when they came to
the Grand Jury.

†These are cases sentenced to the House of Correction and merely put
into the jail directly from court until they can be conveyed the following day
to the House of Correction.

‡Under this heading are grouped the cases for safekeeping either U. S.
or local, the remanded cases, warrants, a few held as witnesses and on writs
of ne exeat.

§Includes 3 for 32 weeks, 1 for 33, 1 for 34, 3 for 35, 3 for 36, 1 for 37,
1 for 38, 2 for 39, 3 for 40, 1 for 41, 1 for 42, 4 for 46, 1 for 48, 1 for 50, and
1 for 54.

||Includes 1 for 32 weeks, 1 for 33, 4 for 34, 1 for 35, 3 for 36, 1 for 37,
2 for 38, 1 for 39, 1 for 43, 4 for 44, 1 for 47, 1 for 50, 3 for 52, 1 for 56, 1 for
60, and 1 for 63.

This table, unfortunately, does not follow the classification in the preceding table. It is not possible, for example, in this table to ascertain how
many of those who were held to the Grand Jury were discharged, for although one group includes "no-billed" cases, it is pointed out that all of the
"no-bills" are not included and the other groups such as "stricken out,"
"nolle prossed," and "tried and found not guilty" are equally impossible of
identification.

In spite of these drawbacks, the table indicates very clearly the great
hardships caused by "the law's delays." Of the "no-billed" cases, for example, 251 were kept in the County Jail for periods ranging from two to sixteen weeks, surely a terrible punishment for people against whom there is
not sufficient evidence even to secure an indictment. Of those held awaiting
hearings before the Grand Jury or continuances, the table shows that 587
"lay in jail," as the saying goes, for periods varying from two to twenty-four
weeks. The longest periods of imprisonment, however, are endured by those
who are awaiting trial after indictment. The table shows that 1,860 persons
unable to secure bail were held in jail for this purpose last year and that 1,409,
or 75 per cent of these men, who it must be remembered are supposed to be
innocent until they are tried, were held in jail awaiting trial for periods
varying from four weeks to one year.

Not only because of the long periods during which these thousands of persons awaiting trial or hearing are confined in the County Jail, but also because of the fact that 455 persons are sentenced to terms of imprisonment there, some of them for periods longer than one year, it is important to know something about the conditions of the jail cell-houses. No investigation of the jail has been made for the Committee, but the report made in May, 1912, by the Inspector of Institutions for the State Charities Commission has been published in the Institution Quarterly* and is fortunately available. Concerning the so-called "newer cell-house," which was built nearly twenty years ago, the State Inspector made the following report:

"The so-called newer cell-house was built in 1895. There are seven tiers of cells in the department; each tier has twenty-six cells which are placed in rows of thirteen.

The jail room has windows on all sides save the south; the east wall is mainly windows, the west and north sides have fewer windows, but good air circulation is provided for the outer corridors.

The fifth, six and seventh tiers of cells are on one floor. Therefore the men of the fifth and sixth tiers exercise on a common corridor, as this corridor is between the two rows of cells, and the solid iron doors are closed during exercise hours, and light is admitted only through the bars at the northern extremity. Artificial light is used throughout the day.

As minors are placed on the seventh tier, they easily communicate with the men. They are not allowed on the ground corridor, but, when they walk on the platform surrounding their cells, they are closely associated with the older men.

Men are locked in their cells save for two hours in the morning, two hours in the afternoon, and one hour in the evening. The boys exercise in the schoolroom during one hour of the evening.

Each cell is of iron, has bars in the back, solid door, sanitary toilet, wash bowl with running water and two bunks.

As the only openings in the cells are the bar backs, those cells which are opposite solid walls are very dark. The wall on the west side has few windows and consequently the cells on this side are very dark. Men who offend in any way are placed on this side, while obedient prisoners receive the cells on the eastern sides. In the dark cells it is necessary to use candle light for reading, as the electric light in the corridor is too far away to light the cells.

Shower baths are accessible to the men, at their option. Every one must bathe twice a week in summer and once a week in winter. Separate towels are provided.

On the first floor are placed four tiers of cells. When it is remembered that there are two men to a cell (when the jail is crowded, additional men are placed in the cells), that each tier has twenty-six cells, one can conceive what it means to have the occupants of all these cells exercising in a common dark corridor."

Concerning the cells in the so-called "old jail," which was built forty-two years ago, but which is still in use, the following report is made:

"The old jail department was built in 1872; where, in the newer section, steel was used in the construction, in this section, stone was used.

There are four tiers of cells arranged in two rows. The cells are placed back to back, seventeen in a row. The windows are in the upper halves of the walls so that the lower cells are dark. There are ten windows on the north side, ten on the south side, two on the west, and none on the east.

The exercise corridor surrounds the cells, and all the men in the old section occupy this common corridor during exercise hours. During the day of inspection about 300 men were confined in this department.

Each cell has a sanitary toilet, a wash bowl, with running water, and two canvass hammocks with blankets. The only ventilation is secured by means of bar doors. As, during the winter months, it is often necessary to confine five men in a single cell, the inadequate provision for light and air cannot be overestimated.

Tubercular and venereal patients are kept on the fourth tier of cells.

Prisoners are transferred to this old cell-house, after they leave the receiving cells; if their behaviour is good, they are transferred to the dark

---

*The Institution Quarterly, vol. IV, No. 3: 83-84. (Sept. 30, 1913.)

side of the new cell-house and thence to the lighter side of the new cell-house."

Certainly this description of dark, crowded, and unventilated cells and of equally dark, crowded corridors is very important in view of the statistics that have been presented. With regard to five men in a single cell, the State Inspector speaks moderately in saying that "the inadequate provision for light and air cannot be overestimated." It is, however, important to recall in the light of these descriptions the fact that the great majority, about 85 per cent, of the prisoners in the County Jail are only there awaiting trial; they have not been found guilty, and in the vast majority of cases if they had not been poor they would have been released on bail.

That a great and wealthy community like Cook County, Illinois, can maintain a public institution so far behind all modern ideals of social justice is, indeed, almost unbelievable. Moreover, it is an accepted theory today that confinement under such conditions must tend not to prevent crime, but to create criminals.

In view of the fact that the report has shown that during the past year more than 14,000 persons were committed to the House of Correction and that 82 per cent were committed merely for the non-payment of fines, it has seemed worth while to include here the statistics of the report of the State Inspector* which deal with the House of Correction.

"The so-called west cell-house is a one-year old building, which extends north and south, having windows on all sides. The building, vauled at $225,000 was built by inmate labor; it is attractive, from an artistic standpoint, whether looked at from the exterior or the interior.

Two rows of cells are arranged on either side of a 30-foot corridor which is itself lighted and ventilated by windows at either end, by sky-light and by windows near the roof. There are four tiers of cells. Each cell is of iron, is 6 x 9 x 8½ feet in size, has concrete floors; each cell has an outside window 2 x 4 feet and a bar door 2½ x 7 feet. Bar transoms extend across the entire front of the cells. A single iron cot, with mattress, sheets, pillows and blankets, a wash bowl with running water, and a sanitary toilet furnish each cell. In addition every man has a stool, his own towel, and books from the library, if he desires them.

The men who are lodged in this cell-house dine at tables placed in the light, cheery corridor. The inspector saw a good meal served with plates, knives and forks. As this cell-house is enjoyed by all the prisoners, and the old building is very undesirable, men who work in the shops are lodged in this department.

South of the main building is a cell-house which is 458 feet long. The wing extends north and south, having windows in the upper half of the wall on the east and west sides. The cells are of concrete, are placed back to back, and are at a distance of about 12 feet from the walls. The only cell ventilation consists of a small opening, in which night buckets are placed, and a bar door 2x5½ feet. A double iron frame arrangement is used for placing two mattresses in each cell. The cells, each 5x8x8 feet, are dark and ill-ventilated. There are 640 cells, arranged in two rows—back to back—and four tiers. The upper tier is rarely used, as the air is especially vile at this height. The approach to the upper cells is by means of wooden platform and stairs; the danger is obvious when it is considered that there are two men to a cell.

Men wash in troughs, provided with running water. Separate towels are used.

The north cell-house is north of the central wing, extends north and south, and has windows on the east and west sides. There are 408 cells, arranged in two rows and four tiers. The cells are of steel, each 5x8x8 feet, and are ventilated by iron bar doors 2x5½ feet. There are openings in the cells, for the reception of night buckets. Air is forced through these openings at night.

The windows are placed in the upper part of the wall so that the lower cells are dark. The cells are at a distance of about 12 feet from the windows, which are in the outside wall. As in the south cell-house, the stairs and platforms are of wood, the cell ventilation is bad, and two men are crowded into a single cell.

Both the north and south cell-houses seem especially undesirable since it is possible to compare them with the new cell-house which is a model of sanitation."

At the time of inspection there were 1,389 men and 117 women confined in the House of Correction, and during that year the reports show that 11,282 persons were committed to the House of Correction for periods of time varying from 1 day to 15 months. It is important to note too that the report by the Civil Service Commission on **Prison Labor and Management House of Correction,** which was made as recently as March, 1914, confirms the report of the State Inspector made two years previously. With regard to housing and sanitation, this report contains the following statements regarding the cell-house of the House of Correction:

"Of the three cell-houses occupied by men inmates, the south cell-house is antiquated and is generally unsuited for its present purpose. The sanitary arrangements are bad and prisoners are not assigned to the top tier of cells, which are the worst except at that season of the year when the population is greatest. This cell-house should be replaced at an early date by one of modern construction. The west cell-house is new and of modern construction, having a toilet and wash basin in every cell. The building is scrupulously clean and the inmates assigned to this cell-house take pride in keeping it so.

Sanitary conditions throughout the institution are fairly good, although in the two old cell-houses occupied by men, viz., the north and south cell-houses, toilet facilities are bad. When the old cell-houses are replaced by modern ones bad conditions will have been removed." *

It will be noted that none of these reports criticises the management either of the County Jail or of the House of Correction; they simply point out that the cell-houses in which thousands of men, many of whom are innocent or are guilty only of minor offenses, are confined are utterly unfit to be occupied by human beings. It would seem, indeed, as if Cook County might be able to find the money to erect a modern building to replace a jail built nearly half a century ago at a time when jails were not expected to be anything more than "whited sepulchers." It has been pointed out that only a small percentage of the persons confined there have been tried and found guilty of any offense; but even if men are guilty, it is no longer considered good public policy to deprive them of light and air and to crowd five men into a cell not large enough for two.

The two following tables were prepared from data obtained from the Jailer's records. Table III shows the number of days each month on which the jail contained a specified number of prisoners. Table IV shows the length of sentence of 455 persons sentenced to imprisonment in the County Jail, together with the actual time spent in jail. This table shows that some prisoners sentenced to imprisonment for only one, two, three or four weeks spent more than that number of months in jail.

TABLE III. DAILY POPULATION OF THE COUNTY JAIL DURING 1913.

Number of days on which jail population was—

Month.	350-399	400-449	450-499	500-549	550-599	600-649	650-699	700-749
January	..	..	..	..	5	17	8	1
February	..	..	..	..	..	..	26	2
March	..	..	..	..	..	1	30	..
April	..	..	..	..	..	..	29	1
May	..	..	..	..	..	4	27	..
June	..	..	..	2	6	10	11	1
July	..	..	2	25	4	..	..	..
August	4	14	13	..	..	..	..	..
September	27	3	..	..	..	..	..	..
October	2	17	12	..	..	..	..	..
November	..	..	28	2	..	..	..	..
December	..	..	..	11	20	..	..	..
Total	33	34	55	40	35	32	131	5

*Report of the Civil Service Commission, City of Chicago, 1914. **Prison Labor and Management House of Correction,** p. 25.

TABLE IV. LENGTH OF SENTENCE OF PERSONS, TOGETHER WITH ACTUAL TIME SPENT IN JAIL. (FROM THE RECORDS OF THE COUNTY JAIL.)

Actual time spent in jail.	Less than 1 week.	1 and less than 2.	2 and less than 3.	3 and less than 4.	30 days or 1 month.	2 months.	3 months.	4 months.	5 months.	6 months.	7 months and over.	‖Un-specified.	Total.
Less than 1 week...........	68	8	2	..	9	4	10	..	..	21	1	52	175
1 and less than 2 weeks....	8	17	1	..	3	2	3	..	..	5	..	9	48
2 and less than 3 weeks....	..	1	3	..	2	..	..	..	..	5	1	6	18
3 and less than 4 weeks....	..	2	1	..	..	..	..	..	..	3	..	6	12
4 and less than 8 weeks....	..	4	2	..	23*	2	3	..	..	5	1	18	58
8 and less than 12 weeks....	..	2	1	..	..	10	1	..	..	3	..	12	29
12 and less than 16 weeks....	3	1	1	..	8	..	8	..	..	1	..	8	30
16 and less than 20 weeks....	..	1	1	..	3	5	4	1	1	..	..	4	20
20 weeks and over..........	..	..	1	..	3	4	5	3	..	18	11	20	65†
Total	79	36	13	..	51	27‡	34§	4	1	61	14	135	455

*Includes one 37, one 40, and one 42 day sentence.

†Includes 1 in jail for 20 weeks, 3 for 21 weeks, 4 for 22, 4 for 23, 3 for 24, 5 for 25, 9 for 26, 1 for 27, 5 for 28, 2 for 30, 1 for 32, 1 for 33, 4 for 34, 1 for 35, 3 for 36, 1 for 37, 2 for 38, 1 for 39, 1 for 43, 4 for 44, 1 for 47, 1 for 50, 3 for 52, 1 for 56, 1 for 60, and 1 for 63 weeks.

‡Includes one 66, one 68, and one 69 day sentence.

§Includes one 105, one 107, and one 114 day sentence.

‖ In "term unspecified" most of the sentences are probably for one day or less for 35 cases where the prisoners were waiting trial after indictment; the rest are judgments against debtors, are attachments, or are fines, and the length of time spent in jail dependent upon the capability of the person convicted to discharge debt or fine or judgment.

The cases of discrepancy between length of sentence and actual time spent in jail are explained usually by the fact of imprisonment while awaiting trial, but partly because the sentence would read so many days in jail or so much money, or perhaps ten days in jail and fine and costs. The inability to pay fine or costs would lengthen the stay; the ability to pay would shorten it.

APPENDIX C

DISCUSSION OF THE VALUE, FOR COMPARATIVE PURPOSES, OF THE STATISTICS OF CRIMINAL COMPLAINTS

In attempting to ascertain the extent of crime, it is, of course, most important to have statistics showing the crimes known to the police. It is important also to have statistics showing the number of offenders arrested in comparison with the number of crimes and the number of offenders convicted. It has already been explained that the Criminal Judicial Statistics of England and Wales furnish such statistics annually. In Chicago, statistics of criminal complaints are available, but after a careful examination of these statistics, the conclusion was unavoidable, for reasons set forth in the following section, that the statistics of criminal complaints could not be legitimately compared with statistics of arrests and convictions.

Statistics were given in Table 1, page 20, of the text showing the number of criminal complaints and arrests on felony charges. These statistics are presented again in the table given below, showing also, over the whole period for which statistics are available, what per cent the arrests are, each year, of complaints. The question of whether or not this comparison between complaints and arrests is legitimate is discussed below.

TABLE I.   CRIMINAL COMPLAINTS AND ARRESTS* ON FELONY CHARGES, 1905-1913.

Date.	Complaints.	Arrests (Felonies), Number.	Per Cent of Complaints.
1905	11,732	12,144	103.5
1906	10,754	12,376	115.1
1907	11,292	10,653	94.3
1908	11,034	10,551	95.6
1909	10,697	9,656	90.3
1910	10,718	9,376	87.5
1911	11,730	9,881	84.2
1912	13,032	10,276	78.9
1913	14,340	11,203	78.1

*Statistics of arrests are really statistics of charges: See note 2, Table 1 in Part 1 of the Report.

The comparison between criminal complaints and arrests on felony charges presented in this table is of value only (1) if all criminal complaints represent actual crimes justifying arrests, and (2) if arrests upon felony charges are made only upon the filing of a criminal complaint. If these suppositions were true, if the complaints represented all of the actual crimes known to the police and if the arrests represented the number of persons charged with those crimes who had been apprehended, then the ratio of arrests to complaints would be significant and would fairly represent the percentage of crime dealt with by the police. Unfortunately, however, it seems to be true that neither of these suppositions is correct. Criminal complaints seem to include all complaints of crimes even when the complaints are unfounded. If "complaints" of burglary and larceny, for example, are made by people who later find their property, their complaints are nevertheless counted along with complaints of actual crimes. On the other hand, the statistics of arrests undoubtedly include a very large number of arrests made without the filing of a criminal complaint. Arrests on felony charges are undoubtedly made by the police "on view," and, even if this is not a common practice, it would render comparisons between complaints and arrests untrustworthy.

A much more serious difficulty in the way of such a comparison is the fact that some offenses that are not felonies are nevertheless classed as felonies in the police statistics. Included in their list of felonies, for example, is the offense "contributing to the delinquency and dependency of children." There were, in 1913, 1,528 arrests on this charge, but no criminal complaints are filed for this offense. It seems to be clear that the police statistics of arrests for felonies include this large group of offenders not included at all in the statistics of criminal complaints.

Looking back at the preceding table in the light of these facts, it is apparent that the percentages in that table are meaningless. The table showed that during the period from 1905 to 1913 the number of arrests on felony charges ranged from 78.1 per cent to 115.1 per cent of the number of criminal complaints. According to this table, in five out of the nine years for which statistics are available, the arrests were 90 per cent or more than 90 per cent of the complaints, and in one year the arrests greatly exceeded the complaints. An excess of arrests or a percentage of arrests as high as 90 per cent is easily explained if arrests on felony charges are made by the police "on view" or in some way other than upon the filing of a criminal complaint. It should be noted, too, that the number of arrests might, of course, be greater than the number of complaints if a large number of individuals were arrested in connection with some one crime the author of which could not be discovered. In the case of the legitimate arrest of several persons who were all involved in one crime there would be a series of complaints, and no excess of arrests could be accounted for in that way. An actual excess of arrests has happened, however, in the year 1906, when arrests were 115.1 per cent of complaints.

It seems to be clear, therefore, that comparison between the total number of criminal complaints and the total number of arrests on felony charges is not legitimate.* Even a comparison of complaints and arrests on specific crimes such as burglary, robbery and larceny, while it eliminates the difficulty caused by the inclusion of such offenses as "contributing to delinquency," is yet open to other objections that have been mentioned.

A clearer idea of the relation between complaints and arrests may be obtained by comparing complaints and arrests for specific crimes. Data for such a comparison are available for a series of years, but are given only for the years 1913 and 1912, and for these years separately.

TABLE II. COMPLAINTS AND ARRESTS FOR BURGLARY, LARCENY, ROBBERY, AND OTHER FELONIES, 1912, 1913.

Offense.	1913			1912		
		Arrests			Arrests	
	Com-plaints.	Num-ber.	Per Cent of Com-plaints.	Com-plaints.	Num-ber.	Per Cent of Com-plaints.
Burglary	6,534	1,053	16.1	5,458	1,117	20.5
Larceny	5,375	4,593	85.5	5,523	4,198	76.0
Robbery	1,389	1,022	73.6	1,277	1,106	86.6
Total Burglary, Larceny and Robbery.	13,298	6,668	50.1	12,258	6,421	52.4
*Other felonies	1,042	4,535	435.2	774	3,855	498.1
Total	14,340	11,203	78.1	13,032	10,276	78.9

*Other felonies included in the table of arrests 1913: Confidence game 681, receiving stolen property 451, murder (including accessory to and assault to commit) 498, mayhem and manslaughter 57, embezzlement and forgery 262, contributing to delinquency 1,528, malicious mischief 250, rape 258, other offenses against public morals 188, kidnaping and threats to kidnap 78, arson 85, other felonies 163, pandering (not a felony) 36.

*Nothing has been said about the possibility of the statistics of complaints not being accurately kept. Such statistics as are furnished by the police department have been assumed to be good of their kind. But the questionable value of all statistics of complaints is indicated in this extract from the **Final Report of the Civil Service Commission on Police Investigation,** 1911-1912 (page 33): "The Commission has heard testimony and has received communications in vast number that complaints, either by writing, by telephone, or by word of mouth, when they affect gambling, street walking, disorderly houses, all-night saloons, and similar violations receive but scant courtesy at the station in precincts where these conditions abound. Some complaint has also been made that the same rule applies to petty thievery, activities of pickpockets, and even of burglaries and robberies. The method in vogue of desk sergeants writing verbal complaints on slips of paper, placing them on

This table shows that according to the statistics furnished by the police department the arrests for burglary in 1913 were 16.1 per cent of the number of complaints, the arrests for larceny 85.5 per cent of the complaints, and the arrests for robbery 73.6 per cent of the complaints. The corresponding percentages for 1912 were 20.5 per cent of the burglary complaints, 76.0 per cent of the larceny complaints, and 86.6 per cent of the robbery complaints. That is, the arrests for burglary, larceny and robbery were 50.1 per cent of the number of complaints in 1913 and 52.4 per cent of the number of complaints in 1912.

The most striking fact in this table, however, is the undue proportion of arrests for "other felonies." Although the arrests for burglary, larceny and robbery were about one-half of the number of complaints on these charges, the arrests for other felonies were four times the number of complaints in 1913 and five times the number of complaints in 1912.

It is clear that statistics of arrests and complaints are not comparable if, as these tables indicate, the arrests for burglary, larceny and robbery constitute only about 50 per cent of the complaints on these charges and the number of arrests for other crimes is four or five times the number of complaints.

A further comparison that should be examined is a comparison between complaints, arrests and convictions. The following tables present such a comparison. The first table, Table III, is compiled from the police statistics, and, therefore, includes under "felonies" some offenses, e. g., "contributing to delinquency" and "petit larceny," that are not felonies. The other table, which has been prepared from statistics furnished by the Municipal Court, is based on a different classification. The court statistics do not classify as felonies offenses that are technically only misdemeanors. This Table, Table IV, shows, together with the number of criminal complaints, the number of preliminary hearings in the Municipal Court, and the disposition during the same year of all cases that finally reached the Criminal Court.

TABLE III. CRIMINAL COMPLAINTS, ARRESTS AND CONVICTIONS, 1913. (STATISTICS FROM REPORT OF SUPERINTENDENT OF POLICE, 1913.)

| | | ——Arrests—— | | ———Convictions——— | |
Charge.	Criminal Complaints.	Number.	Per Cent of Complaints.	Number.	Per Cent of Arrests.	Per Cent of Complaints.
Burglary	6,534	1,053	16.1	289	27.4	4.4
Larceny	5,375	4,593	85.5	2,219	48.3	41.3
Robbery	1,389	1,022	73.6	171	16.7	12.3
Total Burglary, Larceny and Robbery	13,298	6,668	50.1	2,679	40.2	20.1
Other felonies	1,042	4,535	435.2	1,587	35.0	152.3
Total	14,340	11,203	78.1	4,266	38.1	29.7

TABLE IV. CRIMINAL COMPLAINTS (POLICE STATISTICS), PRELIMINARY HEARINGS AND FINAL DISPOSITION IN CRIMINAL COURT OF CASES HEARD THERE, 1912. (MUNICIPAL COURT STATISTICS.)

| | | Preliminary Hearings | | Convictions Criminal Court | |
Charge.	Criminal Complaints.	Number.	Per Cent of Complaints.	Number.	Per Cent of Prelim. Hear.	Per Cent of Complaints.
Burglary	5,379	1,127	21.0	337	29.9	6.3
Larceny	5,458	2,204	40.4	172	7.8	3.2
Robbery	1,225	987	80.6	197	20.0	16.1

a spindle and tearing them up when an officer reports thereon, needs no comment. The matter of running out and reporting on all complaints is of such vital importance to the individual citizen that the common expression by the citizen that it is of no use to make complaint should never be heard in the city of Chicago."

Charge.	*Criminal Com- plaints.	†Preliminary Hear- ings		Convictions Criminal Court		
		Num- ber.	Per Cent of Com- plaints.	Num- ber.	Per Cent of Pre- lim.Hear.	Per Cent of Com- plaints.
Total Burglary, Larceny and Robbery 12,062	12,062	4,318	35.8	706	16.4	5.9
Other felonies 677	677	2,833	418.5	229	8.1	33.8
Total 12,739	12,739	7,151	56.1	935	13.1	7.3

†Cases pending were subtracted from these columns as follows: Burglary 24, Larceny 52, Robbery 28, Other Felonies 107.

*Statistics in this table are all for the year ending Nov. 30, 1912, since comparable statistics from the Criminal and Municipal Courts are available only for this year. For this reason criminal complaints are different from those for 1913 in Table III, which are for the year ending December 31.

A comparison between Tables III and IV shows quite clearly the result of combining and of separating the cases of grand and petit larceny. In the police statistics of felonies where they were not separated, the number of convictions was 48.3 per cent of the number of arrests; in the Municipal Court statistics of felonies which deal only with grand larceny the number of convictions was only 7.8 per cent of the number of preliminary hearings. Larceny convictions, according to the police statistics, were 41.3 per cent of larceny complaints; according to court statistics they were only 3.2 per cent of the complaints. It must, of course, be noted that these two sets of statistics are not for the same year. The police statistics are for the year ending Dec. 31, 1913; the Municipal Court statistics are for the year ending Nov. 30, 1912. There is, however, no reason to suppose that the percentage of convictions has changed very much within a year, and the difference between 48.3 per cent of convictions in the table from the police statistics and 7.8 per cent from the Municipal Court statistics can be explained only by the fact that the latter deals with grand larceny and the former with all larceny cases.

Because of this difference in the police and municipal court classification, it does not seem any more legitimate to make comparisons between criminal complaints and the criminal court convictions in the case of larceny than in the case of "all felonies."

Comparing statistics for burglary and robbery in the two tables we find that the Municipal Court statistics show a somewhat higher percentage of preliminary hearings, "cases disposed of," than the police statistics show of arrests, but the police statistics show a slightly lower percentage of convictions than the court statistics. That is, according to the police statistics, the convictions for robbery in 1913 were 16.7 per cent of the arrests on this charge, and 12.3 per cent of the complaints; the convictions for burglary were 27.4 per cent of the arrests and 4.4 per cent of the complaints. According to the court statistics, the number of convictions for robbery in 1912 were 20 per cent of the preliminary hearings and 16.1 per cent of the complaints; the convictions for burglary equaled 29.9 per cent of the preliminary hearings and 6.3 per cent of the complaints.

Both sets of statistics, therefore, show that convictions on charges of robbery and burglary are a small percentage (between 16.7 per cent and 30 per cent) of the number of arrests or preliminary hearings, and an extremely small percentage (between 4.4 per cent and 16.1 per cent) of the complaints. While it seems rather startling that burglary convictions equal in round numbers only 4 or 6 per cent of the complaints, it is probably true that the small percentages are to be accounted for in part by the fact that burglary complaints are changed sometimes upon arrest and sometimes after trial to charges of larceny.

Questions involved in a comparison of arrests and convictions are discussed with sufficient detail in the text (see pages 23-24 and 29-31). The purpose of this appendix is merely to explain that the statistics of criminal complaints furnished by the police department were not included in Tables 6, 11, 12, 13, because it appeared after a careful analysis that the statistics of complaints could not be legitimately compared with statistics of arrests or convictions. It is scarcely necessary to point out that reliable statistics of "crimes known to the police," similar to the statistics published annually in the Criminal Judicial Statistics of England, should be published each year for Chicago.

Before leaving the subject of criminal complaints, it should be explained that statistics have also been obtained showing the number of complaints received in the forty-five police precincts of Chicago, and these statistics are presented in Table V. Unfortunately, no data are available regarding the population of these various precincts.

After what has been said regarding the value of the statistics of criminal complaints, it has not seemed worth while to use Table V as the basis of a discussion of "crime areas." It should also be explained that, while statistics of arrests by precincts have not been available in the past, the department is now tabulating arrests by precincts and in the future such data will probably be published in the annual report. The sergeant in charge of the records, however, very kindly supplied such data as were already tabulated for the first two months of the year 1914, and these are presented in Table VI. Unfortunately, only the total number of arrests is given for each precinct, and the relative number of felonies and misdemeanors cannot be determined.

TABLE V. CRIMINAL COMPLAINTS RECEIVED 1912 AND 1913—BY POLICE PRECINCTS.

Precinct	Larceny. 1913	Larceny. 1912	Burglary. 1913	Burglary. 1912	Robbery 1913	Robbery 1912	Other Crimes. 1913	Other Crimes. 1912	Total. 1913	Total. 1912
1 180 N. LaSalle....	989	1,077	244	240	30	38	66	42	1,329	1,397
2 625 S. Clark.......	505	538	129	111	74	102	53	38	761	789
3 210 W. 22nd......	192	268	192	180	103	92	98	100	585	640
4 2523 Cottage Gr...	125	111	74	64	48	29	28	19	275	223
5 454 E. 35th.......	219	224	199	160	58	48	55	39	531	471
6 740 W. 35th......	68	73	90	90	56	29	27	20	241	212
7 2913 Loomis	30	24	33	30	28	13	15	7	106	74
8 3900 S. California.	25	13	48	26	6	4	6	5	85	48
9 (Discontinued)		8	....	4	....	1	....	0	....	13
10 5233 Lake	271	159	221	175	42	47	20	10	554	391
11 5001 S. State......	58	90	269	288	32	42	10	9	369	429
12 6344 Rosalie	89	104	191	146	17	25	10	18	307	293
13 834 E. 75th........	15	11	36	43	7	22	15	6	73	82
14 200 E. 115th......	21	15	45	31	2	3	1	0	69	49
15 2938 E. 89th......	35	23	35	32	15	7	15	3	100	65
16 3525 E. 106th......	18	10	18	11	6	3	6	1	48	25
17 6347 Wentworth ..	140	92	424	166	61	38	37	13	662	309
18 8501 S. Green.....	51	52	84	85	6	16	8	3	149	156
19 4736 S. Halsted...	53	62	65	47	36	21	21	15	175	145
20 1700 W. 47th......	46	38	106	71	14	16	15	13	181	138
21 943 Maxwell	234	247	476	282	133	88	98	67	941	684
22 2075 Canalport....	28	46	65	70	9	5	9	23	111	144
23 1700 W. 21st Pl...	61	43	96	101	24	22	23	27	204	193
24 2250 W. 13th......	56	57	187	179	55	50	24	19	322	305
25 2656 Lawndale	25	13	97	54	11	11	2	3	135	81
26 4001 Fillmore.....	84	80	232	207	32	21	53	17	401	325
27 120 N. Desplaines.	236	319	144	238	44	61	25	18	449	636
28 1637 W. Lake.....	195	235	194	188	62	50	20	9	471	482
29 2433 Warren......	93	140	149	146	24	20	13	5	279	311
30 4250 W. Lake.....	40	36	97	65	7	4	4	0	148	105
31 5610 W. Lake.....	27	30	70	78	8	4	5	3	110	115
32 1123 W. Chicago..	53	94	179	201	36	43	7	9	275	347
33 1312 W. North....	14	29	95	94	5	13	5	3	119	139
34 2256 W. North....	69	82	212	199	31	32	15	17	327	330
35 2138 N. California.	34	43	219	158	44	36	29	27	326	264
36 3973 Milwaukee....	80	48	119	65	20	17	41	26	260	156
37 4905 Grand......	21	14	32	18	5	5	12	12	70	49
38 113 W. Chicago...	342	358	328	248	67	64	48	43	785	713
39 1501 Hudson	111	65	122	67	26	16	11	14	270	162
40 2126 N. Halsted...	99	78	117	86	13	16	12	13	241	193
41 2742 Sheffield	96	91	204	161	17	23	19	27	336	302
42 3600 N. Halsted...	196	177	238	173	62	37	25	14	521	401
43 3801 N. Robey....	25	60	75	95	13	9	7	1	120	165
44 1940 Foster.......	127	102	248	198	20	25	23	17	418	342
45 7075 N. Clark.....	67	44	45	87	4	5	2	3	118	139
Total	5,363	5,523	6,543	5,458	1,413	1,277	1,038	774	14,357	13,032

TABLE VI. ARRESTS BY PRECINCTS DURING THE FIRST TWO
MONTHS OF THE YEAR 1914.

Precinct	January	February	Total for 2 months
1	281	248	529
2	492	365	857
3	439	324	763
4	242	165	407
5	298	223	521
6	113	116	229
7	82	150	232
8	39	48	87
9	...	...	...
10	79	41	120
11	234	181	415
12	107	97	204
13	63	63	126
14	118	86	204
15	175	146	321
16	44	55	99
17	173	190	363
18	22	48	70
19	206	196	402
20	148	196	344
21	479	404	883
22	82	121	203
23	127	186	313
24	87	104	191
25	51	51	102
26	88	76	164
27	805	547	1,352
28	197	199	396
29	99	90	189
30	71	127	198
31	25	50	75
32	386	374	760
33	185	386	571
34	116	199	315
35	152	287	439
36	44	59	103
37	32	48	80
38	308	331	639
39	74	121	195
40	50	88	138
41	102	157	259
42	113	106	219
43	47	41	88
44	43	42	85
45	35	24	59
Headquarters	214	44	258
Second Deputy's Office	370	137	507
First Deputy's Office	65	26	91
Detective Bureau	209	173	382
Traffic Division	113	158	271
Motorcycle Squad	3	5	8
Vehicle Bureau	560	490	1,050
Totals	8,687	8,189	16,876

APPENDIX D

DISCUSSIONS OF RECURRENT "CRIME-WAVES" STATISTICS OF ARRESTS BY MONTHS

Discussions of so-called "crime-waves" constantly appear in the news-papers. It is a question of interest to determine whether or not these "crime-waves" occur with any degree of regularity at the same time of the year. The following table, which shows the statistics of arrests (charges) by months, shows that for the last six years there has been a marked increase in arrests in the month of March. The number of arrests has then fallen in April (with the exception of the year 1908) and increased, but less mark-edly, in May (with the exception of the year 1910). In four out of the six years there has been a "crime-wave" in December, in two years in January.

TABLE I. MONTHLY SUMMARY OF CHARGES: 1907 TO 1913.

(From the Annual Reports of the General Superintendent of Police.)

Month.	1913.	1912.	1911.	1910.	1909.	1908.
January	8,462	6,368	5,866	5,856	4,687	4,707
February	8,191	5,672	5,178	5,517	4,556	4,332
March	9,357	6,387	5,881	7,245	5,546	5,329
April	7,817	5,797	5,289	6,011	4,843	5,498
May	8,243	6,927	6,725	5,978	5,119	5,457
June	7,792	7,600	7,605	6,948	6,016	5,850
July	8,800	7,610	7,517	6,661	6,279	6,110
August	8,901	7,770	7,657	7,813	6,023	5,323
September	10,202	7,530	7,337	6,445	6,155	5,834
October	8,874	7,680	7,186	6,592	5,431	4,945
November	8,857	6,885	6,771	6,109	6,630	4,888
December	11,761	7,627	7,637	6,043	5,410	5,112
Total	107,257	83,853	80,649	77,218	66,695	63,385

Unfortunately, the monthly summary of arrests is for "all offenses," and it is not possible to show arrests by months on felony charges and on mis-demeanor charges separately. There are available, however, some statistics of criminal complaints by months for the years 1912 and 1913. The statistics which are given below show that the "crime-wave," as far as the more seri-ous crimes are concerned, is likely to occur in the months of November and December. These are the months when the greatest number of burglaries, larcenies, and robberies occur, but it is important to note that there seems to be a second "crime-wave" in May of almost equal proportions.

TABLE II. MONTHLY SUMMARY OF CRIMINAL COMPLAINTS RE-CEIVED DURING 1912 AND 1913.

Month	1913					1912				
	Larceny	Burglary	Robbery	Other	Total	Larceny	Burglary	Robbery	Other	Total
January	391	545	161	117	1,214	381	348	101	52	882
February	326	469	151	69	1,015	378	475	85	52	990
March	365	506	96	75	1,042	403	430	83	75	991
April	365	541	83	63	1,052	413	428	81	54	976
May	453	576	92	75	1,196	478	540	100	84	1,202
June	421	508	69	82	1,080	532	454	114	75	1,175
July	521	484	73	88	1,166	520	462	83	70	1,135
August	495	471	117	82	1,165	465	435	91	61	1,052
September	483	585	106	93	1,267	496	413	95	62	1,066
October	484	563	118	68	1,233	472	420	121	70	1,083
November	517	657	164	111	1,449	530	511	149	72	1,262
December	554	629	159	119	1,461	455	542	174	47	1,218
Total	5,375	6,534	1,389	1,042	14,340	5,523	5,458	1,277	774	13,032

APPENDIX E
STATISTICS RELATING TO ARRESTS AND CONVIC-
TIONS IN CHICAGO, NEW YORK AND
LONDON COMPARED

The extent of crime or treatment of crime in different countries is not subject to exact comparisons. The laws defining crimes are different, and the procedure varies from one country to another. Nevertheless such comparisons, if made with the understanding that they are subject to reservations, are interesting. The following table shows the number of arrests per 1,000 of the population in Chicago compared with statistics from New York and London. No attempt is made to use statistics for Paris or Berlin, the other cities with which Chicago challenges comparison, because the criminal code and system of courts in France and Germany is so unlike our own. The London statistics are for "persons proceeded against."

ARRESTS OR ARRAIGNMENTS PER 1,000 POPULATION:
CHICAGO, NEW YORK, LONDON.

	Felonies	Mis-demeanors	Total Arrests	Convictions Per 1,000 Population	Per Cent of Arrests
Chicago, 1913	4.78	42.05	46.83	21.83	46.6
New York, 1913*	3.71	19.32	23.03	15.76	68.5
London, 1912†	2.18	15.91	18.09	22.49	87.2‡

*Comparison with New York is hardly legitimate because of the extensive use of the summons in New York in the last few years.

The increasing use of the summons since 1910 in New York has resulted in a decrease in arrests and an increase in the percentage of convictions. In 1913 there were 119,736 arrests excluding juvenile cases, but there were 52,294 summons cases. There were 81,952 convictions and 45,609 convictions on summonses. It does not seem fair to add the summons cases in New York since they are not included in the Chicago figures, but the increasing use of the summons in New York makes the comparison less accurate. If the summons cases were added in, the result would be 33.09 arrests per 1,000 and 24.54 convictions per 1,000. See **Annual Report of the Police Department, City of New York, 1913,** p. 16.

†Statistics for London compiled from **Judicial Statistics, England and Wales, 1912,** Part I. Criminal Statistics, p. 89 (Cd. 7282).

‡The percentage was necessarily computed on the total number proceeded against which includes 55,879 summonsed in addition to 131,167 arrested.

This table shows that Chicago has a high "crime rate," if the arrests per 1,000 of the population for felonies be taken as indicating crime; that is, Chicago has 4.78 arrests on felony charges per 1,000 population in comparison with 3.71 per 1,000 population in New York and 2.18 per 1,000 population in London. The total number of arrests per 1,000 population in Chicago is also high in comparison with these other cities: 46.83 per 1,000 population in Chicago compared with 23.03 in New York and 18.09 in London. On the other hand, if the crime rate were to be determined not by arrests, but by convictions for crime, the results are quite different: 21.83 per 1,000 of the population in Chicago, compared with 15.76 in New York and 22.49 in London. That is, the per cent of needless arrests seems to be very high in Chicago. The figures indicate that we have 46.6 per cent of convictions, compared, for example, with 87.2 per cent in London. It is possible to compare the per cent of convictions for felonies in Chicago and the per cent of convictions for indictable offenses in London with the following result:

LONDON: INDICTABLE OFFENSES, 1912.

Persons proceeded against 16,045
Discharged 2,718   16.9%
    Discharged ....2,326)
    Acquitted .... 392)
Held or convicted 13,195   82.2%

```
Convicted  ............................4,693)
Committed for trial ..................4,454)
Order made without conviction.........4,048)
```
Otherwise disposed of 132   .9%

CHICAGO: FELONIES, 1912.

Total preliminary hearings 7,362
```
Discharged without trial ...........................  5,959      81.0%
    Discharged by Municipal Court............4,749)
    No bills, Grand Jury.......................  783)
    Nolle pros. or stricken off................  427)
```
Held for trial 1,403   19.0%

These figures are of course not comparable in any exact sense. The offenses classified as "felonies" in Illinois are, however, very much like the "indictable offenses" in England. The English statistics include under indictable offenses in round numbers about 500 cases of "attempted suicide," about 200 cases of habitual drunkenness, about 400 "offenses in bankruptcy," about 200 cases of coining or possession of counterfeit money that would not be included here. On the other hand our police statistics include, in round numbers, 1,500 cases of "contributing to delinquency," which would not be included in the English classification. The great difference between the 80 per cent held in London and the 19 per cent held in Chicago is due in part to the fact that arrests cannot be made there without legal evidence of guilt. This would, of course, prevent the great waste involved in the needless arrests made here.

A comparison of the police force in the several cities can be made statistically as to the number of officers per 1,000 of the population and the number per square mile, as follows:

NUMBER OF POLICE IN COMPARISON WITH POPULATION AND AREA.

	‡London, 1911	New York, 1913	Chicago, 1913
Number of police	19,156	10,266	4,430
Population of the city......................	7,251,358	5,198,888	2,344,018
Area of city in square miles...............	692.9	268.8*	184.7*
Police per 10,000 population................	26.42	19.75	18.90
Police per square mile.....................	27.65	35.79	23.98
Per capita expenditure for police..........	$2.21	$2.97†	$2.92†

*This is the land area as given in the United States Bureau of the Census Report on **Financial Statistics of Cities**, 1912, p. 137.

†Statistics of per capita expenditures for New York and for Chicago are from the same report, p. 214. It is of interest to note that similar per capita expenditure for other cities having a population of 500,000 and over is as follows: Philadelphia, $2.69; St. Louis, $2.84; Boston, $3.19; Cleveland, $1.50; Baltimore, $2.21; Pittsburgh, $2.07; Detroit, $2.01. Some question may be raised as to the comparability of these per capita statistics, but the census does not discuss this point.

‡Statistics for London from **London Statistics, 1911-12**, issued by the London County Council.

This table shows that while Chicago has a smaller police force than New York or London, making the comparison both in relation to the population and area of the different cities, the numbers are not enough smaller to explain any very great difference in police methods. New York has only one more officer for every 10,000 of the population than Chicago, London has seven and one-half more. London has per square mile, however, about three and one-half more than Chicago and New York has about eleven and one-half more than Chicago. It is, of course, the population comparison that is important, since crime has a very close relation to numbers of population and a very remote relation to area of the city. The most important question obviously is that of method of organization of the force, and on this point statistics do not throw any light.*

---

*In discussing the inefficiency of the Chicago police organization, the **Final Report of the Civil Service Commission on Police Investigation** contains the following statement: "In its preliminary report the Commission, in commenting upon the large number of patrolmen assigned to special duty,

A comparison of the number of specific offenses of such crimes as murder, burglary, and robbery, committed in different cities and in different countries, cannot be made with any satisfactory degree of accuracy. It is not fair, for example, to compare arrests, for one city may be very lax about apprehending criminals, another very thorough and still another very active in making arrests, but very inefficient in arresting the right persons. On the other hand, it is not fair to compare convictions, since a small number of convictions may be due to the fact that the police have been inefficient in one city or the courts inefficient in another. However, such comparative figures as are available have been brought together below:

STATISTICS RELATING TO THE NUMBER OF CASES OF MURDER, ROBBERY AND BURGLARY, COMPARED IN CHICAGO, NEW YORK AND LONDON.

	Cases Disposed of
Murder and Manslaughter—	
Chicago, 1913	149
Chicago, 1912	127
*New York, 1913	131
New York, 1912	174
London, 1912	87
Robbery and Assault to Rob—	
Chicago, 1913	1,178
Chicago, 1912	1,015
New York, 1913	928
New York, 1912	637
London, 1912	45
Burglary—	
Chicago, 1913	1,320
Chicago, 1912	1,151
New York, 1913	1,755
New York, 1912	1,463
London, 1912	3,270

*The New York classification is "homicide."

With regard to the number of burglaries it should be explained that the Chicago figures are for three felonies, "burglary," "accessory to," and "assault to commit." The New York classification includes "the commission of burglary in any of its degrees." For London, the various forms of burglary were grouped together; they include "burglary," "house-breaking," breaking into shops, etc.," "attempts to break," "entering with intent," "possessing tools."

stated that out of 3,800 patrolmen on duty, about 500 are ordinarily carried in citizen's dress, 350 on wagons and ambulances, 300 on street crossings, rail-crossings and bridges, and about 1,200 on 'special duty;'" and "The Commission further stated that the assignment of patrolmen to duties that could be performed more efficiently and at a lower salary by other types of employes, is an injustice to the taxpayers, and a financial injury to the city" (pp. 42-43). A further criticism with regard to the "secret service" is as follows: "The number of men assigned to this duty is out of all proportion to the work accomplished, and a critical analysis of the work done by plain clothes men at stations should be made with a view of returning to patrol duty as many men as possible. The character of the work to which the plain clothes men are assigned is, to a large extent, such as could better be performed by a man in uniform. The presence of a man in uniform is a most corrective aid against crime, vice and disorder, and the all-important function of a police department is the prevention of crime and disorder and not to make a record for arrests. The detection of criminals is of minor importance if crime is prevented by the presence of an ample uniformed police."

APPENDIX F.

DETAILED TABLES OF FELONIES AND MISDEMEANORS (ALL CHARGES), 1900-1913.

TABLE I. CLASSIFICATION OF CHARGES (FELONIES), 1900 TO 1913.
(From Annual Reports of the Police Department.)

Charge.	1913.	1912.	1911.	1910.	1909.	1908.	1907.	1906.	1905.	1904.	1903.	1902.	1901.	1900.
Abandonment of child under 1 year.	9	11	1	2	6	2	1	1	9	49	45	*	*	*
Abduction	19	36	22	23	18	26	28	24	27	27	33	34	27	18
Abortion	17	25	17	10	17	16	21	11	15	3	2	3	2	3
Arson or attempt to commit arson	85	73	100	45	13	21	19	33	46	21	22	16	25	30
Bigamy	22	35	21	26	26	20	26	19	12	47	44	8	8	7
Burglary	985	1,013	1,183	1,124	1,229	1,634	1,415	1,739	1,780	1,388	1,616	1,653	1,709	1,664
Burglary, accessory to	56	…	29	17	9	40	15	16	16	202	252	23	35	13
Burglary, attempt to commit	131	81	87	58	73	83	68	88	78	97	91	130	122	92
Children, crime against	…	109	80	78	77	…	…	…	…	…	…	…	…	…
Children, contributing to delinquency	1,528	821	666	692	523	…	…	…	…	…	…	…	…	…
Confidence game	681	740	641	599	621	647	497	501	535	304	267	…	…	…
Conspiracy	71	29	53	38	45	49	32	27	23	18	30	43	56	34
Crime against nature	21	29	38	33	31	…	…	…	…	…	…	13	13	20
Embezzlement	199	167	272	234	230	137	150	168	115	110	127	196	205	187
Forgery	63	89	87	59	74	89	73	87	64	85	86	66	77	68
Having burglars' tools	12	23	5	3	8	…	…	…	…	…	…	10	5	15
Incest	19	14	9	7	12	4	15	8	14	9	8	2	3	8
Kidnapping	10	9	21	27	14	9	3	11	8	7	6	6	2	9
Larceny and larceny by bailee	4,532	4,138	3,977	4,007	4,369	5,224	5,420	5,329	5,234	4,732	5,398	5,051	5,841	5,560
Larceny, accessory to	38	41	35	23	40	19	21	34	60	513	666	211	203	163
Larceny, attempt to commit	23	19	18	11	13	…	…	…	…	…	…	74	76	36
Malicious mischief	250	227	212	219	264	231	372	717	553	567	674	665	599	663
Manslaughter	43	41	33	20	22	18	25	33	11	30	7	3	8	2
Mayhem	14	16	25	20	18	27	34	52	39	38	46	34	24	41
Murder	219	170	88	61	73	53	73	68	177	35	50	26	29	26
Murder, accessory to	33	13	15	22	13	10	17	10	46	46	82	…	…	…
Murder, assault to commit	246	238	391	312	261	328	393	915	931	502	567	782	659	602
Pandering	36	68	60	92	73	…	26	…	…	…	…	…	…	…
Perjury	25	53	16	9	19	19	11	11	8	19	13	11	11	14

Charge.	1913.	1912.	1911.	1910.	1909.	1908.	1907.	1906.	1905.	1904.	1903.	1902.	1901.	1900.
Rape	204	250	172	175	205	172	164	139	137	70	71	33	49	70
Rape, assault to commit	54	72	61	69	54	67	54	127	108	73	101	60	58	53
Receiving stolen property	451	340	389	413	465	429	404	485	371	387	445	357	415	374
Robbery	835	866	852	679	507	709	719	1,001	1,200	922	933	832	859	918
Robbery, accessory to	7	16	18	23	9	17	11	16	19	117	201	9	60	20
Robbery, assault to commit	180	224	138	105	165	142	173	191	122	154	186	137	192	125
Threats to kidnap or murder	68	133	....	....	....	....	....	....	....	....	....	....	....	....
Other felonies	17	57	49	41	60	309	384	514	386	544	481	7	11	3
Total felonies	11,203	10,276	9,881	9,376	9,656	10,551	10,653	12,376	12,144	11,116	12,550	10,495	11,383	10,838

*Before 1913 the charges were simply listed and not classified into felonies and misdemeanors. The following offenses appear only in the earlier years and evidently include both felonies and misdemeanors. In addition, therefore, to those listed in the foregoing tables where there were in the years 1900, 1901 and 1902 the following:

	1902.	1901.	1900.
Abandonment	261	288	235
Criminal carelessness	11	9	15
Harboring a female under 18 years in a house of ill fame			2
Horse stealing	154	178	207
Swindling	1,030	933	869
Threats			6
Total	1,456	1,408	1,334

TABLE II. CLASSIFICATION OF CHARGES (MISDEMEANORS), 1900 TO 1913.

(From the Annual Reports of the Police Department.)

Charge.	1913.	1912.	1911.	1910.	1909.	1908.	1907.	1906.	1905.	1904.	1903.	1902.	1901.	1900.
Abandonment of wife or children	1,171	1,017	1,104	1,076	932	965	873	547	424	320	314	....	....	....
Adultery and fornication	477	286	370	342	366	495	295	68	88	82	136	68	78	74
Assault and assault and battery	977	1,241	875	714	682	730	2,325	2,698	2,431	2,648	3,803	4,950	4,614	4,458
Assault with deadly weapon	1,396	1,128	1,193	1,080	993	1,036	1,212	1,054	1,010	868	920	482	525	532
Assignation house, inmates	....	....	....	....	....	....	....	....	15	131	175	211	357	240
Assignation house, keepers	....	....	....	....	....	....	....	....	74	4	12	21	60	42
Bastardy	381	339	388	412	415	421	345	166	116	137	129	71	79	77
Carrying concealed weapons	1,192	1,129	1,203	970	836	948	1,078	1,330	1,160	576	610	911	923	750
Cruelty to animals	255	212	100	368	289	350	388	162	57	28	24	142	104	58
Cruelty to children	1	1	12	14	11	26	35	52	7	3	5	2	12	2

Charge.	1913.	1912.	1911.	1910.	1909.	1908.	1907.	1906.	1905.	1904.	1903.	1902.	1901.	1900.
Disorderly conduct	54,738	43,635	49,386	51,791	43,398	40,875	35,650	49,230	45,847	45,577	40,186	34,405	32,469	34,965
Disorderly house, inmates or keepers	1,654	1,405	660	996	782	530	504	763	408	236	474	703	707	433
Doing business without license			934	1,189	941	392	224	319	276	658	594	221	424	325
Having gaming devices	7	3	29	35	94	112	115	913	689	800	623	21	30	8
Gaming house, inmates	4,127	2,112	2,588	1,230	1,531	1,671	1,561	5,603	4,336	3,803	1,954	1,713	1,306	1,385
Gaming house, keepers	1,256	2,318	330	386	505	454	408	1,258	850	796	184	525	349	213
House of ill fame, inmates	3,195	1,663	617	347	580	236	299	1,209	897	399	566	563	813	1,001
House of ill fame, keepers	486	396	264	149	222	68	90	649	329	261	280	229	292	331
Intimidation	7	10	24	5	5	4	18	42	46	140	33	1	14	17
Impersonating an officer	44	53	43	64	65	60	49	52	44	22	15	20	63	50
False pretenses	375	358	409	413	450	500	446	403	431	457	351	497	538	392
Opium dens, inmates	99	133	34	37	102	176	74	281	232	146	181	223	521	422
Resisting an officer	167	233	350	359	348	372	506	833	626	528	734	684	682	786
Riot		10	18	16	5	32	25	31	241	139	49	5	13	37
Selling liquor to minors or drunks	124	20	36	79	158	160	43	24	1	12	33	5	16	84
Speed ordinances	4,962	2,233	2,357	1,348	138	68								
Street walkers	1,645	1,516	1,730	1,619	1,778	1,731	897	2,434						
Threats, extortion by	20	7	24	15	13	10	9	9	13	70	70			
Vagrancy	935	850	795	1,572	1,040	1,196	542	379	361	68	631	581	750	818
*Other	18,870	14,366	9,086	5,267	4,040	4,051	4,764	9,428	9,791	8,981	12,037	11,109	10,902	10,751
Total	98,561	76,674	74,959	71,893	60,719	57,669	52,775	79,937	70,800	67,890	65,123	58,363	56,641	58,251

*Under "other misdemeanors" for 1900, 1901 and 1902 were included the following violations of ordinances. They are probably included in the "other misdemeanors" of later years, although this is not entirely clear.

Ordinance.	1902.	1901.	1900.
Bathing		15	16
Begging		1	1
Bridges	3		1
Building	33	39	50
Depots			9
Dogs	635	478	705
Express	1		11
Hacks	20	32	16
Health	114	108	156
Junk dealers	6	71	28
Parks	442	221	274

Ordinance.	1902.	1901.	1900.
Pawnbrokers	4	8	3
Porters and runners			2
Railways		675	1,535
Saloons	659	541	280
Sidewalks	514	34	113
Streets	69	92	83
Telegraphs	185		
Vehicles	19	79	6
Weights and measures	54	40	37
Other	7,561	7,418	6,604
Total	10,319	9,852	9,943

APPENDIX G.

Detailed Lists of Offenses, Preliminary Hearings, Criminal (Misdemeanor) Cases and Quasi-Criminal Cases (Violations of Ordinances).

CASES DISPOSED OF IN THE MUNICIPAL COURT OF CHICAGO, 1908 TO 1913.

A.—FELONY AND OTHER CASES ON PRELIMINARY HEARING.

Offense.	1913.	1912.	1911.	1910.	1909.	1908.
Abduction	22	36	38	29	19	20
Abortion	24	21	17	15	21	15
Arson	138	108	68	44	14	40
Assault with intent to kill	344	319	376	227	271	377
Bigamy	32	37	25	34	31	25
Bribery	17	6	13	5	10	17
Burglary	1,320	1,151	1,339	1,128	1,334	1,614
Confidence game	1,035	924	1,149	753	804	645
Conspiracy	72	30	59	24	66	48
Crime against nature	68	49	55	24	31	73
Enticing female into house of prostitution	5	8	2	3	1	....
Permitting female into house of prostitution	....	....	....	....	....	14
Embezzlement	240	193	294	166	127	179
Forgery	89	100	106	66	103	105
Gaming house	....	....	....	....	2	....
Horse stealing	40	17	26	30	33	38
Incest	25	13	14	11	9	8
Larceny	2,150	2,256	3,718	3,077	1,716	2,213
Murder	103	87	116	137	106	43
Manslaughter	46	40	25	22	16	34
Obtaining money under false pretenses	68	67	168	1	50	270
Perjury	25	29	32	8	20	32
Rape	303	347	261	267	278	265
Robbery	1,178	1,015	968	839	882	657
Receiving stolen property	307	194	292	145	191	258
Other felonies	451	315	365	563	325	731
Total	8,102	7,362	9,526	7,618	6,460	7,721

B.—CRIMINAL (MISDEMEANOR) CASES.

Offense.	1913.	1912.	1911.	1910.	1909.	1908.
Abandonment	1,472	1,612	1,769	1,548	1,432	1,063
Adulteration of foods	54	96	67	44	22	98
Adultery and fornication	512	344	402	191	247	252
Assault and battery	999	1,471	819	737	769	1,270
Assault with deadly weapon	1,458	1,327	1,395	1,130	896	555
Automobiles	7,231	4,132	2,996	1,049	145	294
Child labor	366	199	160	114	202	....
Children, delinquent and dependent	1,610	1,119	733	634	361	470
Cruelty to animals	4	....	2	2	4	44
Cocaine	....	11	3	2	....	9
Dental	....	....	2	2	....	13
Employment of females	353	248	173	....	....	....
Embezzlement	....	....	....	34	90	34
False pretenses	374	358	271	357	416	321
Fish and game	5	2	2	5	3	7
Gambling	....	....	....	7	13	86
Kidnapping	10		1	....	....	
Larceny	2,938	2,824	914	1,545	3,316	3,233
Lotteries	....	4	3	2	1	25
Malicious mischief	162	156	166	118	147	134
Obscene books	....	6	3	3	5	18
Pandering	54	72	62	92	....	....
Pharmacy	14	3	....	....	....	3
Receiving stolen property	202	167	131	113	264	199
Seduction	12	11	12	4	10	3
Vagrancy	214	165	151	176	71	166
Other misdemeanors	1,476	1,561	1,533	1,916	1,716	2,170
Total	19,520	15,888	11,770	9,825	10,130	10,467

C.—QUASI-CRIMINAL CASES.

(Violations of City Ordinances and Bastardy Cases.)

Offense.	1913.	1912.	1911.	1910.	1909.	1908.
Bastardy cases	419	590	552	540	488	....
Buildings, unsafe	120	360	305	107	57	104
Carrying concealed weapons	1,181	1,183	1,111	831	758	952
Coal, short weight	34	19	19	17	19	19
Cream, under grade	50	15	18	55	94	194
Disorderly conduct	53,503	47,824	52,100	53,228	44,769	42,127
False weights and measures	190	113	59	94	162	279
Fire escapes	6	11	17	....	5	68
Gambling	4,966	2,323	314	372	1,364	857
Immoral exhibitions	3	6	27	11	14	26
Indecent exposure	56	73	81	136	106	138
Inmates and keepers of gambling houses	211	2,924	1,774	1,040	510	952
Keeping slot machine	6	28	86	2	56	40
Keeping house of ill-fame	3,345	1,863	205	134	182	70
Keeping disorderly house	1,608	1,075	598	934	697	447
Markets, unclean premises	9	6	21	2	27	243
Milk, adulterated	1	....	18	32	6	191
Milk, under grade	202	246	55	218	373	860
Milk dealers, unclean premises	103	21	1	39	106	78
Night walkers	1,846	1,569	1,633	1,619	1,665	1,664
Smoke nuisance	248	381	663	816	320	121
Vagabonds	662	703	842	....	....	....
Violating park ordinances	1,184	2,146	2,545	1,665	1,400	....
Water closets, unclean	26	13	6	28	50	20
Violating other city ordinances	23,732	19,627	8,384	8,559	8,553	7,292
Total	93,711	83,119	71,434	70,479	61,781	56,742

APPENDIX H.

STATISTICS SHOWING DISPOSITION OF CASES IN THE MUNICIPAL COURTS, 1900-1913, FROM THE ANNUAL REPORTS OF THE POLICE DEPARTMENT.

DISPOSITION OF CASES IN MUNICIPAL COURTS, 1900 TO 1913.

Disposition.	1913.	1912.	1911.	1910.	1909.	1908.	1907.	1906.	1905.	1904.	1903.	1902.	1901.	1900.
Held to Grand Jury	2,182	2,725	2,783	2,934	2,315	3,242	2,315	3,438	3,398	3,333	3,440	3,139	3,000	3,574
Held to Juvenile Court	53	24	64	71	252	1,127	1,741	2,061	2,021	1,851	2,021	1,784	1,990	1,312
Sentenced to County Jail	141	128												
Sentenced to House of Correction	1,933	1,209	1,116	1,133	2,039	1,618	1,933							
Sentenced to other correc. institut'ns	2	3										*2,091	†1,975	
Fined	43,690	27,448	30,612	31,647	26,987	26,292	25,307	22,698	22,362	21,542	20,412	17,825	19,063	16,366
Paroled (probation)	1,918	701												
Released on peace bonds	105	88	120	11	95	263	401	1,315	1,243	1,165	1,329			1,274
Ordered to make weekly payments	876	910												
Discharged	56,529	48,563	49,034	44,286	39,000	35,593	29,867	59,706	50,436	43,045	46,597	41,693	40,318	45,247
Nolle pros and stricken from docket	2,003	3,415												
Otherwise disposed of	332	167	872	227	373	423	358	212	1,223	8,383	3,343	‡3,782	‡3,096	§2,663
Total	109,764	85,381	84,601	80,309	71,061	68,558	61,922	89,340	80,683	79,319	77,142	70,314	69,442	70,436

*Includes 292 cases sent to penitentiary or reformatories.
†Includes 388 cases sent to penitentiary or reformatories.
‡Otherwise disposed of and still pending.
§2,533 cases are change of venue to private justices.

Underlying Causes
and
Practical Methods
for
Preventing Crime

by
PROFESSOR ROBERT H. GAULT
NORTHWESTERN UNIVERSITY

GENERAL INTRODUCTION

The causal factors that enter into every form of human behavior, whether criminal or otherwise fall into two groups: psycho-physical and environmental. Thus it is, in part, one's mental or physical make-up, or both mental and physical make-up combined, that determine how one will behave. If one's nervous system is badly out of gear so that nerve impulses, in one part of the system or another, become sidetracked or retarded or accelerated, the parts of the system must fail to work together harmoniously at least, just as an organized body of men fail when there is lacking a co-ordinated system by which the purposes of the organization may be carried into effect. In order, therefore, that one may make intelligent forecast respecting the behavior of a given individual who is about to go forth into the midst of surroundings to which he has not until now been accustomed, or in which he has hitherto failed to fit himself with approximate nicety, it is necessary for one to know, in the first place—first only for convenience of statement—whether that individual has a nervous system so substantial and so nice in its adjustments that it can withstand strains and meet emergencies. It is information of the same nature that one seeks when one has in contemplation the purchase of a new typewriter. If any comment upon the parallelism implied here is required, we have only to say what is perfectly patent to a student of behavior: that man is a machine to a greater degree than he realizes. One needs to know whether this mechanical system is infected with destructive poisons; whether the muscular system is such as to favor adjustment to the conditions of life, and whether the activities of alimentation are capable of supplying the organism with energy producing food. Where all other factors in determining behavior and successful adjustment to the conditions of social life are equal, the conditons implied in the above questions may be wholly decisive.

In the second place—second, again, only for convenience of statement—we want to know whether the individual whose future behavior we would foresee is mentally equal to meeting the difficulties that are incident to living in the sphere to which he belongs. Many, though not all forms of mental alienation, and incapacity, disqualify him for facing those difficulties. Self-control is very largely a matter of emotional control; of attention; of persistence; of ideals and of practical judgment. Deficiencies in one or another of these respects, particularly in emotional control, control of attention, and in persistence, usually go hand in hand with profound defects in the nervous organization.

Studies in the psycho-physical nature of the individual delinquent, therefore, are the cornerstone of investigations in the field of criminology. In the work upon which we are making report in the following pages we have given considerable attention to the phyco-physical problem. The first division is wholly devoted to this problem, and to an estimate of the probable adaptability of certain groups of women and men to a normal social environment, afflicted as they are with profound nervous disorders, destructive infections, phychoses and feeble-mindedness.

In each of the remaining sections of the report the psycho-physical factor receives more or less attention. It is particularly emphasized in the first three sections of the third division, where we set forth the results of our examinations of 63 boys in the John Worthy School; our follow-up of certain juvenile cases whose phyco-physical conditions were determined in the Juvenile Phychopathic Institute in the years 1910, 1911 and 1912, and our study of the psycho-physical condition and the behavior of Cook County boys who are now in the State Reformatory at St. Charles, Illinois.

At the outset in this introduction I gave the environmental factor a place as a cause of every form of behavior. From this the psycho-physical cause is never isolated. Behavior, whether of a saint or a sinner, of an imbecile or a savant, is invariably modified by the conditions that surround the actor, if it is not wholly occasioned by external stimulation. What we shall do, and for that matter what we shall become, is the resultant of two forces: our disposition or our psycho-physical nature on the one hand, and on the other hand the stimulations that we receive from our friends and our enemies, our books and playthings, the houses in which we live, the streets in which we walk, the work of our hands, etc., etc. Were it not so we should dispense with our schools.

In the faith that the environmental factor does contribute to behavior or actually determine its character; that the behavior of the delinquent and the upright alike is a reaction of an individual with given disposition and capacities, stable or unstable, normal or distorted as they may be, to the stimulations afforded by the surroundings in the midst of which he lives; in this faith we set about to arrange the surroundings or the environment of our wards to the best of our ability—to control the stimulations, in other words, so as to get the kind of behavior that we approve, and in getting that behavior, ultimately to develop the dispositions in those with whom we deal that will guarantee approved behavior in future. This is what we are doing when we improve our school buildings, devise school currimula, assign tasks, etc., to our children; we are arranging the external or environmental conditions of behavior so as to get certain desired responses, e. g., familiarity with numbers and facility in handling them, habitual co-operation with others, etc., etc. We are doing all this in our schools, to repeat, in the expectation that we may develop habits or dispositions that will guarantee future behavior. Happy are we if our educational experts can tell us in particular instances what are the dispositions and capacities upon which we may begin our building.

It is precisely the same problem in which the student of criminology is involved. The question is not only as to the present psycho-physical nature of the delinquent. This, it is true, may be a burden transmitted to him from a tainted ancestry. If not so the question is as to the environmental stimulations that have played their part in occasioning the behavior of the delinquent and ultimately, it may be, the delinquent disposition.

Furthermore, when we are confronted by thousands of criminals of all ages the very critical question arises as to how we can so arrange the external conditions into which we place these people as to secure the utmost human salvage possible through a modification of their dispositions and their behavior consequently. This is a question of social protection as well as of reformation, and it is not essentially altered in the face of that host of delinquents who are undoubtedly unredeemable.

The above considerations are reflected in the following report in the second division entitled, Adult Probation and later in the third division in the section on the employment of juvenile delinquents, in which we are interested in the development of an educational system and a plan for vocational guidance that will minimize the chances of the youth's entering upon a career of truancy, juvenile delinquency and crime. In that section, too, our thought is directed toward surrounding the youthful delinquent with such an environment of occupations and practical schools as will give material assistance in the development of dispositions toward the behavior that society approves.

To some it will appear that in what follows we are perniciously confusing juvenile delinquency which is not crime with adult delinquency which is crime. Such a criticism is likely to arise from those who are troubled, even though unwittingly, with the ancient and speculative problem of individual responsibility. It is only as educators in the broad sense of the word that we are justified in assuming an attitude toward youths that is different from that assumed towards adults. We have no more necessarily to do with responsibility here than has the teacher in the school room. In dealing with pupils in school or children at home we administer praise or blame or punishment, corporal or otherwise, such as experience suggests may produce desirable reactions, and desirable dispositions finally, on the part of individuals whose psycho-physical natures are more or less well known to begin with. Such is (or will be) our attitude toward delinquents, old or young. This justifies the discussion of juvenile delinquency in our report.

Furthermore the development of a full blown criminal is like the development of a professional man. He grows out of the youth. If it is our design to develop a strong lawyer we control the environment of a youth who has been selected for the purpose. If we would prevent the development of other professional men and women called criminals we will look again to the control of the surroundings of our plastic youths—and we cannot know too much about their psycho-physical nature. The proper study of criminology is our youth in their reactions to their environment throughout a period of development. In this sense it is precisely analogous to our study of the lawyer or any other professional or business man. Every complex is best studied from its beginnings and throughout its developmental period.

The report does not refer specifically to the problem of alcoholism in relation to crime. No search for such a relationship was made. From the work that we have done, however, one or the other of two inferences may be drawn: that habitual indulgence in alcohol will load an organism with poisons, disorganize the system, produce mental weakness, and so render one unreliable in one's responses to environmental stimuli; or that such mental weakness and lack of resistance as are directly the cause of crime express themselves also in alcoholic indulgence. For that matter both these inferences may be drawn. Alcoholism undoubtedly is both effect and cause of some weaknesses that are directly the cause of crime. Studies of the problem that show the relatively high degree of alcoholism among criminals really go no further than is indicated here, excepting to show that alcohol, even when it is not taken in such quantity or so persistently as to produce degeneration, causes crime by breaking down normal inhibitions and arousing passion consequently. The number of annual convictions in Germany could be reduced one-fifth by killing the abuse of alcohol. (Aschaffenburg, Crime and its Repression, p. 228.)

On the basis of all the information that is available at present relating to the causal relation of crime and venereal or other infections we can make no statement different from that above concerning alcoholism. These infections are both effect and cause of some of the weaknesses that are directly responsible for criminal behavior.

The economic question invites investigation also. One is tempted often to believe that if the economic strain could be lightened crime would be sensibly diminished. No doubt there are hundreds of cases in which an unusually adverse economic situation has stimulated men and women and children to the performance of acts of delinquency. Breckenridge and Abbott in "The Delinquent Child and the Home" showed a striking parallelism between poverty and juvenile delinquency. If both father and mother must work away from home all day in order to buy food, the opportunities for truancy among the children, and consequently for the development of irresponsible and reckless dispositions, multiply.

It is a fair question whether the relief from economic strain, such as is effected by the system of Mother's Pensions, will correct juvenile delinquency in the homes that profit by the pension. An unequivocal answer to this question would bear upon the causation of delinquency and consequently of crime. Whatever correction of this sort may be found, of course, could not be attributed without question to economic relief. It might be due as well to the friendly supervision of the officer which is always available with the relief.

We made a preliminary attempt at this problem. For our purpose we selected 100 families from the pension list, families that were especially low on the economic scale, and compared them with an equal group from the non-pensioned County Agent's list from the point of view of the prevalence of delinquency. The County Agent's families selected were technically eligible to the pension. But we could not find in the pension list a sufficient number of families in which delinquency had appeared to make a comparison fruitful. We were unable to follow up the families from the County Agent's records, and in a few cases the delinquents on the pensioned list attained the age of 14 and automatically passed out from the influence of the Pension Department so soon after the family was admitted to its benefit that, whatever the development of the youth, it could hardly be laid to the credit or to the discredit of the Pension system. We are not, therefore, in a position to offer a report on this question. We believe, however, that the method of investigation that we have followed in this preliminary inquiry is one that promises to supply reliable scientific data if only a thousand or more families can be brought under observation and kept under observation for a prolonged period.

This brings us to a consideration of the economic situation as a cause of the crimes of adults. On this point we have made no investigation whatever. Our statistics of unemployment, of wages and the cost of living, not to speak of our criminal statistics, are in such an undeveloped state that one is in the realm of opinion only when one expresses a decision in the matter without prolonged and exhaustive investigation of our conditions here at home. If we are justified in saying, as we have said in the earlier part of this introduction, that infections, etc., that reduce the adaptability of an organism favor the yielding to opportunities and the committing of crimes, then we are undoubtedly justified in saying that lack of sufficient food will have a similar effect, and that consequently unemployment or low wages and high costs, making it impossible to procure food and other necessaries of life, are causes of a certain weakness that is itself directly a cause of crime. Similarly we could go further, and with good logic, to say that even after the very necessaries of life are provided economic pressure may be made, by our desire for luxuries, too intense for us to bear, until the breaking point is reached and crimes, therefore, committed. Such discussion as this, however, does not allay one's scientific craving. For satisfaction we turn to European literature where we find how involved the question really is, and even that authorities are contradictory.

We find Garofalo, for example (Criminology, Criminal Science Series, Boston, 1914, p. 165) saying, "the economic condition of the proletariat . . . is entirely without influence upon criminality, as a whole; its influence is exerted only upon certain special forms which constitute the specific criminality of the lower classes. . . . Extreme indigence ordinarily results in mendicancy, sometimes in vagabondage; the only crimes for which it is clearly accountable are such trivial offenses as the stealing of firewood, articles of food and other articles of insignificant value." But economic stress does not end with those who receive low wages. Garofalo says further: "There is nothing to show that the disproportion between desires and the means of satisfying them is any greater in any one class than in another." (P. 148.) Hugo Herz, who discusses the economic status of the people in relation to criminality in Austria, says that such atavistic forms of criminality as deeds of violence, theft and robbery are directly dependent on the prices of food. Those offenses, however, that are better adapted to modern conditions, in which falsehood and deceit, instead of violence, are employed, have left this primitive dependence on the price of food behind them, and seek their opportunity in the complex life of the modern business world. (Monatschr. f. Kriminal Psychol, II, 292. See Aschaffenburg, Crime and Its Repression, Criminal Science Series, 1913; p. 117.) The decrease in theft and the increase in fraud and embezzlement that go along with increasing freedom from the economic pressure in the struggle for the necessaries of life, balance each other. This suggests certain data that is presented by Aschaffenburg relating to Juvenile Offenders in Germany (ibid., p. 149). Since 1892, German youths have been increasingly active in remunerative occupations. But notwithstanding their steadily improving economic condition, juvenile offenses during the period have alarmingly increased; assault and battery by 123 per cent; breach of the peace by 128.6 per cent; fraud and embezzlement by 40 per cent; theft by but 8 per cent. Only the statistics relating to thieving by juveniles deny the general increase of juvenile offenses in the face of their improving economic conditions. It seems that if youth are given the means of "enjoying life" they lose their blameless reputation. Their felt needs grow with prosperity more rapidly than their inhibitions, and the dancing hall, the picture show and the saloon too soon become habits of life. "More important," says Aschaffenburg, in speaking of the general situation (p. 114) "than absolute need is the inability to adapt one's self to changed conditions. Whoever is accustomed to spend a good deal on amusement cannot easily give up doing so when times are hard. The more a man earns, the greater are his demands," etc.

This all seems to me to throw us back for reliance upon the training and education of the home, the school, the church and other educational agencies. These in the long run must control crime, by means of developing adaptable, self-controllable individuals and equipping them with the work habit.

It follows from all of this that the improvement of the economic status of the home in which there are growing children will afford a better opportunity than otherwise exists for these educational agencies to perform their normal function, always assuming that the heads of the family are capable of using their advantage wisely in the interest of the children. This, to revert to the preceding subject, is precisely what our system of mother's pensions seeks to guarantee. With every grant of a pension there goes the certainty of supervision by a probation officer who attends to it that a family budget is properly prepared and followed, and that the children are made primarily the beneficiaries through the increase of their educational opportunities. It follows, too, that the improvement of the economic status of adults will favorably affect their own behavior at once only if their native and acquired dispositions are favorable to begin with.

Our conclusion on this point is that economic conditions may and should be made to afford opportunities for the development of dispositions that can withstand the strain of living; that to improve the economic condition in advance of the disposition—which includes the capacities, judgment, motives, ideals, etc.—of an individual is not a measure for social protection; that the improvement of the economic condition of the home, by any system, in behalf of the children is a measure for social protection against the development of criminals, provided the system provides careful supervision of the way in which the economic advantage is employed.

Finally, attention must be drawn to means for protecting the offender against the unscrupulous who pose as his defender, but who in their greed exploit the offender, make him resentful, deprive him of confidence in men, take away his courage and make him in future ten times the menace he has been before. On this point we present a section on The Defense of Poor Persons Accused of Crime in Chicago. We acknowledge indebtedness to Harry K. Herwitz for the data and composition of this portion of the report.

This report on the Causes of Crime in Chicago covers at best but a beginning of investigations in a very few subjects. The field is so large and complex that a few months is as nothing compared to the time that is required for a thorough study of a limited area. We have attempted to make the work, as far as possible, a study of individual cases. Ths is necessarily a slow and tedious procedure.

We present our results as follows:

FIRST.—Investigations among prisoners confined in the House of Correction. (a) Mental and physical examination of 61 female prisoners in the House of Correction; (b) An investigation of insane prisoners in the House of Correction.

SECOND.—A study of adult probation.

THIRD.—Some studies of juvenile delinquents in Chicago. (a) Mental and physical examination of 63 boys in the John Worthy School; (b) effectiveness of Juvenile Court procedure considered in relation to certain groups of offenders; (c) study of Cook County boys now in St. Charles Reformatory; (d) delinquent boys in employment.

FOURTH.—Defense of poor persons accused of crime in Chicago.

FIFTH.—General summary of conclusions and recommendations in above investigations.

I

INVESTIGATIONS AMONG PRISONERS CONFINED IN THE HOUSE OF CORRECTION

Every considerable group of prisoners that has been the subject of investigation includes many who, by reason of either mental or physical deficiency or both, are unable to adjust themselves to the conditions of normal life, once they are released from prison. This is the conclusion of students of criminology in all parts of the world who have given time to this problem. Wherever such persons are found, therefore, in our prison population, we are likely to find a large degree of recidivism, provided they are committed to prison for a short term on account of the minor offenses of which so many of them are guilty, and released again indiscriminately at the expiration of their term. If this is the case, it is probable that our prisons, as far as they affect certain classes of prisoners at any rate, prevent crime only while these prisoners are in confinement. It is appropriate then to inquire what is the mental and physical condition of certain classes in the Chicago House of Correction.

We report in Section A on the condition of 61 women prisoners who are addicted to the drug habit in one or another form. Our means for identification of offenders in Chicago are so unsatisfactory that it is not possible to say to what extent these people are recidivists. Putting together, however, what records are available with the prisoners' statements, it is safe to say that considerably more than half of the cases have been arrested heretofore and committed several times here or elsewhere.

The medical examination consisted in an investigation of the condition of the sense organs, vital organs and reflexes as indicative of the condition of the nervous system. What other examinations were made including the Wasserman test, are indicated in the analysis below. The mental status was determined by the Binet test. The physical and mental examinations were made by Dr. H. C. Stevens of the University of Chicago.

A

A MENTAL AND PHYSICAL EXAMINATION OF 61 FEMALE PRISONERS IN THE HOUSE OF CORRECTION

The statistics of recidivism suggest an inquiry into the mental and physical condition of adult prisoners who have been convicted more than once. Such investigations conducted elsewhere show that persons who have been convicted several times are, on the whole, of such a nature that they cannot be expected to respond normally to their environment. Persons who have been convicted more than three times in Prussia, e. g., are regarded as not capable of being rehabilitated. Dr. Paul Bower's study of the diagnosis of 100 recidivists in the Michigan City, Indiana, prison, who had been committed four or more times, reveals a condition that leaves no hope for improvement.

If these statements truly represent the case it is probable that our prisons prevent crime—in the case of many people—only while the prisoners are confined. This thought, or question rather, prompts the investigation that is reported below.

The general outcome of this study, which is only as yet a preliminary investigation, shows:

1. That the mentality of the female prisoners is of the moron class.
2. That there are evidences of serious disturbances of the nervous system in at least 50 per cent of the cases. The disturbance of the nervous system are such that prolonged treatment will be necessary to cure them.

The detailed report which follows includes the results of the investigation of:

1. Mental age of 126 female prisoners, as determined by the Binet test.
2. Neurological examination of 61 female prisoners.
3. The Wassermann test on the blood serum of 11, and the Wassermann test on the spinal fluid of 9 female prisoners.

4. Venereal infection in 45 female prisoners.
5. Gyneological examination of 17 female prisoners.

BINET TEST.

The mental age of 126 female prisoners was determined by means of the Binet Test. The co-operation of the prisoners with the examiner was good. In only two instances was there any refusal on the part of the prisoner to answer the question. These two instances are not included in the report. There is no pretense that the result of this test is the last word relating to the psychological status of these adult women. It is entirely probable, however, that our data on this point is not far from correct. The results of this test are shown in the following summary:

SUMMARY.

Number ranking between 5 and 6 years........ 1
Number ranking between 6 and 7 years........ 1
Number ranking between 7 and 8 years........ 5
Number ranking between 8 and 9 years........ 8
Number ranking between 9 and 10 years........ 32
Number ranking between 10 and 11 years........ 29
Number ranking between 11 and 12 years........ 36
Number ranking between 12 and 13 years........ 12
Number ranking between 13 and 14 years........ 2
Refused to answer............................... 2

Total 138

It will be seen from this summary that 86 per cent of these women fall between 9 and 13 years of mental age. Probably some correction in favor of the women should be made on account of illiteracy, due to the lack of opportunity. There can be no doubt, however, that the result of the test is in general a fair indication of the mentality of the prisoners.

NERVOUS SYSTEM.

The condition of the nervous system was evidenced by changes in the reflexes, sensation and muscular power. Sixty-one women were examined with reference to these three points. These 61 cases have been grouped according to offenses for which the prisoner was committed. The classification is as follows:

Drug Addiction 13
Alcoholism 20
Disorderly Conduct, Vagrancy and Soliciting.... 25
Larceny 2

Total 61

The incidence of nervous systems is shown in per cent in the following table:

Offense.	Symptoms. Nervous Per Cent.
Drug Addiction	54
Alcoholism	70
Disorderly Conduct, Vagrancy and Soliciting	50

Although the number of cases is not sufficient to justify general conclusions, it is significant that 50 per cent of these women show nervous symptoms of a marked sort.

WASSERMANN TEST.

The blood serum was taken for examination for the Wassermann test in 11 cases. Nine of the 11, or 82 per cent, gave a positive reaction. Four of these cases have been diagnosed as syphilitic. The result of the Wassermann reaction was never contradictory to the clinical diagnosis. In 9 cases the spinal fluid was taken for examination for the presence of syphilis. In one case only was the Wassermann reaction positive. This case is undoubtedly an early case of cerebro spinal syphilis.

VENEREAL INFECTION.

The results given in this portion of the report were derived from the records of the Women's Hospital in the House of Correction. An examination for the presence of venereal disease is made only in those cases in which the patient complains of trouble. The results are as follows:

Gonorrheal infection alone...................... 24
Syphilitic infection alone...................... 9
Gonorrhea and Syphilis Chancroid.............. 11
Chancroid 1

                                             ——
Total 45

The distribution of venereal infection, according to the offenses for which
the patient was committed, is shown in the following table:

Offense.   Venereal Infection.
Drug Addiction 77%
Alcoholism 35%
Disorderly Conduct, Vagrancy and Soliciting... 50%

RECOMMENDATION.

Such prisoners as these, because they, in all probability have not the
mental and physical stamina to bear up under unfavorable conditions, and
to adjust themselves to normal society, should be segregated on farm colonies
or in hospitals until cured. The medical staffs of our penal institutions should
be empowered to commit such patients to appropriate institutions. (See
conclusion to Sec. B following and Sec. A, Part III.)

B

AN INVESTIGATION OF INSANE PRISONERS IN THE HOUSE OF CORRECTION

We present herein data showing the number of insane of all types who
have been discovered by the hospital staff in the House of Correction between
January 1, 1914, and August 20, 1914. The total number is 132. Of these, 56
were in such condition that by the usual process of law, namely, by the jury
that acts on such cases, it was possible to send them immediately to one or
another of the state institutions for the insane.

I. SHOWING THE MENTAL CASES EXAMINED IN HOUSE OF
CORRECTION FROM JAN. 1, 1914, TO AUG. 20, 1914, AND SENT
THENCE TO DETENTION HOSPITAL FOR COMMIT-
MENT TO INSTITUTIONS FOR INSANE.

Diagnosis.   No. of Cases.
General Paresis 24
Dementia Precox 14
Paranoia 5
Alcoholic Hallucinosis 6
Other Cases 7

                                       ——
Total 56

II. SHOWING THE MENTAL CASES EXAMINED IN THE HOUSE
OF CORRECTION FROM JAN. 1, 1914, TO AUG. 20, 1914, AND
KEPT THERE TO SERVE OUT THEIR SENTENCES.

Diagnosis	No. of Cases.	Av. Length of Term.	Range.
General Paresis	9	108 days	33 days to 213 days
Dementia	14	106 days	33 days to 213 days
Paranoia	2	122 days	63 days to 180 days
Imbeciles	6	59 days	10 days to 6 mo.
Alcoholics	28	163 days	23 days to 1 year
Other Cases	17	210 days	53 days to 1 year

Total............... 76

The remainder of this group, 76 in all, are positively determined to be
suffering from mental diseases. They are victims of paranoia, of general
paresis, and of practically every other form of insanity in the catalogue. They
are not, however, in such condition that it is possible to have them committed
by a jury of laymen to an institution for the insane. They are a part of the
great army of borderland cases whose mental alienation is not readily apparent to a layman. When they shall have served the term in the House of
Correction for which they were committed, the duration of which varies from
a month to a year, or more than a year in some cases in which a heavy fine

has been assessed in addition to the House of Correction sentence, they will once more be free men in the streets. Experience both in this city and elsewhere indicates that there is a strong probability that these offenders will be repeated transgressors against the law. They will probably return again and again to such institutions as the House of Correction or the state penitentiary, a constant burden upon taxpayers of the city or the state, and a source of danger as well to law abiding members of the community.

It must be borne in mind that the patients referred to above are by no means all of such cases that could be found by definite diagnosis in the House of Correction. That total of 132 diagnoses are only those that were made for one reason or another by the hospital staff. In many cases, the friends of the prisoners requested the examination. In a few cases the diagnosis was made at the request of the prisoner himself. The remainder of the examinations were conducted on the initiative of the hospital staff, or on the suggestion of guards or other prison officials, who observed some striking peculiarities in the prisoners. The only way to determine the full number of mentally deranged cases in the House of Correction is· to make a careful, painstaking diagnosis of the 2,000-odd inmates of the institution. That is a task so exacting as to be beyond the ability of the staff, confronted as it is with a vast amount of professional work that requires, day by day, immediate attention. Indeed, it would hardly add to the force of this section of our report to show the full number of prisoners in this institution who are of the types designated. It is sufficient to know that there is a considerable number of these cases, and, furthermore, that they are a source of recurring offenses and consequent prosecution and imprisonment. That this is a correct statement of the case is sufficiently indicated by the following brief descriptions of typical cases:

CASE 1. Has been in and out of the House of Correction during a period of at least 14 years. Cherishes the delusion that she is the rightful owner of a great estate that is being withheld from her. Paranoiac. She is usually committed for a term of a few months on charges of disorderly conduct. When she has served her term she is able to live within the law for but a few months at most, when she is returned as a prisoner charged with a new violation. The beautiful symbolic embroidery that she produces impresses the uninitiated as evidence of a high degree of intelligence and artistic skill. She is one of the great army whose repeated minor offenses retard· the courts, add to our sense of social insecurity and to the financial burdens of the municipality.

CASE 2. This patient was last arrested on a charge of soliciting. She has been positively diagnosed as a victim of General Paresis. She was sent to the Detention Hospital, where the jury refused to commit her to an institution for the insane. After a few months she had served her term and was out again in the street. She will never be fit to be at large.

CASE 3. This patient has been arrested 15 times in Syracuse, N. Y., four·times in Chicago, and several times in other cities. There are definite indications of General Paresis in her case. She is, furthermore, alcoholic. Her paretic condition indicates that there is no possibility of her ever being able to adjust herself to normal life.

CASE 4. This woman led a decent life until four years ago, when she suffered an injury to her skull, and thereafter, as is often the case, developed alcoholism. For four years she has been in and out of the institution. It is a case of mental aberration following head injury. She will surely continue as a repeatedly disorderly person.

These are not extreme cases. They are typical of a great number, any one of which could be appropriately selected in this connection. Dr. Sydney Kuh, the alienist on the staff of the House of Correction, is authority for the statement that each week as many as 25 such characters as the above are committed to the House of Correction. Only those who are especially noticeable or disturbing elements in the institution are brought to the attention of the medical staff. Undoubtedly the majority of those other extreme cases of recidivism, the statistical consideration of which enters into Miss Abbott's report to your committee, are sufferers from one or another type of mental aberration. We are wasting our human and financial resources by handling the problem they present as we are doing today. What is to be done?

RECOMMENDATIONS.

In the Illinois Revised Statutes, 1913, Ch. 85, Sec. 12, relating to the transfer of certain prisoners in the State Penitentiary to the asylum for insane criminals, we have the following language:

"Insane convicts in the State Penitentiary may be committed to the asylum for insane criminals, without formal inquest, on the certificate of the penitentiary physician."

It would seem that a simple amendment to this law would make it applicable to such institutions as the Chicago House of Correction as well so that prisoners in such institutions who suffer from mental disease might, without appeal to a jury, be sent to an institution for the insane, to be kept there until cured. In our judgment this should be done. Protection against the unjustified use of such power in the hands of a prison physician or medical staff can be secured by requiring that penal institutions to which the law is to apply should maintain a certain standard of fitness in its psychopathic or medical department.

There is sufficient precedent for such a procedure as that recommended here. In the Revised Statutes of Connecticut, 1902, Sec. 2782, we have language to this effect: That when the jailer of any common jail believes that a prisoner has become insane he may report to the Governor of the state, whose duty it then becomes to appoint a commission of three experts to examine the prisoner. On their report, if affirmative, the jailer is authorized to commit the prisoner to the state hospital for the insane. California provides a procedure to the same end, which, at any rate, to a large extent, avoids the necessity of taking cases before a lay jury.

Furthermore, the difficulty of getting a lay jury to commit to an insane asylum many of our most troublesome borderland cases could be obviated in a very large measure by the appointment of a commission on insanity to sit at the House of Correction, subject to whose findings alone a patient could be sent to an appropriate institution or held at the House of Correction. This commission could not handle the case that demands a jury hearing. Neither could the prison physician or medical staff. Such a one must go to the jury according to the present practice, but undoubtedly hundreds would not demand such a hearing, and we would therefore find substantial relief.

If some such procedure as the above were adopted, and if our penal institutions were equipped with adequate medical staffs, it would be possible to stop up a large source of supply of our criminal population.

In an ideal system those offenders who were suffering from mental alienation at the time of trial would be detected in the court and committed directly to an institution in which they could receive proper attention and remain until cured. This requires the equipment of the courts with facilities for making psycho-physical examinations, and the equipment, as well, of a detention hospital in which those offenders who are suspected of being victims of insanity may be kept for as long a period as may be necessary to satisfy the psychopathologist in attendance of his real condition.

The first requirement for relief in our city, to conclude, is such an amendment to our state law as would enable our medical staff, in default of an appeal for a jury hearing, to commit an insane prisoner to an institution for the insane. If such a provision should become effective, however, it would be necessary for the state immediately to enlarge her facilities for caring for patients of this character.

The farm colony plan has been found useful in handling the class of cases described herein, and we recommend that the plan be adopted here. (See the preceding Section and especially the third division of this report.)

II

A STUDY OF ADULT PROBATION

In connection with adult probation the first fundamental problem that claims attention is the selection of suitable subjects for probation.

Probation is a method of education, and, therefore, it must not be applied in a hit and miss fashion. There is the same justification for extreme care in the selection of fit subjects for probation as there is for carefulness in the choice of boys for this or that sort of instruction or training in school. If this is true then there should be a careful investigation of each individual before he is admitted to the privilege of probation. Of 95 per cent of Cook County adult probationers there is no trace of the results of an investigation, other than that that occurs in the usual course of a trial at court. The adult probation law does not make it mandatory for the court to seek the co-operation of the probation officer in making investigations into the history and character of prospective probationers. Some judges, no doubt, leave no stone unturned in their effort to unearth the life history of prospective probationers. In such cases it may be a very rare occasion when one who is unfit is unwittingly released on probation. But the probation office has no record by which to check up this matter to determine to what extent preliminary investigation is conducted in a given case by any and all agencies.

It is stated above that in the case of 95 per cent of Cook County adult probationers there is no record of a preliminary investigation. Such an investigation is made each year on a few cases that come before the Chicago Municipal Court. With the number of probation officers at the service of the court and 2,522 cases admitted during the year ending Sept. 30, 1913, to probation by this court alone, it should be possible for the officers to make a sufficiently thorough investigation of the life history of each case to determine his fitness for probation, provided that but a minimum of time were required of them in following up cases in the field, yet they make but few investigations either before or after admission to probation. It is, by the way, the opinion of students of the subject that one day spent in a careful preliminary investigation to select the probationer is worth three spent in following him up after he has been admitted to probation.

The above statement relating to the Municipal Court does not present a true picture of the situation in Chicago. There are 20 adult probation officers in Cook County, and the number of adults admitted to probation during the year ending last September 30th, was 4,696, or over 234 to each officer. It does not need a special investigation to show that it is impossible for one officer to handle so many; to make a careful preliminary investigation and to follow up the cases afterward, assisting them to secure employment, giving them counsel when required, and receiving their periodical reports. In an ideal situation the officer should not be responsible for more than fifty.

Below we show how Chicago compares with other cities in the matters of preliminary investigation of probationers and number of probation officers. Excepting as otherwise noted, the figures are for the year 1912.

Name of Court.	Number of Probation Officers.	Number Placed on Probation, 1912.	Number per Officer During Year.	Investigations Before Trial.	Number on Probation at One Time.	Number per Officer at One Time.
Municipal Court of Boston	17	4,259	250	All	1,800	105
Municipal Court of West Roxbury	1	331	331	All	85	85
N. Y. City Magistrate's Court, 1st Div	29	1,632	56	None	1,100	37
N. Y. City Magistrate's Court, 2nd Div	29	2,241	77	Rare	2,500	86
Philadelphia Quarter Sessions	2	123	61	Some	240	120
Washington, D. C., Police Court	2	306	153	All	300	150
Milwaukee Municipal	2	300	150	None	400	200
St. Paul District and Police Court	5	400	80	50%	....	....
All Cook County Courts (year ending September 30, 1914)	20	4,696	234	5%	....	....
Chicago Municipal Court	14	2,522	180	....	....	....

It will be seen from the above that as far as the number of probationers assigned to each officer is concerned, Chicago courts do not compare unfavorably with those of Boston, where approximately the same number of cases are handled. The New York City Magistrate's Court, first and second divisions, have fifty-eight (58) probation officers at their disposal and both divisions together place on probation only three thousand eight hundred and seventy-three (3,873) cases, making an average of only sixty-six plus for each officer as against two hundred and thirty-four plus for each officer in all Cook County courts. The New York Court referred to makes, through the probation officers, practically no preliminary investigations which is the rule in Chicago. This leaves the way open in New York for especially thorough follow-up work during the period of probation. We call attention to the data in the table relating to the Municipal Court of Boston, where during a year almost as many persons are placed on probation as in all of Cook County, yet with an average of 250 to each probation officer the claim is made that each case was investigated before trial. At the same time the Chief Justice of the Municipal Court of Boston has said (Annals Amer. Acad. Pol. & Soc. Sci., March, 1914, p. 135): "In adequate supervision of persons on probation lies the very heart of the system." Before the ideals of preliminary investigation by probation officers and thorough field work cannot be maintained in Chicago or elsewhere if each officer is responsible for upwards of 250 cases.

In the next place, we inquire what are the classes of offenders from whom the least satisfactory results are obtained in adult probation. Domestic relations cases are reported as yielding poorest results by the courts in Cook County, the Municipal Court of Boston, Dorchester and West Roxbury, New York City Magistrate court, 1st Division, Erie Superior and County Court, Portland, Maine, Municipal Court, Houghton, Michigan, Circuit Court, Muskegon Circuit Court, Washington, D. C., Police Court and the Superior Courts of California. In the Milwaukee Municipal Court poorest results are obtained from men over forty years of age. In the District Court of Worcester, Massachusetts, poorest results are obtained from drunkards and old persons. The unemployed are reported by the Municipal Court of Brighton, Massachusetts, as poor material for probation. This is as far as data can be obtained on the point in question. Each of the courts referred to annually places on probation from one hundred to several thousand adults. The reports are almost unanimous to the effect that drunkards are not good material for probation. Of course, the term "drunkard" is a loose one, but, nevertheless, the data referred to has an important bearing upon the selection of fit cases for probation.

When we inquire concerning the best material in the experience of various courts we find no such unanimity. In the light of what is presented above we can exclude drunkards, but when this has been said we can genealize no further. First offenders come more nearly than others to being good subjects, but there are too many exceptions to allow even this to stand as a general rule. Whether legally or not, judges here and elsewhere occasionally admit second offenders to probation, and results do not always afford a basis for condemning the practice. Failure or success on probation depends upon the strength or weakness of the probationer more than upon any other one factor. To be sure, strong ties of family and friends, other accidental factors in the environment, etc., assist a man to hold his own, and consequently they must be taken account of in selecting probationers. But when all these things are equal, the determining factor will be the make-up of the prospective probationer as a psycho-physical organism. This is the reason for our inability to say that burglars with revolvers on their hips, and second offenders of any sort, are never good subjects for probation. In isolated instances they are so. Experience proves that we cannot classify fit subjects for probation on the basis of the kind or seriousness of offenses they have committed.

Observation of cases suggests the following criteria of fitness: (1) Habits of industry; (2) Abstention from alcohol and drugs, or at least habitual temperance, (3) Mental normality; (4) Physical health of a sufficient degree to enable the probationer to engage successfully in his occupation; (a) Negative Wassermann reaction, and other evidence of freedom from all dangerous infections; (5) Proof of employment which can be undertaken at once at a living wage; (6) Possession of friends of good character who will co-operate with the officer in touch with the probationer; (7) Proof of first offense, unless on the other points the offender has exceptionally strong recommendations.

The above criteria would involve the employment of a psychopathic and chemical laboratory to assist other agencies in making the selection of probationers. If there is strong objection to employing in investigation those officers who are subsequently to keep in touch with probationers in the field, a number of specially fitted officers could be attached permanently to the psychopathic laboratory to conduct the social phases of the investigations.

The second, third and fourth criteria above should be insisted upon in every case chiefly for two reasons: (1) Alcoholics, drug fiends, the mentally subnormal and the victims of syphilitic infection, as other portions of this report will show, present anomalies of the nervous system that render them unstable in their responses to the surroundings and so enhance the probability of their going wrong again; (2) the negative Wassermann reaction should be insisted upon, if for no other reason, as a means of protecting the health of the community. Every offender should be denied the freedom of probation, and should be kept in detention, at any rate until such time as he may have lost the infectious character of his disorder, when he may be given the full freedom of probation, turned over to prison authorities, or released, according to the nature of the case.

If the above criteria had been in force in Cook County during the year ending Sept. 30, 1914, it is fair to estimate that there would have been at least one thousand fewer undesirables admitted to full freedom of probation. Most of those charged with disorderly conduct would have been eliminated on the ground of addiction to the drink habit. Those charged with soliciting, with patronizing houses of ill fame, and with being inmates of disorderly houses would in all probability be thrown out on the ground of syphilitic infection.

Detaining these people would be a problem in itself at present because of our meager institutional equipment. A plan for meeting that difficulty will be proposed in another chapter of this report. Suffice it to say here that additional institutional equipment contemplated in other connections will be of service here, and that during the detention of an offender who is fitted for probation but for his alcoholic habits or his infectious condition, and who under the present practice would be admitted to probation, those who are dependent upon him for support will have to be provided for by means now at public disposal.

If extreme care in the selection of probationers along the lines suggested herein were to be made the rule, the choice of probation officers at once becomes a first-rate problem. The present law (Ill. Dec. 8th, 1912, Ch. 38, 509j, Sec. 10) provides as follows: "Any reputable private person who shall be of the age of 25 years or upwards may be appointed a probation officer." We recommend that the law be so amended as to make it the duty of the Governor of the State to appoint a non-partisan, unpaid Probation Commission, whose duty it shall be to provide a certified list of persons who are fitted for serving as probation officers. The amendment also should make it the duty of the courts to select officers from this list. The commission should be empowered to lay down courses of study and training as a prerequisite for certification, and should be required to publish an annual report setting forth the progress and needs of the probation system in the state.

Descriptions of Specific Cases Illustrating the Failure of the Adult Probation Law in Illinois to Distinguish Those Who Are Good Subjects for the Freedom of Probation, from Those Who Are Bad Subjects.

We present below two groups of adults, aged now from 23 to 35 years, who have, at one time or another, been on probation by the Courts of Cook County or the City of Chicago, within the space of three years preceding December 1st, 1914. The cases included in these groups have all been personally investigated by your investigators. No one has been visited by us fewer than three times. The statements made by the individuals in the first group have been completely verified by consultation of the court and police records. The statements of the remainder have been partially verified.

In the first group, comprising 17 persons, we have, without exception, men who have been guilty of robbery and burglary. In several instances the persons when arrested had concealed weapons on their persons. In no case was the value of the property stolen less than $125.00. In each case there was an indictment by the Grand Jury, subsequently the plea of guilty of larceny was accepted, and admission to probation followed.

Case 1.—Burglary of house at age of 22. Stole jewelry to value of $150.00.

Juvenile Court record. Vigorous physically. Under probation got into touch with.................. Term of probation expired.................. Discharged. Now employed as clerk in department store. Has been in this position 8 months. Doing well.

Case 2.—Burglary. Stole property valued at $125.00 at age 22. Good physical type. Gives one an impression of intelligence. When arrested had revolver on his person. Discharged from probation. Now salesman in grocery store. Held this position 9 months.

Case 3.—Robbed employer at age of 21 of $400.00. Two Juvenile Court records. Good physical type. Discharged from probation on................. .... Has held present bookkeeping position 11 months. Trusted.

Case 4.——Burglary at age 20, value $200.00. Carrying a weapon. No previous offense. Plead larceny of $15.00. Probation. Discharged on .... For 13 months has satisfactorily held a position as department store salesman.

Case 5.—Robbery. Took $125.00 from till at age 20. Juvenile Court record. Made good connections under probation officer. Discharged from probation on .... Now salesman in department store. Has held three jobs in 15 months. Improves self with each move.

Case 6.—Burglary at age 22. Value of property $500.00. Plead larceny. Probation. Discharged. Previous police record. For 10 months salesman in department store.

Case 7.—Burglary at age 23. Property taken valued at $350.00. Larceny. Since day of probation has been serving as hotel waiter in one place continuously. Married and living honestly.

Case 8.—Burglary at age 20. Goods taken valued at $200.00. Since day of probation has worked continuously 8 months as machinist. Saving his money to buy house and get married.

Case 9.—Burglary at age 25. Goods taken valued at $300.00. Working since day of probation as machinist, 9 months.

Case 10.—Burglary at age 30. Value of goods taken $550.00. Plumber. Steady worker. Doing exceptionally well.

Case 11.—Burglary at age 25. Value of goods taken $130.00. Now bookkeeper. Reliable. Has made a circle of friends among good, reliable people.

Case 12.—Burglary at age 21. Value of goods taken $600.00. Carried a gun when arrested. Juvenile Court record. Worked up into bookkeeping position since day of probation. Has made good connections in church, etc.

Case 13.—Burglary at age 22. Goods stolen $300.00. Arrested once before; discharged. For seven months has been working faithfully as a bookkeeper. Has a good circle of friends.

Case 14.—Burglary at age 24. Goods stolen $225.00. Carried a gun. During probation and since discharge for nearly four months has been working faithfully as machinist.

Case 15.—Burglary at age 24. Value of goods taken $169.00. Worked in store during probation. Since discharge has been salesman in department store. Lodges in good surroundings and has formed good associations.

Case 16.—Burglary at age 22. Value of goods taken approximately $175.00. Carried a gun. Record of incorrigibility in school. Machinist. Doing well.

Case 17.—Burglary at age 23. Value of goods taken $140.00. Salesman in provision store. Third job since day of probation. Each move an improvement. Doing well.

Judging from the behavior of these men since the day on which they were placed on probation, one is forced to the conclusion that an injustice would have been done them had the present law been strictly applied. They should have been committed for a term of imprisonment. As far as these men are concerned, society would be no better, if as well, protected by making them suffer the legal penalty for burglary, than it is protected against them at present. These men, without exception, impress the observer as strong men physically and as intelligent persons as well.

In the second group of 13 men we have cases who were discovered in the House of Correction. They have been committed on the charge of larceny, though they were originally indicted for burglary. Each of these men has had more or less of a criminal history. Each one had at one time been on adult probation (acording to their statements) and had violated the conditions of probation, or, having lived through the probationary period successfully, had subsequently committed crime. We were not able in every case to find in the court records the data relating to the action that led up to the probation. If a certain group of seven among them had been admitted to probation, it was under other names than those by which they were known at the House of Correction. The remaining six do have court records under the names given to us and were at one time admitted to probation. Each of these five shows external symptoms of alcoholic habits or venereal infection or both. One is undoubtedly feeble-minded. Each one had a bad history of delinquency. The date of their admission to probation was in no case more than 13 months previous to December 1, 1914. If they were at that time in the condition in which they now are, an adequate preliminary investigation, as described in the earlier part of this report, should have prevented probation. Their history itself excludes them from probation according to the law. This last group clearly shows inadequate investigation in these cases at any rate. On the other hand, such investigations as are now made might easily have excluded all of the first group.

RECOMMENDATIONS

To carry out the recommendations of this report relative to the selection of probationers, the present law requires certain amendments. Some of the changes proposed here have already been considered and adopted by a committee of the Civic Federation of Chicago: (1) Only those defendants who are guilty of murder or treason should be absolutely denied probationary treatment. Those who have been previously convicted of a crime should not be eligible to probation excepting on the unanimous agreement of those who have investigated the case. (2) An amendment should require the court to order the probation officers and the Director of the Psychopathic Laboratory to determine the personal characteristics, habits, health of body and mind of the defendant, the character of his associates within his family and outside of it, and whatever other facts may aid the court in determining the defendant's fitness for the full freedom of probation. In case the examination reveals a condition of mental subnormality or of dangerous infection or other disorder that makes him unable to pursue his occupation in life, it should be made the duty of the court to place the defendant on probation to the superintendent of a detention hospital for treatment or to an institution for the feeble minded, as the case may require. All reports presented by the probation officers and by the psychopathic laboratory should be filed as parts of the proceedings in the case.

III

SOME STUDIES OF JUVENILE DELINQUENTS IN CHICAGO

The proper study of criminology is the juvenile delinquent. He is not a criminal, but may be one in the making. He will become a criminal unless we understand him and act upon our knowledge. The more complete our knowledge and control of him the more successful shall we be in preventing the development of criminals. Investigations in this field, therefore, should first challenge the interest of the criminologist. The measure of the constructive ability of a state or municipality in its treatment of the problem growing out of the presence of criminals within its borders is found in the broad minded efficiency that it demonstrates in dealing with its juvenile delinquents, and, for that matter, with its juvenile population in general.

It was in this faith that we undertook the investigations on which we report in the following sections. No one of these studies comes near to satisfying one's instinct for completeness. Each of them, however, we believe, exposes important facts with which the public is not sufficiently acquainted and discloses the way by which further research and practical remediable measures should proceed.

In Section A we report on the physical and mental condition of 63 juvenile delinquents—boys—who are confined in the John Worthy School, Chicago. Dr. H. C. Stevens, Director of the Psychopathic Laboratory at the University of Chicago, made the physical examinations and did a part of the mental testing in these cases.

In Section B we report on the history of 116 juvenile delinquents since their conditions were subject to diagnosis in the Juvenile Psychopathic Institue in 1910, 1911 and 1912. Miss Kawin, Probation Officer of the Juvenile Court, secured the records of examination in these cases and collected the details relating to their history during their probationary and post-probationary periods. Mr. Edwin Booz assisted in putting the material into the form in which it stands in this report.

Secton C is a report on the 280 Cook County boys who are now in the State Reformatory at St. Charles. Mr. Edwin Booz, with great care, collected the data and assisted in putting it into the form in which it stands.

In Section D is a report on the occupations of juvenile delinquent boys who were on probation on September 1, 1914, and during four months preceding. For this material we are indebted to the co-operation of Mr. Joel Hunter, Chief Juvenile Probation Officer of Cook County, who distributed our questionaire among his officers and collected their returns.

We are indebted also to Dr. D. P. MacMillen, Director of the Child Study Bureau of the Board of Education of Chicago; to Dr. William Healy, Director of the Juvenile Psychopathic Institute; to the Juvenile Court; to Principal Mortensen of the Chicago Parental School, and Principal Milliken of the John Worthy School, for granting the freedom of their offices.

A

MENTAL AND PHYSICAL EXAMINATION OF 63 JUVENILE DELINQUENTS IN THE JOHN WORTHY SCHOOL

This investigation was applied to 63 boys in the John Worthy School of Chicago. The ages of the boys range from 10 to 16 years. The school in which they are confined is conducted and maintained by the Board of Education of the City of Chicago. It is, however, a semi-penal institution, and is a place of commitment and detention. Many of these boys are detained here pending an opening for them in the State Reformatory at St. Charles. We have examined the conditon of the eyes, teeth, throats, ears, vital organs, muscular power, co-ordination, reflexes, as indications of nervous function, blood, as indicated by the Wasserman test, and finally the mental condition of each subject as indicated by the Binet and Kent-Rosanoff tests.

The boys were brought to the examining room by attendant at the school just as they happened to be available when the examiner was at the institution. There was no principle of selection, therefore, excepting that we aimed to get the most recent arrivals at the school. Since the number we examined, 63, is approximately one-half of the population of the school, it is fair to assume that our results are indicative of conditions throughout the institution.

Following, in detail, are the results of the investigation:

The results obtained point to the necessity of a prolonged and intensive study of delinquent boys. The study should be directed toward the acquirement of information with regard to the general mental age of the individual, the condition of the nervous system, and the examination of the blood for the presence of infectious disease. Sixty-three cases are altogether too few in number to permit drawing valid general conclusions, but the results are sufficiently suggestive to indicate the need of further research along the line indicated for this study.

The ages of the boys of this group varied from 12 to 17. The offenses for which they were committed were larceny, truancy and disorderly conduct. The report shows specifically the results obtained.

1. Binet test.
2. Wasserman test of the blood serum.
3. Nervous symptoms as determined by a physical examination.
4. Pathological conditions within the chest.
5. Pathological conditions of the mouth, nose and throat.
6. Pathological conditions of the abdomen and genitals.

BINET TEST

The Binet test was performed on 34 boys. The correlation between the actual age in years and the mental age, as determined by this test, is shown in Table I.

TABLE I. BINET TEST.

Actual Age.	6	7	8	9	10	11	12	13	15	Adult	Binet Age
12	...	...	...	...	...	...	2	...	...	...	2
13	...	...	...	...	...	...	...	...	...	...	0
14	...	...	...	2	...	...	1	...	1	...	4
15	...	...	...	...	2	2	...	...	2	...	6
16	1	...	...	1	...	...	4	...	...	5	15
17	...	...	...	...	...	...	2	...	...	...	2
18	...	...	...	...	...	...	...	...	...	...	...
	1	0	0	3	2	2	9	0	7	5	

GRAPH I, BINET TEST

6   7   8   9   10   11   12   13   15   Adult

DEGREE OF RETARDATION

TABLE II

No. of Boys		Years Retarded
1	....	10
1	....	7
6	....	5
6	....	4
1	....	2
4	....	1

From Table II it appears that fourteen boys out of thirty-four, or 41 per cent, are four years or more retarded. Of the same thirty-four, the Kent-Rosanoff test indicates that thirteen are subnormal.

WASSERMAN REACTION

TABLE III

Results of Wasserman test on the blood serum:

10	....	16
1	....	1.6
6	....	10
6	....	10
2	....	3.3
35	....	58.3
Total..60		98.3
Certainly affected	....	26%
Doubtful	....	13%
Negative	....	61%

The positive reaction is indicated by a plus sign and a negative reaction by a minus sign. The strength of the positive reaction is indicated by the number of plus signs. The strongest reaction is indicated by four pluses, the next strongest by three pluses, the next by two pluses, and the weakest by a single plus. The doubtful positive reaction is indicated by a plus sign and a question mark. It will be seen from the table that 26% of the boys tested show a two-plus reaction or stronger. This means that at least 26% are certainly affected with syphilis. In view of the fact that at least two of the boys have acquired gonorrheal urothritis, it is possible that some of those affected with syphilis have also acquired it by sexual contact. In view of the youthfulness of the boys, it is perhaps more reasonable to suppose that the syphilis came from their parents. It is, therefore, of the congenital variety. A comparison of the results of the Binet test with the results of the Wasserman test does not show that mental retardation coincides with the syphilitic infection, at least in every case. In view of the 26% of undoubted syphilitic infections it is reasonable to suppose that the presence of this disease is in part responsible for the criminal behavior of the boys, although it cannot be said to produce criminal behavior by first producing mental deficiency.

NERVOUS SYMPTOMS

Nervous symptoms are of three sorts, changes in reflexes, sensation and co-ordination. The occurrence of these symptoms is shown in Table IV.

TABLE IV

	Number.	Per Cent.
Nystagmus	48	76
Anisocoria	10	16
Reflexes changed	7	11
Inco-ordination	15	24
Sensation	4	6
Deafness	1	

Nystagmus is an abnormal, oscillatory movement of the eyes. Anisocoria is inequality in the size of the pupils of the eyes. Changes in the reflexes are inequalities in the reflexes of the two sides of the body. Inco-ordination means faulty movements in certain parts of the body. Changes in sensation are loss or diminution of the normal power to feel.

PATHOLOGICAL CONDITIONS OF THE CHEST

Pathological findings of the chest are shown in Table V. The table shows that in nine out of sixty-three cases, or 14%, there is evidence of cardiac disease in the nature of a mitral regurgitation. In twenty-one out of sixty-three, approximately 34%, pathological conditions were found to be present in the lungs.

TABLE V, CHEST

	Number.	Per Cent.
Mitral regurgitation	9	14.3
Rales	21	33.3
Thyroid enlarged	3	4.8
Arhythmia of heart	4	6.3

PATHOLOGICAL CONDITIONS OF MOUTH, NOSE AND THROAT

Pathological conditions of the mouth, nose and throat are exhibited in Table VI. The most comon defect is enlarged tonsils in approximately 44% of the cases. Of secondary importance is the condition of the teeth. There is pyorrhea alveolaris present in approximately 41% of the cases.

TABLE VI

	Number.	Per Cent.
Pyorrhea	26	41
Tonsils enlarged	28	44
Palate asymmetrical	18	29.8
Mouth breathing	7	11
Hutchinsonian teeth	5	7.9

PATHOLOGICAL CONDITIONS OF ABDOMEN AND GENITALS

The condition of the abdomen and genitals is shown in Table VII.

TABLE VII

	Number.	Per Cent.
Inguinal glands enlarged	35	55
Hernia (Inguinal 1, Umbilical 2)	3	4.7
Phimosis	6	9.5
Gonorrheal urethritis	2	3.5

Enlargement of the inguinal glands is exceedingly common. A condition requiring circumcision was found in six cases, or 9%. Inguinal hernia was present in one case, and umbilical hernia in two cases. Two of the boys reported gonorrheal urethritis. This diagnosis, however, was not made by the

RACE

The distribution of the boys with respect to race is shown in Table VIII.

TABLE VIII

	Number.	Per Cent.
Negro	13	20.7
White	50	79.3

The distribution of the boys with respect to the offenses for which they were committed is shown in Table IX.

TABLE IX

	Number.	Per Cent.
Larceny	49	77.7
Truancy	11	17.5
Disorderly conduct	3	4.8

The following are notes on the life histories of typical cases among those whose mental and physical conditions furnish the basis of this report. They afford a concrete picture of the boys whom we are studying. Judging from the histories disclosed here, one would asume that many of these boys are already at least fairly well confirmed delinquents.

CASE 1.—Born December 25, 1897.

March 5, 1910, charged with cutting out plumbing in a vacant house. Damage $20.00. Father depicted as a bad man and the home environment was bad.

March 24, 1910, disposition. Continued generally.

June 1, 1912, charged with using insulting language to a young girl.

June 10, 1912, disposition—committed to J. W. S.

April 2, 1914, charged with stealing coal from cars.

July 4, 1914, charged with stealing two sacks of potatoes, assisted by two other boys.

July 13, 1914, disposition J. W. S.

Wasserman reaction strongly positive. Romberg negative.

CASE 2.—Born May 27, 1898.

March 3, 1914, charged with general vagrancy and incorrigibility.

March 16, 1914, disposition—paroled.

April 9, 1914, charged with leaving home and stealing $9.00.

April 10, 1914, physical examination by Dr. Yerger—O. K.

May 5, 1914, disposition—paroled. Held in detention home for four months.

October 13, 1914, charged with stealing and pawning a ring and watch and forging a few small checks in S. D.

October 28, 1914, disposition—J. W. S.

Wasserman reaction positive—mild. Romberg negative.

CASE 3.—Born May 30, 1898.

January 3, 1911, Parental School.

September 27, 1914, charged with burglary; stole phonograph ($25.00) and records ($8.00) with two other boys.

December 2, 1912, disposition—continued generally.

September 2, 1913, charged with receiving a stolen suit of clothes and sweater; acknowledged sexual intercourse.

September 29, 1913, disposition—J. W. S.; released on good record, December 24, 1913.

October 11, 1914, charged with holding up and robbing a man of watch and $17.00. Education, cannot read English.

October 14, 1914, dispositon—J. W. S.

Tremor in fingers.

CASE 4.—Born September 4, 1899.

July 1, 1911, charged with stealing potatoes, assisted by three others. Disposition—continued generally.

January 26, 1912, Parental School.

July 21, 1913, charged with taking a horse and wagon in the Loop district and driving to Melrose Park on his way west.

August 6, 1913, disposition—paroled. ..

August 28, 1913, burglary; rifles and revolvers.

September 2, 1913, sent to J. W. S.

December 24, 1913, released to uncle.

July 23, 1914, paroled to father.

August 18, 1914, charged with stealing automobile tire from Adams Express Co.

August 27, 1914, disposition—continued to get work.

October 8, 1914, disposition—J. W. S.

Wasserman reaction strongly positive; tremor of eyelash; nails bitten. Romberg negative.

CASE 5.—Born July 30, 1900.

August 6, 1911, charged with stealing newspapers, with several others.

September 26, 1913, charged with stealing goods from delivery and peddlers' wagons with others.

October 10, 1913, disposition—paroled.

September 24, 1913, charged with systematically robbing ticket agents of elevated road.

January 23, 1914, disposition—Chicago Parental School.

July 25, 1914, charged with assault and battery.

September 12, 1914, charged with entering and stealing a coat and pair of trousers from tailor shop.

September 5, 1914, disposition—J. W. S.

Wasserman reaction negative. Romberg negative.

CASE 6.—Born December 27, 1898.

August 20 1914, charged with stealing laundry. Prior to this he ran away from an industrial school in St. Louis and "beat" his way to Chicago. He is a vagrant here.

August 28, 1914, disposition—committed to J. W. S., arrangements being made for his return to his home in St. Louis.

CASE 7.—Born October 18, 1898.

July 7, 1910, charged with general incorrigibility. Disposition—paroled, to be placed on a farm.

March 28, 1911, charged with truancy and general incorrigibility. Disposition—continued for Parental School petition.

April 7, 1911, committed to St. Charles 16 months.

June 16, 1914, charged with incorrigibility. Disposition—J. W. S.

Wasserman reaction negative; termor in fingers. Romberg negative.

CASE 8.—Born September 29, 1899.

June 10, 1909, mother is mentally weak, and father's work compels him to sleep day times, so that he cannot look after the education of his boys. They are habitual truants. Disposition—Manual Training School.

August 1, 1910, the child's mother has been living illegally with (   ) for the past 14 years. On the night of July 23 she deserted her family. At no time have the children had proper care or guardianship. At various times the mother has deserted the family for indefinite periods.

August 8, 1910, a good home found for these children.

April 28, 1912, charged with stealing rubber heels.

May 17, 1913, disposition—committed to St. Charles; released in June, 1914.

July 28, 1914, charged with stealing a revolver from a saloon while in company with two others. "This boy has no home; he has been sleeping in outhouses and barns."

Wasserman reaction strongly positive. Romberg negative.

CASE 9.—Born July 12, 1899.

August 11, 1914, charged with attempting to hold up and rob a junk dealer in his own basement.

September 18, 1914, charged with sleeping out. He is suffering from venereal disease.

September 18, 1914, disposition—J. W. S. for treatment for gonorrhea.

Wasserman reaction negative; fine tremor. Romberg negative.

CASE 10.—Born March 19, 1898.

August, 1914, charged with incorrigibility.

August 17, 1914, charged with stealing a motorcycle.

August 17, 1914, disposition—paroled.

September 15, 1914, charged with stealing a case of oranges and pears.

September 24, 1914, disposition—J. W. S. Has been in this county one year.

Wasserman reaction mildly positive; co-ordination poor. Romberg negative.

CASE 11.—Born August 28, 1898.

March 20, 1914, charged with general incorrigibility and vagrancy. Bad neighborhood and home conditions.

May 5, 1914, disposition—paroled.

June 11, 1914, charged with general vagrancy. Disposition—J. W. S.

Wasserman reaction strongly positive. Romberg negative.

CASE 12.—Born November 23, 1890.

July 30, 1912, charged with stealing two bicycles. Dispositon—dismissed when the damages and cost were adjusted.

September 19, 1912, charged with entering and stealing from a cutlery store two revolvers and one gold filled watch, value $8.50, with an-other boy.

October 14, 1912, disposition—continued generally.

September 26, 1913, charged with stealing.

October 5, 1913, this boy is a kleptomaniac. I am confident that the boy, who is of high nervous temperament, is not really a bad boy.

October 10, 1913, dispositon—continued until December 19.

December 3, 1913, charged with entering and stealing from a box-ball alley $5.00 in cash and candies and cigars to the extent of $3.00.

December 16, 1913, disposition—committed to St. Charles. At request of father stayed in J. W. S. 2 1-2 months.

April 16, 1914, charged with stealing a check and trying to pass it.

July 16, 1914, disposition—paroled; put on a farm.

July 25, 1914, charged with stealing a horse and buggy valued at $250.00.

August 24, 1914, disposition—continued and held in Detention Home until September 10, 1914.

September 10, 1914, charged with breaking in and stealing stamps. Dis-position—J. W. S.

Wasserman reaction negative. Romberg negative.

CASE 13.—Born December 15, 1900.

August 22, 1911, charged with general incorrigibility.

October 9, 1911, disposition—adjudged dependent.

December 22, 1911, charged with running away.

December 27, 1911, disposition—released three times to the mother on parole.

January 31, 1912, charged with general incorrigibility. Disposition—St. Charles.

May 18, 1914, charged with stealing coal; not brought into court; settled outside.

September 29, 1914, charged with stealing fruit valued at $13.00, with five or six other boys.

October 5, 1914, disposition—J. W. S.

Wasserman reaction negative. Romberg negative.

CONCLUSION

The results of the examinations on approximately one-half the population of the John Worthy School demonstrate a deplorable condition. One-quar-ter, perhaps even 39%, of these boys suffer from venereal infection. Their nervous symptoms point to profound disorder of the nervous system and suggest that at best their reaction to a normal environment will be unre-liable. Their physical condition, besides offering no guarantee even of the probability of the establishment of steady habits, leaves no doubt in our minds that these boys, if they were at liberty now, would be as great a menace to the health of the community as those adults in the House of Correction reported on in another section of this report.

The prevalence of the infectious condition we have found to exist in these boys is not far different from that which is reported from the Psychopathic Hospital of Boston (Contributions from the Psychopathic Hospital, 1913, pp. 57-62). Out of eleven children, aged two to eighteen years, who had been consecutively examined in the out-patient department of that hospital, 31.5%

yielded a positive reaction to the Wassermann test. But 78% of this group were delinquents in any form, and of these 78, only 11 were Juvenile Court cases. The remaining 67 had been brought to the hospital for examination on account of truancy (15), incorrigibility (14), immorality (11), stealing (14), untruthfulness (11), and forgery (2). It is interesting to observe that 45.7% of the mentally defective in this group from the Boston hospital gave a positive reaction to the Wasserman test. It would be profitable to inquire, experimentally, whether syphilitic infection may produce mental defectiveness.

RECOMMENDATIONS

The above data and conclusions suggest the following recommendation: That the farm colonies and hospitals recommended in another section of the report (Section B, first division on the treatment of mentally alienated and otherwise abnormal adult prisoners) be supplemented by places of detention for such youths as those reported on here until they are pronounced by a competent medical staff to be fit to move in a normal community without being a social menace and a source of danger as well to public health. Whatever may be said of the advantages of farm colonies in this connection applies equally in the case of adults.

Such places of detention should be in the nature of farm villages or colonies simlar to that for adults at Occoquan, Va. Institutions of this sort should be provided and maintained by the State of Illinois, and others by the City of Chicago. There should be provision in such institutions for delinquents, and particularly for such boys as those discovered in our investigations in the John Worthy School who are unfit, by reason of mental and physical condition and confirmed habits, either for probation or for early parole. Similar equipment should be provided for non-delinquent juvenile defectives also.

Commitment to such an institution should be with or without the consent of the parent or guardian of the child. Release should be obtained: (a) only on the certification of the medical staff of the institution that the individual whose release is considered will not be a menace to public health; (b) on certification by the same staff that the indivdual is mentally and physicaly able to support himself; (c) on assurance that competent friends are at hand to render assistance and encouragement when needful.

This institution should include such features as a farm, a dairy, carpenter shop, machine shop, painting, printing and repair shops, bricklaying school, playgrounds, power and heating plant and hospital. The control of the city institution should be vested in a non-partisan board of five or seven appointed by the Mayor, and since the purpose of the plant is educational, their appointment should be approved by the Superintendent of Schools.

A committee on legislation under the chairmanship of Mr. Sherman Kingsley, appointed by President A. A. McCormick of the Cook County Board, is charged with the duty of preparing bills providing for the following:

1. A new institution on the colony plan, situated within 60 miles of Chicago, which will provide a permanent home and suitable industrial training and occupation for feeble minded persons of all ages.

2. The admission of feeble minded persons of all ages to the Lincoln State School and Colony.

3. The commitment of defective delinquents both to the Lincoln State School and Colony and to the proposed institution.

4. The permanent detention, without parole, of all feeble minded persons, inmates of the Lincoln State School and Colony and the institution to be established.

Such measures as the above would give us great relief. In our opinion, however, in whatever provision we make for the feeble minded we should have in mind also the control of the dangerously infected, whether old or young, who are a menace to public health, and who, as our results suggest, cannot be depended upon for stable behavior.

The plan for making a substitute for the John Worthy School on the outskirts of the city will give but partial relief to our situation. Besides, the new plant is too close to the city to meet the needs of the larger proportion of the population we have under consideration.

COST

After the initial outlay for a site and the plant needed for beginning operations much of the work of construction and other work incident to running the institution can be done by the residents, which is the rule in institutions of the sort we are contemplating. On the basis of a populaton of 500 on a farm of 600 acres, the gross cost of maintenance would amount to approximately 50 cents a day for each inhabitant, and this figure, according to the experience of West Virginia, Arkansas and Texas, could be further reduced as the farm becomes productive.

What has been said here relating to the cost of farm colonies would apply equally well to colonies for adults, which are recommended in another section of this report.

The work-house for the District of Columbia at Occoquan, Virginia, provides for a population of about 6,500 different men and women in the course of a year. The average daily population is approximately 720 officers and prisoners. The value of buildings and equipment is estimated at $657,847.00. The net cost of maintenance is $0.48 a day for each person. Leaving the cost of the site out of account, we believe that the maintenance cost of a farm colony in Illinois should be comparable with the cost of a similar institution in Virginia.

B

THE EFFECTIVENESS OF JUVENILE COURT PROCEDURE CONSIDERED IN RELATION TO CERTAIN GROUPS OF OFFENDERS

In this section of our report we are fundamentally interested again in the prevention of the development of criminals. Whether the function of the Juvenile Court is to facilitate the reformation of the boy or girl delinquent, or to protect the community from his depredations, or whether these are both equally the functions of the court, is of little moment here. In any case, the court, through the agencies at its command, must exercise control over its wards. In this labor of control the court is aided by the Juvenile Psychopathic Institute, the probation officers, and the institutions to which commitment is made. A study of the history of juvenile delinquents, therefore, subsequent to their disposition by the court, ought to afford a test of the effectiveness of that control—or of one or more agencies through which control is exercised. Such a study, therefore, might be expected to uncover points of weakness, if there are any, and to suggest remedies.

With this idea in mind, we have undertaken to trace out the history of each individual in two groups of juvenile delinquents, all of whom have had their mental and physical conditions diagnosed in the Chicago Juvenile Psychopathic Institute, an arm of the Juvenile Court. In one group are 55 boys and girls who were declared after examination to be mentally normal. In the other group or 61, all of whom were diagnosed as subnormal. The cases in each of these groups were taken in their chronological order as they appear on the records of the Psychopathic Institute, beginning with January 1, 1910. We have made an analysis of the histories of individuals in these groups respectively, subsequent to their treatment by the court.

As the tabulations on succeeding pages are reviewed, it will be apparent that considerable attention has been given to the recommendations by the Psychopathic Institute, following diagnoses, for disposition of the subnormal cases. In many cases the recommendations were not followed, and the histories of these cases make a fruitful study as compared with others. In still other cases the recommendations were followed, but the parents or the relatives of the children affected, exercising their legal right, after a too brief period removed the child from the institution to which commitment had been made. In general we may say here, in anticipation of closer study, that as far as our cases give proof, the control of subnormal children by their parents, when that power of control is exercised to remove the children from institutions to which they have been committed, is not conducive to the good either of the children or of the community.

THE NORMAL GROUP

First we turn attention to the mentally normal group, and we have in Tables I and II the distribution of this group as to age and sex respectively. The ages of the cases were taken at the time of diagnosis. It will be observed that one-half of them are aged sixteen and seventeen years.

TABLE I
SUMMARY OF NORMAL CASES
Total number of cases, 55.
Ages of the cases.

Years.	No. Cases.
6	2
7	1
8	1
9	3
10	12
12	4
13	5
14	4
15	7
16	13
17	10
18	1
19	1
Not given	1
Total	55

TABLE II
Sex of the cases.

Female	22
Male	33
Total	55

In Tables III and IV respectively we have the charges on which our normal cases were brought to court and statistics relating to their institutional history prior to their court appearance. Only a total of eleven had had any institutional history prior to the Juvenile Court incident.

TABLE III
Court Charges.
(Some were charged with more than one offense)

Males.		Females.	
Stealing	19	Sex delinquency	8
Running away	9	Stealing	4
Truancy	5	Shop-lifting	2
Bad sex practices	3	Lying	2
Petty thievery	2	Bad sex practices	2
Burglary	2	Running away	2
Mistreating mother	2	Prostitution	1
Dependency	2	Drinking	1
Loafing	2	Flirting	1
Stabbing fellow	2	Impudent to parents	1
Hold-up	1	Attempted suicide	1
Sex delinquency	1	Truancy	1
Vagrancy	1	Incorrigibility	1
Wanderlust	1		
Breaking windows	1		
Lying	1		
Picking pockets	1		
General incorrigibility	1		
Minor in saloon	1		

TABLE IV
Institutional history prior to this court appearance.

Parental School	4 cases
John Worthy School	3 "
St. Charles School	1 "
House of Correction	1 "
Reform School	2 "
Total	11 "

TABLE VII. NORMAL CASES.

Showing causal factors in delinquency as determined by the Psychopathic Institute and also the cases in which recommendation was made by the Institute, and whether the recommendation was followed or not (see note); showing also under the headings "Making Good," etc., the development subsequent to Juvenile Court action (see note).

Number of Case.	Cause of Delinquency.			The Remedy.		Making Good.	No Progress.	Deterioration.	Lost.
	Physical.	Mental.	Environmental.	Recommendation.	Disposition.				
1			X	N.R.	P.				X
2	X			X	F.		X		
3	X			X	F.	X			
4	X			X	F.	X			
5			X	X	D.				X
6			X	X	N.F.				X
7			X	N.R.	P.	X			
8	X		X	X	N.F.	X			
9			X	N.R.	P.			X	
10			X	X	N.F.	X			
11			X	X	F.				X
12			X	X	F.	X			
13	X		X	X	N.F.	X			
14			X	X	F.	X			
15			X	X	F.	X			
16			X	X	F.			X	
17	X		X	X	D.				X
18	X		X	X	F.		X		
19			X	X	N.F.				X
20			X	X	F.		X		
21	X		X	X	F.				X
22			X	X	F.	X			
23	X		X	X	N.F.				X
24	X			X	F.	X			
25	X			X	F.	X			
26			X	N.R.					X
27			X	X	F.	X			
28			X	X	F.	X			
29	X			X	F.			X	
30			X	N.R.	P.	X			
31		X	X	N.R.	P.				X
32			X	X	F.	X			
33			X	X	F.			X	
34	X			N.R.	J.W.S.			X	
35	X		X	N.R.	P.		X		
36			X	X	F.				X
37	X		X	X	F.	X			
38			X	X	N.F.	X			
39		X	X	X	F.	X			
40			X	X	F.		X		
41			X	X	F.		X		
42	X		X	X	F.		X		
43			X	N.R.	G.	X(?)			
44			X	X	F.	X			X
45	X			X	F.	X			
46	X		X	X	F.	X			X
47	X		X	X	N.F.				X
48	X		X	X	N.F.	X			
49			X	X	N.F.		X		
50			X	N.R.	P.	X			
51			X	X	F.				X
52	X			X	F.	X			
53			X	X	F.		X		
54			X	X	F.				X
55		X		X	N.F.				X

Note.—R. indicates recommendation; N. R., no recommendation; F., recommendation was followed; N. F., recommendation was not followed; D., doubtful whether recommendation was followed; P., probationed; G., Geneva.

Table VII shows: (1) The cause of delinquency among normal cases ·to be predominantly environmental. (2) Recommendations were followed in 60 per cent of the cases. Not followed in 18 per cent of the cases. No recommendation was made in 18 per cent of the cases. In 4 per cent of the cases we could not tell whether the recommendation had been followed or not.

TABLE V.
Summary of Physical Diagnosis.

Excellent condition	5
Excellent condition with exception	2
Good condition	8
Good condition with exception	15
Poor condition	16
Very poor condition	1
Disorders of vital organs	4
Infected (otherwise O. K.)	4
Total	55

TABLE VI.
Summary of Mental Diagnosis.

Good average ability	49
Good ability with exception	6
Total	55

A glance at Tables V and VI suffices to indicate that the group we are considering here is, on the whole, mentally of good average ability, and that considerably more than one-half of them are in good physical condition.

TABLE VIII.
Development of 55 Normal Cases.

Making good	26	47.3%
No progress	8	14.5%
Deterioration	5	9.1%
Lost	16	29.1%
Total	55	100. %

TABLE IX.
Recommendation Followed.

Making good	19	55.9%
No progress	6	17.6%
Deterioration	3	8.8%
Lost	3	17.7%
Total	34	100.0%

TABLE X.
Recommendation Not Followed.

Making good	3	30%
No progress	2	20%
Lost	5	50%
Total	10	100%

TABLE XI.
Recommendation Not Made.

Making good	3	33⅓%
No progress	1	11.1%
Deterioration	2	22.2%
Lost	3	33⅓%
Total	9	100%

In tables VIII, IX, X and XI we have set forth in statistical form the developmental history of these normal cases subsequent to their treatment by the Juvenile Court. It shows that, on the whole, 47.3 per cent of the whole group are "making good." We use this phrase to describe the youth who is working for his own support, or to assist in supporting others, and who is at least not a nuisance in his community. He is keeping out of trouble with the public authorities. On the whole, again, there are 14.5 per cent of this group who are making "no progress" toward self-support and who, while not actually coming into conflict with public authority, are nevertheless somewhat doubtful characters. Of the same group 9.1 per cent have deteriorated in both of these respects and 29.1 per cent have been lost. In tables IX, X and XI we summarize the history of the normal group under three heads to set forth the results of following or not following the recommendations of the Psychopathic Institute, and finaly the results in those cases in which no recommendation whatever was made. Of course, our figures are too small to afford a first rate basis for statistics, but as far as they go they indicate a decided advantage on the side of following the recommendations of the Psychopathic Institute. The basis for this statement is found in the per-

Note.—R. indicates recommendation; N. R., no recommendation; F., recommendation was followed; N. F., recommendation was not followed; D., doubtful whether recommendation was followed; P., probationed; G., Geneva.

Table VII shows: (1) The cause of delinquency among normal cases to be predominantly environmental. (2) Recommendations were followed in 60 per cent of the cases. Not followed in 18 per cent of the cases. No recommendation was made in 18 per cent of the cases. In 4 per cent of the cases we could not tell whether the recommendation had been followed or not.

TABLE V.
Summary of Physical Diagnosis.

Excellent condition	5
Excellent condition with exception	2
Good condition	8
Good condition with exception	15
Poor condition	16
Very poor condition	1
Disorders of vital organs	4
Infected (otherwise O. K.)	4
Total	55

TABLE VI.
Summary of Mental Diagnosis.

Good average ability	49
Good ability with exception	6
Total	55

A glance at Tables V and VI suffices to indicate that the group we are considering here is, on the whole, mentally of good average ability, and that considerably more than one-half of them are in good physical condition.

TABLE VIII.			TABLE IX.		
Development of 55 Normal Cases.			Recommendation Followed.		
Making good	26	47.3%	Making good	19	55.9%
No progress	8	14.5%	No progress	6	17.6%
Deterioration	5	9.1%	Deterioration	3	8.8%
Lost	16	29.1%	Lost	3	17.7%
Total	55	100. %	Total	34	100.0%

TABLE X.			TABLE XI.		
Recommendation Not Followed.			Recommendation Not Made.		
Making good	3	30%	Making good	3	33⅓%
No progress	2	20%	No progress	1	11.1%
Lost	5	50%	Deterioration	2	22.2%
			Lost	3	33⅓%
Total	10	100%	Total	9	100%

In tables VIII, IX, X and XI we have set forth in statistical form the developmental history of these normal cases subsequent to their treatment by the Juvenile Court. It shows that, on the whole, 47.3 per cent of the whole group are "making good." We use this phrase to describe the youth who is working for his own support, or to assist in supporting others, and who is at least not a nuisance in his community. He is keeping out of trouble with the public authorities. On the whole, again, there are 14.5 per cent of this group who are making "no progress" toward self-support and who, while not actually coming into conflict with public authority, are nevertheless somewhat doubtful characters. Of the same group 9.1 per cent have deteriorated in both of these respects and 29.1 per cent have been lost. In tables IX, X and XI we summarize the history of the normal group under three heads to set forth the results of following or not following the recommendations of the Psychopathic Institute, and finaly the results in those cases in which no recommendation whatever was made. Of course, our figures are too small to afford a first rate basis for statistics, but as far as they go they indicate a decided advantage on the side of following the recommendations of the Psychopathic Institute. The basis for this statement is found in the per-

centages oppósite. The basis for this statement is found in the percentages opposite "making good" and "lost" respectively in the tables.

By comparing the case numbers in Tables XII and XIII respectively with those in Table VII we are able at a glance to associate the present status of each case with other data that has been presented.

TABLE XII.   DISTRIBUTION OF CASES ON BASIS OF RECOMMENDATIONS.

A. Recommendation was followed:
    1. Making good: Cases 3, 4, 8, 12, 14, 15, 23, 26, 27, 29, 30, 36, 41, 44, 46, 49, 51, 55, 59.
    2. No progress: Cases 2, 18, 20, 45, 60.
    3. Deterioration: Cases 16, 37.
    4. Lost: Cases 11, 22, 40, 50, 58, 61.
B. Recommendation not followed:
    1. Making good: Cases 10, 13, 43.
    2. No progress: Cases 47, 57.
    3. Deterioration: Cases 31.
    4. Lost: Cases 6, 19, 35, 54, 62.
C. No recommendation:
    1. Making good: Cases 7, 33, 48, 57.
    2. No progress: Case 39.
    3. Deterioration: Cases 9, 38.
    4. Lost: Cases 1, 28, 34.
D. Cannot tell whether recommendation was followed:
    a. Unable to trace boy: Cases 5, 17.

TABLE XIII.   PRESENT STATUS OF NORMAL CASES.

	No. of Cases.
Returned home—making good: 4, 7, 8, 10, 12, 13, 14, 15, 23, 27, 29, 30, 33, 36, 41, 46, 49, 51, 55, 57, 59	21
Returned home—no progress: 2, 18, 20, 47, 60	5
Returned home—deterioration: 16, 31, 37	3
In an institution—making good: 43	1
In an institution—no progress: 39, 45, 56	3
In an institution—deterioration: 9, 38	2
Married—making good: 26, 44, 48	3
Married—no report: 1, 34	2
Living with relative—making good: 3	1
Departed to Europe: 62	1
Lost: 5, 11, 17, 19, 22, 25, 28, 40, 50, 61, 6, 54, 58	13
Total	55

THE SUBNORMAL GROUP

Now we come to a discussion of the group of 61 subnormal cases. In Table XIV we have displayed, in addition to the age and sex of each child, the charge on which he was brought to court. Furthermore, there is set forth here a group of causal factors: viz., physical, mental and environmental factors. The legend "F. M." indicates feeble-minded. In each case the record has been copied from the cards in the Juvenile Phychopathic Institute.

In Table XIV we have also set forth the recommendation that the Psychopathic Institute made in each of the sixty-one cases. The sign "L" indicates that the recommendation was that the subject should be sent to the Lincoln State School and Colony for Feeble-Minded. In case 56 the recommendation was that the child be sent to Geneva. In a few other cases, as in 6 and 7, no recommendation was made.

In the next place, the table shows the remedy that was applied to each case, or the disposition that was made of it. Thus the sign "L" indicates that the case was disposed of by sending it to Lincoln; J. W. S. indicates that the subject was sent to the John Worthy School; N. F. indicates that the recommendation in the particular case was not followed. In a few cases the sign "F" is used to indicate that the recommendation, whatever it was in the particular case, was followed. In the remaining columns of the table we have tried to show what was the effect of the treatment in each instance. Each case is making good, in the sense described earlier in this section; he is at a standstill, is deteriorating or he has been lost. **Thus we have in this** table a basis for estimating the importance to the individual and to the community following or failing to follow the recommendations of the **Juvenile** Psychopathic Institute.

Upon the special study of the subsequent history of those who, on **recommendation** of the institute, were sent to Lincoln, we enter in Table XVI. Here we have a study of the 35 cases among the 61 that were sent to Lincoln. We see the length of time during which they have remained in the institution, their disposition on release (applying, of course, only to those who are no longer in the institution), and the date at which they left the place.

The summary of this table shows that but fifteen of the original thirty-five subnormal cases that were sent to Lincoln are still in that institution. The remaining twenty have been released at the request of parents or other relatives, have run away, or have been dischargd.

TABLE XV.

SPECIAL STUDY OF 35 LINCOLN CASES.

Case No.	Age.	Sex.	Length of time in Lincoln.	Cause of Leaving.	Time of Leaving.
1	17	M.	4½ years	Released to mother............	October 30, 1914.
2	12	M.	3⅙ years	(Still there)	
3	14	F.	3⅓ years	Paroled to aunt..................	August, 1913.
4	8	F.	1⅓ years	Paroled to foster mother.......	December 19, 1911.
5	13	F.	4½ years	(Still there)......................	
8	8	M.	2¼ years	(Still there)	
9	9	F.	2¾ years	Discharged	April 16, 1913.
10	16	M.	4½ years	Released to sister to fulfill promise to dying mohter.....	Spring, 1912.
17	17	F.	1⅓ years	(Still there)	
18	16	M.	4 years	(Still there)	
19	25	M.	3½ years	(Still there)	
20	15	M.	⅙ year	Request of parents.............	February 3, 1911.
21	14	M.	1¼ years	Released to parents............	March, 1912.
22	13	M.	2¼ years	Fahter claims doctor said boy was mentally capable........	November 13, 1913
23	12	M.	3¾ years	(Still there)......................	
25	13	M.	2⅔ years	Ran away	July 7, 1914.
26	13	M.	2⅔ years	Mother's request	June 23, 1913.
27	13	F.	2 years	Parents' request; decided they were wasting money.........	June, 1913.
29	12	F.	1½ years	Request of parents.............	(?)
30	14	M.	(?)	Discharged for escaping several times	(?)
32	12	M.	½ year	(Still there)	
37	15	F.	3⅙ years	(Still there)......................	
38	11	M.	⅓ year	(Still there)......................	
39	12	F.	1¾ years	Request of married sister.......	July, 1913.
40	15	M.	½ year	Request of uncle to go to Russia	May 8, 1912.
44	12	M.	1½ years	(Still there)......................	
49	14	M.	¾ year	Ran away, father's request.....	August 3, 1914.
50	14	M.	2 years	Ran away	June 22, 1914.
52	13	F.	2½ years	(Still there)......................	
53	8	M.	2¼ years	(Still there)......................	
55	18	F.	½ year	Mother wanted money, wages of girl	Spring, 1913.
60	12	F.	1½ years	Parents' request	December 4, 1913.
62	13	M.	1¾ years	(Still there)......................	
64	15	F.	1 year	(Still there)......................	
65	17	M.	½ year	Ran away	July 7, 1913.

Total, 35 cases.

SUMMARY OF TABLE XV.

Ages.		Time.	Final Disposition and Cause.
Yrs.	No.		
2	3	Shortest time ....2½ months	Still there 15
9	1	Longest time ....4½ years	Ran away 4
11	1	Average time ....2 years	Parents' request 10
12	7		Relative's request ... 4
13	7	Sex.	Discharged 1
14	3		Doctor's approval,
15	4	Males 22	claimed by father.. 1
16	2	Females 13	
17	4		
18	1	Total.................... 35	Total........... 35
Total...... 35			

In Table XVI we have tried to show the present condition of the thirty-five cases that were sent to Lincoln. Three of these, or 4.1 per cent, have been lost. Of them we can say nothing further. Twenty-seven, or 75.8 per cent of the total, are either gradually deteriorating or are no more able to care for themselves than they were when they were brought to the Psychopathic Institute for examination. Five, or 14.3 per cent of the total, are reported as making good. We mean by the phrase "making good" that each of the five is at least not a disturbing element in his community and that he is assisting to maintain himself. The five cases are Numbers 3, 4, 9, 21, and 25. By referring to Table XVIII it will be seen that the first four of these were paroled or discharged to friends and that the fifth ran away. We see there, furthermore, what the history of each of these cases has been since he left Lincoln. In this connection we should draw attention to the fact that case 26 escaped from the institution as late as July 7, 1914. He had been at liberty therefore hardly more than three months when the data on which this report is based was collected. It is a fair question, therefore, whether we have a sufficient test of his ability to adjust himself.

TABLE XVI.

SPECIAL STUDY OF 35 LINCOLN CASES SHOWING DEGREE OF ADJUSTMENT. (Note.)

Case No.	Making Good.	No Progress.	Deterioration.	Lost.
1	......	×	......	......
2	......	×	......	......
3	×	......	......	......
4	×	......	......	......
5	......	×	......	......
8	......	......	×	......
9	× (?)	......	......	......
10	......	×	......	......
17	......	×	......	......
18	......	×	......	......
19	......	×	......	......
20	×	......	......	......
22	......	......	×	......
24	......	×	......	......
25	×	......	......	......
26	......	×	......	......
27	......	×	......	......
29	......	......	×	......
30	......	......	×	......
32	......	......	×	......
37	......	×	......	......
38	......	×	......	......
39	......	......	......	×
40	......	......	......	×
44	×	......	......	......
49	......	×	......	......
50	......	......	×	......

Case No.	Making Good.	No Progress.	Deterioration.	Lost.
52	......	×	......	......
53	......	......	×	......
55	......	×	......	......
60	......	×	......	......
62	......	×	......	......
64	......	......	×	......
65	......	......	×	......

SUMMARY OF TABLE XVI.

Cases making good	5	14.3%
No progress	17	47 %
Deterioration	10	28.6%
Lost	3	7.1%
Total	35	100 %

We now turn to a special study of those cases who have been released from Lincoln for whatever cause. The history of these persons subsequent to their release should in itself be a comment upon our methods of handling our subnormal population.

TABLE XVII.

SPECIAL STUDY OF RELEASED AND ESCAPED LINCOLN CASES, SHOWING CAUSE OF LEAVING, TIME SPENT IN LINCOLN, DEGREE OF ADJUSTMENT, AND SUBSEQUENT HISTORY.

Case No.	Age.	Sex.	Cause of Leaving.	Time in Lincoln.	Time of Admission.	Time of Leaving.
1	17	M.	Mother's request	4½ yrs. (3)	1908.	Oct. 30, 1913 (last)
3	14	F.	Aunt's request	3½ "	April 12, 1910.	August, 1913.
4	8	F.	Foster mother's request	1 1/12 "	Nov. 2, 1910.	Dec. 19, 1911.
9	9	F.	Discharged	2¾ "	June, 1910.	April 16, 1913.
17	17	F.	Sister's request	1⅓ "	Dec. 16, 1910.	Spring, 1912.
20	15	M.	Parent's request	⅙ "	Dec. 16, 1910.	Feb. 3, 1911.
21	14	M.	Parent's request	1⅙ "	Jan. 18, 1911.	March 27, 1912.
22	13	M.	Father's request, doctor's O. K.	2¾ "	Feb. 8, 1911.	Nov. 13, 1913.
25	13	M.	Ran away	2⅔ "	Nov. 21, 1911.	July 7, 1914.
26	13	M.	Mother's request, decided wasting money	2 "	May 9, 1911.	June 23, 1913.
27	17	F.	Parents' request	2½ "	May 9, 1911.	June, 1914.
29	12	F.	Parents' request	1½ "	(?)	(?)
30	14	M.	Discharged after escaping three times.		(?)	(?)
39	12	F.	Married sister's reques	1¾ "	Oct., 1911.	July, 1913.
40	15	M.	Uncle's request	1½ "	Dec. 6, 1911.	May 8, 1912.
49	14	M.	Father's request	¾ " (2)	April, 1912.	August 3, 1914.
50	14	M.	Ran away	2 "	May 8, 1912.	June 22, 1914.
55	18	F.	Mother's request; wanted girl's wages	½ "	Nov. 27, 1912.	Spring, 1913.
60	12	F.	Parent's request	1½ "	Nov. 27, 1912.	Dec. 4, 1913.
65	17	M.	Ran away	½ "	Jan. 22, 1913.	July 7, 1913.

SPECIAL STUDY OF RELEASED AND ESCAPED LINCOLN CASES.

Case No.	M.G.	N.P.	D.	L.	Subsequent History.
1	....	×	....	....	Worked in piano factory; $7.00 per week. Whenever he worked he was likely to remain away from home till his pay was gone. Mother preparing to open lunch room for him.
3	×	....	....	....	Has job in printing shop at $5.00 a week; has held htis position over a year.
4	×	....	....	....	At home found her unmanageable; in court February, 1912; committed to Illinois Technical School; still there; making good.

No. Case	M.G.	N.P.	D.	L.	Subsequent History
9	X				Public school, 4th grade; promoted to 5th. Trouble with parents. Sent to an orphanage; has been there 5 weeks; making good.
17		X			At sister's home; troublesome; implied immorality. Married Sept., 1913; lives in doubtful neighborhood.
20				X	Could not locate.
21	X				There has been no difficulty with him since that time.
22			X		Worked part time; too lazy to succeed. Chooses small children as playmates. Left home to Tennessee, May, 1914, to October. Has not worked.
25	X				No room at home; lives with aunt; earns $7.50 a week
26		X			At home. Missouri farm. Picked up January 14. 1914, as half starved by another boy. Taken to Detention Home and then sent home.
27		X			Worked as domestic servant till July, 1914; now wears good clothes, but refuses to say where she works.
29			X		Home; runs away to places unknown; has been picked up several times; probationed to parents not to be sent to work.
30			X		Has no tfound work since return; has been in a couple of thefts since. Still looking for work. (?)
39				X	Could not locate family.
40				X	May 8, 1912. Uncle said he wanted to return the boy to Russia. Unable ot locate either.
49			X		Has not worked since his return; still aimlessly looking for work.
50			X		Reported working at $6.00 a week. Not located.
55		X			Has had practically no work since her return; mother had her sent to House of Correction for disorderly conduct. Will be released February, 1915.
60		X			Home until May 13, 1914. Nickel show fiend. Mother could not control her; returned to Lincoln.
65			X		Home with bad companions. August, 1914, arrested for larceny. Studied by Dr. Healy; sent to Detention Hospital. Diagnosed as an idot. At Kankakee.

SUMMARY OF TABLE XVII.

XVIII. Cause of Leaving.

Parents' request	11	55%
Relatives' request	4	20%
Ran away	4	20%
Discharged	1	5%
Total	20	100%

XX. Time of Admission.

First ....April 12, 1910
Last ....January 22, 1913

XXII. Ages.

8 years	1	case
9 "	1	"
12 "	3	"
13 "	3	"
14 "	5	"
15 "	2	"
17 "	4	"
18 "	1	"
Total	20	cases

Sixty per cent of these cases are at a standstill or are deteriorating.

XIX. Time in Lincoln.

Shortest time ....2½ months
Longest time ....4½ years
Average time ....1 7/12 years

XXI. Time of Leaving.

First ....February 3, 1911
Last ....July 7, 1914

XXIII. Sex.

Males	11
Females	9

XXIV.

School age	8	40%
Over school age	12	60%

XXV. Showing Degree of Adjustment.

Making good	5	25%
No progress	6	30%
Deterioration	6	30%
Lost	3	15%
Total	20	100%

In Table XXVI we show the history of those who were released from Lincoln at the request of parents and other friends. Of these there are fifteen, as shown in Table XIX. Of this number five have been lost. But four are reported as making good. The remaining six are either at a standstill or actually deteriorating.

TABLE XXVI. SUBSEQUENT HISTORY OF THE FIFTEEN CASES RELEASED BY REQUEST.

	Parent's Requests.					Relative's Requests.			
Case No.	M.G.	N.P.	D.	L.	Case No.	M.G.	N.P.	D.	L.
1		X			3	X			
4	X				17		X		
20				X	39				X
21	X				40				X
22			X		Made good 1				25%
26		X			No progress 1				25%
27		X			Lost 2				50%
29			X						
49			X			Combined Requests.			
55		X			Making Good 3				20%
60	X				No progress 6				40%
Made good..........2	18.2%				Deterioration 3				20%
No progress..........5	45.6%				Lost 3				20%
Deterioration 3	27.3%								
Lost 1	9.1%								

It will be seen by comparing previous tables that the three released to parents and other relatives, and reported as lost, are the only ones among the entire 35 Lincoln cases who have been lost.

The phrases quoted below from case histories of those designated in the above table show in brief space what kind of individuals these are who have been released to parents and other relatives. Case 1.—When he has money he stays away from home until it is spent. Case 4.—Unmanageable at home. Sent away. Case 20.—Lost. Case 21.—Conduct satisfactory. Case 22.—Vagrant. Case 26.—Ward of the court. Case 27.—Refuses to say where she works. Case 29.—Vogrant. Case 49.—Not working. Case 55.—In House of Correction; disorderly conduct. Case 60.—Nickel show fiend. Case 3.—Satisfactory. Case 17.—Immoral. Case 29.—Lost. Case 40.—Lost.

This is anything but a good showing for the practice of release from Lincoln at the solicitation of friends.

Table XXVII follows in which we have brought together those of the 20 released and escaped Lincoln cases who are making good, who are making no progress, who are deteriorating, and who have been lost respectively. We show in these groupings, once more, the physical and mental diagnoses, the environment through which each case grew up, and his history subsequent to his Juvenile Court appearance. This gives opportunity easily to compare one of these groups with another in point of mental and physical condition, environment and subsequent history. All are alike in point of feeble-mindedness. As to physical condition and environmental conditions the "deterioration" cases appear at a distinct disadvantage in comparison with the other groups.

XXVII. SPECIAL STUDY OF TWENTY RELEASED AND ESCAPED LINCOLN CASES.

Comparison of Groups With Reference to Diagnosis.

Making Good Cases.	Physical Diagnosis.	Mental Diagnosis.
3	Poorly nourished	F. M.
4	Fair condition	F. M.
9	Fair condition	F. M.
21	General condition good. Defective hearing and speech	F. M., dull from physical cause.
25	Development and nutrition poor..................	F. M.

No Progress
  Cases.
  1   O. K., but speech defective.......................   F. M.
  17   O. K,. development and nutrition poor...........   F. M.
  26   O. K. ....   F. M.
  27   O. K. ....   F. M.
  55   Strong and healthy. Defective vision.............   F. M.
  60   Well at present. Has had mony illnesses. Enuresis. F. M.
Deterioration
  Cases.
  22   O. K., except enuresis...........................   F. M.
  29   Development poor; nutrition fair; color fair; epi-
             leptic ....   F. M.
  30   Development poor; nutrition poor.................   F. M.
  49   Fairly good condition, except enlarged tonsils...... F. M.
  50   Development and nutrition poor; defective vision..   F. M.
  65   Development and nutrition fair...................   F. M.
Lost Cases.
  20   Development and nutrition fair; poorly developed
             chest; suspected epilepsy......................   F. M.
  39   Undersized; very nervous........................   F. M.
  40   Developmen tand nutrition O. K.; backward
             puberty; possible epilepsy....................F. M., or else
                                                            psychosis, or
                                                            else dull from
                                                            epilepsy.

Making Good Cases.	Environment.	Subsequent History.
3	Very bad. Father alcoholic. Mother dead.	Has job in printing shop at $5 a week.
4	Adopted by good people, with a good home.	Found her unmanageable at home. In court February, 1912. Sent to Illinois Technical School. tSill htere. Making good.
9	Very poor, but respectable. Italians. In Chicago 5 years. Bad sanitary condition.	Public school, 4th grade; promoted to 5th. Trouble with parents. Sent to an orphanage. Has been there 5 weeks. Making good.
21	Parents poor, but respectable. Mother dead 3 years. Father remarried.	There has been no diculty with him.
25	Mother dead 7 years. Father drinking. Deserted. Boy with married sister.	No room at home; lives with aunt. Earns $7.50 a week as packer. Still working.

No Progress Cases.	Environment.	Subsequent History.
1	Crowded tenement neighborhood.	Worked in piano factory at $7.50 a week. Whenever he worked he was likely to remain away from home until his pay was spent. Mother preparing to open lunch room for him.
17	Poor, but good neighborhood. Good parents. Mother "nags."	At sister's home. Rather troublesome. Implied immoral relations. Married September, 1913. Lives in doubtful neighborhood.
26	Lived in very poor neighborhood.	Home. Missouri farm. Picked up January 14 as half starved by another boy. Ward of the court. Taken to Detention Home and then sent home.
27	Poor, but respectable parents.	Worked as domestic servant till July, 1914. Now wears good clothes, but refuses to say where she works. Not heard of very often. Calls by telephone.

55   Very poor Polish home, no   Has had practically no work since her
      English.   Very ignorant.   return. Mother had her sent to House
      Father paralyzed.   of Correction for disorderly conduct.
                                   Will be released February, 1915.
60   Very large family; all said to Home until May 13, 1914. Nickel show
      be peculiar. Decent neigh-   fiend. Mother could not control her.
      borhood.   Had her returned to Lincoln.

Deterioration
   Cases.
22   Boy   is   illegitimate child.   Worked part time; too lazy to succeed.
      Mother drank before his   Chooses small children as playmates.
      birth. Immoral. Now step-   Left home, beat way to Tennessee,
      mother.   May, 1914, to October, 1914. Has not
                                    worked at all.
29   Parents poor, but decent.   Runs away to places unknown. Has
      Large family.   Poor home   been picked up on streets several
      control.   times. Probationed to parents, not to
                                    be sent to work.
30   Very bad.   M.o t h e r blind Has not found work since his return.
      Father old and worn out at   Has been in a couple of thefts since.
      time of boy's birth. Sister- Still looking for work. (?)
      in-law drinks.
49   Poor, but respectable parents. Has not worked since his return. Still
      Decent n e i g h b o r h o o d. aimlessly looking for work.
      Mother over-indulgent.
50   Very bad. Father a criminal. Working, according to brohter's report,
      Aunt immoral. Unsanitary   at $6.00 a week. He or his sister,
      and dilapidated home.   with whom he is supposed to live, not
                                    located.
65   Mother epileptic; not strong. Home with bad companions. August,
      Father drank some. Good   1914, arrested for larceny. Studied
      neighborhood.   Well-mean-   by Dr. Healy. Sent to Detention
      ing people.   Hospital, thence to Kankakee. Diag-
                                    nosed, idiot.

Lost Cases.
20   Fairly good home. Mother   Could not locate.
      ignorant.
39   Early environment very bad.   Could not locate the family.
      Mother erratic;   married
      three times.
40   Little known of early en-   May 3, 1912. Uncle said he wanted to
      vironment. Came from Rus-   return the boy to Russia. Unable to
      sia two yeasr ago. Parents   locate either.
      dead. Lives with uncle.

All the above cases are feeble-minded. Between the "making good" and
the "deterioration" groups one cannot find in the diagnosis, as reported here,
any great differences. In the "deterioration" cases, however, the environmental factor is described as distinctly bad.

SUBNORMAL CASES DISPOSED OF OTHERWISE THAN BY A LINCOLN COMMITMENT.

In Table XXIX we summarize the data relating to the 26 cases who were
disposed of otherwise than by sending them to the School for Feeble-minded
at Lincoln. We have treated this data exactly as that pertaining to the 35
Lincoln cases.

It will be seen that cases 13, 16, 23, 35, 51, 58, 59, and 67, a little more
than a third of the total, should have gone to Lincoln had the recommendation of the Psychopathic Institute been adopted. With three exceptions (16,
23, 51) they were allowed to return to their homes.

Let us see the subsequent history of these cases: No. 13, social menace;
No. 16, missing 6 months; No. 23, arrested four times; No. 35, couple of burglaries; No. 51, failing in school; No. 58, continual stealing; No. 59, attacked
teacher with knife; No. 67, incorrigible. Six of this total of 26 have been
lost. When we add this to the eight who are incorrigible we have a distinctly
bad report of those cases just referred to.

We also find almost invariably bad reports of cases 14, 15, 28, 42, 47,
56, 61, and 63, in which other than Lincoln recommendations were made.

XXVIII. TWENTY-SIX SUBNORMAL CASES DISPOSED OF OTHER-WISE THAN BY LINCOLN COMMITMENT. DIAGNOSIS AND HISTORY.

Case No.	Age.	Sex.	Recommendation.	Disposition.	Date of Disposition.
6	13	M.	....	J. W. S.	May, 1912.
7	16	M.	....	J. W. S.	(?)
11	18	F.	....	Farm	....
13	13	F.	L.	Home	....
14	19	M.	Farm	Farm	(?)
15	17	F.	Institutional care....	Home	....
16	16	M.	L.	Ran away	....
23	12	M.	L.	Farm	....
28*	7	M.	Farm	Farm	....
31	12	M.	....	Dependent Home ...	November, 1911.
33	16	M.	....	Sent East	....
34	50	F.	....	Dunning	August, 1911.
35	6	M.	L.	Home	....
42*	12	M.	Parental and treat-ment	Parental	....
47	16	M.	Farm with good home	Farm	....
48	17	M.	....	Reform School......	....
51	10	F.	L.	Illinois Tech. School.	April 15, 1912.
54	10	M.	....	Home for F. M.	....
56	18	F.	Geneva	Geneva	....
58*	13	M.	L.	Home	....
59	12	M.	L.	Home	....
61	14	M.	Institutional care....	Home	....
63	15	F.	F. M. Institution of Inst. Home	Geneva	November, 1912.
66	16	M.	....	....	....
67	13	M.	L.	Home	January, 1913.
68	27	F.	....	....	....

26 Total cases.

Ages. Summary of above.

6	.... 1 case	Males	18
7	.... 1 "	Females	8
10	.... 2 "		
12	.... 4 "	Total	26
13	.... 4 "		
14	.... 1 "		
15	.... 1 "		
16	.... 5 "		
17	.... 2 "		
18	.... 2 "		
19	.... 1 "		
27	.... 1 "		
40	.... 1 "		

Total .... 26 cases

Case No.	M. G.	N. P.	D.	L.	Subsequent History.
6	×	......	......	Died.	In J. W. S. two months, to be treated for gonorrhea. Released to aunt. Making good when he died of pneumonia.
7	......	......	......	Died.	Released. Arrested for stealing horse and buggy. Sent to House of Correction. Died of tuberculosis.
11	......	......	......	×	Could not be kept there because of bad be-havior toward men. Geneva, July, 1910 Released to sister. Could not locate.

Case No.	M. G.	N. P.	D.	L.	Subsequent History.
			Effect		
13	......	......	×	......	Parents objected to Lincoln. March, 1914, in court. Assaulted by several men. House of Good Shepherd. Still there. Social menace.
14	......	×	......	......	On a farm in Indiana, off and on for the last few years. Comes to Chicago when he gets tired. Filthy in habits. Deteriorating.
15	......	×	......	......	Dr. Healy, November, 1912. Oak Forest could not keep her. Ran after men. Detention Hospital. Kankakee few months. Home servant. No progress.
16	......	......	......	×	Later application was made for Lincoln, rejected. Continued habit of running away. Reported to have held one job one year. Now missing six months.
23	......	......	×	......	Arrested four times from December, 1911, to July 17, 1914. Parents refuse Lincoln. P. O. feels his work is useless. Deterioration.
28*	......	×	......	......	Did well for few months. Then started old habits of running away. Dependent Home. Ran away, 1912. Lincoln to May, 1913. Arrested three times. Still at Lincoln.
31	......	×	......	......	Still in Dependent Home; no report.
33	......	×	......	......	Sent East by a society interested in him. Unable to trace boy.
34	......	×	......	......	Still in Dunning; diagnosed as an imbecile.
35	......	×	......	......	February, 1912, arrested as incorrigible. June, 1913, to Feehanville; ran away in July, 1913. July 11, 1913, ran away from Juvenile Home. August, 1913, in a couple of burglaries. Parental October, 1913, to April, 1914. Paroled. Returned to Parental.
42*	......	......	......	×	September, 1912, in court for stealing. Lincoln October 15, 1912, to August 22, 1913. Arrested for stealing; returned to Lincoln January, 1914. Escaped August, 1914. Cannot be located.
47	......	×	......	......	August, 1913, was still on farm. Unable to find present whereabouts.
48	......	......	......	×	The boy was sent to a reform school in the South.
51	......	×	......	......	In Illinois Technical School until (?); over two years. Returned to third grade of public school. Not making it go.
54	......	×	......	......	Still in private institution for F. M.
56	......	×	......	......	Brought back by an organization interested in her. Working and carefully guarded. Progress doubtful.
58*	......	......	......	×	January, 1913, in court for stealing; April again. Continued stealing. At last sent to Lincoln, September, 1914. Escaped October, 1914. Unable to locate.
59	.. ...	......	×	......	Expelled from Subnormal room for attacking teacher with knife. Still at home doing odd jobs.
61	......	×	......	......	Neer any treatment. Now poor condition. Age 16 in third grade. Expect to keep him in school.
63	......	×	......	......	Paroled, and later returned to Geneva. Was unable to find out why.
66	×	......	......	......	Released from probation December, 1913, as over age. In court January, 1914, for stealing. Lied about age. Now with brother as porter in cheap barber shop.

Case ——————— Effect.—————
No. M. G. N. P. D. L.   Subsequent History.
67 X   ...... Went back to public school. Expelled for
                               throwing stones at children. Put in indus-
                               trial room. Runs away. Parents now plan-
                               ning to send him to Lincoln.
68 X   Could not locate.

*Note. These three cases eventually came to Lincoln.
Case No. 28 is there now.
Case No. 42 escaped August, 1914.
Case No. 58 escaped October, 1914.

Eight cases recommended to Lincoln. One of these eventually came to Lincoln.
　　　Development of these 8.　　　　　　Summary of above cases.

No progress 2	25%	Making good 2	7.7%
Deterioration 4	50%	No progress 11	42.3%
Lost 2	25%	Deterioration 5	19.2%
	—	Lost 6	23.1%
Total 8	100%	Died 2	7.7%
		Total 26	100.0%

CONCLUSION.

1. Somewhat less than one-half of our group of normal subjects (47.3%) have made good since their Juvenile Court experience.

2. Somewhat more than one-half (55.9%) of these cases in which the recommendations made by the Psychopathic Institute were followed have made good.

3. Only 30% among those cases in which the recommendation of the Psychopathic Institute was not followed have made good.

4. Fifty per cent are lost track of among those cases in which the recommendation of the Psychopathic Institute was not followed. Only 17.7% were lost among those cases in which the recommendation was followed.

5. Of the 35 subnormal cases sent to Lincoln, but 15 remain there. The remaining 20 have escaped, have been discharged, or have been released to parents or other friends.

6. Of 15 released at the solicitation of friends, but three are making good, three cannot be traced, and the remainder are making no progress or are deteriorating.

7. The nine who are traceable and who are not making good exhibit histories such as the following in their subsequent careers. (See Table XVIII.) Nickel show fiend; House of Correction for disorderly conduct; idle; seldom heard from; refuses to say where she works; runs away to places unknown; idle; immoral relations; unmanageable, etc.

8. Among the cases released to parents and friends and escaped we cannot find profound differences between the "making good" cases and the "Deteriorating" cases as far as physical diagnosis are concerned. All are alike in point of feeble-mindedness. We do find great differences between these groups as far as the environmental factor is concerned.

9. Of the 26 subnormal cases who were disposed of otherwise than by commitment to Lincoln but two have made good, six have been lost, two have died and considerably more than one-half, 16, are at a standstil, or are deteriorating.

RECOMMENDATIONS.

1. That state and municipal authorities take steps to provide suitable institutions for the segregation of feeble-minded children, as recommended in the preceding section.

2. Proposals for legislative enactment to this end have been prepared by a committee appointed for the purpose by President McCormick of the Cook County Board. We recommend that legislation along the lines proposed by that committee be had in this state to correct our failures in our attempts to control the feeble-minded. (See recommendations at the end of preceding section.)

We call attention to the fact that the provision for denying parents and their relatives the right to interfere with commitment of a feeble-minded child to an institution for such cases has precedent in the laws of the following states: Connecticut, Idaho, Indiana, Iowa, Kentucky, Maine, Massachusetts, Michigan, Minnesota, New Hampshire, New Jersey, North Carolina, North Dakota, Ohio, Pennsylvania, Rhode Island, South Dakota, Texas, Vermont, Washington, West Virginia, and Wisconsin.

C

A STUDY OF COOK COUNTY BOYS NOW IN THE ST. CHARLES REFORMATORY

In this section of our investigation it was our purpose to get as complete an account as possible of the developmental history of the 280 Cook County boys who, when we began this phase of our work on September 10, 1914, were in the State Reformatory for Boys at St. Charles. This soon proved to be a program, however, for which the time at our disposal was wholly inadequate. After obtaining certain data on the whole group from the records of the Juvenile Probation Office, set forth in the first table below, our attention was drawn to the very interesting fact that approximately 10% (29 cases), of the total group had already, before commitment to St. Charles, come to the attention of one or several of those public agencies, in addition to the Juvenile Court proper, by which we seek to protect the community against the juvenile weakling and the juvenile delinquent, and to establish or re-establish him in the ways in which society elects that he should go.

We were able, for example, to obtain a view of these cases not only through the records of the Probation Office, but through those of the Juvenile Psychopathic Institute where a diagnosis of their mental and physical condition was made; through the records of the Child Study Bureau of the Board of Education, where in many instances a diagnosis had been made of the mental and physical condition very much earlier than the commitment to St. Charles. In such cases it was evident that at that earlier time the boys had been recognized by the school authorities as sufficiently troublesome problems to lead their teachers to send them to the Bureau for diagnosis and for the advice of the Bureau as to the most appropriate educational treatment in each case. In these cases also we consulted the records and the Principal of the Chicago Parental School, from which source further data was obtained relating to the characteristics and development of the youths in question. Finally we consulted the St. Charles Reformatory itself, both by written inquiry and by personal visit, for information relating to the developmental history of the boys since they reached the institution, and for the practical judgment of experienced officials at the Reformatory on the question whether each boy in the list will give a satisfactory account of himself on his release.

The detailed results of this study are set forth below. Table I will show which of these cases, by case number, have been in the Parental School (P. S.); have a record of the Child Study Department (C. S. D.) of the Public School System, and which of them have a record in the Juvenile Psychopathic Institute (J. P. I.).

TWO HUNDRED AND EIGHTY ST. CHARLES BOYS, DESIGNATING CASES THAT HAVE PASSED THROUGH THE CHICAGO PARENTAL SCHOOL AND HAVE BEEN DIAGNOSED IN THE CHILD STUDY DEPARTMENT OF THE BOARD OF EDUCATION AND JUVENILE PSYCHOPATHIC INSTITUTE.

Case No.	P. S.	C. S. D.	J. P. I.	Case No.	P. S.	C. S. D.	J. P. I.
1				9			
2				10			
3				11			
4	×			12			
5†			×	13	×		
6				14			
7*‡	×	×	×	15			
8				16†			

Case No.	P.S.	C.S.D.	J.P.I.	Case No.	P.S.	C.S.D.	J.P.I.
17				81†			×
18				82			
19				83			
20†		×		84†			×
21				85			
22			×	86			
23				87			
24	×			88			
25	×			89			
26				90			
27				91			
28				92			
29†‡	×	×	×	93*‡	×	×	
30	×			94†		×	
31†‡	×	×	×	95†			×
32				96			
33				97			
34				98	×		
35	×			99†			
36			×	100			
37			×	101	×		
38			×	102*‡	×	×	×
39			×	103			
40				104†			×
41				105†			×
42	×			106			
43	×			107			
44		×		108†		×	
45		×		109	×		
46				110			
47	×			111			
48				112			
49				113			
50‡	×			114†			×
51†		×		115*‡	×	×	
52				116			
53‡	×		×	117			
54				118†			×
55*‡	×	×	×	119†			×
56	×			120†			×
57	×			121			
58	×			122†			×
59	×			123	×		
60				124	×		
61				125			
62				126			
63				127†			×
64				128		×	
65				129	×		
66	×			130			
67				131†			×
68‡	×		×	132			
69*				133	×		
70*				134			
71‡	×		×	135			
72				136†			×
73*‡		×	×	137‡	×		×
74				138*‡	×	×	×
75				139			
76				140	×	×	
77				141†		×	
78				142†			×
79	×			143			
80				144†	×		×

Case No.	P. S.	C. S. D.	J. P. I.
145			
146			
147	X		
148	X		
149			
150			
151			
152*‡	X	X	
153†			X
154			
155†			X
156	X		
157			
158‡	X		X
159			
160	X		
161			
162			
163			
164†		X	
165†		X	
166			
167			
168	X		
169	X		
170†			X
171†			X
172†			X
173	X		
174			
175	X		
176‡	X		X
177			
178	X		
179			
180	X		
181			
182‡	X		X
183‡	X		X
184			
185‡	X		X
186	X		
187			
188	X		
189‡	X		X
190†		X	X
191			
192			
193	X		
194			X
195†‡			X
196			
197			
198	X		
199			
200	X		
201	X		
202	X		
203†			X
204		X	
205			
206			
207			
208			
209	X		
210			
211			
212	X		
213			
214‡	X		X
215†			X
216	X		
217			
218†			X
219	X		
220*‡	X	X	X
221			
222			
223	X		
224	X		
225			
226†			X
227†			X
228*‡§		X	X
229			
230			
231			
232			
233	X		
234	X		
235			
236			
237†			X
238			
239			
240			
241			
242			
243			
244			
245			
246			
247			
248	X		
249			
250‡	X		X
251			
252			
253			
254†			X
255†			X
256			
257	X		
258†			X
259			X
260			
261	X		
262			
263			
264			
265			
266			
267			
268			
269			
270	X		
271			
272			

Case No.	P. S.	C. S. D.	J. P. I.	Case No.	P. S.	C. S. D.	J. P. I.
273				277	×		
274*‡	×	×		278	×		
275†			×	279‡	×		×
276				280			

TOTALS.

Parental School ....82 cases
Child Study Department...............................26 cases
Juvenile Psychopathic Institute ....66 cases
Examined in common .... 9 cases

*Cases studied by both J. P. I. and C. S. D.

†Forty-eight St. Charles cases, examined, but not in P. S.

‡The 29 selected cases.

§Two of the 29 selected cases not in Parental School.

The insignia in the table above, as explained in the introduction to the table, designate those cases that have a record at the Chicago Parental School, at the Juvenile Psychopathic Institute, and at the Child Welfare Study Bureau of the Chicago Department of Education. There are designated also those cases that have been examined in both the Psychopathic Institute and the Child Study Department as well as those who were examined in one or other of these agencies but have no record in the Parental School. The totals show that 82 of these cases, or 29.2%, have a Parental School record. In other words the records show that almost a third of these boys have been recognized as truants. Twenty-six of them had, while they were yet in the regular public schools, been brought to the child study department as difficult cases for expert advice as to the disposition that should be made of them. Sixty-six, before commitment to St. Charles, by the Juvenile Court, were examined in the Psychopathic Institute.

Let us turn now to the 29 cases referred to above who had, in addition to Parental School history, a record of diagnosis in either the Juvenile Psychopathic Institute or the Child Study Bureau of the Department of Education, or both. They were regarded as particularly troublesome cases before commitment to St. Charles. We insert below the history of several of these 29 cases which sets forth the date of birth, the first school report that brought the boy to the attention of custodial agencies, the diagnosis, Parental School reports, the nature of the environment in which the youth grew up, the date of his arrest and the charge, disposition by the Court, school progress in St. Charles and the estimate of the officer of the Reformatory as to whether he will "make good" outside. All these details are arranged chronologically.

When such histories as these are brought together they present an especially valuable view of each case. In almost every instance we have reports covering several years and comprising data that is contributed by skilled observers. By reason of the length of the period that is covered in most of these histories, and the nature of the observers, the data affords a good basis for prognosis in each case. Space does not allow the publication of all the records in this form. The reader is referred to a greatly abbreviated summary of the 29 histories that follows the illustrative cases.

I. EDUCATIONAL HISTORY OF ST. CHARLES REFORMATORY BOYS, WITH DATE OF EARLIEST REPORTED DELINQUENCY. DATA ARRANGED CHRONOLOGICALLY.

(C. S. D.—Child Study Department of the Public Schools.)

(J. P. I.—Juvenile Psychopathic Institute.)

CASE 7.—Born Aug. 17, 1897. Nationality—Canadian.

October 18, 1910. Principal's report of Aggassiz School. "This boy is a habitual truant. He is a little subnormal mentally."

November 11, 1910. Parental School until March 8, 1911. Four months. School grade, 1st. Cause of discharge—Age limit.

April 11, 1911. C. S. D. "Subnormal, does not know how to read. Should have the training of special subnormal centre.

May 22, 1914. J. P. I.

Mentally—Subnormal. Excessive bad habits.

Physically—Exceedingly dissipated. Various physical defects, although well grown.

Heredity—One parent addicted to drugs before conception. Very premature birth.

Environment—Poverty. Mother works out. Poor home control.

June 12, 1914. Arrested. Charge—General incorrigibility.

July 6, 1914. Disposition—St. Charles. (Temporarily John Worthy School.) Grade on entering St. Charles, 1st.

October 15, 1914. St. Charles report by School Principal: Present grade, 1st. Progress in school of letters, bad. Will he "make good" outside? No.

Note: Mother of this boy once received a pension from County. Stayed because of bad reports.

CASE 29.—Born October 22, 1909. Nationality—American (German).

May 9, 1912. Principal's report to Wentworth School. Boy is a habitual truant beyond control of his mother.

May 17, 1912. Parental School until October 16, 1912. Five months. School grade, 4th. Cause of discharge—Satisfactory conduct.

October 31, 1912. C. S. D. "Vision is only half normal; some adenoids; is run down physically. Has a number of physical stigmata indicating rickets in early childhood. Bad school habits due more to the matter of inherent constitution than lack of training. If the conduct should again become intolerable, it would be a good plan to return the boy to the Parental School where they have the facilities for handling the case."

April 10, 1913. Parental School until September 17, 1913. Cause of discharge—Satisfactory conduct and kidney trouble. The latter caused nightly urination in bed. Hence refused to take him back.

December 26, 1913. St. Charles until April 24, 1914. Paroled to Officer O'Brien. Put him in John Worthy School temporarily. School grade on entering St. Charles, 4th.

April 24, 1914. Released from St. Charles (John Worthy School temporarily) to mother.

May 24, 1914. Arrested. Charge—General truancy and loafing.

May 24, 1914. J. P. I.

Mentally—Normal.

Physically—Nervous. Defective vision. Developmental convulsions during childhood and excessive difficulty in control of sphincters. On account of the latter, a great dislike for school has arisen.

Heredity—Parent mild epileptic.

May 26, 1914. Committed to St. Charles; temporarily John Worthy. Delivered to St. Charles July 20, 1914.

May 26, 1914. Dr. Yerger, M. D.: "Has defective vision and adenoids. Urine does not show any abnormality."

October 15, 1914. St. Charles report. Present grade, 4th. Progress, bad. Will he make good outside? Probably.

CASE 31.—Born July 4, 1898. Nationality—Russian Jew.

January 7, 1906. C. S. D. "Wholly a case of poor home conditions. Picks things out of barrels in alleys for food. Poor hearing due to enlarged tonsils." Mentally bright.

July 12, 1907. P. O. report. "This boy was picked up at 4 a. m., July 11, 1907, at Washington and Clark Streets trying to sell papers. He told the officer that he had nothing to eat since noon the day before. This boy came from a very poor home. I hope your Honor may see your way clear to send him to some home."

July 16, 1907. Judge Tuthill. Sent to orphanage. Ran away several times.

October 11, 1907. Principal's report, Washburn School. "Truancy has become chronic. Had him placed in Orphans' Home. Conditions in his home vile beyond description.

October 31, 1907. Arrested. P. O. report—"Sleeping in the rear of Chicago Examiner's building. Lack of parental care."

November 4, 1907. Ran away from Orphans' Home.

December 13, 1907. Parental School until May 6, 1908. Five and one-half months. School grade, 3rd.

September 14, 1908. P. O. report—"Has not proper parental care or guardianship, also has not sufficient means of subsistence. On September 12, 1908, at 11 o'clock, I found him at 5th Avenue and Madison Street in destitute condition. He said he had been wandering about the streets and alleys for a week, both day and night. I would recommend that he be placed in some institution."

September 21, 1908. Parental School. Second term until January 13, 1909. Four months. Dismissed as dependent.

January 20, 1909. Industrial school. Ran away May 10, 1911.

November 11, 1911. J. P. I.

Mentally—Ability very good, but is aberrational in type. Very defective in self-control. On the basis of defective heredity, etc.

Physically—Fairly good.

Hededity—Parent insane. Father unknown.

Environment—Excessively bad on account of poverty and the above.

December 19, 1911. Released to mother from Industrial School by Judge Pinckney. P. O. record.

April 14, 1912. Placed in a good private home.

May 26, 1914. Ran away to New York.

October 21, 1912. Arrested. Charge—Criminal assault of a little three-year-old girl.

October 28, 1912. Committed to St. Charles School. School grade on entering St. Charles, 7th.

April 3, 1914. Paroled. Returned July 9, 1914.

October 15, 1914. St. Charles report. Progress good. Will he make good outside? No.

CASE 50.—Born March 25, 1897. Nationality—American.

September 16, 1907. Principal's report, Doolittle School—"Should receive immediate attention. Truant. Mother helpless."

October 11, 1907. Parental School until October 27, 1909, 2 years. School grade, 2nd. Reason of discharge—Satisfactory conduct.

April 4, 1912. Arrested. Charge—Breaking bulbs at 60th Street on the Illinois Central R. R.

June 16, 1913. Arrested. Charge—Stealing cigars and watch.

July 18, 1914. Arrested. Charge—Breaking into a locker at Jackson Park.

July 18, 1913. Disposition—St. Charles. Released to mother before commitment.

November 10, 1913. Arrested. Charge—Misapplying funds, $10.00.

November 10, 1913. J. P. I.

Mentally—Capable and intelligent. Lacking in self-control.

Physically—Strong and well developed, but nervous.

Environment—Poverty. Poor home conditions. Mother works out. Father died while the boy was a baby. Long association with bad companions. Lack of wholesome interests.

Nov. 10, 1913. Committed to St. Charles. School grade, 5th.

October 15, 1914. St. Charles report. Present grade, 5th. Progress indifferent. Will he make good outside? Probably.

The 29 histories similar to the foregoing illustrations are briefly summarized in the following table. In the summary the data is presented chronologically from left to right.

It will be seen in the summary above that approximately 37% of these youths have spent from two to four years in institutional life, and that 69% of them will not or probably will not make good outside—in the judgment of practical and experienced observers. Neither of these items suggests a hopeful prognosis.

The foregoing histories afford a good opportunity to observe the diagnosis on the one hand and to set over on the other hand the time that has lapsed between admission to the Parental School and to the St. Charles Reformatory as well as the school progress made in the interval and the prospect for the future as estimated by the progress now being made in St. Charles. It is unsatisfactory to set this kind of data down in tabular form and we refer hack therefore by number to the summarized histories in Table II:

CASE 7.—Advanced no grade in 4 years. St. Charles record bad. Subnormal, dissipated. Make good? No.

CASE 29.—Advanced no grade in 1 year. St. Charles record bad. Normal, nervous, bad vision. Make good? No.

CASE 31.—Advanced 4 grades in 5 years. St. Charles record good. Normal, bad home. Make good? No.

CASE 50.—Advanced 3 grades in 5½ years. St. Charles record indifferent. Normal, and physically strong. Make good? Probably.

CASE 53.—Advanced 1 grade in 4½ years. St. Charles record good. Fair ability. Bad home. Make good? Yes.

CASE 55.—Advanced 2 grades in 2½ years. St. Charles record good. Defective hearing, nervous. Make good? Yes.

CASE 57.—Advanced 1 grade in 2½ years. St. Charles record bad. Fair ability. Alcoholic environment. Make good? No.

CASE 68.—Advanced 3 grades in 2½ years. St. Charles record good. Normal. Defective vision. Make good? Yes.

CASE 71.—Fell back 1 grade in 3 years. St. Charles record indifferent. Fair ability. Epileptic. Make good? Yes.

CASE 93.—Advanced 1 grade in 5 years. St. Charles record bad. Restless. Adenoids. Make good? Yes.

CASE 102.—Advanced 5 grades in 5½ years. St. Charles record good. Slow but accurate. Good physical development. Make good? Yes.

CASE 115.—Advanced 1 grade in 3 years. St. Charles record bad. Normal. Physical defects. Make good? No.

CASE 137.—Advanced 3 grades in 5 years. St. Charles record bad. Normal. Neurotic. Make good? Probably.

CASE 158.—Advanced 1 grade in 2½ years. St. Charles record bad. Fair mentally. Healthy. Bad home. Make good? No.

CASE 176.—Advanced 2 grades in 4½ years. St. Charles record indifferent. Subnormal. Poor general physical condition. Make good? No.

CASE 183.—Advanced 3 grades in 4 years. St. Charles record indifferent. Normal. Poorly developed. Make good? Probably.

CASE 183.—Advanced 3 grades in 3½ years. St. Charles record good. Adolescent instability. Make good? Yes.

CASE 185.—Advanced 1 grade in 4½ years. St. Charles record indifferent. Normal. Good condition. Make good? Probably.

CASE 195.—Advanced 3 grades in 2½ years. St. Charles record good. Normal. Good condition. Make good? Probably.

CASE 124.—Advanced 1 grade in 1 year. St. Charles record good. Normal. Make good? No.

CASE 220.—Advanced no grade in 2 years. St. Charles record bad. Subnormal. Not feeble-minded. Adenoids. Make good? Probably.

CASE 250.—Advanced no grade in 3 years. St. Charles record bad. Feebleminded. Defective vision. Make good? No.

CASE 279.—Advanced 3 grades in 4 years. St. Charles record good. Good ability. Good condition. Make good? No.

Failure to show school progress (Compare Tables V and XIV) in these cases is, of course, not always traceable to inability. They may not have continued in school after discharge from the Parental School, although they should have done so under the compulsory education law until the age of 14 years should be attained, and even to the age of 16 in case the youth was not legally employed. These cases were below 14 years of age when discharged from the Parental School excepting the following: Nos. 7, 53, 55, 71, 102, 115, 137, 138, 158, 182, 183, 195, 214, 220, 250, and 274. (Table II.) These are somewhat more than half of our cases. By reason of having reached the age of 14 years at the time of discharge from the Parental School they had no formal opportunity to advance their school grade before their subsequent admission to St. Charles. Of course there is the possibility that some of them continued in school by reason of their not being able to plead employment, but of this we have no evidence, and it is improbable. Yet all these cases excepting six (7, 29, 71, 58, 220, 250) had increased their school standing before entering St. Charles. Those excepted merely held their own, or lost ground. (No. 71.) Their record is "bad" or "indifferent" at the Reformatory and the estimate as to the future of three of them (7, 158, and 250) is that they will not make good outside. Of two of them (29 and 220) it is reported that he will make good. All, excepting 158, have a very unfavorable mental and physical diagnosis. Case 71 is mentally normal, but is described as epileptic.

TABLE II. SUMMARY OF THE HISTORY OF TWENTY-NINE ST. CHARLES BOYS WHO HAVE BEEN DIAGNOSED BY THE PSYCHOPATHIC INSTITUTE OR THE CHILD STUDY DEPARTMENT OF THE BOARD OF EDUCATION, OR I

No. of Case	Date of Birth	Nationality	Date and Age Entering Parental School	Grade	No. of Times in Par. Sch.	Total Time	Cause of Discharge	No. of Times Arrested	Court Charges	No. of Times in J.W.S.	No. of Times in J.W.S.	Date and Age of Commitment at St. Charles	Length of time at St. Charles	School Gr. on Ent. St. Charles	Progress at St. Charles	Present Grade
7	3/17/97	Croatian	11/13/10 13 years	1st	1	4 months	Age limit	1	Gen. incor., truancy, etc.	1	(Temp.)	7/16/14 17 years	4 months	1st	Bad	1st
30	10/22/01	American	5/7/12 11½ "	4th	2	10 "	Satisfactory conduct	1	Truancy and loafing	2	(?)	12/21/13 12 "	1 "	4th	Bad	4th
31	7/4/98	Russian Jew	12/3/07 9 "	3d	1	9½ "	Dependency	1	Vagrancy, assault	..		10/26/12 14 "	2 "	7th	Good	8th
33	3/25/97	American	10/11/08 10½ "	3d	1	24 "	Satisfactory conduct	4	Breaking lights, lockers, stealing	..		7/18/13 16 "		5th	Indifferent	5th
59	5/24/97	Irish	11/10/08 11½ "	4th	2	16 "	Age limit	5	Shooting lights and man, burglary	1	1 month	3/9/14 17 "		5th	Good	6th
55	12/15/97	Russian Jew	3/12/09 11½ "	5th	2	26 "	Age limit	1	Vagrancy, general incorrigibility	1	15 days	7/1/13 15 "	1 "	7th	Good	8th
57	4/10/98	Italian	11/13/09 11½ "	3d	1	4 "	Satisfactory conduct	3	Begging, gen. inc., vagrancy, stealing	..		7/30/08 15 "	1 "	4th	Bad	5th
55	11/09/02	Polish	4/26/12 9½ "	2d	2	15 "	Satisfactory conduct	2	General incorrigibility	1	(Temp.)	7/27/14 12 "		5th	Good	5th
71	1/1/98	German	2/25/10 12 "	3d	1	16 "	Age limit	3	Snatching pocketbooks, stealing	..		2/12/12 13 "	2 "	2d	Indifferent	4th
77	4/24/00	Italian						2	Cutting and stealing wirts and cable	..		4/16/14 14 "		4th	Bad	4th
81	10/25/98	Finn	1/22/09 10 "	3d	2	15 "	Satisfactory conduct	1	Hold-up for money and watch	..		3/18/13 15 "		4th	Bad	5th
82	10/27/96	Bohemian	10/11/07 9½ "	3d	3	26½ "	Age limit	2	General incorrigibility	1	(Temp.)	1/4/13 15 "	2 "	6th	Good	8th
115	7/15/00	Swedish	3/26/11 11 "	3d	2	15 "	Age limit	2	Robbery, stealing	..		4/9/14 14 "	1 "	4th	Bad	5th
137	7/00/00	German Jew	5/21/09 9 "	2d	3	22 "	Age limit	1	General incorrigibility	..		4/28/14 14 "	½ "	4th	Bad	4th
138	8/ /96	German	6/7/12 15½ "	4th	1	6 "	Age limit	4	General incorrigibility	1	(Temp.)	7/ /14 15 "				
152	12/18/99	American	11/17/11 11 "	5th	1	12 "	Delinquent (St. Charles)	5	Stealing	..		4/21/13 14 "	1 "		Indifferent	
155	7/16/98	American	12/8/11 13½ "	6th	1	6 "	Age limit	2	Vagrancy, burglary, stealing	1	(Temp.)	4/27/14 16 "		5th	Bad	4th
176	4/2/01	Polish	11/26/09 8½ "	1st	4	28 "	Satisfactory conduct	2	Incendiary, burglary (4)	..		4/27/14 13 "		3d	Indifferent	3d
182	7/4/96	Irish	10/15/09 11 "	3d	3	16½ "	Age limit	3	Vagrancy and general incorrigibility	..		7/15/13 15 "	1 "	4th	Indifferent	5th
183	9/22/97	American	2/3/11 13½ "	5th	1	7 "	Age limit	2	General incorrigibility and stealing	2	6 months	6/11/14 17 "		8th	Good	8th
185	11/11/01	Polish	5/13/10 8½ "	2d	1	9 "	Dependent	4	Vagrancy and stealing	..		3/31/14 13 "	½ "	3d	Indifferent	3d
189	6/25/02	American	8/21/12 10 "	2d	1	9 "	Subnormal	2	General incorrigibility	1	8 months	3/28/14 12 "			Bad	4th
195	3/ /99	Italian	3/29/12 12½ "	6th	2	10 "	Age limit	5	Stealing, snatching bags	..		3/ 6/14 15 "		8th	Good	8th
211	5/11/00	Polish	3/28/13 13 "	2d	1	10 "	Age limit	2	Vagrancy	..		3/29/14 14 "		3d	Good	3d
220	4/12/99	German	5/30/12 13 "	4th	1	8½ "	Age limit	2	Burglary, stealing	..		10/ 6/13 15 "	1 "	4th	Bad	4th
228	10/ 1/97	German						4	Bribery, stealing	..		11/30/09 12 "	3 "	4th	Good	
251	7/29/98	Polish	6/ 9/11 13 "	2d	1	9 "	Age limit	4	General incorrigibility	..		4/ 9/14 16 "		2d	Bad	2d
274	5/22/99	Russian Jew	3/23/12 13 "	2d	1	8 "	Age limit	2	Robbery, vagrancy	..		8/20/14 14 "				
278	8/10/98	Swiss	6/17/10 12 "	5th	1	6 "	Delinquent (St. Charles)	3	Stealing, forgery	1	(Temp.)	5/26/14 16 "		8th	Good	8th

ANALYTICAL SUMMARY OF THE HISTORY OF TWENTY-NINE ST. CHARLES BOYS WHO HAVE BEEN DIAGNOSED BY THE PSYCHOPATHIC INSTITUTE OR THE CHILD WELFARE DEPARTMENT OF THE BOARD OF EDUCATION,

Table III. Nationality.

	Cases.	Per Cent.
American	5	17.25
German	5	17.25
Polish	5	17.25
Italian	3	10.3
Russian	3	10.3
Irish	2	6.9
Austria	1	3.45
Bohemian	1	3.45
Canadian	1	3.45
Finnish	1	3.45
Swedish	1	3.45
Total	29	100

Table IV. Age at Parental School.

	Cases.	Per Cent.
8 years	2	6.9
9 "	4	13.8
10 "	3	10.35
11 "	7	24.15
12 "	5	10.35
13 "	8	27.6
0 "	2	6.9
Total	29	100

Table V. Grade at Parental School.

	Cases.	Per Cent.
1st	2	6.9
2nd	9	31.5
3d	6	20.7
4th	4	13.8
5th	4	13.8
6th	2	6.9
0	2	6.9
Total	29	100

Table VI. Number of Times at Parental School.

	Cases.	Per Cent.
1 time	15	51.7
2 "	8	27.6
3 "	3	10.35
4 "	1	3.45
Total	29	100

Table VII. Total Time at Parental School.

	Cases.	Per Cent.
2 months	1	3.45
4 "	2	6.9
6 "	3	10.35
7–9 "	6	20.7
10–12 "	5	13.8
13–18 "	6	20.7
19–28 "	5	17.2
0	2	6.9
Total	29	100

Table VIII. Cause of Discharge.

	Cases.	Per Cent.
Age limit	16	59.5
Satisfactory conduct	6	22.2
Dependent	2	7.4
Delinquent	2	7.4
Subnormal	1	3.7
Total	29	100

Table IX. Number of Times Arrested.

	Cases.	Per Cent.
1 time	7	24.15
2 "	8	27.6
3 "	4	13.8
4 "	5	17.2
5 "	5	17.2
Total	29	100

Table X. Age Entering St. Charles.

	Cases.	Per Cent.
10 years	1	3.45
12 "	5	17.25
13 "	3	10.3
14 "	9	31.05
15 "	6	20.7
16 "	3	10.35
17 "	3	10.35
Total	29	100

Table XI. Length of Time at St. Charles.

Range 3 Months to 32 Months.

	Cases.	Per Cent.
3 to 6 months	12	41.4
7–9 "	4	13.8
10–12 "	6	20.7
13–18 "	1	3.45
19–24 "	3	10.35
25–32 "	1	3.45
No time	1	3.45
Total	29	100

Table XII. Grade on Entering St. Charles.

	Cases.	Per Cent.
1st grade	1	3.45
2nd "	2	6.9
3rd "	3	10.35
4th "	10	34.5
5th "	4	12.8
6th "	2	6.9
7th "	3	10.35
8th "	1	3.45
No grade given	4	13.8
Total	29	100

Table XIII. Progress at St. Charles.

	Cases.	Per Cent.
Good	10	34.5
Bad	11	37.9
Indifferent	6	20.7
No answer	2	6.9
Total	29	100

Table XIV. Present Grade at St. Charles.

	Cases.	Per Cent.
1st grade	1	3.45
2nd "	2	6.9
3rd "	3	10.35
4th "	8	27.6
5th "	5	17.2
6th "	1	3.45
7th "	4	20.7
No grade given	4	13.8
Total	29	100

Table XV. Will He Make Good?

	Cases.	Per Cent.
Yes	7	24.1
No	12	41.4
Probably	8	27.6
No answer	2	6.9
Total	29	100

Table XVI.

Range 6 M

6 months	
7–12	
13–18	
19–24	
25–30	
31–48	
Total	

Leaving these six cases and returning to the remainder of the list cited above, i. e., Nos. 50, 57, 93, 115, 137, 182, 183, 193, and 214, we find that only three (183, 195, and 214) are making good progress at St. Charles. Only No. 183 is expected to make good outside. These three present good diagnoses. Excluding now this group of three cases the remainder of this last list, i. e., 50, 57, 93, 115, 117, and 182, are all making bad or indifferent records at St. Charles. They had all increased their school standing by from 1 to 3 grades between the time of entering the Parental School and the time of entering St. Charles. Number 50 presents a good diagnosis; he will probably make good. Fifty-seven, fair; he will not make good. Numbers 93 and 137 give evidence of unstable nervous systems, but mentally they are declared to be normal. No. 93 will make good; 137 probably. Number 116 suffers from sensory defects. He will not make good. Number 182 is of fair mental ability, but is physically poorly developed. He will probably make good. From the data we have at hand no very definite statement can be made relating to a correlation between the mental and physical diagnoses we have quoted on the one hand, and the character of the record at St. Charles and the prognosis of practical officials on the other.

PHYSICAL AND MENTAL DIAGNOSES OF TYPICAL CASES FROM AMONG 41 OF THE 280 ST. CHARLES BOYS.

Diagnoses by Psychopathic Institute. No Parental School record. (None of these included in the 29 cases foregoing):

No. of Case.	Physical Diagnosis.	Mental Diagnosis.
119	Poor general development. No defects.	Bright.
120	General condition fair. Formerly had epilepsy. Chorea. St. Vitus Dance. Now minor epilepsy.	Dull from physical causes.
122	Well developed and nourished. Scar and bone envolment from old injury.	Poor in ability and advantages. Only two years schooling in U. S.
127	In good condition.	Tentatively diagnosed as fairly good ability. Poor educational advantages.
121	Good general condition.	Poor in ability and advantages.
136	Very small. Fairly well nourished but poorly developed.	Tentatively subnormal. Appeared to be pretending to know less than he really did. May be dull from physical causes.
140	Strong. Sturdy. Some defective hearing on one side.	Fair in ability and advantages.
142	Strabismus. Scar of old corneal ulcer.	Bright.
144	Poor general development and nutrition.	Fair in ability.
153	Good condition except defective vision.	Extremely bright.

Of the 41 cases illustrated above whose conditions were examined at the Psychopathic Institute, but 14 were in good or fair physical condition at the time of diagnosis. The remainder present various signs of profound neurotic disturbance. But 25 are of good or fair mental ability. The remainder are distinctly subnormal.

CASES DIAGNOSED ONLY BY THE CHILD STUDY DEPARTMENT OF THE BOARD OF EDUCATION. (NO ONE OF THESE INCLUDED IN THE 29 SELECTED CASES.)

No. of Case.	Remarks and Recommendations.
16	He is a dull, stupid child who will require individual attention to accomplish anything in the way of school work. His nervous system is in a wretched condition, no doubt in consequence of poor food and unsanitary home conditions.
20	It is a question of poor heredity and moving about from place to place. Ought to be approached wholly through concrete methods.

No. of
Case.   Remarks and Recommendations.
44 His case calls for more individual treatment. Raymond School. Until
     the mother can locate in that neighborhood, the boy may as well
     remain at home.
45 A boy of more than average brightness. Has only been in U. S. 14
     months. Simply a case of not being acquainted with the language.
     Not a case for the ungraded room.
51 Not aggressive. Hardly defends himself. Occasionally cranky about
     eating. Plays vigorously. Sleeps well.
94 Teacher says cannot do anything. This is again a physical case. Boy
     is extremely nervous, is tense and physically depleted. Probably will
     get on satisfactorily with school work for he has gotten hold of his
     symbol work fairly well.
128 Needs to be aroused and interested in motor methods. Also consider-
     able drill with symbols in the way of giving them a concrete basis.
     Brother who is in St. Charles is about as low as this fellow. Very
     tense and erratic. Some hereditary taint has induced neurosis. Rec-
     ommended the transfer to grade 3 in Seward School.
141
164 Cannot stand on one foot.
165 Some aberration.
190 Was in Feehanville July to December, 1909. Uncontrollable. Boy seems
     wholly untrained. Good instincts. Parents do not understand him or
     wish to get rid of him.
214 This boy is 16 years 11 months, but practically less than the size of an
     11 year old. He has been greatly stunted in early life, first by reason
     of his inheritance which is tubercular, and likewise on account of his
     sickness during early life. Not feeble-minded. He is able to work
     with number combinations in the concrete to 50. He seems to have
     a good memory for simple things and his perception is fairly keen,
     though slow. He shows a great number of physical defects both on
     the side of growth and movement. These can be attended to later.
     We recommend his admittance to the ungraded room at Seward School.
     Trial.
                          CONCLUSIONS.
   Only nine among the 29 cases are physically in good condition. The
remainder are suffering from various types of disorder which signify more or
less neurotic dispositions.
   But 14 cases in a group of 41 among the 280 at St. Charles, who have
been diagnosed at the Psychopathic Institute, are described as of good or
fair physical condition. The remainder of this group present indications of
neurotic disturbances. Only 26 of this number are described as of good or
fair mental ability.
   In Table .... we have 11 additional cases whose physical and mental
diagnosis is recorded in the Child Study Department. (Case 190 in this group
is included with the 41 in Table .....) Seven of this number are in bad
physical and mental condition.
   Out of a total therefore of 82 St. Charles boys (nearly 30% of the Chicago
contingent), whose diagnoses we have been able to secure, 54 are unstable
physically or mentally or in both respects. If the conclusion reached by
Dr. Stevens in the first section of this portion of our investigation is correct
—that these unstable youths require special and prolonged attention in order
to give them an even start in life—then we have with these boys the same
problem that presents us in the case of the John Worthy boys and the Lincoln cases. (See Sections A and B II.)
   One other thing that stands out prominently in the history of these cases
is the length of time they have spent in institutional life and the unfavorable
home surroundings from which they have come. With these diagnoses and
histories in mind the practical question that confronts us is, what becomes
of these youths and others when they are paroled from St. Charles? The
answer to that question is the test of our methods. It has been impossible
in the course of this investigation to take up this problem. It would involve
the tedious process of following up the history of several hundred paroled
boys throughout several years. In this connection we are at liberty to
quote a letter on the subject of parole from St. Charles, addressed to Mr. Joel
D. Hunter, Chief Juvenile Probation Officer for Cook County.

Mr. Joel D. Hunter,
    Chief Probation Officer, Juvenile Court.
Dear Mr. Hunter:

With regard to the parole situation at the St. Charles School for Boys, I would say the St. Charles School for Boys has, since its establishment, had but one parole officer who gave attention to the boys paroled from that institution. This officer is known as a Home Visitor and is supposed to have the same qualifications as the visitors who attend dependent children for the Illinois State Board of Administration.

The St. Charles School has in the neighborhood of 1,000 boys on parole, and approximately one-half of this number come from Chicago. This officer has no special training for the care of delinquent boys but is examined for his fitness for visiting dependent children (boys and girls) placed in homes. He is paid for this service $75.00 per month. The law creating the St. Charles School specifically states that the officer shalll be a parole agent.

According to the report of the Juvenile Court, submitted to the County Board for the year 1913, there were committed to the St. Charles School for the year 1913, 183 boys from Cook County. For the last two years the Home Visitor, so-called, of the St. Charles School has not visited in Chicago at all. It would be a physical impossibility for one Parole Officer for the St. Charles School, assigned to the City of Chicago alone, to attend properly to all the parole cases that are allowed to return from that institution to the city. As it is they have no supervision whatever. It is small wonder that so large a number of these boys are re-arrested and brought back into this Court, or into the Boys' Court for new offenses. It is generally conceded by people experienced in correctional institutions that the most critical period with the person whom you are attempting to correct, follows his release from the correctional institution, and extends over a period of a year or more from that date. These boys coming out of St. Charles have had the advantage of a very high grade correctional training, and are then once more allowed to return to the old environment without the guiding influence of a Parole Officer to assist them to get re-established.

The State of Massachusetts maintains a school at Westboro for Delinquent Boys under the age of 16. That institution has seven parole officers—one Chief Parole Officer who receives $150 a month. The other officers are paid salaries that make it possible for the Superintendent to secure high class men. It is useless to attempt to set forth the advantage of such a plan, as that will seem obvious. It is my firm belief that a large number of the boys who come from St. Charles on parole could, under proper parole supervision, be kept from committing new offenses. Another serious disadvantage is that boys who escape from that institution are very frequently able to avoid being returned as a result of the failure of adequate parole supervision in the institution to apprehend and return these boys.

Respectfully yours

HARRY HILL.

RECOMMENDATIONS.

In the light of the unfavorable nature of the Chicago boys in St. Charles, as far as it has been set forth in this study, it is of prime importance to know what becomes of them, in order that we may intelligently check our methods. On this account and in the light of the letter quoted above, we recommend that the City of Chicago make some provision for studying the history of Chicago boys subsequent to their parole from St. Charles. We ought to know where the 500 Chicago boys are who have been paroled from St. Charles. Such a study should begin with boys who were placed on parole four or five years ago, and include all who have been paroled since from that date up to the present.

2. If the condition discovered among John Worthy School boys reported in the first section of this portion of the report obtain also among the St. Charles Boys—and it is fair to assume that this is the case—it is necessary for the sake of public health and safety to exercise the same care of discharge and parole from St. Charles as has been recommended in the case of

John Worthy boys. We recommend that physical and mental examination of St. Charles boys be made and recorded repeatedly, and that authority be given to the medical staff to discharge or hold according to its findings.

3. The adoption of the preceding recommendation would make it necessary to enlarge the facilities of the state and city for taking care of delinquent boys. These facilities are already inadequate.

D

DELINQUENT BOYS IN EMPLOYMENT

Our task with the delinquent boy is on one side the problem of mental deficiency. On another side it is the problem of the unfit home—unfit on account of poverty or on account of the character of parents, brothers and sisters, or for both reasons. Once more, it is the problem of employment. Of course, all three of these problems may come together in the person of a single delinquent.

Here it is our purpose to set forth the facts as we find them, relating to the employment of all juvenile boys over the age of 14 years who were on probation on September 1, 1914, and who also had been on probation during the four months preceding that date. We are indebted to the Juvenile Probation Office of Cook County for the data that is summarized herein.

On September 1, 1914, there were on probation in Cook County 436 delinquent boys over the age of 14 years. Of these 242 were employed on that day and 194 were unemployed. The following table presents the data with respect to the proportion of time employed during the four months preceding the date named above:

I. SHOWING THE PROPORTIONATE TIME EMPLOYED.

No. employed full time during 4 mo. preceding Sept. 1........... 88
No. employed ¾ to full time during 4 mo. preceding Sept. 1...... 66
No. employed ½ to ¾ time during 4 mo. preceding Sept. 1.......: 89
No. employed less than ½ time during 4 mo. preceding Sept. 1.... 134
No. not working during 4 mo. preceding Sept. 1................. 11

Total... 388

In Table II we have the wages received by these boys while they were working within the period covered by the report:

II. SHOWING THE WAGES OF DELINQUENT BOYS.

No. receiving less than $5.00 per week......................... 78
No. receiving $5.00 to $6.00 per week......................... 138
No. receiving $6.00 to $7.00 per week......................... 75
No. receiving $7.00 to $8.00 per week......................... 42
No. receiving $8.00 to $9.00 per week......................... 17
No. receiving $9.00 to $10.00 per week........................ 16
No. receiving $10.00 and more per week........................ 6
No. receiving board only (in country)......................... 5
No. not working 11

Total... 388

In Table III is set forth our data relating to the constancy of boys in their several occupations:

III. SHOWING THE NUMBER OF JOBS HELD BY DELINQUENT BOYS.

No. holding 1 job during 4 mos. preceding Sept. 1.............. 162
No. holding 2 jobs during 4 mos. preceding Sept. 1............. 125
No. holding 3 jobs during 4 mos. preceding Sept. 1............. 47
No. holding 4 jobs during 4 mos. preceding Sept. 1............. 24
No. holding 5 jobs during 4 mos. preceding Sept. 1............. 14
No. holding 6 jobs during 4 mos. preceding Sept. 1............. 0
No. holding 7 jobs during 4 mos. preceding Sept. 1............. 5
Not working 11

Total... 388

The types of occupations followed by these boys cover a wide field. It will be noticed that the errand boy, the wagon boy, the messenger and the shop boy occur in considerable numbers. These are occupations—like many others in the list—from which there are not many open avenues for advancement.

IV. SHOWING TYPES OF OCCUPATIONS FOLLOWED BY DELINQUENT BOYS.

Errand Boy	Packer	Timekeeper
Wagon Boy	Shop	Butcher Boy
Water Carrier	Grocery	Elevator Boy
Bellboy	Chauffeur	Gordon Feeder
Machine Worker	Livery Attendant	Team Boy
Farm Boy	Leading Ponies	Picture Frame Worker
Stock Boy	Office Boy	Printing
Teamster	Plumber's Apprentice	Peddler
Electrician's Helper	Blockman	Cook's Assistant
Box Maker	Sorter	Deckhand
Envelope Maker	Bottle Washer	Handy Boy
Helping Sawyers	Painter's Helper	
News Stand	Messenger	

Of errand boys there were 93 on September 1, 1914; wagon boys, 47; shop boys, 27; office boys, 14; messenger boys, 24; machine workers, 16; farm boys, 10; teamsters, 10. The remaining boys were distributed in smaller numbers among the other occupations listed above.

In the report of the Cook County Juvenile Court for the fiscal year ending November 30, 1913, pp. 71 FF., data similar to the foregoing is presented. It is the experience of the Court that in the majority of cases "probation will not succeed with a delinquent boy over 14 unless he can be kept steadily at work or in school." Common sense would dictate such a statement as this. It is essential, therefore, to the success of the juvenile probation system that intelligent effort and co-operation be taken to secure steady and suitable employment for probationers. There is appended here a letter from Probation Officer I. Levin addressed to Mr. Joel Hunter, Chief Probation Officer. It is pertinent to the general problem of juvenile employment:

Chicago, Ilinois, Sept. 23, 1914.
"Dear Sir:

"I beg leave to present to you my interpretation of the figures shown on the enclosed statistical sheet, and such other comment as I think is appropriate to the discussion of the problem of employment of delinquent boys.

"I think I am correct in stating that the opportunity of securing employment has diminished more and more since a year and a half ago. I believe that if statistics were compiled for the first four months of 1913, when industrial conditions were more nearly normal, there would be shown fewer boys who have worked part time, and also fewer boys who have not worked at all.

"You will notice that of the sixty-three boys probationed to me there are twenty-one attending school, leaving forty-two boys who should be at work. Of this number, eighteen boys, or 43%, have worked full time, while thirteen boys, or 30%, have worked part time.

"Let us turn to the eleven boys who have not worked at all in the four months under consideration. They are designated below by numbers:

(1) "This lad is subnormal. His mother is insane, and has been in Dunning. The father is subnormal (information from Dr. Healy). The boy and his brother, a year older, have each one been in St. Charles for eighteen months. I find it almost impossible to get him to keep an appointment. His irregular behavior is such that no employer will keep him.

(2) "This lad has worked as a driver, and has earned by that means $8.00 a week, although he was only fourteen years old at that time. When he lost this job, he would not work as an errand boy, the only occupation open to a boy under sixteen. This lad has the height and weight of a boy seventeen or eighteen.

(3) "This lad was reared without the aid of his father, who was a man of uncontrollable temper. The boy worked one day at a job in a japanning factory. He is of low mentality. I doubt whether he will ever earn his livelihood by honest labor.

(4) "This boy is of low mentality. Every effort to get him to work has failed.

(5) "This lad is an immigrant from Russia. He is of slight frame and can do no heavy work. He has not learned to speak English.

(6) "This boy is of low mentality, is undersized, and the mother, a very stupid woman, will not co-operate with the probation officer.

(7) "This boy's desire to wander away from home, and from town to town, is the cause of his unemployment. It is interesting to note that this boy has a sister who is an imbecile. The probability is that he too is sub-normal.

(8) "This boy's mother is very stupid. He himself is subnormal, though he has exceptional talent for mechanics. Out of scrap material he has built an auto truck and a steam engine. Secured for him a job with a scientific instrument house where the Superintendent planned to have him run errands until he is sixteen, and then place him in the shop. As soon as he knows the trade of instrument maker, he will earn as high as $8.00 a day. He turned the job down, and talked impertinently to the manager. Secured other jobs for him at which he worked a few days and quit. He will have to wait until he is sixteen before he can lawfully work with machinery.

(9) "Worked in a picture-frame factory at piecework, earning from $3.00 to $6.00 a week. Became discouraged because of the low wages and quit.

(10) "This boy is of small size, and of low mentality. His father is dead, and his mother has little control over him.

(11) "Same condition as in that of No. 10, excepting that the mother, instead of the father, is dead.

"In the above eleven cases, we find five boys who are definitely subnormal (pronounced as such by our Dr. Healy). There is a strong probability that eight of the eleven are subnormal, judging by their family history and their behavior on probation. Very little can be done toward getting the subnormal boy to hold his job after one has been found for him. The chance for this type of boy to secure and hold a job is getting smaller and smaller as the Taylor system is being installed, and the aim at increased shop efficiency is being applied to industry.

"Of the five unemployed boys designated as being of low mentality and probable subnormality, three are of undersize. When a boy has made little progress at school, plays checkers, as in the cases of these boys, as an infant does, will not keep an appointment, has no sense of social obligation, and seems never to think of consequences; and when his associates nickname him "Bonehead," "Goofy," "Ivory," or "Sawdust," there is little chance of erring when we size up the boy as one of low mentality. The boy with a poor mentality is the first one to be let out when a retrenchment policy is adopted; and because he makes more errors than the normal boy, his value to his foreman is little and at the least provocation, general retrenchment or not, the boy is discharged.

'You will observe that one boy is too large for his age. Having earned more money than what is generally paid a boy, he will not work for a boy's wages. This boy reminds us of another 15-year-old boy, probationed to one of the juvenile probation officers. He weighs about 150 pounds, and has the strength of a well-developed man, but the only employment open to him is that of errand or office boy. This boy feels too old to go to school, and feels too manly to do a boy's job. And until he is sixteen years old, he will tramp the streets, asociate with idlers, and in time become a delinquent. In talking this problem over with Miss Cook, teacher at the Juvenile Detention Home, she suggested that the limitations to labor be defined on the basis of bodily strength instead of age.

"The unemployment of one of the boys can probably be traced to his small earnings. The boy of fourteen when he leaves school and works as an errand boy, will receive from $4.00 to $6.00 a week. Whenever he quits his job and finds another he receives the same pay, or perhaps less pay. In time, as the boy grows older, and his value to his employer has not increased and his wages are, therefore, constant, he becomes discontented. The boy will not work until he finds a job which will pay him the wage he wants.

"Surely, this condition argues for a system of vocational education, to the end that the boy may enter the shop equipped with the essential knowledge, to learn more, to become more skillful and efficient, and thus be able to command a better wage.

"One boy's unemployment can be charged up to his ignorance of the

English language. This impediment will be removed under the supervision of the Probation Officer to whom the boy is assigned.

"One boy's unemployment can be charged up to his ignorance of the English language. This impediment will be removed under the supervision of the Probation Officer to whom the boy is assigned.

"Among the boys assigned to me are five who are employed on farms. At least two of these are of low mentality, and were a constant menace to the boys in their neighborhoods when they lived in the city. Apparently country life is the best obtainable environment for such boys.

"There are of course many factors which are not disclosed by figures. Many a boy would not have quit a position, or would have found one when out of work were it not for the fact that his companions are not working. The unemployment of one boy is a strong factor in encouraging other boys to be idle.

"In one of my boys is an instance of a lad who, through contact with the Juvenile Court, secured a job in a printing plant, and to the surprise of his parents and neighbors, worked for about a year steadily. Perhaps this boy did not get the "right kind of a job" until he was adjudged a delinquent and was placed on probation.

"While we are endeavoring to place every boy of working age, it should not be forgotten that some kinds of employment are worse for the boy than no employment at all. As a case in point: ———— worked as a messenger for the Western Union Telegraph Company. Through the medium of his job, he was introduced to a knowledge of the drug traffic and prostitution. Since he quit this occupation his health has improved, he sleeps at home, bathes regularly, and has become a manly fellow.

"Quite a number of boys and their parents, as well, cannot understand the school certificate requirement of the child labor law. Many a boy will be unemployed because he fails to exchange his original certificate issued for a certificate issued at the Jones School. And many a boy, who has lost, destroyed or given away his school certificate, has not the courage to ask for another, and he will, consequently, remain idle. The suggestion offered by Mr. Sherman Booth, of the Association of Commerce, to take the certificate out of the boy's hands, but have the Board of Education issue the certificate to the employer, the same to be returned to the Board of Education when the boy leaves, is a timely one.

"Since Mr. Nelson, the Chief Factory Inspector, has taken office, employers have informed me that they want to observe the child labor law strictly; and so many of them have made it a rule not to employ any one under sixteen years of age. The employer thinks that for the same money he can get a sixteen-year-old boy to work, as long as the shop is open, in excess of eight hours, without becoming liable to a fine. And I am informed by some concerns that the insurance companies which underwrite their personal injury liabilities specify in their policies that no boy under sixteen shall be employed on the premises.

"The law ought to be amended to compel every child to attend school until he is sixteen years old. It is needless to say that the curricula of our school will have to be revised to successfully conform to such a change in the law. Frequently a boy will not learn at school, and the older he grows the less interested he is in his school work. The curriculum will have to include a variety of courses that have a vocational trend.

"Many boys who agree to work on farms come back soon because of the low wages paid. Perhaps if they would secure jobs on farms located at a considerable distance from Chicago, where labor is less plentiful, they could command better wages, which would induce them to stay on the farm.

"Several institutions, such as the Lewis Institute, the University of Chicago, the Typothetæ Association, and R. R. Donnelly & Co., have volunteered to co-operate with the Juvenile Court by placing their apprenticeship system at the disposal of our boys. We have been unable to take advantage of the offer because most of the boys placed on probation leave school in the fifth, sixth and seventh grades. It is the exceptional boy who has a grammar school diploma. And the boy qualified to take an apprentice course is generally able to find a job that pays two or three dollars a week more, and this increase in income lures the boy to the job that gets him nowhere, in preference to the apprenticeship with a future.

"A few recommendations in connection with the Juvenile Court's endeavor to find positions for its dependent and delinquent boys suggest themselves:

1. "To install two telephones, one to be used exclusively for calling up employers.

2. "To answer all blind 'ads' for boys by dropping a prepared form in the box for the advertiser. This form should briefly explain why the Juvenile Court desires the co-operation of employers in finding jobs for the Court's boys.

3. "Constant advertising by arranging to have each boy present a leaflet to the prospective employer.

4. "An arrangement with the Board of Education to change its telephone system, so that when a police or probation officer sees a 'Boy Wanted' sign, he can walk up to the nearest school and telephone the information to the Juvenile Court's employment head.

5. "The reservation of a room where the boy may read, dress, wash and make himself neat generally. And, following the precedent established by the State of New York in paying the railroad fare when sending an unemployed man to a job at a distance, Cook County should furnish the noon hour meal and the necessary carfare for the boy sent by the Court to and from a prospective employer.

"In closing this letter, I want to draw your attention to the fact that my experience in securing jobs for boys bears out the proposition that, in the main, every job secured by our boys lessens the number of jobs for the army of boys looking for work, thus not affecting the total number of unemployed boys by the above artificial endeavor to find work for boys. This lesson was strongly impressed upon me when at one time I rushed in front of a sign 'Boy Wanted,' for fear that a boy, who appeared as if he were looking for work, would come near, being afraid that if he saw the sign he would walk into the store and compete with my boy for the job. One of the boys understood this so thoroughly that when he saw this sign he tore it off the door and walked up with it under his arm in quest of the job without fear of competition.

"This certainly would tend to lead me to believe that our work is futile. But when we bear in mind that society can better afford to have ten moral boys out of work than an equal number of boys who are delinquent, a more cheerful aspect presents itself."

CONCLUSION AND RECOMMENDATIONS.

The data and the correspondence included in the foregoing pages emphasizes several points for consideration.

We have no adequate knowledge of the youths for whom we seek employment. It is futile to look for good results from the haphazard employment of subnormal youths. Only five of the subnormal cases described in Mr. Levin's letter had had their conditions definitely diagnosed in the Psychopathic Institute. It was left for casual observation, subsequent to admission to probation, to determine the condition of the remainder. This ought not to be so. Before any boy is admitted to probation, he should be detained in a suitable home for a period sufficiently long to enable a corps of well-trained specialists to make a searching analysis of his mental and physical condition, and his vocational aptitudes. That is not a fifteen minute task. When such analysis and recommendations based thereupon are in the hands of a well organized place-finding department of the Juvenile Probation Office, we should be in a position to place the juvenile probationer into better than "blind alley" jobs. At any rate, such jobs should not figure so prominently in the occupation of probationary youths as they do at present, and the hopeless condition set forth in Tables I and III above, showing the inconstancy of employment among the wards of the Juvenile Court, should be relieved. To this end, as suggested in Mr. Levin's letter above, co-operation with employers must be secured, and it must be a part of the business of police officers to assist in keeping the Probation Office informed of opportunities for employment in their respective districts. Plans for the wider social use of the police in this and other respects are being developed in New York City, and, according to report, in Los Angeles, as well.

At the best, however, suitable employment of youths just above fourteen years of age at gainful occupations in inevitably a hard problem by reason of youth, if for no other cause. The problem would be canceled to a great degree by extending the period of compulsory education to sixteen years and ultimately to eighteen years of age; by extending opportunities for public vocational education which, as experience in Chicago already indicates, will keep many a youth in school who would otherwise be out in the streets with no healthful interest to steady his career. This statement is supported by the following extract from the 1914 Year Book of the Lane Technical High School:

"On September 24, 1912, the Prevocational department was organized in the Lane Technical School with an assignment of 152 boys. Each boy had previously taken the required examination—an examination significant only as a factor in determining in what grade he shall be placed. The students who are eligible are boys of fourteen years who have not finished the sixth grade, and the boys of fifteen or more who have not completed the seventh or eighth grades. It does not naturally follow that these boys are mentally defective. The following extracts from the survey of causes show that financial conditions, change of residence, illness, travel, discouragement, or lack of application and interest have interrupted their progress.

" 'I had trouble with a teacher in fourth grade and then all the teachers had it in for me.'

" ' My twin brother is in second year High School and I am only in low seventh. My people say it is because I am the weak twin. But I can do all the athletic games better than my brother. The teachers at Lane say I am all right.'

" 'I had an operation performed and I was sick for a month. Then I went to Europe for two months. When I came back I had to go into a low grade.'

" 'I had to leave school when I was fourteen because my father couldn't get any work. I was out for two years.'

" 'My father is a traveling man and I have lived in thirteen towns. That is one reason why I am behind.'

" 'I was always in trouble with the teachers. My father got tired of coming to school and he was going to put me to work. Then the principal told him of the Lane and I came here. My record has been good for a year and a half.'

" 'I quit school when I was fourteen and in the sixth grade. I couldn't get along with the teachers, and I wasn't interested because we had to wait and listen while a whole class read the same lesson. I used to read library books, and that made the teacher sore. I got a pretty good job near my home. I had to make temperature records in a chemical institute. I got as high as twelve dolars some weeks, but when I was eighteen I couldn't get any more. I heard of the Prevocational department for backward boys and I came. I thought I could get chemistry, but I didn't know enough for that, so I am taking all the academic work and no shop. I double up on each subject. I expect to get through in June, and when I enter High School I shall try and specialize in chemistry.'

" 'I had to quit school when I was twelve. I was large for my age and it was easy to get work. I helped my mother to support five other children until I was eighteen years old. Then my mother let me start out for myself.'

" 'I came to Chicago and I found I was handicapped because I had had so little schooling. One day I got a pretty good night job in a drug store. I got it through the Y. M. C. A. agency. I had plenty of time on my hands then, for I only worked from five to twelve o'clock at night. Every day I had to pass a school and I could see the pupils inside, and I got to thinking that this was my chance to get an education. It took a lot of courage to begin, and I was discouraged, for my size and awkwardness gave a great deal of amusement to the other students. I decided to quit, but the principal urged me to enter the prevocational class at Lane, and I did. I have felt at home from the start, for no one knows what class you belong to and the boys are all large.'

"Restless pupils long for change and release from their confinement, but their protests are classified as defiance and lawlessness rather than an appeal for freedom. The record of one boy who came to Lane was eighty-four weeks and one month in one grade on account of misconduct. He gave no trouble after entering Lane."

It should be optional with the pupil and his advisers to determine at what time, if at all, he should pass from the regular to the vocational school, or vice versa. The school, whether or not it is of vocational nature, ought to be a better character builder than the best form of gainful occupation that the boy of fourteen to sixteen years of age can enter, because of the systematic exercise that it enforces during the habit-building period. The vocational school holds many to a systematic regimen whom the regular school allows to slip away, and the converse is true also. Those habits and ideals of industry, of seriousness, etc., the sum total of which is nearly or quite all of character, are worth more than a knowledge of either Latin or mechanical drawing. It ill becomes the friends of one type of education to cavil at another type provided only that boys and girls are not slipping away from systematic, character building exercise, but are standing by them interestedly and persistently.

But even with the extension of the period of compulsory education, we will still have to struggle with the employment problem, including that of the inconstant employment of youths on probation. The part time night or day school should assist in its solution. It is easily within the range of possibility to compel every youthful probationer at least, to attend a part time school each day or night during the term of his probation. In these schools emphasis should rest upon stimulating talks, demonstrations, etc., relating to the work that engages the youths. One of the immediate aims should be to show each youth what are the outlooks from his particular occupation; what possibilities for reward of diligent service it offers. A youth who enters at the bottom in a large establishment may be bewildered and discouraged because he is blind to the way up.

It is now apparent that the study of the mental and physical condition and vocational aptitudes of prospective juvenile probationers, which has been suggested above, is only a part of a much wider problem. Such examinations for vocational guidance and weeding out the unfit should be prosecuted throughout the school population in an intensive way, and repeatedly. A beginning of such guidance has been made in Chicago. For illustration, we quote here from the 1914 Year Book of the Lane Technical High School:

"The work consists of a study (1) of the boy, his likes, his natural aptitudes, his character, his parents' plan for him, and his teachers' opinions of him. . . . We depend upon the elementary school from which the boy comes to give us facts about the neighborhood life and the home life which the high school cannot readily obtain.

"We make a study (2) of the industrial opportunities open to boys and of the sort of work which should be avoided—the so-called 'blind-alley' trades which have no future—and the work of large initial wage, which is detrimental to his future. This work is done by the study of the industries, by visits to factories, by lectures given by business men, and by the 'part time' scheme—a scheme in which boys work and go to school alternate weeks. Lane at present has the co-operation of several hundred local firms in the Vocational Guidance and Placement Plans. Five firms, the Chicago Telephone Company, the Western Electric Company, the Automatic Electric Company, the Western Union Telegraph Company, and the Commonwealth Edison Company, are co-operating in the part time project.

(3) "The next step in the problem of vocational guidance is that of keeping a sort of guardianship over the boy for a time, and of acting as an intermediary between him and his employer. For this we must depend upon the boy's keeping the department informed of his progress or lack of progress."

This work should ultimately develop into intensive investigation of each pupil by trained specialists comprising a Bureau of Vocational Guidance.

IV

THE DEFENSE OF POOR PERSONS ACCUSED OF CRIME IN CHICAGO

The defense in our criminal courts of a person accused of crime financially unable to employ an attorney, is intrusted to a lawyer appointed by the judge before whom the prisoner is arraigned for indictment. At a recent arraignment of twenty-seven persons, after indictment in the Criminal Court, fourteen asked the court to appoint attorneys to defend them, as they were unable to employ lawyers themselves. Twelve had engaged counsel and one asked that he be allowed to plead his own case. The judge made his selections from the list of lawyers who handed in their business cards to him, thus indicating that they were willing to accept an appointment. The attorneys volunteering for this service are, as a rule, either young, inexperienced lawyers, who wish in this way to gain experience in the handling of criminal cases, or criminal lawyers of only mediocre ability.

The attorney assigned by the court receives no compensation for his services and there is therefore little incentive for him to properly prepare the case for trial. The Bar Association is commenting on the present system and says in its report for 1913, "defense under our present system of appointment is inadequate, particularly because of the lack of preparation. Counsel so appointed usually has no time to make adequate preparation, and possibly has no inclination to do it. Preparation as to the law of the case does not matter so much, but preparation getting facts is extremely important. The court may try to exercise special diligence in securing precise justice for defendants unable to employ counsel, but he is more or less helpless unless all the facts can be presented." In cases where the accused is financially unable to employ counsel the situation is made more serious by the fact that the accused is ordinarily confined in jail, being, of course, unable to furnish bail, and is therefore unable to help in the preparation of his own case. He furthermore has no means to employ any one to gather the necessary facts in the case so that his attorney may present his side of the case to the jury. The public defender of Los Angeles, in speaking of the need of proper preparation for the poor person confined in jail awaiting trial in the criminal courts, said, "probably the class of cases that calls for the service of the public defender most is that class where it is necessary to do some investigating to verify the stories of the accused and to find witnesses in his or their behalf. Often a defendant, upon asserting his innocence, will give the names of witnesses who might testify to facts tending to substantiate his contention. If no means are provided for making investigation, or for examining witnesses for him, and if the attorney appointed by the court and working without pay does not care to do this work, the accused will be left without proper representation and all the facts will not be brought to the attention of the jury." The position of the accused should be contrasted with the facilities furnished the prosecution by the state, or with the protection the accused would have from the law if he were able, as a matter of dollars and cents, to remain out of jail until he was actually found guilty and to provide himself with able counsel so that the facts and law favorable to him could also be put before the jury for consideration.

The practice now in vogue of assigning attorneys to defend prisoners without compensation, also places a premium upon the entry of a plea of guilty by the attorney so as to avoid the trouble and loss of time incidental to the trying of the case. This was illustrated in a case tried in the East Chicago Avenue branch of the Municipal Court, at which the writer was present. A young man on trial for larceny who was without funds asked the judge to appoint an attorney to defend him. The attorney assigned to the case, who happened to be in the courtroom on another matter at the time, consulted with the prisoner for less than five minutes and then asked the court to enter a plea of guilty to a less serious offense which did not require that the case be tried in the Criminal Court. The judge then sentenced the young man to a year in the Bridewell. It was apparent to the on-looker that the attorney had little opportunity to go into the details of such a serious case in such a short time as the attorney devoted to the matter, and the prisoner did not have full opportunity to present his case with proper legal advice. Lawyers acquainted with Criminal Court practice are of the opinion that guilty pleas are often entered after but little attention to the case by the attorneys with the view of getting through with the unprofitable case as soon as possible.

The present method of assigning unpaid counsel to the defense of prisoners, besides frequently resulting in inadequate defense of the accused persons because of the inexperience of counsel, or his inability or disinclination to give the same attention to the case as to that of a private client, frequently gives an unscrupulous attorney an opportunity to exploit the friends or family of the prisoner. Attorneys assigned by the court, after investigating the resources of the prisoner's family or friends, may, if they find it worth while, bring pressure to bear upon them so as to secure a fee for their legal services. This is frequently done by continuing the case at the request of the attorney on the plea that he is gathering evidence for the defense and the accused is kept in jail awaiting trial an unusually long period until the fee is forthcoming from the prisoner's friends.

The need for an improvement in the practice of the defense of persons accused of crime is not measured only by the number of cases in which the judge assigns counsel because the prisoner has prior to his arraignment been unable to employ one. Unscrupulous lawyers, either through arrangements with professional bondsmen, or by taking advantage of the serious position in which a poor person accused of crime and ignorant of the workings of our judicial machinery finds himself, have taken advantage of the situation to exploit the prisoners or their friends. The prisoner is frequently forced to pay fees incommensurate with the services rendered and his family is put to very heavy expense, which in many cases proves a serious financial burden, in order to provide adequate defense. Instances are on record where attorneys of this kind have forgotten their clients after the initial fee has been paid, and have paid no further attention to the case, or where they have even suggested the plea of guilty so that their work in connection with the case could be reduced to a minimum.

A number of cases illustrating this system have been collected by social workers of the County Bureau of Public Welfare detailed at the County Jail and are here presented:

John Schmidt, 17 years old, 1543 Clifton Park Avenue, was held to the grand jury on a charge of burglary, after a preliminary hearing in the Boys' Court, August 24, 1914.

His father, Charles Schmidt, stated that Attorney C. D. Bradley came to him at the county jail and offered to take John's case. Mr. Schmidt paid him $25.00, taking a receipt which he still holds. Later he went to Mr. Bradley's rooms as given on his letterhead, 1214 Ashland Block, but was informed that Mr. Bradley was not located there. I telephoned Central 776 (telephone number given on Mr. Bradley's letterhead) and found it to be the firm of Burres & Wamsley. They informed me that Mr. Bradley had desk room in their office two years ago and a few times since for a day or two, but that he has not any right to use their rooms and telephone number on his letterhead. They have had frequent complaints of him and say he is not to be trusted; that he hangs around Criminal Court most of the time. I have never been able to reach Mr. Bradley at his home telephone, Rogers Park 5273.

Julius Kerhove, cell 625, county jail, told his attorney that he paid an Italian bondsman, 1837 W. Van Buren Street, to secure his release on bond. When he was indicted, his bond was raised and he paid him $50 more; yet a very short time later his bondsman surrendered him and he is now in jail.

Wm. E. Buckney, 224 N. California Avenue, an attorney, having secured as a client the boy referred to above, suggested to his widowed mother, 62 years of age, living at 146 N. Hermitage Avenue, that she sell her furniture in order to pay him. To this the boy objected and took his case from Mr. Buckner's hands.

Mr. Buckner was counsel for three boys implicated in a robbery—Walter Gulczynski, 1623 W. 17th Street, whose parents live at 2846 S. Throop Street; John Wass, 2815 S. Kolin Avenue, and A. Guzynski, boy whose address I cannot find. He secured about $50 in all and because he could not get more, quietly told the judge that they were a "bad lot."

These lawyers and bondsmen also take their places in the entrance to the jail; as the relatives and friends of the prisoners come in they engage in conversation with them. By appearing to show interest and sympathy for the ones in trouble they get at the finanacial situation in the family, which aids them in deciding whether the case is worth going after or not.

It is obvious that the practice of defending poor persons by unpaid counsel has not resulted in giving them an adequate defense, which they are supposed to be given under the law. It is to be expcted that a system which penalizes a conscientious attorney who accepts an appointment and which offers no incentive to the attorney handling the case for the faithful performance of his duty would necessarily result in placing a handicap upon the poor person in securing justice in the Criminal Court. Certain measures have been taken under private auspices to meet this situation in this city. The Bar Association sent out a circular in 1913 to those of its members who were acquainted with criminal practice asking them to volunteer to act as counsel when a person too poor to pay an attorney was arraigned in court. About 35 members of the association responded to this letter and volunteered their services in one or more cases and the chief justice of the Criminal Court made assignments off this list until it was exhausted. The results obtained under this system were very much better than under the usual plan of assigning an attorney in the ordinary manner, but the success of this plan depends solely upon the co-operation of public-spirited lawyers who are willing to give their time and ability to this kind of charitable service.

The Legal Aid Society has also done some work along this line. It is represented by an attorney stationed in the Boys' Court, who presents the law and facts from the point of view of the defendant and advises others coming into this court as to their legal rights and co-operates with the court and the probation officer in the handling of cases. During the period this attorney has been in the Boys' Court, approximately 75 boys have been defended by the attorney each month. When cases are transferred from this court to the Criminal Court the representative of the Legal Aid Society makes arrangements for an attorney, if that is necessary under the circumstances. I have been informed, also, that the facts gathered by this lawyer in the preliminary investigation of the case have in many instances been helpful to the judge in settling the case and to the other administrative agencies, such as probation officers, in following up the case after decision has been made. The experience in this court has been that preliminary investigations of this kind, conducted so as to give a fair trial to the defendant, are very helpful to the court and to the probation officers in making proper disposal of the case.

The County of Los Angeles has, under new charter of 1913, put on efficient basis the defense of poor persons in the courts though the creation of the position of Public Defender. Under the provisions of the Los Angeles law the public defender represents every person accused of any offense in the Superior Court (analagous to our Criminal Court) who is financially unable to employ an attorney, upon the request of the prisoner or upon order of the court; prosecutes appeals in proper cases; and, on the civil side, handles cases, where the claim does not exceed $100, for poor people. In the civil cases the office of the public defender may represent either the plaintiff or the defendant. No provision is made, under the present law, for the appearance of the public defender in the police courts. A volunteer defender is now at work in the police courts and an amendment extending the jurisdiction of the defender to these courts is recommended by those who are acquainted with the work of the public defender in the higher courts. The public defender and his deputies are appointed from a civil service eligible list after examination.

Walton J. Woods, Public Defender of Los Angeles, says in regard to the work of his office:

"In Los Angeles the district attorney and the public defender are working harmoniously together. We are doing what the district attorney tried to do in many cases but which, on account of conditions which could not be overcome, he was unable to do. We are daily advising the accused of their rights. We are informing them of the law covering the crime of which they may be charged. We are listening to their side of the story and are bringing out whatever points there may be in favor of the defendants, at the same time doing nothing to hamper or delay the administration of justice. Many of our clients come by recommendation from the office of the district attorney, others come from officials at the county jail and others at the request of the judges.

"I call attention to the statement in the letter of Judge Willis that our office 'has been a great saving to the county in the matter of expense.' This is a very remarkable statement, yet I believe it is absolutely true. We have had a number of cases dismissed by talking frankly with the district attorney and showing him that a trial would result in acquital. He has, in such cases, dismissed the prosecution. In other cases we have been able to avoid delays, and by having attorneys who are familiar with criminal procedure in court at all times, the court has been able to dispatch business much more rapidly. In the matter of expense the same condition to some extent prevails in the civil department of our work, where we relieve the courts of many congested cases by adjusting them without filing suit."

The appointment of a public defender in Chicago, with powers and duties in the Criminal Courts, similar to the public defender of Los Angeles, has been endorsed by Chief Justice Kersten of the Criminal Court, Chief Justice Olson of the Municipal Court, Dean Wigmore and others, to whom the question has been presented. It would be the function of the public defender to defend and give legal advice and assistance to all persons who are held to the Criminal Court and who are unable to hire counsel. The existence of such official in Chicago would provide an efficient and adequate means of defense for indigent persons accused of crime and should lessen considerably the "shyster" lawyer business in connection with our Criminal Courts. Some provision should also be made to assist prisoners in the police courts in bringing out their side of the story to the court. The procedure in the Municipal Courts is not as technical as in the Criminal Court and the need of a legal adviser for defendants is not so apparent. If lawyers are not assigned to these courts, arrangements should be made for the appointment of investigators who can gather the facts in regard to cases so that substantial justice for the defendant may be secured. The precedent established at Los Angeles in selecting the public defender and his assistants on a civil service basis should be followed.

V

GENERAL SUMMARY OF CONCLUSIONS REACHED IN THE COURSE OF THIS INVESTIGATION

1. Of 61 women offenders at the House of Correction, 50% suffer from such profound nervous disturbances that prolonged treatment is necessary to place them in such a physical condition that there can be reasonable certainty of their adjusting themselves to normal conditions of life.

Of these 61, 45 suffer from venereal infection.

The mental condition of these 61 prisoners and of 65 others, a total of 126, is of the moron class.

One-half of this total group has been committed either to the House of Correction, or to other similar institutions elsewhere, more than twice.

The mental condition of the entire group is such as to make it probable that after they shall have served their short terms here they will still be sources of danger to the health of the community.

Those who suffer from venereal infection, 45, will be a danger to public health on their release.

2. Of 132 men patients in the House of Correction who were examined by the medical staff and found insane between January 1 and August 20, 1914, 56 were committed by process of jury to institutions for the insane. The remaining 76 were held at the House of Correction to serve out the terms for which they were committed because it was deemed by the medical staff impossible to get a lay jury to commit them to an insane asylum; this for the reason that to the inexpert each one of the 76 would in all probability appear sane.

These 132 were not found on a thorough investigation of the entire population of the House of Correction. They are only among those who because of their symptoms were brought to the attention of the staff. The probability is (judging by experience elsewhere) that all those who have been committed four or more times are suffering from mental alienation. If this is true we may have 1,000 or more such persons in the House of Correction. Judging again by experience both here and elsewhere we are preventing these people from committing offenses only while they are imprisoned.

3. The letter of the adult probation law utterly fails to establish a satisfactory criterion of fitness for probation. Seventeen cases are presented of persons who have made good during a period of at least 14 months since the date of probation. Yet, under the probation law as it stands, strictly applied, they should have been denied probation. Thirteen cases are presented of persons who have in the past been admitted to probation and failed. At the time at which the investigation was made they were in the House of Correction. If, at the time of probation their mental and physical condition approximated present conditions, an adequate investigation should have excluded them from probation and the city should have been spared the annoyance and cost of a repeated offense, arrest, and trial.

Twenty probation officers are a wholly inadequate force to handle 4,696 probationers. The adult probation office is doing the best it can in the circumstances.

4. Of 63 boys examined in the John Worthy School 26% are certainly suffering from syphilitic infection. Thirteen per cent are doubtful cases.

The Binet test on 34 of these boys shows that 14 are retarded 4 years or more.

As to the nervous condition, 48 suffer from nystagmus; 15 from incoordination; in 7 the reflexes are changed.

All these conditions mean that the individuals to whom the above statements apply cannot be put into a normal condition without prolonged and special attention. They will be a menace to safety and health as long as these conditions prevail.

Farm colonies could be provided and maintained for such cases as these, for the insane and others described in Section A and B, Part I, and for those who but for the condition of their mind and body should be admitted to probation. The construction of buildings and equipment—provided the inmates are employed at building, etc., should not cost at a higher rate per population than the construction and equipment at the District of Columbia Workhouse at Occaquan, Va. That institution accommodates an average daily population of 716 prisoners and officers and the estimated value of buildings and equipment is $657,847.00. The net cost of maintenance for the population named above is $0.489 a day. This can be reduced as the farm increases in productiveness.

5. Of 55 mentally normal juvenile delinquents who passed through the Juvenile Court of Cook County in the years 1910, 1911, 1912, 14.5% have made no improvement; 9.1% have deteriorated; 29.1% have been lost. In 33 of these cases the Juvenile Psychopathic Institute made a recommendation as to treatment or disposition by the court, and the recommendation was followed. Of these, 55.9% have made good; 17.6% have made no progress; 8.5% have deteriorated; 17.2% have been lost. In 10 cases the recommendations made by the Institute was not followed. Of these 30% have made good; 20% have made no progress, and 50% have been lost. As to the remainder, in which no recommendation was made, 33% have made good; 11.1% have made no progress; 22.2% have deteriorated; 33⅓% have been lost. The above review shows an advantage on the side of following the recommendation of the Institute.

Of 61 subnormal cases 35 were sent to the Lincoln State School and Colony for the Feeble-minded on recommendation of the Institute. Of these but 15 are still there; 4 ran away; 15 have been released on requests of parents and other relatives, and 2 have been discharged.

Of those who have been released from Lincoln on request of parents and other relatives (15) 20% are making good; 40% are at a standstill; 20% have deteriorated, and 20% have been lost. Two of the three who are lost were released at the request of other relatives than parents.

Of 26 subnormal cases disposed of otherwise than by a Lincoln commitment, only 7.7% are making good; 42.3% have made no progress; 19.2% have deteriorated, and 23% have been lost. Two of the 26 have died. In 8 of these cases Lincoln had been recommended but the recommendation was not followed. Each of these eight has an exceptionally bad history subsequent to the Juvenile Court record—with one possible exception.

The general outcome of this study is favorable to (a) securing and following the recommendations of the Juvenile Psychopathic Institute, at any rate in doubtful cases; (b) denying to parents and friends jurisdiction over children who have been sent to Lincoln or with respect to whom commitment to Lincoln has been advised by the Institute.

6. Chicago boys in the St. Charles Reformatory—at least 29 of them of whom a more particular study was made—have a history in the records of the Child Study Bureau of the Department of Education, the Psychopathic Institute, the Probation Office, the Parental School, and in St. Charles that emphasizes their abnormality and the need of a study of paroled boys who have been sent out from St. Charles. About 500 Chicago boys are paroled from St. Charles and there is but one Parole Officer. No one can give a satisfactory history of these boys subsequent to parole.

Out of a total of 82 of these St. Charles Boys, including the 29 to which extended reference has been made, 42 who have a record in the Psychopathic Institute but have not been in the Parental School, and 11 others who have a record in the Child Study Department but have not been in Parental School, 54 are unstable mentally or physically or in both respects. These boys, if our conclusion 4 above is correct, are liable to failure in social adjustment as long as the unfavorable conditions persist.

7. A study of 388 boys on probation on September 1, 1914, and during 4 months preceding shows that 134 of them worked less than one-half time; that they were inconstant in employment; that the feeble-minded within this group are without occupation.

Further data has been presented that is suggestive of the steadying influence of a vocational element in education upon a certain type of boy.

GENERAL SUMMARY OF RECOMMENDATIONS

1. That the City of Chicago and the State of Illinois establish farm colonies (a) for adult prisoners; especially for several times repeated offenders who are found to be victims of feeble-mindedness or mental alienation, or of infections that make them sources of danger to the health or safety of the

community, or of any other disorder that, in the judgment of psycho-pathological and medical experts, makes it impossible for them to adjust themselves
to the conditions of normal life; (b) for those applicants for the freedom
of adult probation who are declared by psycho-pathological and medical experts to be suffering from feeble-mindedness, or mental alienation, or infections that make them sources of danger to the health or safety of the community, or of any other disorder that, in the judgment of psycho-pathological
and medical experts, makes it impossible for them to adjust themselves to
the conditions of normal life.

2. That the state law relating to the transfer to an insane asylum of
prisoners found to be insane in the state penitentiaries on the recommendation
of the prison physician, be so amended as to apply to the medical staff in such
institutions as the Chicago House of Correction and to the Psychopathic
Laboratory, or that new legislation be enacted to that effect.

3. That the adult probation law be so amended as to make it obligatory
upon the court to (a) secure from probation officers a written report on a
complete investigation of each applicant for probation, touching the question
of previous convictions, arrests, habits of life, and family history. (b) Secure
from the Psychopathic Laboratory a complete written report on his mental
and physical condition. (c) File these reports with other proceedings in each
case. (d) Make these reports decisive in determining the question of probation within the limits of the law. (e) Forbid probation in cases of feeble-
mindedness, insanity, dangerous infections, and such unstable conditions as
render the applicant, in the judgment of experts, unable to adjust himself to
normal conditions. (f) Commit all such persons, on the recommendation of
the probation officers and the Psychopathic Laboratory, to a farm colony
or hospital "until cured." (g) Amend the law by removing the upper limit
to the number of probation officers. (h) Make only murderers and traitors
exempt from probation. (i) Create a non-partisan State Probation Commission with authority to fix the qualifications of probation officers, both adult
and juvenile, and to prepare a certified list from which the court shall make
appointments.

4. That the city and state provide farm colonies at least 60 miles from
Chicago for juvenile delinquents. These may be in conjunction with the institution recommended above for adults. The city colony should be under the
management of a board appointed by the Mayor with the approval of the
Superintendent of Schools. They should afford opportunities for agricultural
pursuits and shop work, in addition to formal education, and the construction
and repair work, should be, as far as possible, conducted by the boys. Hospital treatment should be provided and release on parole or otherwise should
be denied on the certicate of the medical staff that one for whom parole is
considered is in such condition that he would be a menace to public safety
or health or both.

5. That the state law relating to the commitment of feeble-minded to
the Lincoln State Farm and Colony be so amended as to (a) make commitment and release independent of the wishes of parents and guardians, but dependent solely upon the Juvenile Court and its branches. (b) Make possible
commitment of dangerously infected youths "until cured."

6. (a) That the city enlarge its facilities for vocational education and
vocational guidance as a means of tying our youth to an occupation. (b)
That the age limit for compulsory education be raised to 16 years. (c) That
the system of part time night schools in the city be extended and that the
Juvenile Court law be amended to require each juvenile probationer to attend
such a school during the period of probation.

7. Finally we recommend that investigations, of which the foregoing is
only the beginning, be provided for the city, and the attention be directed
particularly to (a) an examination of 1,200 or more prisoners in the House of
Correction who have been committed in this city o relsewhere more than three
times. (b) A search for the history of 500 or more Chicago boys during the
period subsequent to the date of their parole from St. Charles. (e) A search
for the history of Chicago men and women during the period subsequent to
the date of their parole from the penal institutions of the state.

Description and Analysis
of Criminal Conditions

by

MORGAN L. DAVIES, Attorney for Committee

and

FLETCHER DOBYNS, Associate Counsel for Committee

I

REPORT OF ATTORNEY FOR COMMITTEE
BY MORGAN L. DAVIES

To the Honorable Charles E. Merriam,
  Chairman, Committee on Crime,
    Of the City Council, Chicago, Illinois.

I have the honor to submit herewith the findings and recommendations which seem to me to follow from the testimony heard before the Committee.

Before enumerating them, a word should be said about the first work undertaken in this investigation.

Immediately after the organization of your Committee in June, 1914, and the appropriation of the sum of $10,000 for carrying on the work, a number of discussions were held as to the best means of approaching this enormous subject matter in a city as large as Chicago. It was decided that it was necessary for the Committee to know the exact amount of crime in this community as a foundation for its work.

Miss Abbott, an expert statistician, was employed by the Committee and presented a very complete report on the statistics available with reference to the various crimes committed and the apprehension, prosecution, and subsequent treatment of offenders.

The subject of crime was then considered from three broad, general viewpoints. First, the nature and causes of crime in Chicago. Second, the apprehension of the offender, and its relation to the police department. Third, the prosecution of the offender with relation to the courts, the city, and the state's attorney.

The first subject matter, namely, the nature and causes of crime in Chicago, was studied, and investigated at length by an expert criminologist, Robert H. Gault. Some eight judges, including the chief justice of the Municipal Court, appeared before the Committee and discussed this subject matter from the viewpoint of the judge having to deal with the offenders brought before the court. Dr. Hickson, of the Psychopathic Laboratory of the Municipal Court also presented to the Committee the subject matter of the offenders with relation to their mental capacity and the results of the work done in the Municipal Court along those lines.

With reference to the second subject matter, the responsibilities and functions of the police department, a rather extended investigation was made. In the early part of the work it was learned that there was some reason to believe that members of the detective bureau of the police department of the City of Chicago were working in active partnership and collusion with professional criminals. It was then thought nothing could be accomplished with reference to additional aid to the police department, and that increased efficiency on the part of the police department was impossible, if the integrity of any portion of its members were in question.

The subject matter of inefficiency, judicial delays, complicated machinery for dealing with crime and the criminal, civic movements for the betterment of conditions which tend to produce crime, all become of secondary importance when the instrument which the public has for dealing with crime and criminals is questioned as to its integrity.

The police officer is the representative of government who comes in contact with the individual citizen most intimately, and the character of that representative is the criterion by which the citizen judges his government. Consequently corruption on the part of a police official poisons at the foundation all efforts to deal with crime and criminal conditions.

Your Committee, therefore, determined at once to go to the bottom of this subject, and, by way of gossip and information received indirectly from professional criminals, the investigators were lead to believe that such a condition did exist in the Detective Bureau of the Police Department of the City of Chicago. It was apparent that such corruption was of a long existing nature and that many important individuals were involved in it. It was also apparent that this system of collusion was so long entrenched, and its powers were so great, the charge was appalling, that the committee could not afford to have testimony presented to it, making this charge based on indirect statements of professional criminals or other sources of information of a similar character. It was deemed essential that direct, real and undisputable evidence must be had of such collusion if the same existed. It is not easy to realize at this time, when the whole subject matter has been brought out and proved, with subsequent indictment of a number of these individuals by the state's attorney of Cook County, coupled also with the fact that a shooting affair occurred on a prominent street in the city of Chicago, which was alleged to have arisen from a possible disclosure, the enormous difficulties that confronted the task of showing up and proving this collusion.

It was learned that a reporter for one of Chicago's leading newspapers had successfully posed as a professional criminal and mingled with the professional criminals of Chicago at some time prior to the formation of this committee for the purpose of securing information as to the criminal conditions in Chicago. Immediately this reporter was sent for. He explained at length the manner in which he had posed as a pickpocket, lived with certain groups of them, how he had learned their language and all their plans and the nature of their operation. The Committee secured the services of two young men as investigators, and with this reporter, they laid and carried out the plans which resulted in the complete and undeniable disclosure of the criminal collusion existing between certain members of the detective bureau and the criminal underworld. The stories of these three courageous and efficient young men, setting forth the manner in which they went to one of the railroad stations of Chicago acting the part of confidence men, and then notified members of the detective bureau by indirect means of their presence there, and their subsequent arrest, whereby they were put through the detective bureau "mill," graduating them into the class of professional criminals with a record, by means of which they were able to come in contact with the professional criminal system of Chicago, are set forth at length in the testimony of the Committee and need not be gone into further here.

It seems to me, however, that before leaving this subject the committee ought to express in some way its appreciation of the keen, courageous and splendid manner in which these three men carried out the plan of the investigation. In a manner their work made possible a great many other things that this committee has sought to accomplish, and too much credit for the breaking up of this system of criminal collusion cannot be given to these men.

Attached hereto is an excerpt from Captain Meagher's testimony which gives a complete picture of criminal environment to which attention ought to be called.

Mr. Davies: "How about Butch Carroll?"
Captain Meagher: "Butch Carroll had a saloon on Madison street."
Mr. Davies: "Did he ever have one at 941 W. Washington street."
Captain Meagher: "Not that I remember of."
Mr. Davies: "Butch Carroll?"
Captain Meagher: "Yes, and George C.—"
Mr. Davies: "One of the Carroll's is serving time?"
Captain Meagher: "Yes."
Mr. Davies: "Which one?"
Captain Meagher: "A fellow that we call John Bunker. He is a pickpocket."
Mr. Davies: "Butch Carroll, has he ever had a place at 941 W. Washington street?"
Captain Meagher: "He came there from his present place?"
Mr. Davies: "Do you know anything about that saloon at 948 Madison street?"
Captain Meagher: "Yes."
Mr. Davies: "Do you know what Carroll's real name is?"
Captain Meagher: "Yes, Wainwright."
Mr. Davies: "He is from Cincinnati, isn't he?"
Captain Meagher: "Said to be."
Mr. Davies: "Butch Carroll had a place at 947 W. Madison street, didn't he?"
Captain Meagher: "Yes."
Mr. Davies: "How long ago was that license revoked?"
Captain Meagher: "Two years ago."

Mr. Davies: "Do you know whether Butch has any record or not?"

Captain Meagher: "I think it would be a safe thing to say yes."

Mr. Davies: "He has a saloon at the present time, han't he, Captain?"

Captain Meagher: "I have heard he has, but he is not in my district, and I don't know whether he has any license there or not."

Mr. Davies: "He is operating over there in another district, isn't he?"

Captain Meagher: "Yes."

Mr. Davies: "Where is that place?"

Captain Meagher: "I would call it Madison and Elizabeth streets, I think."

Mr. Davies: "Where is Butch Carroll's saloon now, or the one you think he has an interest in?"

Captain Meagher: "I think it is Elizabeth and Madison streets. You might describe it at the northwest corner."

Mr. Davies: "The northwest corner of Elizabeth and Madison?"

Captain Meagher: "Yes."

Mr. Davies: "What kind of a building is it at 948 Madison street?'

Captain Meagher: "That is a three-story building."

Mr. Davies: "Butch Carroll's saloon is down stairs?"

Captain Meagher: "Yes."

Mr. Davies: "There are two flats upstairs?"

Captain Meagher: "Yes."

Mr. Davies: "How many rooms in these flats—how large flats were they?"

Captain Meagher: "I never was inside, but I think I am safe in saying— I have a book at home with a collection of all the rooming houses in, and the number of rooms, and the persons there, etc."

Mr. Davies: "How large would you say they were?"

Captain Meagher: "If there are two flats, it would be 20 rooms, halls and all."

Mr. Davies: "I have a list here labeled 'Registered voters, 18th Ward, Precinct 10,' dated August 14, 1914, and under the registered voters from 948 W. Madison street, I find the folowing names—about 25 in number. I would like to have you examine that."

Captain Meagher: "I have seen that list before. I have a list of every voter in the 18th Ward, and also the 19th."

Mr. Davies: "You know of this list?'

Captain Meagher: "Yes, sir, I know of the list, and I have seen the names. I only know them by name."

Mr. Davies: "Now, under 948 the first name is Frank Weaver."

Captain Meagher: "Yes, sir."

Mr. Davies: "Do you know who he is?"

Captain Meagher: "Yes, sir."

Mr. Davies: "Has he a record?"

Captain Meagher: "I think he has."

Mr. Davies: "Do you know whether or not he has served time?"

Captain Meagher: "I think he has."

Mr. Davies: "What was he sentenced for, Captain, do you know?"

Captain Meagher: "I don't know, but I feel that Weaver has a criminal record. I have had him arrested several times."

Mr. Davies: "He was arrested two or three months ago for holding up a man, wasn't he, in connection with another man by the name of Bisman?"

Captain Meagher: "Yes."

Mr. Davies: "They held up a saloon at Aberdeen street?"

Captain Meagher: "Yes, sir."

Mr. Davies: Now, in this list of names at 948 W. Madison street, is the name of Margaret Lane. Do you know of any complaint ever being brought against her?"

Captain Meagher: "She may be in that name or some other name for having maintained a house of prostitution. I presume she is one of the housekeepers there. That is a house of assignation, a house of prostitution, or was at one time. It is not above suspicion today."

Mr. Davies: "How about James Tyler?"

Captain Meagher: "I don't know him."

Mr. Davies: "How about Anna M. Shields?"

Captain Meagher: "Does it was man or woman?"

Mr. Davies: "Yes, Miss Anna Shields."

Captain Meagher: "I think she is one of the women there, one of the housekeepers there, too."

Mr. Davies: "She is registered from that number."

Captain Meagher: "I don't know her."

Mr. Davies: "How about Charles Kennedy, do you know him?"

Captain Meagher: "No."

Mr. Davies: "How about Jeffries?"

Captain Meagher: "He is an ex-convict."

Mr. Davies: "He has a record?"

Captain Meagher: "Yes."

Mr. Davies: "Do you know what he was sent in for?"

Captain Meagher: "I think he was brought back here from Leavenworth, Kan., the last time."

Mr. Davies: "What for?"

Captain Meagher: "I don't know what the United States had him out there for."

Mr. Davies: "This is dated August 9, 1914. Do you know whether Jeffries is over there now or not?"

Captain Meagher: "No, I don't know."

Mr. Davies: "Do you know about Thomas Gleason, or James Gleason?"

Captain Meagher: "I don't know him."

Mr. Davies: "How about Thomas Gannon?"

Captain Meagher: "I don't know him."

Mr. Davies: "How about Charles Gray?"

Captain Meagher: "I don't know him."

Mr. Davies: "How about John Edwards?"

Captain Meagher: "I don't know Edwards."

Mr. Davies: "Do you know whether he tends bar for Bruder or not?"

Captain Meagher: "I don't know. Is Bruder keeping a saloon?"

Mr. Davies: "I think he has a place."

Captain Meagher: "No, he has a club at 1044 W. Madison street. I don't know whether you would call him a bartender or not."

Mr. Davies: "You don't know whether Edwards works for him or not?"

Captain Meagher: "No, sir."

Mr. Davies: "At that same number?"

Captain Meagher: "I don't know."

Mr. Davies: "How about W. J. Havirt?"

Captain Meagher: "I don't know him."

Mr. Davies: "How about Dan Gibbons?"

Captain Meagher: "I don't know him."

Mr. Davies: "How about Fred J. Rooney?"

Captain Meagher: "He is an ex-convict. I know I had him in some time ago."

Mr. Davies: "What was he in for?"

Captain Meagher: "I think it was a burglary."

Mr. Davies: "Burglary?"

Captain Meagher: "Yes."

Mr. Davies: "How about James Duffy?"

Captain Meagher: "I don't know Duffy personally."

Mr. Davies: "How about James Smiley, do you know him?"

Captain Meagher: "No, I don't think I know Smiley."

Mr. Davies: "How about F. J. Mitchell?"

Captain Meagher: "I don't know him."

Mr. Davies: "How about Joseph Milton?"

Captain Meagher: "I don't know him."

Mr. Davies: "George Carroll—that would be the brother of Butch Carroll. What is Butch Carroll's right name?"

Captain Meagher: "Butch is John."

Mr. Davies: "Butch is John. He is registered from the same place?"

Captain Meagher: "Yes."

Mr. Davies: "Now, is George Carroll, the fellow that is now named Joe Bunker, the pickpocket? Do you know him?"

Captain Meagher: "No, Joe is Bunker."

Mr. Davies: "His name is now Bunker?"

Captain Meagher: "Yes, Joe Bunker, yes."

Mr. Davies: "And George Carrol?"

Captain Meagher: "He has another brother."

Mr. Davies: "Their original name is Wainwright?"

Captain Meagher: "According to the criminal records."

Mr. Davies: "What is your impression about George and John, have they got any records?"

Captain Meagher: "I don't think George has."

Mr. Davies: "And about John?"

Captain Meagher: "I think he has, yes."

Mr. Davies: "And how about Harry Adams?"

Captain Meagher: "He is an ex-convict, I think we call him 'Red Adams.'"

Mr. Davies: "What was he up for?"

Captain Meagher: "Pickpocket."

Mr. Davies: "Now, 'Red Adams,' Harry Adams, I didn't quite get what he was up for?"

Captain Meagher: "He was an ex-convict."

Mr. Davies: "And Brush?"

Captain Meagher: "Brush, I don't know him."

Mr. Davies: So, out of this number, 948 Madison, there are twenty-five in the list of people who registered from there, and there are eight, I think you have given eight, at any rate the record will show, that have records?"

Captain Meagher: "Yes, sir. But pardon me, I think you will find that they don't live there."

Mr. Davies: "I will agree with you on that, but they vote from there, don't they?"

Captain Meagher: "Yes, but that is up to the election commissioners to look after the registration."

Mr. Davies: "But, according to this list here they have a right to vote from there?"

Captain Meagher: "I am not clear on the election law, as to the residenceship and so on that was. I have got something else to do you know."

Mr. Davies: "They are on the list. Are any of them around there now, Captain?"

Captain Meagher: "They are liable to be seen on the street at any time and in any place in the city of Chicago. If you would put races out in Elgin why, tomorrow I would not be a bit surprised to see them out in Elgin. If you would put races out in Belvidere, why, they would be out in Belvidere."

Mr. Davies: "Do you know any of them who are working, except at their profession?"

Captain Meagher: "No, I don't know of any of them who have lawful employment."

Mr. Davies: "Who runs that building, Butch Carroll, doesn't he?"

Captain Meagher: "Oh, yes.'

Mr. Davies: "Do you know who leases the whole building?"

Captain Meagher: "I did at the time of this investigation, but previous to the time of the revocation of the license, I think the book shows all of the houses and all the leases in the past, and who the owner was, and every one of them knew that when we caught them we sent in the records to the chief of police and he looks up the owners and agents and serves a notice on them."

Mr. Davies: "Did you examine this particular precinct list before with reference to the people who registered from that place?"

Captain Meagher: "It is the only one I recall in that precinct."

Mr. Davies: "I mean have you seen this precinct list before?"

Captain Meagher: "I have seen that, yes."

Mr. Davies: "Did you look at it to see who was registered from 948 Madison street?'

Captain Meagher: "We discussed it in the station."

Mr. Davies: "All of it?"

Captain Meagher: "Yes, sir. I keep a list of every person registered."

Mr. Davies: "Would you say that this was the worst case that there ever was in your district?"

Captain Meagher: "Yes, I would emphatically say I don't know of another place where they would permit it. If those people are legal residents, which I claim they are not, they are not living there the same as I am on Turner Avenue."

Mr. Davies: "Did you arrest any of these fellows under the vagrancy section, Captain?"

Captain Meagher: "Yes, sir."

Mr. Davies: "Who, if any of them, have been arrested under this particular section?"

Captain Meagher: "We had Adams in court five or six months ago."

Mr. Davies: "You would have to keep arresting them every day, wouldn't you?"

Captain Meagher: (continuing) "I think he was in on what you would call a regular vagrancy charge. I think Red Adams had a sentence here in court to get out of town within two weeks."

Mr. Davies: "And those fellows are passing in and out all of the time. They would have to spend all of the time in jail, because they don't work at anything else?"

Captain Meagher: "They don't seem to spend very much time in jail."

Mr. Davies: "When one of them gets arrested, the rest of them get busy, don't they?"

Captain Meagher: "I don't think the wagon hardly arrives with one of them before he gets away. The wagon don't hardly arrive at the station before some one is there to get him out."

Mr. Davies: "Some lawyer?"

Captain Meagher: "It is hard to judge."

FINDINGS AND RECOMMENDATIONS.

Suggested by Mr. Davies for consideration of the Committee*

The pressure of economic conditions has an enormous influence in producing crime. Unsanitary housing and working conditions, unemployment, wages inadequate to maintain a human standard of living inevitably lead to the crushed or distorted bodies and minds from which the army of crime is recruited. The crime problem is not merely a question of police and courts. It leads to the broader problems of public sanitation, education, home care, the living wage and the attainments of industrial democracy.

These, however, are indirect causes and the Committee has confined itself to direct causes, and makes, with respect thereto, the following findings and recommendations:

A. The Committee finds that the drug traffic directly increases crime. That 75% of the drug users are of the criminal classes; that if the drug could not be secured in Chicago, they would leave. That users of drugs become physically incapable of earning their livelihood at any occupation requiring sustained effort. Frequently a resort to crime is the result.

The Committee recommends an active co-operation between the police department and Federal Government; that there be an interchange of all information; that a special city attorney be assigned to co-operate with the office of the United States Attorney to break up this traffic.

That a hospital be provided for the treatment of prisoners addicted to the use of drugs.

B. The Committee finds that there are a large number of saloons and poolrooms where criminals hang out, plan their operations and secure new recruits. The Committee found as many as 100 of such places and that of these, twenty (20) are owned or operated by ex-convicts.

The Committee believes that the retail liquor dealers of Chicago are opposed to the issuance of licenses to such places, and are best equipped to deal with this evil. It is, therefore, recommended that no license shall be issued unless the same is first recommended by a duly authorized and constituted committee, representing the retail liquor dealers of Chicago, and that all revocations of licenses be made on the recommendation of such a committee.

C. There was much discussion concerning the psychopathic examinations of juvenile offenders, and the advisability of a farm colony for the segregation of subnormals, or so-called morons. The Committee believes that this subject matter, so far as Chicago is concerned, is in an experimental stage. That such a treatment might furnish another loophole of escape from responsibility on the part of the officers, for their acts. The Committee, therefore, make no recommendation on this subject matter.

---

*See Pages 9 to 17 for findings and recommendations made by the Committee. A tentative summary covering certain of these points had previously been submitted by Ald. Merriam.

D. The Committee has no testimony before it which would reflect any discredit on the great body of men and officers who compose the Police Department of Chicago; the Committee has no testimony before it which gives the comparative efficiency of the police department in Chicago with that of other large cities. There is no evidence before this Committee with reference to the relative efficiency of the police now as compared to any other time.

There has, however, been presented to this Committee, testimony to show that certain members of the Detective Bureau were in active collusion with various classes of criminals and that in some cases, not only were the proceeds of crime divided, but criminals were forced to ply their occupations, that the corrupt officials might have the plunder. There is every reason to believe that this system has been in existence for a great many years. As a result of the disclosure of this Committee and the indictments by the state's attorney, this system has been greatly checked and large numbers of professional criminals have left Chicago. Only constant vigilance will prevent the return of this evil.

Police collusion with crime is a crime in itself and the power of responsibility to deal with it rests entirely on the state's attorney. The McCann case in Chicago, the Becker case in New York City, and the recent indictments here show the manner this must be dealt with.

E. The corrupt officials heretofore referred to, maintained their power over the criminal world by the method of arresting the criminal, who refused to obey orders or divide the plunder, and holding them in custody under shocking physical surroundings and refusing to bring them before a court for the fixing of bonds and admission to bail. This is a violation of the law of Illinois, but there is no punishment prescribed for it. The Committee recommended that the unwarranted holding of a prisoner be made a crime by the laws of Illinois.

F. The Committee recommends that every police officer be compelled to make in writing, immediately after the occurrence of a crime, a statement in writing of the facts as stated to him or witnessed by him.

G. It is recommended that professional criminals be prosecuted under the State Vagrancy Law in accordance with the plan submitted by this Committee and enforced in other states, such as Massachusetts.

H. It is recommended that joint action be taken by the courts, the state's attorney and the chief of police to remove in some degree, the sinister pressure and harassment of the police by the criminal system of defense, composed in part of the "crooked bondsmen," the "crooked lawyer," and the "fixer.'

When the power activities and methods of this system are understood it is amazing that there are so many honest and efficient policemen.

I. The Committee finds that the police force of Chicago is smaller in proportion to that of other large cities and recommends an additional number to the department.

J. It is recommended all criminal branches of the Municipal Court be consolidated in one central building.

K. The Committee recommends the employment of an additional number of assistant state's attorneys, so that there will be an assistant state's attorney both day and night in the police stations, located in the larger crime zones of Chicago.

L. The Committee finds that the great power and responsibility of dealing with evil conditions shown before this Committee rests with the state's attorney. That the state's attorney in the performance of his duties, must incur the ill will of powerful interests. In view of the great responsibility, the dangers incurred, it is the belief that the salary of the state's attorney is wholly insufficient and that some method should be found by which the city of Chicago should make this adequate.

M. It is recommended that this Committee be made a permanent Committee, with an appropriation to continue the work. That it should have referred to it all reports of the Police Department required in the subject of crime from time to time.

Respectfully yours,

MORGAN L. DAVIES.

II

DESCRIPTION AND ANALYSIS OF CRIMINAL CONDITIONS

BY FLETCHER DOBYNS

In the investigation of Criminal Conditions the following subjects were given special attention:

1. Hangouts of professional criminals.
2. The number and classification of professional criminals.
3. Fences for the disposition of stolen property.
4. The use of the Vagrancy Act as a means of driving out professional criminals.
5. Relation of crime to prostitution, the drug habit and gambling, and the excessive use of liquor.
6. Police organization and methods.
7. Police collusion with crime.
8. Professional bondsmen, disreputable lawyers and fixers.
9. The prosecution of crime.

1. HANGOUTS OF PROFESSIONAL CRIMINALS

The first investigation of criminal conditions was directed toward hangouts of professional criminals. The greater part of this work was conducted with the assistance of Mr. Edward Altz, chief investigator, and various other investigators, operating under his direction.

Mr. John P. Mortimer and Mr. Paul R. Classen were especially useful in this work, and Officers Loose and Gray, detailed to the Committee by Chief Gleason, rendered very valuable service. The detailed report on the patrolmen and night shifts and other conditions in the Police Department was made by Mr. W. C. Dannenberg. Mr. Altz and his assistants mingled with the different pickpockets and known criminals of the city, associating with them day after day, night after night. They passed as crooks of various kinds, and in this capacity obtained direct information regarding the places where criminals assembled. These investigators reported a list of about one hundred meeting places or hangouts of professional criminals.

The greater number of these hangouts were found to be saloons, with a smaller number of poolrooms and a few restaurants. In twenty instances these saloons are operated by men with criminal records. Some of these hangouts are the resorts of definite classes of criminals, while others are the meeting places of almost every kind of crooks. Some, for example, are the hangouts of pick-pockets, others of "strong-arm men," while others are frequented more commonly by confidence men, or by panderers. Sometimes they are used as clearing houses for stolen property, and very often they are operated in close connection with houses of prostitution.

A typical illustration from testimony submitted follows:

"Saloon, hangout for criminals. Sherwood Smith hangs out there. . . . Oliver Harquist, Mushmouth Kline, one Buddy, William Burns, and a number of others whose names we have not been able to find. I have found this place on two or three different occasions in company with crooks. I have heard conversations between the crooks and the bartender, in which they discussed the best places for operation at that time."

—— Saloon. Red Lewis, Eddy Lewis, Harry Knouton, Doc Dobis, Chicken, Charles Davis, Kinky Jew, Tear-a-way Kid, Eddy Bowler, Fred Kerwin, Eddy Creely and George Hogarty hang out there. . . . While I was in there two policemen came in and both of them took a drink at the bar without paying for the drinks, and both spoke to these men that were in there at this time, among them the Kinky Jew and the Tear-a-way Kid, and Eddy Bowler." . . .

"After they went out these men boasted of the fact that they were safe in there." . . .

"That policemen did not dare to take them out of there." . . .

"Pool Room, ——, ——, is a very bad place and a good many dope users hang out there. Most of the pickpockets that frequent that

vicinity hang out in that place, also boosters, shop-lifters, etc., that work
the stores in that vicinity and frequent that vicinity."
"————— Cigar Store. Little Hugo, John Saunders, Mendel Simon,
Harry Stein, Patsy Keegan, Moe Feinberg and Tom White hang out
there." (Out of this place ————— was taken by the investigators of the
Committee, and sentenced to six months in the House of Correction
under the Vagrancy Act.)

As a rule these resorts are not molested and, indeed, in many instances
criminals seem to think that they are immune in these places. They appear
to regard them as cities of refuge from which they cannot lawfully be taken.
Such resorts are sinister breeding places of crime, and their continued existence is a standing menace to the safety of persons and property in Chicago.
In these places criminal acquaintances are made, prospective "jobs" are discussed and past ones related. From these haunts criminals go forth to make
their raids and return after their work is done. It is, of course, impossible to
prevent the assembly of groups of criminals as long as their presence in the
community is tolerated, but they should not be permitted to meet in public
places, such as saloons, poolrooms and restaurants. That a large number of
these dangerous resorts exist is due to one of two causes, or possibly both—
either fear or indifference on the part of the authorities or incompetence in the
securing of adequate evidence to convict the criminal characters who frequent
them. If the licenses of known rendezvous of criminals are revoked and not
restored, either to the same person or place, the practice of harboring these
criminals will speedily be ended; or if the inmates of these places were taken
under the Vagrancy Act, discussed in the latter part of the report of the
Committee, they could undoubtedly be convicted and restrained from running
at large.

2. NUMBER AND CLASSIFICATION OF PROFESSIONAL CRIMINALS

The investigation covered the number and kind of professional criminals
in Chicago. This list includes men of criminal records and reputation who in
the main are not pursuing any lawful occupation, and who in most instances
are actually engaged in the practice of their criminal profession. A detailed
list of 500 such criminals was supplied to the Committee by our investigators
and it is estimated by the chief investigator that there are many times this
number of this class operating in the city. The list of 500 includes only such
names as were actually checked up in the course of the investigation. In this
group various types of criminals are included. The principal classes are as
follows:

Pickpockets, or "dips."
Burglars, or "prowlers," divided into "day prowlers" and "night prowlers."
Shop-lifters, or "boosters."
Hold-up men, or "stick-up" men.
Confidence men of all grades from high class "con men" to low class.
Safe blowers, known as "peter men," or "yegg men."
Gamblers of all types and descriptions, from crap shooters to those in
   the "big games."
Panderers, living on the wages of woman's prostitution.
All around crooks, who have not specialized in any particular branch of
   crime, or perhaps have specialized in several lines of criminal activity.

These men carry on their work from year to year apparently without fear
of successful interference with their occupation. Occasionally raids, arrests
and round-ups are made, and in some instances convictions are secured, but
broadly speaking this group of enemies of society have entrenched themselves
in such a manner as to have little to fear from the law. They have formed
a crime system which gives its members a reasonable sense of security.
Among the members of this fraternity the rates for insurance against conviction of crime ought not to be much higher than the prevailing rates, outside
of the fraternity, for burglary insurance, or hold-up insurance. It is possible
that a pickpocket may be arrested and convicted, just as it is possible that
the citizen may have his pocket picked, but the chances are equally great in
either case. They have built up lines of defense consisting in part of the
corrupt lawyer, the fixer, the corrupt politician, with the further assistance of
our antiquated system of criminal procedure, until they have made their business about as safe from governmental interference as any other form of business. A "fall" (that is to say an arrest and conviction) is possible in the
underworld of crime. Indeed, many groups of thieves provide what they call

"fall money," for such an emergency. But the chances for such an occurence are not very great.

The statistics prepared for the Commission by Miss Abbott, show in the case of criminal complaints that the convictions amount to only 12 per cent, and of these only one in thirty receives any other punishment than that of a jail or a Bridewell sentence for a felony, which is legally punishable by imprisonment in the penitentiary.

The crime system is not a system in the sense that it is centrally organized, that is completely centralized, and under fairly close control. The degree of centralization differs in the various branches of crime. The pickpockets for example, are probably the best organized, while burglars and hold-up men are regarded as the lower grade of criminals. There are dukes, counts and lords in the criminal group, but there is no king who rules over the entire population. The closest approach to centralization is found in the lines of political influence that converge toward a small group of men, characterized as the men, or sometimes even the man "higher up." While this criminal group is not by any means completely organized, it has many of the characteristics of a system. It has its own language; it has its own laws; its own history; its tradition and customs; its own method and technique; its highly specialized machinery for attack upon persons, and particularly upon property; its own highly specialized modes of defense. These professionals have interurban, interstate, and sometimes international connections. In fact, when we consider the opportunities for escape from detection, by collusion or connivance, or incompetence of the police, by the work of the professional fixer; by the pressure of political influence; by the inactivity and incompetence of prosecutors; the spineless attitude of some judges, or by some loophole of escape in the mazes of criminal law, we must admit that professional crime is better organized for defense against the law than society is for the apprehension and conviction of the professional criminal. The details of this system will be outlined in the pages of this report so far as its ramifications have been investigated and exposed. It is not to be presumed, however, that the inquiry made is by any means exhaustive, of a group so subtle, shifty and secret in their methods as the professional criminals in a great city like Chicago. The roots of their system strike deep, and they also reach high and wide. It is not been possible to follow them all.

One of the most highly specialized groups in the criminal class, is that of pickpockets or "dips." A special investigation of this group was made, under my supervision, and lists of notorious pickpockets and of their hangouts, and detailed descriptions of their methods of adequate defense, were supplied to the Committee in the course of public hearings upon this question. The testimony showed that there are approximately 500 pickpockets in Chicago, and a list furnished contained the names of a large number.

The testimony showed that pickpockets almost invariably work in what is known as "mobs," or "gangs," of from two to five men. A complete mob consists of a "fan," who "locates the office," that is to say, locates the pocket book or "poke." The next member is the "stall," whose duty is to make the victim change his position in such a manner that the "instrument," can get at his pocket. This can be done by having the stall step on his toes or give him a shove. The man known as the "instrument," or "wire," then takes the "poke" or pocket book, which he immediately passes to the person known as the "switch." The "switch" makes his escape or in some instances relays it to still another member of the mob. The "stall" in the meantime may interfere in the pursuit, if the theft is discovered. There are, of course, many variations in the method, depending upon the size of the mob, and the peculiar methods of working. It is reported that in some instances that three men constitute a mob, one acting as an instrument, the other as a switch, and the police officer acting as a stall. Favorite places of operation were also indicated by our investigator, including Halsted street between Madison and Sixteenth, Halsted and Sixty-third, Madison street, from Canal west to Roby, Riverview Park, Ashland and Forty-seventh. Pickpockets also work in banks, elevators, office buildings, and in department stores. In the latter case their work is called "moll buzzing.' Many of these gangs operate constantly in Chicago, while others, particularly during the summer time, leave the city in order to make the race tracks and county fairs near the city.

Pickpockets have several main lines of defense. The strongest of these is direct collusion with officials on the police force. The nature and extent

of this co-operation will be discussed in that section of this report dea
with the general subject of police collusion with criminals.

In other instances they are defended by certain lawyers, regularly en.
ployed for that purpose. These attorneys secure the release of the pick-
picket by means of a writ of habeas corpus, when the case is not promptly
booked at the station or through insufficiency of evidence, where cases come
to trial; or through various other legal technicalities in the use of which their
long experience gives them great skill. Pickpockets appear to be better defended from the legal point of view than any other group of habitual criminals.

A striking illustration of the ease with which they evade the law is found
in the case of Eddy Jackson, a well known dip, who for so many years escaped
punishment that he came to be known as "Eddy the Immune."

A few of these pickpockets operate with the knowledge of the police
officials, who allow them to operate either because of corrupt connivance, as
indicated above, or because of alleged inability to secure evidence leading
to a conviction.

Another group of professional criminals is made up of the burglars of
various classes. Some of them are known as "night prowlers," who operate
after dark, and "day prowlers," who work during the day. A special branch
of this class is the "booster," who works the department stores, and other
shops. Further there are innumerable special classes of automobile thieves,
freight-car thieves, jewelry thieves, horse thieves, wagon thieves, and many
other persons who make some brand of larceny a specialty. They do not
seem as a rule to be as intelligent or as well organized as the pickpockets,
nor do they have as complete arrangements made for their defense as do
the "dips." While the percentage of conviction for larceny is somewhat
higher than other cases, yet on the whole the professional prowler may carry
on his occupation for a considerable time without much danger of interrup-
tion.

Safe-blowers, otherwise known as "peter man," or "yegg-men," are also
found in considerable numbers in Chicago. Many of these men do not operate
in this city, but make Chicago their headquarters. From this point, as a
center, they go out to do "jobs' in cities or towns within a radius of several
hundred miles. When their work is done, they take refuge in Chicago, where
the possibilities of detection are not very great. Safe-blowing is by no means
unknown in Chicago, yet in the main, the Chicago safe crackers regard this
as their dormitory rather than their workshop. They are likely to be known
to the police, however, and, therefore, must provide themselves with defense
against the arm of the law.

This protection must be some form of political influence, or a cash payment to secure silence. "Peter men" are among the aristocrats of the criminal
world. They regard themselves, and are regarded by the professional criminal
as superior to such types as the prowler, or the stick-up man. The vigorous
attempts made by the various banking interests to run down and punish safe-
crackers, makes their pursuit much more hazardous than most crimes. The
men who follow it, therefore, require a degree of nerve and ability which is
not necessary in the sneak thief or hold-up man.

The hold-up men include a rather ill defined group of "strong-arm" men,
who are ready to do any rough job, as strike breakers, labor sluggers, or otherwise. The "stick-up" men who are professionally engaged in the hold-up business and gun-men are ready for almost any kind of a job. "Stick-up" men
may follow some other line of criminal work. They sometimes work in
gangs like the Gilhooley boys, the Dooley boys, or Rooney's gang, who are
ready for any sort of strong-arm work regardless of consequences to themselves or others. Others work individually in the hold-up business or sometimes they operate in pairs. One of the striking features about hold-up cases
is the large number of instances in which the robbery is committed by very
young persons, not infrequently by boys under 21 years of age.

Another class of professional criminals is the so-called "con" men or
confidence men. There are many varieties of these, from the short-change
men up to the perpetrators of more pretentious schemes of fraud, such as
those of the wire-tappers, and the organizers of fake or fraudulent businesses.
"Con men" is a flexible term and does not ndicate whether the particular
person is "high class" or "low class." They frequently perpetrate the most
bare-faced and apparently impossible frauds, especially upon visitors to the
city, who are ignorant of their ways. Offering to sell the Masonic Temple

nt device, but it has been accomplished more than once.
Clairvoyant Trust and of the wire-tappers have recently
now matters of general knowledge. These ingenious
atively little fear of interference. Their defense con-
protection by the police department, as conviction for
..s is not very difficult to procure. In general, therefore, they
..ue their earnings with those who give them immunity from police
..ence.

Our investigation also shows the existence of gambling on a large scale.
The chief investigator estimated the number of "hand books" alone in Chicago at about 300, and of these, 50 were actually checked up. Investigators
made bets or heard bets made, and saw the money passed in fifty places
scattered around the city of Chicago. The Committee also found that there
are a number of "clearing houses" for gambling in Chicago. A clearing
house is a place where the news is received direct from the race track as to
the different horses about to run, the riders, and whether the horse is scratchd,
and so on. A wire is leased and race track news from all over the country
obtained over it. Then this in turn is distributed to the smaller clearing
houses, and from them sent to the different hand-book makers. One clearing
house was located at 2032 West Madison street. Here the wire was tapped
and the investigators reported the conversation. The following is a report of
an investigator on Saturday, November 28, 1914:

I went to 2040 West Madison street at 11 o'clock a. m. Both phones were
working, Bell and automatic. The following is what I got over the Bell phone:
Somebody called up and said: "Hello, Ed." Ed said: "Yes." The other
party said: "$10." Then Ed said: "All right." Somebody called up and
said: "Hello, Ed, how is the track?" Ed said: "Fair." The other party
said: "Has Hester Pryne got a rider?" Ed said: "Yes." The other party
said: "$10 on Hester Pryne, $10 on Fairy Godmother." Ed said: "All right."
Some fellow called up and said: "Hello, Long, this is Billy. Got that
pony?" Ed said: "No." The other fellow said: "Will you call up?" Ed
said: "Yes.'
Somebody called up and said: "Hello, Ed, who won the second?" Ed
said "Chupadero." The other fellow said: "All right." Ed called up Monroe 230, and said: "Is that you, Smith?" Other party said: "Yes." Ed said:
"Hester Pryne, Thistle Blue and Montpelier entry on the 4th race." The
other fellow said, "$10 on each, that makes $30 in bets that I owe you." Ed
said: "All right."
Ed called up Monroe 230 and said: "Hello, Smith, Hester Pryne scratched."
Smth said: "What odds." Ed said: "Two and two and one-half to one."
Smith said: "Put two on Flitter Gold, two on Thistle Blue, and two on Ten
Points. Here is some more money for you, Ed, from Harry. My bets go the
way I laid them."
Ed called up Canal 5095, and said to the party that answered: "One, Four,
Six winners."

Our investigator further reported that there is a general understanding
among the persons frequenting these places that the handbook system is con-
trolled by one person. It is a matter of general understanding among the
handbook fraternity that these books are operated under police protection.
It is stated that $50 a week is received for each book run. If there are three
hundred books, as estimated, then on that basis the total amount paid for
police protection would aggregate nearly $800,000 a year.

3. "FENCES" FOR THE DISPOSITION OF STOLEN PROPERTY

A large number of burglary and larceny cases, amounting in the year 1913
to 11,906, indicated the desirability of a thoroughgoing inquiry into this
subject. Obviously such extensive stealing could not take place unless the
disposition of stolen goods was well organized. Very shortly after the investigations were begun the story came to our attention constantly that one of the
largest and most complete organizations for the protection of crime in this
city is that between burglars, thieves, shoplifters, and the receivers of stolen
property, usually called "fences." Investigation of these reports was undertaken
for the purpose of finding the system and recommending remedial measures.

The system is operated in the following manner. A man who is known
as a "fence," receives stolen property from any accredited thieves who may
bring it to him. He is an individual fence. But there are many of these
fences who are "wholesalers." They have regular crews of burglars and

shoplifters who go out and obtain goods for them. They have wagons marked as milk wagons, or bakery wagons, so that they can make their deliveries in the early morning hours. In other words, these fences are the center of a spider's web of thieves and burglars who are on intimate relations and between whom there is more or less well defined working partnership. Another class of thieves have their representatives in other cities. A buyer from another city wishes, for example, so much cloth of a certain kind, or it may be jewelry. He sends his order to the fence, who takes the matter up with his burglars or shoplifters and they in turn send out their buyer who goes to the various places where he thinks these goods may be found. This buyer goes in and under a pretense of wanting to buy the goods, will look over the place and see what is there, notices what exits there are, and finds out where the goods he wants are located. At night the burglars have their milk wagons or bakery wagons at the shop, and the "job" is "pulled off." The goods are then delivered and immediately sent out of the city to fill the order.

There are also gangs who get orders not only from out of the city, but from in the city for quantities of goods. They say to the fences, "We want so much goods," then the fences get in touch with their mobs or gangs, who go out and steal this material. It is then delivered to the wholesaler, all marks of identification being removed, and the goods are delivered, either in or out of the city. This practice is the very foundation of shoplifting, burglary and thieving of every kind.

The statement of Officer Loose, detailed on this investigation, is as follows:

"Wholesalers deal with people usually from out of town, who know the kind of property they are buying when they deal with the wholesaler. The wholesaler will receive in total, an order for a large amount of stuff, a large mass of stuff. The wholesaler don't run a mob of burglars, except the larger size fences do. Now when the wholesaler receives sufficient orders totaling a large amount, he communicates with the different fences, those that run mobs, and the fences then send out what they call the fence "buyer" into the store that carries a line of stock that the wholesaler requires to fill his order. He visits a sufficient number of stores containing stock to fill the total amount of the wholesaler's order. The buyer then reports back to the fence the list of stores containing this stock. Then the fence sends out what they call the head burglar, and he looks over the list that has been submitted by the fence's buyer and notes the best entrance. Then he reports back again to the fence, and then, on the report of the buyer and the chief burglar for the fence, the fence and the wholesaler then agree on the burglary of these stores to fill the order that the wholesaler has. Now, to see that the fence's buyer has not reported wrong about the class and quality of the stock there may be in the store to be burglarized, the wholesaler has a man that they call the wholesaler's buyer, and sometimes, not alone the wholesaler's buyer, but the wholesaler himself goes there and looks the situation over, and rechecks the list furnished at the time, for the series of burglaries to be made to fill the contract of the wholesaler, and if the goods come up to their requirements in quantity and quality, the fence then gets the job, and in the afternoon of the day that a certain burglarly is going to be made, the wholesaler is then communicated with, and he knows what places are going to be "busted" that night, and he knows what the contents are, and to what customer that will fit that he has an order from, and then the job is done, and the stuff is not taken to the fence at all then. It is taken directly to the wholesaler, and the wholesaler has his boxes ready, and he snips off all identification marks, and packs the stuff in boxes, and by the time the man gets down to his store, and finds that he is burglarized, the stuff is on the way out of town. That is the system."

Occasionally the system goes wrong as the officer indicated:

"A big job came off on the North Side a little while ago in which there was a mass of fine handkerchiefs stolen. The fence came into possession of the handkerchiefs and sent out what they call the fence's salesman with samples of the handkerchiefs. Unfortunately he visited the very man from whom the handkerchiefs were stolen, with a sample handkerchief to sell them to him. Of course, he bought them there, and when they came there to deliver them, there were two officers there, and they grabbed them, and they had a big bundle of handkerchiefs."

The man who steals something to put in his own pocket would not raise petty stealing to the dignity of a business or organization. The largest part of the theft is what may be called "syndicated stealing." Probably 95% of the thefts are connected in some more or less closely organized way with the professional fences. In short, the fence is the center of burglary and all other forms of thieving in Chicago.

The amount of property stolen each year, the systematic manner in which it is done, and the innumerable ramifications of the system, have taxed the credulity even of those somewhat familiar with the workings of the criminal world.

There are a large number of fences scattered over the city. The number is estimated at 300 and the investigators located 50 of these definitely. The fences deal in various kinds of commodities. They handle groceries, leather, shoes, toilet goods, woolens, silks, and other like goods. Jewelry is handled by pawnbrokers as a rule, or by special kinds of fences. Those saloons which are used as criminal hangouts are also likely to fence jewelry.

Investigators for the Commission obtained definite information regarding the fence system in the following way:

Two of the investigators posed as thieves. They obtained addresses of supposed fences, cards of introduction to them, or in other cases, passwords, numbers or names, all for the purpose of assuring the fence that he was dealing with persons handling stolen property. They secured a room and placed in it stocks of goods, consisting of woolens, ready made suits, trousers, ladies' dress coats, groceries, shoes, leather, grain, oats, spool silk and feathers. With this room a dictagraph was connected in order that conversation with those who came to buy supposed stolen property might be recorded. The dictagraph work was done by A. J. McGurn, an expert dictagraph shorthand writer. These supposed burglars then went out for the purpose of locating presumed fences. One of the investigators says: "We would naturally appear to be very suspicious all the time. When we went to a place we would be absolutely sure to get the man we were sent to, so that there could be no slip anywhere. As soon as we could, we made our connection right away, either by the pass word, or sometimes it was necessary that we would say that a man had been in to see him three or four days or a week previously, and told us to come in to see him about buying a certain line of goods. If he was still doubtful or reluctant to talk to us, we produced a card, and in almost every case that settled the matter right there."

A typical case reported by the investigators is as follows:

We went to ———— and told him that a friend of ours told us to call and show him some samples of some woolens which we had. It appears from Mr. ——— conversation that the man who had gained entrance there had been there some three weeks before, and ——— did not remember the connection very well, and hesitated to do business with us, saying, that we could not blame him for being careful. We told him that we would send our connection around again and would see him later.

Three days later, to make our proposition more genuine, we called at ———— and secured from them several samples of high grade selvidged woolens, and then went to ————. When we arrived there, Mr. ——— was just arising. He remarked that he had been out to 2:30 a. m. that morning, and said that sometimes it was necessary in business to stay out late. We then proceeded to business. We showed Mr. ——— the samples, and he wanted to know how many yards of each piece we had. We informed him that we did not know exactly, but had approximately about 250 yards of each kind (or about 1,600 yards in all). He then said: "Boys, I can see you are new in this business. Let me give you some advice. When you steal this stuff, there is always a ticket on each bolt, giving the number of the goods and the number of yards in the bolt. Take a piece of paper; make your own numbers for your samples, and then write the number of yards. Then take the original ticket and burn it up. Then there is no check on it, and you can tell the man you sell it to just how many yards of each kind you have." We asked him if he could use the 1,600 yards. He said: "I could use 16,000 yards if you had it, or all you can get. There is not limit to me. The man I do business with is as solid as a rock. Away up high." We then talked about price. We asked him if he would give 50 cents a yard for it. He said: "To a user, it would be worth that much, but to me, a dealer, it would not. Of course, you know I would not use this goods here myself. I dispose of it to other people. Will you boys trust me to give you a square deal?" We said if he would be square with us he could do a lot of business with us.

He said: "I can use anything you get—suits, shoes or anything there is any money in.") He said: "The fellow who sent you here is a coward." He said: "Well, I will go downtown right after my breakfast and see my man. If he gives me 60 cents a yard, I will give you 50 cents. If he gives me 50 cents a yard, I will give you 40 cents. You see, I am entitled to 10 cents a yard for my trouble, anyway." We then asked him where he wanted the stuff delivered. He said: "That's my business. I don't ask you where you got your stuff stored. I don't want to know. You don't know where any stuff goes, so we are all safe." He said: "I will send an expressman to you. You give him the goods, pay for the expressage, and he will take it where I send him. That is all there is to it." He said: "Why I do this, is this: If you get an expressman, and he knows what kind of stuff you have got, and knows where it comes from, he will haul it about two blocks, and then say he wants $25, or he won't go another foot of the road. If you get an outside party, and a different expressman each time, nobody knows your business, and he just gets so much for doing his job, and that is all there is to it." He then asked us what kind of stuff we had. We told him that we had sold 100 suits just the other day for $3 a suit. He said he could use all we could get. He said it would be best for us to come back tonight to close the deal, as he would then know just how much he could pay us, and he showed us the kind of lining he wanted in the suits. We professed not to know what kind of lining was in our suits, and he took us over to a case and showed us a suit with a black serge lining. He said: "If you can get those kind of suits, with those kinds of linings, that is the best kind to get. They are easier to get off your hands. When you come in tonight, if there is any customers in the store, just take the sample book and pick out the goods and order a suit." We agreed, and left, and promised to return at 7 p. m. We agreed to steal 100 suits for him later on in the week, and left his store at 11:35 a. m.

As per arrangements made with —— this morning, we called at his place of business at about 7:30 p. m. —— was in the act of pressing a suit, and was the only one in the place. He said: "Come over, boys, let's get better acquainted. Now, boys, we have talked several times. This morning when we were here, we talked long, framed a deal, and everything is all right, but one thing, if you had one little word, we could open up and talk business freely. You cannot blame me for being careful. You fellows were in here the other day and didn't have the pass word." So I remarked: "How would 'Innocent' do?" (which is the password). He shook hands very warmly and said: "Now we are brothers." And from then on appeared to be more free with his information. The first thing he said was: "I do a little job myself now and then. In fact, I was out on a job last night. I am well protected, and pay for it, and I help my friends when they are in trouble, so you see we will have no trouble in our dealings." He then asked us about how many suits we had. We told him about one hundred. He said: 'Well, bring me out a pants, coat or vest of each kind, but it would be better to bring the coat." He then said: "It is a little harder to get rid of suits than it is the cloth." He said he could handle everything. He said: "You see this room here? Many a time I had that full of cigars, leather, cloth or anything. A safety pin is small (indicating with his fingers). A diamond, that's large. So we can handle anything from a safety pin to a diamond." We remarked that we could steal some leather, but it would be Chicago stuff. He said: "That's all right; I have a mighty good friend in Kansas City, but I always like to know if it is Chicago stuff or not, for if it is I ship it out to Kansas City quick." He then said: "Call me up on the automatic at the United Cigar Company Store at Twelfth and Halsted Streets tomorrow morning at 9 o'clock, and ask for me if it is this number. When I say 'yes' you say, 'give me the watch.' I will say, 'All right, how many.' Then you tell me the number of yards you have of each stuff." He said: 'When this deal goes through, and everything is all right, when I meet you on the street we are friends no more. You don't know me, and I don't know you. When I get in trouble, I don't know your name; I don't know anything about you, and I cannot tell anything. You don't know anything about me. Man for man, we get a square deal." He then said: "But whenever you get some stuff, of course, we know you are all right. You come right here, and we will clean up the deal. Now, boys, when we make a deal, a deal is a deal. If I tell you you get $1.00 a yard, you get $1.00 a yard. If

I say 50 cents, you get 50 cents. Once the price is given, you get it. There is no come back at all."

In view of the fact that the location of these fences may be easily ascertained by investigation, and in view of the enormous importance of the fence business in relation to organized theft, we draw the conclusion that the regular police have not pursued receivers of stolen property vigorously. It is not at all difficult to obtain the names and addresses of fences, to demonstrate their practice of receiving stolen goods, and having done this, to establish such a surveillance over them as to put an end to their unlawful business. If the business of receiving stolen property was broken up the amount of theft in Chicago would rapidly decline. The enormous amount of thieving now going on depends primarily upon a broad market for stolen goods. With the destruction of that market the organized business of thieving would practically cease. Too great emphasis cannot be placed on the fact that the fence is the center of the whole system of organized thievery, and that with the elimination of the fence the system collapses. There would then remain only such casual theft as an individual might commit. This occasional theft is so small a proportion of organized theft that the amount remaining would be of relatively little importance. Ninety-five per cent of the stealing in Chicago is syndicated stealing, and the fence is the center of the syndicate.

4. VAGRANCY ACT

As a direct means of ridding the city of professional criminals, counsel for the Committee undertook to demonstrate how the Vagrancy Law might be used for this purpose. This act provides a sentence of six months for vagrants.

The method of procedure was as follows: In each of the different parts of the city a man with a criminal record was picked up by investigators and placed under observation in order to determine whether he had any visible means of support or lawful occupation. The records of these men were looked up; they were watched from time to time to ascertain what occupation they followed. It was found that they were living without working, hanging around saloons and gambling places with no visible means of support and that they, therefore, came within the scope of the Vagrancy Act. Complaints were then signed by the Chairman of the Committee, warrants were issued and placed in the hands of officers and three men were arrested and brought before the court. These men were represented by counsel and their evidence was heard. Witnesses were examined on both sides, with the result that the defendants were found guilty of vagrancy and sentenced to six months in the Bridewell.

Ordinarily when persons of this type are arrested by police, they are charged with disorderly conduct without any definite evidence or a prepared case. In most instances, the result will be a discharge of the prisoner or possibly a very light fine. The purpose of the Commission's counsel was to show that there is an effective method under the existing law of imprisoning professional criminals for a period of six months. If they are given a small fine and cannot pay it themselves, the "fraternity" helps them to pay it and we find that these men go back to their work at once. Consequently the fine is very ineffective. Your counsel is of the opinion that if these men were taken up under the State Vagrancy Act rather than under the Disorderly Conduct Ordinance, which is known as 2012, the courts will enforce it, giving a sentence in the Bridewell, and that these men will be afraid to hang around and would not hang around the city. If this vagrancy law were enforced this would clear the city of those criminals, because they will not work. Rather than engage in any steady industry, they will leave the town. Consequently, we believe that the enforcement of this law would be the most effective way of ridding the town of the habitual criminals who commit 90% of the crime.

The Court stated from the bench that it was the first time that he had ever seen cases properly prosecuted under the State Vagrancy Act. There is no doubt that practically the entire body of professional criminals who now infest the city would be driven out by a vigorous application of this effective law.

The two difficulties ordinarily encountered are, first, the absence of definite evidence showing that the defendant has no lawful occupation. This can be overcome either by the method employed in the above cases—namely, by special investigators—or it may be done by the regular police force. A card index system could be kept, keeping record of all the suspicious characters and indicating, for instance, the following items: "the defendant, ————, was seen hanging about, not doing any work." Another officer from the same district might send in the same report another day. If this information was put together properly, when assembled it would constitute sufficient evidence that the accused did not have any regular or lawful occupation; that he had a criminal record, and that he hung about saloons or gambling places. If Slim, for example, having a criminal record, was seen hanging around today by one officer and tomorrow by another, or by the same officer on a series of days, it could easily be shown that he had no lawful occupation.

The second defense is by means of the alibi. The defendant usually comes in and declares that he is employed at some place, and he will have a witness or witnesses to swear that he has been so occupied. In the cases handled for the Committee, the moment the arrest was made the officer was instructed to ask the men what they were doing and where they were working. The officer questioned them with the greatest thoroughness about their employment for the past month and obtained names and addresses. The officer was instructed immediately after the arrest to go directly to these persons and ascertain whether the statements made by the defendants were correct. It can be made perfectly plain to the parties whose names are given as employers that the entire truth is sought, and if it is not given that anyone who suppresses it will be liable to charges of perjury, and in addition to a charge of criminal conspiracy. In that event, the alibi furnished as waiters and bartenders, or like favorite devices, would be far less frequent and useful. Energetic and intelligent handling of this situation would make effective enforcement of the Vagrancy Act possible. It would destroy the principal obstacle that has defeated the law and the court and prevented judges from acting vigorously under it. As an illustration of the frequency of the alibi practice, the following report is illuminating:

"One of the investigators went to one of these notorious hangouts that has been given. The head of that hangout agreed to take any jewelry from him that he might get. He further said: 'I will give you the name of a man that you can see if you are arrested for vagrancy. You call him up and you can have him tell them that you are working for him.' He said: 'You give them the telephone number and if the police call up he will say, yes, he is working for me.'"

Illustrating the importance of physical and mental examination of persons found guilty of any charge before sentence is the experience of the Committee with the three persons found guilty under the Vagrancy Law. Two of these submitted to an examination by Dr. Hickson of the Psychopathic Laboratory. One of them was found to be a dope-fiend and the other an alcoholic. In imposing the six months' sentence, therefore, note was made of the fact that one should be given the cure for the drug habit and the other should be given the cure for alcoholism. The third defendant refused to permit an examination, but after some weeks in the Bridewell asked voluntarily for an examination. His family history on both sides was found to be extremely bad, with melancholia on one side and suicide on the other. He was pronounced by Dr. Hickson a sociopath, that is a person of higher grade than a moron, but one who finds great difficulty in getting on with those around him. Such a defendant really requires a sheltered life in which he may be so far as possible protected from evil associates and environments.

The following concrete practical suggestions on the subject of vagrancy were presented to the Committee by Mr. Dannenberg:

"The reorganization system provided for a series of records, to keep a check on vagrants, as well as other offenders, and at present there is a printed report blank (see exhibit "C"), to be filled out in case a vagrant is found. Upon investigation, however, it has been ascertained that this form is not as practical as many others might be. I have taken this phase of the work up with some of the municipal judges, and explained to them a card system, which I have advocated for some time, in regard to vagrants. All of the judges to whom I have spoken have approved of this simple and convenient method, which is as follows: It would simply be a small printed card, running something like this: Name, address, place of employment, employer's name, description, where found, remarks, date, and officer. Each officer would be required to carry a number of these cards with him at all times, and whenever he had occasion to believe that any individual upon his post did not have any lawful means of support, it would be his duty to fill out one of these cards. He would then ascertain whether it was true that the person worked at the place he claimed. If not, the card would be filed in the alphabetical file in the station. The next time this officer found the same individual on his post, he would do likewise, and, in turn, every other officer who found him on his or any other post. The result would be that in a very short time, there would be five or six cards turned in on one individual. That would constitute sufficient evidence to secure a conviction under the vagrancy statute. The captain or some other subordinate should go through those files every so often, and pick out all cases where there was sufficient evidence to secure warrants, and cause the arrest of the offender. This would be a very simple way of securing sufficient evidence to secure convictions on the vagrancy law, and the cards would all be admissible as evidence, because of the fact that they were taken in the presence of the defendant, and at the time the questions were asked.

"Under the present system, there is not any organized attempt being made to keep a thorough and up-to-date record on various characters which are to be found in any police district.

"If a report system, as I have outlined, was in force, it would be a simple matter to have a card index file on every bad character in every district. What they have now does not amount to anything.

"As an example, I will cite some personal experiences along this line:

"A year ago about this time I was in charge of all vice work. In the various districts where vice flourished I found nearly every place operating with the aid of one, two or more 'look-outs.' A 'look-out' was an individual (I would not disgrace the word man by classifying them as such), whose duty it was to remain outside the premises occupied by his employer and watch for the police, my men, or myself. If he saw any one of the three mentioned he would signal those within to lay low or hide. I have seen as many as thirty or thirty-five such characters in a district six blocks long and four blocks wide, while ten or twelve patrolmen patroled the streets, hour after hour, without molesting one of them. They, in fact, paid no attention to a patrolman, but would run when I appeared, because I was ousting them from time to time. I asked them why they were not molested by the police of the district, and was told they could not get anything on them, nor could they drive them out. After some weeks of activity on my part, they organized a so-called club, thinking that if they ran to the club house when I appeared, that they would be immune. I then had the cards printed, as I have advocated, and one night entered the so-called club and took the names, addresses, places of employment, etc., of every one, about thirty or more in number. The result was, the club broke up and they all quit the district almost at once.

"What's the matter with doing this same thing with tough pool-rooms, saloons, and other places of bad repute? All you need, is to find them there a few times, after you find they have no lawful means of support, and then you can arrest all for vagrancy. It is not hard to secure convictions under this statute, if handled properly."

5. RELATION OF CRIME TO PROSTITUTION, DOPE, LIQUOR and GAMBLING

The work of the investigators developed a close inter-relationship between prostitution, the use of habit-forming drugs, the excessive use of liquor, gambling, and professional crime. In general these various forms of activity are linked together very closely, and their study in combination throws much light on the characteristics of the so-called underworld.

The habitual criminal is very likely to live with some woman whose protector he is, and who prostitutes herself for his profit. He may be merely the "lover" of this woman. He may be working as a pimp, who procures trade for her, or he may be serving as a go-between with the police. The use of habit-forming drugs, such a morphine, cocaine, opium, heroin, and other similar derivatives, is extremely common, not only among prostitutes but also among criminals. The habitual criminal is likely to be not only the protector of a woman, but, with her, to use some one of the habit-forming drugs.

Alcoholism is also closely connected with professional criminality. This is true, however, not so much of the higher grade criminals who require intelligence and nerve as of the lower types, such as the stick-up man or so-called cheap thief. The alcoholic cannot easily become a member of an expert gang because of the danger that he will not be able to control himself while conducting a "job," or that his tongue may be loosened to such an extent that he will talk too freely after the commission of a crime.

The same thing is true of the dope fiend who in his last stages becomes incapable of work at any time, except the desultory activity of a sneak thief, or the casual sticking up of some person, under the spur of necessity, for money to buy the drug desired. Gambling is, of course, a comon practice among professional criminals, who while away their leisure hours in various games of chance. The psychology of the crook inclines him to take a chance rather than to engage in any steady industry.

A desire for dope is especially powerful in the creation of criminals. Once the deadly habit is formed, its victim will resort to any method to obtain his favorite drug. The sense of morality is deadened and the woman victim usually becomes a prostitute or a thief, while the man may become a pimp, pickpocket, prowler, or member of some criminal gang. One of our investigators testified that 75% of the users of drugs are composed of the criminal class. It is also known that the termination of the dope traffic would have an important effect in reducing the amount of crime.

In the hearings before the Commission, the following testimony was given:

The Chairman: One of the most practical ways of making the city an unpleasant place for criminals, would be to cut off the dope?

Mr. Altz: Absolutely. There is no question about that at all.

The Chairman: They do not want to hang around where there is not any dope? Or, where there is not a red-light district?

Mr. Altz: That is true, those two things together, are, I think, great causes for crime.

The Chairman: If the city broke up the dope traffic and broke up the red-light district, wouldn't it be avoided by many professional criminals and crooks?

Mr. Altz: Yes, that is true. No one will dispute that.

The dope habit is often formed either in a house of prostitution or a poolroom. Ninety per cent of the prostitutes use drugs in one form or another, and they frequently initiate their visitors into these drug using habits. Or the drug may be obtained around various poolrooms or other places, where so-called "runners" peddle their dope. They build up regular "routes" along which they deliver to their several customers the various drugs. These "routes" cover saloons, poolrooms, houses of prostitution and so forth. It is estimated that there are from 75 to 100 runners in Chicago who are engaged in the retail sale of cocaine, heroin, opium, morphine, and so on. The investigation shows that high-class criminals and prostitutes use opium, while boosters, shoplifters and pickpockets are addicted to cocaine and heroin, which is obtained at less expense.

Once in the clutches of the drug, the victim is readily recruited into the criminal ranks. A specific instance of this was reported as follows:

"————, international safe blower, makes safe jobs all over the United States. This man was a country boy and came to Chicago, entering a machine shop to learn the trade of a machinist. After working at the trade about two years, he married a girl named ————, and went to keeping house in a nearby suburb, near to where he worked. In company with his wife he visited Sunday night dances. At one of these dances he met a prostitute known as ————, who became very much infatuated with him. After meeting him several times, the prostitute induced him to abandon his wife, and go with her to St. Louis, where she opened up a house of prostitution, and ———— was her pimp. While in St. Louis, acting as a pimp, he became acquainted with a number of other men who were acting as pimps for other women. As usual, these groups of men are composed of criminals, and because of his early training as a machinist, safe-blowing became easy to him. He soon became very efficient in the business. He made lots of money and she gave up her house of prostitution in St. Louis and removed to Chicago, and she is working as a prostitute occasionally when the burglar and safe-blowing business is bad."

"————, 19 years old, mother and father both dead since boy was seven years old. Brought up by relatives in Peoria, Illlinois. Came to Chicago and worked for ———— at ———— street. Frequented poolrooms and met ————. ———— was a user of habit-forming drugs, and induced him to begin the habit. While under the influence of drugs, he burglarized a tailor shop. He was arrested, plead guilty to the charge of burglary and held to the grand jury."

"————, 20 years old, mother dead, father an engineer. He had been previously arrested on a disorderly conduct charge, but was discharged by the court. Drunk at the time of his arrest. Constantly employed; never got into any trouble except when under the influence of liquor. While employed by the Lake Shore Railroad Company as a brakeman at a salary of $88 a month, he and another young man got drunk and held up a street car at 63rd and Wabash avenue, taking $6 from the conductor. He was caught and identified by the conductor, while still drunk."

"A young man frequented a house of prostitution on 22nd street. This is where he acquired the dope habit. He had a girl there, a sweetheart, and it was not long before he was not able to perform any work at all. It was not long before he branched out into a first-class pickpocket. He was arrested a number of times as a pickpocket and shoplifter. After he started using the drug, it was not long before he had associated with thieves and pickpockets, because most of those people around in that district used drugs."

After a course in the use of dope, the victim becomes incapable of expert criminal work, and then many of the most serious crimes, such as stick-ups and even murder, are committed in order to obtain money to buy the drug. A professional criminal runs down the scale of crime. He may start as a rather "high-class" crook. If he acquires the dope habit, he goes on to easier and simpler crimes. He may finally reach such a condition physically, that he is unable to work with mobs. He may go then, get a gun and hold somebody up. This requires some nerve, but under the influence of the drug, he is able to summon nerve for a short time. There can be no doubt that the general suppression of the dope traffic, prostitution, gambling, and the sale of liquor to minors and habitual drunkards, would very materially reduce the amount of crime. The city in which these commodities are not easily obtainable would not long be inhabited by criminals of the professional type. They would soon seek other quarters more congenial. The pickpocket without his dope and his prostitute, would not linger long if there was any place else for him to go. The very fact that congenial groups of criminals may be found in a great city at well-known rendezvous where prostitutes, dope, and gambling are easily available, is one of the factors in drawing the groups of professional thieves, safe-crackers and others to Chicago.

In this connection, it has been suggested that the present law regarding the use of habit-forming drugs be so amended as to provide a prison term instead of a fine for those engaging in the dope traffic, or for those who have been convicted of a crime and are found to be under the influence of the dope habit. It is also suggested that the state law be so amended as to leave no doubt as to the inclusion of drugs other than cocaine, the only one specified in the statute. Under the present ordinance, the maximum fine is $100. Under the state law, of course, a heavier sentence may be imposed.

In conclusion, attention is drawn to the following considerations:

FIRST: The enormous influence of dope, drink, prostitution and gambling, as recruiting agencies for new generations of criminals.

SECOND: The influence, particularly of alcohol and dope commonly used by professional criminals in driving them to desperate deeds of violence, such as hold-ups, assault, and even murders.

THIRD: The intimate relation between professional criminality, the use of habit forming drugs, excessive use of alcohol, gambling and prostitution. These are the pillars of the underworld, and whenever one is weakened, the power of the others is correspondingly reduced.

6. POLICE ORGANIZATION AND METHODS

Th matter of police organization was considered under various heads, namely:

1. The effectiveness of the patrol system.
2. The reports made by detective sergeants.
3. Operators' pull sheets.
4. The police attorney.
5. Handling of cases before Civil Service Commission.
6. Handling of vice reports.
7. Schooling of members of department.
8. Refusal of warrants in certain cases.

The major part of this work was conducted by Mr. W. C. Dannenberg under the supervision of Mr. Dobyns.

Effectiveness of the Patrol System.

The purpose of this investigation was to show the general activities of the uniformed branch of the Police Department. It was frequently asserted that one of the chief causes of the various crime waves, such as hold-ups, robberies, and burglaries of all descriptions, was the neglect of duty on the part of the uniformed branch of the service, which has to do with the patrolling of the various precincts, which includes patrolmen, patrol sergeants, and the commanding officer of the precinct.

A certain number of patrolmen are assigned to every district on each tour of duty, their post being proportioned off according to the size of the precinct, and the number of men assigned. The first duty of the patrolman is to walk his post and keep track, in general, of everything that is going on on his post. The patrol sergeant's duty is to leave his precinct headquarters with the patrolmen, and remain in the precinct, overseeing the work of the patrolmen, meeting each occasionally, and keeping in communication with his station until the tour of duty is at an end. It is up to the commanding officer of any precinct or district to see that the patrolmen and patrol sergeants are doing their full duty. The officer in command is also expected to get around his district occasionally during his tour of duty, so that he will know, of his own knowledge, what is going on.

It therefore resolves itself into this issue: If the patrolman spends his time in saloons, theaters and other places, instead of patrolling his beat in the proper manner, not only is he guilty of neglect of duty and inefficiency, but the patrol sergeant, his immediate superior, should be held strictly responsible for allowing such conditions to prevail.

If a patrol sergeant should spend six of seven hours of his tour of duty lying around his station, instead of being in the precinct with his men, not only is he guilty of neglect of duty and inefficiency, but the commanding officer, whether he be lieutenant or captain, is equally as guilty for allowing the patrol sergeant to lie around the station. It surely must be considered one of the commanding officer's duties to see that his subordinates are doing their duty.

The fundamental principle of proper patrolling of any precinct is an honest and industrious patrol sergeant, for with such a sergeant, the conditions I am about to relate could not exist. If the patrolman sees his immediate superior loafing, what can be expected of him? When he knows that the patrol sergeant is not out in the precinct, why should he have any fear about spending his time in saloons, theaters, or other warm and comfortable places? Mr. Dannenberg says:

"On more than one occasion I have actually searched for over two hours in a given precinct on the main thoroughfares, and side streets as well, for a patrolman, but could not find one. On the other hand, I could visit various saloons in a precinct and find an officer in a few minutes. We looked for over an hour for an officer one night, without finding one, then entered three consecutive saloons, and found an officer in each one.

Another interesting sidelight on this situation is, that with but few exceptions my assistants could pick up any patrolman they happened to find, and sooner or later, find him loafing on his post. While, on the other hand, they would report to me that they had a certain patrolman in a certain saloon or theater at a certain time, and the next night or two nights thereafter I was able to visit the saloon or theater in question, at the times specified, and find the same officer thereat.

I am only citing such cases as those in which we were able to identify the officer. There were innumerable cases where various officers were found in saloons, theaters and other places, but we could not ascertain their identity, as in a number of places I was recognized by either the officer or some one else connected with the place where the officer was found, with the result the officer usually made such haste to depart that he left his drink on the bar unconsumed."

The following conditions are typical examples of conditions which we found during this investigation: The star numbers listed below were, in most cases, taken by the investigator or investigators securing the evidence. The names were secured through the Police Department files, and in all cases every attempt possible was made to verify the number of the star with the files in the Secretary's office, so there will not be any undue criticism against an innocent officer.

At about 11:15 p. m., I was advised by one of our investigators that he had followed two officers to the Rienzi saloon, Clark and Diversey. This place was kept under surveillance and at 11:30 p. m. officer A left the saloon. This was on January 22, 1915.

At about 9:30 p. m. officer B was seen entering the Crawford saloon, 1600 South Wabash avenue, where he remained until 10:05 p. m., when he proceeded to a saloon at 65-67 East Sixteenth street, entering the same at 10:10 p. m., where he remained until 10:25 p. m.

At about 8:15 p. m. on January 22, 1015, officers C and D were seen in a saloon at Milwaukee and Grand avenues, remaining there but a few minutes, when they went to another saloon at Sangamon and Ohio, where they remained until 8:55 p. m. At about 9 p. m. they entered still another saloon at Ohio and Morgan, where they remained for 25 minutes.

This officer D on January 25, 1915, at about 11 p. m., entered the saloon on the northwest corner of Ohio and Sangamon streets, where he remained for 25 minutes.

On January 23, 1915, at about 8:25 p. m., officer E was found in a saloon at Elizabeth and Austin streets, where he drank some wine, which he did not pay for. At about 11:10 p. m. he was found in a saloon at 1057 Grand avenue, where he remained until about midnight.

At about 12:15 a. m., on January 24, 1915, he entered the Grand Buffet, at Halsted and Grand avenue, where he remained until 12:30 a. m., when he entered still another saloon at 503 North Halsted street, where he had a drink and a cigar for which he did not pay, after which he left by the rear exit and could not be found thereafter.

At about 12:45 a. m., on January 23, 1915, officer F was found in a saloon at Superior and Noble streets, where he remained until 1 a. m.

This same officer was, on January 26, 1915, at 8:05 p. m., in a motion picture show, 1005 West Chicago avenue, where he remained five minutes, when he left and entered the Alvin Motion Picture Show, which is near by. He remained there until 8:45 p. m., when he proceeded to the Hub Theater, also in the near vicinity, where he remained until 9 p. m., when he pulled the box at Chicago avenue and Wood street. He then returned directly to the Hub Theater, where he remained until 9:45 p. m., at which time he went to a cigar store, where he remained until time to pull, after which he entered what appeared to be a dance hall at Superior and Noble streets, where a Polish wedding was in progress. He remained here until 10:55 p. m., when he pulled his box and went immediately to Pudla's saloon, at Huron and Bickerdike streets, where he remained for 20 minutes; thence to a saloon on the northeast corner of Superior and Bickerdike streets, where he remained for ten minutes; thence to a saloon on the northwest corner of Superior and Armour streets, where he remained for 20 minutes, and then boarded a westbound Chicago avenue car.

At about 12:30 a. m., on January 24, 1915, officer G was found in the saloon of Joseph Ginochio, at 503 North Halsted street, where he remained for at least 15 minutes.

At about 9 p. m., on January 25, 1915, officer H entered the tailor shop at 58 East Twelfth street, where he remained for 10 minutes, after which he entered the saloon of one Mahoney, a few doors west of the tailor shop, where he remained until 10:35 p. m., at which time he left and pulled the box at Fourteenth and State streets, which he did at 10:40 p. m., and then returned directly to a saloon on Michigan avenue, just north of Twelfth street, which he entered by the alley entrance. He remained here until 11:35 p. m., when he entered a restaurant in the Mayer Hotel, at Twelfth street and Wabash avenue, where he remained for fifteen minutes. Leaving here he went directly to a saloon on the northeast corner of Twelfth and State streets, where he remained for ten minutes, after which he proceeded immediately to a saloon on the southwest corner of Wabash and Thirteenth street.

According to the operator's record in the Second Precinct, this officer is credited with pulling at Twelfth and State streets at 11:40 p. m. I happened to be assisting in watching this officer myself, and know positively that he did not pull between the hours of 10:40 p. m. and 12:15 a. m., when we left him in a saloon at Wabash and Thirteenth street

At about 8:55 p. m. officer I entered the saloon at about 1207 South Wabash avenue, where he remained for ten minutes. At 9:45 p. m., the same date, he again entered this same saloon and remained ten minutes. Again at 11:12 p. m. he visited this saloon the third time, and remained there until 11:20 p. m. This was on January 25, 1915.

At about 8:20 p. m., on January 25, 1915, officer J went into a side door of the Wells School, on Ashland avenue, where he remained until 8:45 p m. At 9 p. m. he entered the side door of a saloon at 1460 West Chicago avenue, where he remained until 9:45 p. m., when he left by the side door and disappeared up the alley.

At about 11:05 p. m., on January 25, 1915, officer K was seen to enter the Lomax saloon, at Harrison and State streets, where he remained for five minutes. He then went to the Gayety Theater, on State street, where he remained for twenty minutes, and then proceeded to the Kuntz-Remler saloon, on Wabash avenue. He was still within at 11:45 p. m.

At about 8:15 p. m., on January 25, 1915, officer L was seen entering the Dearborn Street Station, where he remained until 9:35 p. m.

At about 10:35 p. m., on January 26, 1915, officer M was found in Horn's saloon, at Southport and Belmont avenues, where he sat down and conversed with a proprietor until 11:05 p. m.

At about 7:05 p. m., on January 26, 1915, officer N was seen leaving the Second Precinct Station, when he proceeded directly to the Dearborn Street Station, where he remained for fifty minutes.

At about 10:30 p. m., on January 26, 1915, officer O was seen entering a pool room at 631 South State street, where he remained for thirty minutes. He then entered a barber shop at 645 south State street, and remained until 11:25 p. m., when he pulled the box at Harrison and State streets, at 11:30 p. m. He then proceeded directly to the Alma Mater saloon, on South State street, where he remained until 12:25 a. m., and then proceeded to the Wabash Hotel, where he disappeared within.

At about 9:05 p. m., on January 27, 1915. officer P was seen entering a motion picture show on Madison street, just east of Karlov avenue, where he remained until 9:50 p. m

At about 10:05 p. m., on January 27, 1915, officer Q was seen entering the Victoria Theater, Sheffield and Belmont avenues, where he remained until 10:25 p. m., at which time he went to a saloon at 3100 Sheffield avenue, where he remained until 11:05 p. m.

At about 7:10 p. m., on January 27, officer R was seen entering a motion picture show at 2419 Wentworth avenue, where he remained until 8:05 p. m., then proceeded to a saloon at 2556 Wentworth avenue, where he remained fifteen minutes, after which he went dirctly to another saloon at the northwest corner of Twenty-fifth and La Salle streets. At about 9:10 p. m. he pulled the box at Twenty-third and Wentworth avenue, and then returned to the motion picture show at 2419 Wentworth avenue, where he remained until 10 p. m., when he returned to the saloon on the northwest corner of Twenty-fifth and La Salle Streets.

At about 9:10 p. m., on January 28, 1915, this same officer was seen entering a motion picture theater at 2419 Wentworth avenue, where he remained until 10 p. m. At about 10:15 p. m., he entered a saloon on the northwest corner of Twenty-fifth and La Salle streets, where he remained until 10:30 p. m., at which time he left and went to a saloon at 300 West Twenty-fourth place, where he remained until 10:55 p. m.

At about 11 p. m., on January 27, 1915, officer S was seen entering a saloon on the northwest corner of Harrison and St. Louis avenue, where he had a drink and remained until 11:23 p. m.

At about 8:20 p. m., on January 28, 1915, officer T was seen in a saloon on the northwest corner of Twenty-third and State streets, where he remained until 9:15 p. m. At abou 10:20 p. m., the same date, he again entered the same saloon, and was still within at 11 p. m.

On January 28, 1915. officer U was found in a saloon on the northwest corner of Twenty-fifth and La Salle streets, at 10:15 p. m., where he remained until 10:30 p. m., at which time he proceeded to another saloon at 300 West Twenty-fourth place, where he remained until 10:55 p. m.

At about 8:30 p. m., on January 28, 1915, officer V was seen in Max Schmid's saloon. Madison and Robey streets, where he remained until 9:25 p m., during which time he was playing cards with the patrons of the place.

At 9:30 p. m. he pulled the box at Hoyne and Madison street and went directly back to Schmid's saloon and continued the card game until 10:30 p. m., at which time he pulled the box at Robey and Madison streets and again went directly to Schmid's saloon and continued the card game until 11:30 p. m.

He did not even see fit to walk his post to Hoyne avenue, but rode on a street car, pulled his box, and then caught another car to Robey and Madison, and re-entered Schmid's saloon and continued the card game until 12:30 a. m.

At 11:05 p. m., on January 28, 1915, officer W was seen entering the Verhoven saloon, Twenty-fourth and State streets.

The same officer, on January 30, 1915, at about 8 p. m., was seen entering a "shanty" on the southwest corner of Twenty-fourth and Federal streets, where he aided in kindling a fire, remaining there until 8:55 p. m

At about 8:07 p. m., on January 28, 1915, officer X was seen in a motion picture show, Medora Theater, Harrison street, near Tripp avenue, where he remained until 8:55 p. m., when he pulled the box at Forty-fourth and Harrison streets. He then went to Frugoli's saloon, southeast corner of Harrison and Kostner avenue, and had a drink of whisky, which he did not pay for, and then returned directly to the Medora Theater and remained there until 9:50 p. m., when he visited Minucciani's saloon, northeast corner of Van Buren street and Keeler avenue. He remained only a few minutes and then pulled the box at Keeler avenue and Jackson boulevard, and returned to the Medora Theater at 10:05 p. m., where he remained until 10:35 p. m. At 10:40 p. m. and at 1:05 a. m. he disappeared in a narrow passageway about 4246 Harrison street, which leads to a bakery At 1:50 a. m. he reappeared from the same passageway and pulled the box and returned to the same passageway.

This same officer, on January 29, 1915, at about 9:30 p. m., was found in the Medora Theater, Harrison street, near Tripp avenue, where he remained until 10 p. m.

On January 29, 1915, officer Y entered the Rex Theater, Madison street, near Wood street, where he remained until 9 p. m. At about 10 p. m., same date, he entered the motion picture show on Madison street, three doors west of Western avenue. About five minutes later a street car stopped at the corner looking for an officer Some one directed the conductor into the theater. This officer came out with the conductor, but other officers had arrived in the meantime. This officer then re-entered the theater, where he remained until 11 p. m.

At about 8:10 p. m., on January 29, 1915, officer Z was seen entering the Yale Theater, where he remained until 8:55 p. m., when he left to make a pull at Sixty-third and Steward avenue, after which he proceeded to the Marlowe Theater, Sixty-third and Stewart avenue, arriving there at 9:05 p. m., and remained until 9:45 p. m., then went to Fifty-ninth and Wentworth avenue and pulled the box at 10 p. m., and then entered an alley leading to the Marlowe Theater, where he disappeared until 10:55 p. m., when he came out of the same alley, and pulled the box at Sixty-third and Stewart. At 11:05 p. m. he entered Schultz's bakery, 356 West Sixty-third street, where he remained until 11:45 p. m. At 12:15 p. m. he returned to Schultz's bakery, where he remained until 12:55 a. m. Again at 1:05 a. m., he returned to Schultz's bakery, remaining until 1:50 a. m., and returning still again at 2:25 a. m., where he remained until 2:55 a. m., at which time he pulled box at Sixty-third and Stewart, and returned to station.

This same officer, on January 30, at about 10 p. m., was seen entering pasageway to bakery on Wentworth avenue, between Fifty-ninth and Sixtieth streets, near a motion picture theater. At 11:15 p. m. he came out of the motion picture theater.

At about 10:25 p. m., on January 30, 1915, officer A1 was seen entering a motion picture show on Wentworth avenue, near Fifty-ninth street, where he remained until 11:15 p. m.

On January 30, 1915, at about 8:15 p. m., a shanty was being watched at Twenty-fourth and Federal streets. No one entered or left this place until 8:55 p. m., when officer B1 left, in company with another officer. Between 8:15 p. m. and 8:55 p. m. two officers could be seen in the "shanty," and could be heard kindling a fire.

At about 8:40 p. m., on January 31, 1915, officer C1 was seen entering the Imperial Theater, 1210 East Sixty-third street, where he remained until 9:25 p. m. He then pulled the box at Sixty-third and Dorchester at 9:30 p. m., and went directly to 1406 East Sixty-third street, a laundry company, where he remained until 10:25 p. m., when he pulled the box at Sixty-third and Wood-lawn avenue. He then proceeded to Parmelee Express Co., near the I. C. tracks, where he remained until 11:25 p. m. At 11:30 p. m. he pulled the box at Sixty-third and Dorchester avenue, after which he returned to the laundry at 1406 East Sixty-third street, where he remained until 12:25 a. m.

After pulling the box at Sixty-third and Woodlawn avenue, at 12:40 a. m., he returned to the Parmelee Express Co., and remained there until 1:20 a. m., when he again pulled the box at Sixty-third and Dorchester, and again proceeded to the laundry at 1406 East Sixty-third street, where he remained until 2:25 a. m., when he again pulled the box at Sixty-third and Woodlawn avenue.

At about 1 a. m., February 2, 1915, officer D1 was seen in a laundry at 1406 East Sixty-third street, where he remained until 1:55 a. m.

During the course of this investigation, especial attention has been paid to the general activities of patrol sergeants in the various precincts all over the city. It was quite a rare occasion that either I, or any of my assistants, were able to find a patrol sergeant out in his precinct. The fact that we were out for that purpose must not be lost sight of in this regard.

Out of four precinct stations that were put under surveillance from 7 p. m. to 3 a. m. the following morning, or, in other words, covering an entire tour of duty, our men found but one patrol sergeant out of the four who was out in his precinct doing patrol sergeant duty. He spent about three and one-half hours out of the eight out in his district.

By looking into the general conditions one night of recent date, a visit was made to the Thirty-third Precinct, where we found about a dozen or four-teen officers seated around two tables in the squad room, playing cards. One table was an ordinary saloon card table, with beer pockets on the corners, while the other was an oblong table. The games being played appeared to be poker. Money was on the table, and the conversation could be heard about losing or winning so much on a certain hand. You could even hear money rattle on the tables from the sidewalk.

About two months ago, while I was Inspector of Morals Conditions, I took the necessary steps to stop a poker game that was running there at that time.

At about 9:10 p. m., on January 30, 1915, officer E1 was seen entering a motion picture theater on Crawford avenue, between Harrison and Congress streets, east side of the street, where he remained until 10 p. m., when he came out and boarded an eastbound Harrison street car, riding to Inde-pendence boulevard, where he pulled his box, caught another car back to Crawford, where he entered the elevated station at Crawford and Colorado avenues, where it was found he was collecting fares in the cashier's booth. He remained here for twenty minutes. At about 10:30 p. m. he entered the same motion picture theater, where he remained until 10:55 p. m.

On January 29, 1915, at about 7:10 p. m., officer F1 entered an alley be-tween Congress and Van Buren streets, from Crawford avenue, which leads to his residence at 4012 West Congress street. He disappeared toward the rear door of his residence. His house was covered until 8:05 p. m., but he was not seen leaving during that time. At about 9 p. m. this same officer was seen going north on Crawford avenue, just south of Congress street, when he disappeared up the same alley, and apparently entered the same yard as he did previously. This house was again watched until 10 p. m., but the officer was not seen leaving his home.

At about 7:05 p. m., on January 30, 1915, this same officer pulled the box at the corner of Crawford and Harrison street, after which he went down the alley to 4012 West Congress street to his home and entered his back door. The rear and front entrances of this house were watched until 8:35 p. m., but the officer did not reappear. At 11:20 p. m. the same evening, was the next time this officer was seen, when he stood at the box at Crawford and Har-rison until 11:30 p. m., at which time he pulled the box and reported to the lieutenant that he had hurt his back, after which he went directly to his home."

Reports Made by Deputy Sergeants.

There are between five and six hundred plain-clothes officers, known as first and second class detective sergeants, stationed at the Central Bureau and in the various precincts. No effective attempt is made on the part of commanding officers and other executives of the department, to keep a de-tailed check on what each man is doing. Mr. Dannenberg says that "until recently there was really no regular report system. The reorganization ordinance, however, stipulated that all detective sergeants should make daily reports, and in this connection report blanks have been furnished. This form is not practical for such work, for various reasons. What is there about this report to prevent a plain-clothes officer from loafing in some saloon, or elsewhere, during the entire time of his supposed tour of duty. Suppose a plain clothes officer reports at the Detective Bureau, or his station, at 7 p. m., goes out and does not do one minute of police duty, except ring up every two hours, and reports in at 3 a. m., makes out his report on the form used, filling in all spaces—how is a commanding officer going to know what he has done from that report? Now, take a form such as I recommended to the Committee when I appeared before it at its public hearing or one very similar. The plain clothes officer must assign the title of the case he is working on, the time he spent on that particular case, what he actually did, name and address of any and all witnesses, and, briefly, what they know. If he works on more than one case he repeats this same form. What is the result? The commanding officer, or any other interested or authorized person could ascertain at a glance what each officer was doing; besides all evidence in any given case would be before him. If a commanding officer doubted any officer, he could easily check the report. If false, prefer charges against the author of same and discharge him. Further, the commanding officer could quickly tell whether the officer in question knows his business and was using good judgment. Make the report in duplicate, send the original to headquarters, and retain the copy at the station, filed in proper form.

"Take the present system; when a complaint of a burglary, hold-up or murder is made, and an investigation is made, but not sufficient evidence secured to indict; when a year later a similar complaint, accusing the same individual, is made, who has any record of the evidence in the former complaint? If you could go to a file and secure that, it would aid in the second complaint to a great extent.

"Furthermore, it would probably result in greater activity on the part of detective sergeants, for the following reasons: Under the present form of reports a sergeant might not do anything during his tour of duty, and still it would not show any discredit upon his part, while, under the system of reports advocated, he would be obliged to state that he did nothing during the tour of duty he was on. In the first place, an officer would hesitate about making a report, as it would hold him subject to criticism by his superior at the time the report was rendered.

"Taking up the detective sergeants who are assigned to travel beat:

"The sergeant should be obliged to visit saloons, pool rooms and other known hang-outs, of vagrants, criminals, and all other persons of bad repute; and their reports should show that they visited such and such a saloon, and such and such a pool room, and such and such a disorderly resort, stating the exact conditions found therein, naming all persons of known bad repute, and all persons who can be classed as vagrants; with the result that other officers of the department could then very easily and quickly ascertain where they should look for certain characters."

Operators' Pull Sheets.

Mr. Dannenberg's report showed that the patrolman's call from the patrol box was liable to manipulation at the police station.

"Not infrequently it has been ascertained," he says, "that some of the police operators were recording the alleged pulls of police officers, when, as a matter of fact, the officer did not pull. Further than this, it has been reported to me that some of the operators who complete their tour of duty at 8 a. m. quite frequently close their sheets, or, in other words, record the pulls of all officers at that time on duty in the precinct, between the hour of 7 a. m. and 7:30 a. m., which is anywhere from thirty to forty-five minutes ahead of the time the officer actually pulled. The object of the operator in doing this is to have his sheets closed as early as possible. He, in other words, takes chances and guesses at about what time a certain officer will pull.

"At the present time there are a certain number of police operators assigned to each station. Every operator has and makes friends at the various stations to which he is assigned, with the result that a certain per cent. of all the men traveling post at a given period stand in with the operators, and in case the officers should miss a pull, the friendly operator will take care of him.

On the other hand, if an officer wishes to leave his post, he can tip off the operator, and the operator will again take care of him by recording pulls every hour at a given place. Taking this into consideration, it must be remembered that there are forty-five precincts in Chicago, with the result that there are probably no less than a hundred officers on friendly terms with the operators on every shift. The result, consequently, means that a hundred officers every shift, or three hundred men a day, could be guilty of neglect of duty with the aid of the operator.

"If a central bureau was established, whereby patrolmen and other officers traveling beats in the entire city could ring up, it would go a long way toward remedying the above conditions. In the first place, the operator and the patrolmen would be separated, and there would not be so many officers who would have friends as operators. Furthermore, they would not need the number of operators they have at the present time. There should be a direct wire from each station to the operators' headquarters, whereby commanding officers could get into immediate communication, should they desire to call any particular man, to give him any orders."

Police Attorney.

Under the present system an attorney is employed and paid by the City for the purpose of defending policemen who are brought before the Police Trial Board when charges are preferred against them. It is of the utmost importance that this official should be wholly impartial. He must not be actively allied with any party or factional organization, and he should not engage in criminal practice where the testimony of police officers is likely to be important.

On this subject Mr. Dannenberg says: "Radical changes should be made. In the first place, nobody with political affiliations should have any position in the department of police. In the second place, any lawyer holding the position as police attorney should not be allowed to practice criminal law outside of the police department (or any other practice, for that matter), as the department needs all of the time of the man holding this position." The present police attorney, Miles Devine, is engaged in the practice of criminal law, representing the defense in a large number of criminal cases, in a great number of which the police are prosecuting witnesses. In these instances the officer is fighting the very man he looks to for advice and for protection in case the officer gets into trouble. Therefore, is it not more than probable that some officers would be inclined to lay down at times, when they see this situation in front of them? The following are a number of cases:

Case No. 2835.—Defendant, Paul Kabajoropolas; charge, attempted murder; filed March 25, 1914.

Case No. 2844.—Defendant, Harry Schoffman; charge, larceny; filed March 26, 1914.

Case No. 3243.—Defendant, John P. Cummings; charge, rape; filed May 19, 1914.

Case No. 3529.—Defendent, Kate Sauer; charge, abortion; filed June 26, 1914.

Case No. 3785.—Defendant, Jacob Cohen; charge, receiving stolen property; filed August 4, 1914.

Case No. 3786.—Defendant, Robert Coleman; charge, larceny; filed August 4, 1914.

Case No. 3799.—Defendant, Louis Schaffer; charge, embezzlement; filed August 4, 1914.

Case No. 4139.—Defendant, Max Rovech; charge, conspiracy; filed October 25, 1914.

"Further than this, the present attorney is president of the Cook County Democracy, the organization of one faction of the Democratic party. Only lately this organization, for the purpose of raising funds, gave a ball at the La Salle Hotel. Tickets to this affair were distributed among various commanding officers, who, in turn, were to dispose of them to officers, and others. An able lawyer should be chosen as police attorney, and there should be a sufficient salary appropriated to insure this. He should not be allowed to take up the practice of law outside of the police department. When he is not engaged in representing officers before the trial board, provision should be made that he should appear at certain times, at various stations, to give lectures to members of the department as a whole, commanding officers included, on City Ordinances, State Statutes, Evidence, Court

Procedure, Power of Arrest, Police Authority, and all other matters pertaining to police business; thereby increasing the general efficiency of the department. In this manner, the city would soon recover the sum paid to the attorney selected, in the increase in fines and amounts thereof. The lack of such knowledge among the various members of the department, is largely responsible for the now large number of dismissals in the various courts."

The Handling of Cases Before the Civil Service Commission.

Upon this point Mr. Dannenberg, who for some time represented the city in cases before the Board, says:

"There seems to be a tendency to let violators of police rules off with but little punishment, and, in some cases, where serious charges are made against an officer, as where they have been found guilty of even criminal offenses by the Trial Board, and discharged, they have been, subsequently, reinstated by the same board. There are some cases in which officers have been before the Trial Board, in which, had they been private citzens they would have, undoubtedly, been brought to trial in the Criminal Court, and received a term in the penitentiary. Some of the cases I have in mind are as follows:

"Officers Fay and Wilcox, motorcycle officers, being assigned mostly to violation of the speed ordinance, a year or so ago, arrested a chauffeur of a West Side liquor merchant for violating the speed ordinance. Taking him to the station, they questioned him as to his identity. He gave them a false name, later admitting his identity. Subsequently they asked him by whom he was employed. The officers then phoned to his employer's wife, advising her that they had her chauffeur under arrest, and that he had committed perjury, and that it would take $1,000 to get him out. The employer was out of town. His wife advised the officer that they would have to lock him up, as she would not furnish any $1,000. A day or two later, upon the return of the employer, these two officers visited him at his office. The evidence showed considerable conversation, and two or three visits made there by the officers to the employer, attempting to fix up the case. The evidence further showed that complaint had been filed at that time, and that the matter was before the court; that the employer met the two officers in question in court, and agreed to pay them the sum of $10 each, and give them a jug or two of whisky for the dismissal of the charges against his chauffeur. The evidence further showed that the papers had been removed from the court, and that the employer took the two officers to a store across from the City Hall, and paid them the sum of $10 each, and arranged to send them a jug of whisky. The two officers were found guilty and discharged from the department on February 27, 1914. They were reinstated on May 4, 1914.

"Lacey Case (charged with being engaged in other business besides that of a police officer). The evidence showed that he was the part owner or owner of taxicab company, which was catering mostly to houses of prostitution and assignation in the Thirty-first street district, to which Lacey was assigned as desk sergeant. The evidence further showed that some such places had signs, advertising Lacey's motor livery, in their premises, although it was not operated under his name. The evidence also showed he took orders for cabs over the police 'phone while on duty as desk sergeant at the police station. Lacey was found guilty and discharged on October 9, 1913. He was reinstated on January 17, 1914, and is now sergeant of police."

There are several other cases along similar lines.

The Handling of Vice Reports.

In this connection Mr. Dannenberg, for some time in charge of the "vice squad," says:

"Under the reorganization ordinance, the second deputy superintendent is required to report to the general superintendent the vice conditions in the city as a whole. The purpose of these reports is to serve as a check on the various commanding officers, and enable the chief to ascertain whether or not the various commanding officers are doing their duty in this connection. A number of reports, called 'Inspector of Moral Conditions Reports,' were made to the general superintendent at periods of from two to four weeks, covering a period of about ten months or more. These reports took up precinct by precinct, and listed only such violations as to which the Inspector of Morals Conditions had secured sufficient evidence to warrant prosecution; giving locations of places, proprietors, class of violations, and other data. The general superintendent subdivided these reports and sent them to the various commanding officers. For a considerable period of time the commanding officers were reporting back that the violations did not exist. The object of these reports was to show the general inefficiency and neglect of duty on the part of the commanding officer and officers assigned, when they did not rectify the conditions reported. The conditions, as complained of, were not rectified until I was instructed to proceed and make raids upon the places against which I had been reporting. This, according to my point, proved conclusively that the commanding officer, as well as others of his command, was either inefficient or was guilty of neglect of duty, if nothing more serious, and under the reorganization ordinance, where a commanding officer is supposed to be held strictly responsible for the conditions, I contended that that was sufficient proof and evidence upon which charges should have been filed against the various commanding officers, and other subordinates. These reports were guarded very closely from the public, every effort being made to prevent any of the contents from becoming known to the public. Being as familiar with the situation as I am, I am unable to find any good reason why these reports should not be made public. If the second deputy superintendent of police makes such reports to the general superintendent, and the press and public are aware of their contents, the citizens of the district to which each report refers will immediately take such steps as are necessary to force the commanding officer of that district to eradicate the evils complained of. Second: The commanding officer would not care to see a newspaper account of a long list of violations found in his precinct every two to four weeks, which he claims to know nothing about. Consequently, he would be obliged to be more active in this respect. Third: The general public and the neighbors in the immediate vicinity of any one place reported as being a house of prostitution, or other place where vice was flourishing, would take such steps as were necessary to drive out the nuisance. Fourth: A number of people who conduct such places could not conduct them if every few weeks the public were advised of their activities. I suggest that the committee go over some of these reports and read them into the record."

Schooling of Members of the Department.

There is at present a police school where recruits are required to prepare themselves for public work. This school has been successful, so far as it has gone, but additional provision should be made for the development of this work.

Mr. Dannenberg suggests that the police attorney should appear two or three times a week at the school of instructions and lecture to these men on various points of law, evidence and police authority with which they must come in contact daily.

"The school of instructions also attempts to educate other members of the department who have been on the force for a number of years. This is done by a set of questions and answers, but it is a very slow and inadequate method. There is no reason why, if the police attorney, as has been suggested above, would visit the station at roll call, or a set time, one or two days a week, at which all members of the department must attend, and give lectures, it would not aid wonderfully in aiding the work of a policeman. One of the greatest evils along this line is the fact that it is very seldom that a commanding officer is familiar with the evidence in any of the cases of his subordinates. For instance, an officer, either plain clothes or uniform, makes an arrest, sometimes on a serious charge, goes into court, and the defendant is discharged on account of some weak point in the case. This could be entirely eradicated if every commanding officer would insist that every one of his subordinates should come before him, prior to the time of the hearing of the case, and submit to him what evidence he has on the case in question. It would then be discovered if there was any weak point or if additional evidence was needed to secure a conviction. If this condition was found the commanding officer should see that a continuance was obtained in the case, so as to allow the officer sufficient time to secure the additional evidence.

I found this system of wonderful value in vice work, which I handled for several months. If arrests were made by officers assigned to me, and I found, in going over the case, a weak point which they had overlooked, I immediately appeared before the court, asked for a continuance, and sent the officer back to secure the additional information, with the result that I could then go ahead and secure convictions, where otherwise they would have been discharges, a nuber of which would have been mostly technical."

Captains Should Make Written Reports to the Chief on All Cases Where Warrants Are Refused; Also Should Not Be Retained in One District Too Long.

Not infrequently have officers appeared before a court for a warrant, and for various reasons the court has refused the warrant. The refusal of a warrant may be justified or not, with the result, usually, a controversy arises between the commanding officer and the presiding judge. Often the officer is at fault—in such cases as this. For example: An officer sees a well-known pickpocket on a street car, but sees him commit no offense. The pickpocket is simply riding on the car as he is. The officer arrests him and takes him to the station and attempts to secure a warrant for the pickpocket for vagrancy, or on similar charge. As a matter of fact, there is no evidence to constitute the charge. Still, the police department criticises the court for not issuing a warrant. In order to avoid the criticism, I am of the opinion it would be much better if the commanding officer would make a detailed report of all the facts to the general superintendent. If he believed the court was at fault, he should forward the report to the Chief Justice. Thereby the head of each branch of the municipal government would be able to judge who was right and who was wrong, and thereby eradicate the evil.

Commanding officers are very often kept in one precinct for a number of years. If vice, gambling or saloons should be prevalent in the district, it is especially bad, for the fact that sooner or later some one or other of these elements will secure the friendship of the commanding officer, with the result that they will be given more leniency than should be allowed under ordinary circumstances. If a new captain or commanding officer was sent into the district from time to time, those elements would not have sufficient time to work into the friendship or good graces of the officers in question.

7. POLICE COLLUSION WITH CRIME

Early in the investigation information was received indicating that there was collusion between certain members of the police force and certain criminals. This was verified by detailed work of our investigators. Our action was followed by the State's Attorney in returning indictments against a number of police officials. There can be no doubt that one of the chief causes of crime in Chicago is that members of the police force, and particularly of the plain clothes staff, are hand in glove with criminals. Instead of punishing the criminal, they protect him. Instead of using the power of the law for the protection of society, they use it for their own personal profit. They form a working agreement with pickpockets, prowlers, confidence men, gamblers, and other classes of offenders. The basis of this agreement is a division of profits between the lawbreaker and the public official. The exact extent of this system it is impossible to determine, but there is no doubt that its ramifications are so wide as to cripple the machinery for the enforcement of the law.

The reason why many professional criminals are permitted to remain in Chicago and ply their sinister trade must be found either in the incompetence of the police, or in the corruption of part of the force. It is plain that even with an absolutely competent force, the amount of corruption now existing is sufficient to make proper protection of the public from crime impossible. A relatively small percentage of police officers may betray the public into the hands of the pickpockets, burglars and crooks of all descriptions. The ease with which knowledge of criminal hang-outs and familiar figures in the criminal world may be obtained by investigators makes it incredible that the police are ignorant of these places and persons. Not only is this true, but in some instances information regarding these hang-outs and their habitues was given by the police themselves. In fact, officers even speak with pride of the fact that they know the leading crooks in town and that they can point them out when they are in sight.

It is incredible that the police do not have fairly full information regarding the location and habits of most of the professional criminals in Chicago. Consequently, the only conclusion that can be drawn is that some influence holds them back from vigorous prosecution of these persons. What are these influences? In some instances, police are held back because they use petty criminals as "stool pigeons" or "snitchers." Cheap thieves may be employed as a source of information regarding other thieves, the reward being immunity from arrest.

Again they may be held back by political influence or fear of official punishment and they do not wish to incur the displeasure of those who secure their appointment or promotion, or whose official favor or disfavor may affect their future promotion or location. They do not wish to incur the displeasure of the powers that prey. Testimony on this point was given by Lieutenant McWeeney, as follows:

THE CHAIRMAN: You spoke of pressure being brought to bear upon the prosecutors. Is that same kind of pressure being brought to bear upon officers?

MR. McWEENEY: Yes, it is the custom. I know I have had people ask me several times to be easy, to go easy on such and such a fellow.

THE CHAIRMAN: Men of political influence, you mean?

MR. McWEENEY: Yes, political influence and friends both. Generally friends.

THE CHAIRMAN: They bring a good deal of pressure to bear?

MR. McWEENEY: They do.

THE CHAIRMAN: Do they bring the same kind of pressure to bear on officers under you?

MR. McWEENEY: The same kind exactly.

THE CHAIRMAN: And sometimes they get away with it?

MR. McWEENEY: Often they use me as a go-between. They use me to influence the officer. I don't take their way of looking at it at all.

THE CHAIRMAN: You mean they want you to influence the officer's testimony?

MR. McWEENEY: No, but they want me to ask the officer to be easy.

THE CHAIRMAN: What do they mean by being easy, going a little easy on the testimony?

MR. McWEENEY: Certainly, going a little easy on the testimony. That is what they want.

Punishment may be visited upon these officers either in the form of a transfer to some undesirable post, or failure to secure merited promotion or even trumped up charges preferred against the official. In such cases the real blame for criminal conditions rests upon the man higher up, who is willing to co-operate with the criminal group in order to secure their political support. Such a person in office or out, is willing to permit the traffic in crime or wink at crime in order to hold or secure some high position or special privilege.

In other instances, however, the police relation with criminals consists in a direct partnership between the official and the lawbreaker. The most familiar forms of this are found in connection with prostitution and gambling, but they extend far beyond these limits and over into the sinister relationships with all forms of misdemeanor and felony. They not only tolerate the woman of the street and the gambler, because of the personal profit involved in such toleration, but they reach out for the professional pickpocket, the prowler, the confidence man, and the other denizens of the underworld who traffic in crime.

In order to demonstrate this system, a systematic effort was made. Three investigators were selected who posed as confidence men. Two of them were arrested and confined for about two days in the Central Police Station. They secured their release through a bondsman and attorney and then later made their headquarters at a well-known hang-out. Here they made the acquaintance of many professional criminals and of certain police officers. They formed partnerships with these officials according to the terms of which the profits of their enterprises were to be divided equally between the police and the presumed criminals. The investigators purported to be carrying on the business of picking pockets, and actually divided the presumed proceeds of their thefts with the police officials.

They were informed by these officers, who were detective sergeants, as to the most desirable places for theft, and on occasion they were accompanied by an officer in plain clothes to Sixty-third and Halsted streets, which had been indicated as a harvest field for pickpockets. They were protected by this officer during the time they went through the motions of a pickpocket mob, in order to prevent interference by any uniformed official. This is known as working "under cover," the practices described by one of our investigators being as follows:

"A good many of the gangs work under the protection of the police officers. Sometimes the officers work right with the mobs on the street cars. For instance, they will work in the rear end or on the back platform, obstructing the victim as he gives chase to the pickpocket, after he has been victimized. Sometimes the officer will butt in and grab the victim if he is chasing the pickpocket, pretending that he thinks there is a fight on the car, and he will detain the man who has been the victim just long enough to allow the pickpocket to make his escape. If the victim squawks, the officer doing the covering will step in and make an arrest, in order to prevent some other officer, some honest officer, from making a genuine arrest. He pretends to make an arrest of the men he is working with."

The statement of one of the investigators working on this case is given herewith:

"During one period of inquiry running over nearly a month we made regular visits to Foley's place and became well acquainted with him. His place is a loafing place for numerous detectives.

"One morning a few days ago (September 29, to be exact), we went downtown and as we passed a hotel on Randolph street we met Foley talking to two men at the door.

"Foley called us over and invited the two men and ourselves in the bar to have a drink. As we walked in one of the men with Foley looked at us and laughed. Then he placed both his hands on his pockets as if afraid of losing something and said:

"'You bunch of burglars, you. I'll have to watch you to keep you from picking my pockets.'

"One of the men was introduced to us as a detective. (I will call him 'A.') The other man was said to be a bailiff.

"'How are you fellows making out?' 'A' asked.

"'Oh, we're getting away with a little junk now and then,' I said.

"'Well you know you've got to go 50-50,' said 'A.'

"'Oh, sure, sure,' we replied, 'we're wise to that. But it's just cost us a lot of cash to get out of jail.' We told him it cost us nearly $200.

"'I know all about that,' he said. 'I made you in a minute, but you were fools to pay $200 to get out when I could have fixed it up for $50.'

"'Yes, but we didn't know anybody in the town and we haven't had a chance to make a working arrangement. We're in with Foley now and he is protecting us, but we don't know any coppers.'

"'Well, if you ever get nailed again just call on me.' He said.

"Then he (Detective A.) wrote out his name and telephone number on a slip of paper and handed it to us.

"'We are willing to split if we can fix it all right,' we said.

"'Well, just depend on me and call on me when you get in trouble and I'll go to the front for you,' he said.

"Then he told us of a case which he and Foley were interested in.

"'Foley soaked those two guys for $100, and I told him he would have to give $50 of it back,' he said. 'The guys are all right, and they need the money, because they're nearly broke. Foley wanted to give $25 back, but I won't stand for it. He's got to give $50 of it back.'

"Then 'A.' told us he was going to St. Louis to bring back a prisoner. He had the papers in his pocket and was going to the State's Attorney's office to have them fixed up. Then we told him we knew where a bunch of stolen sealskins were stored in St. Louis, and that if he was going there we would 'tip him off.'

"Then we made arrangements to meet him next day. We called him up early the next morning (September 30) and made a 'date' to meet him at Foley's saloon. We met him (A.) and his partner (B.) and another detective in the back room.

"We sat down at a table and ordered a drink. Then we told the detectives that we had just been over to the fire on Wabash avenue and that we had got nine pocketbooks, but that most of them contained rent receipts and didn't net us much profit. Then I called Detective A. to another room and talked to him a while. I told him we could only give him $25, because it had been a bad day for pocketbooks.

"Then I put $25 in a small match box and handed it to Detective A. He took the match box containing the money and put it in his pocket. Then I bought a drink with a $10 bill and received $9.50 change. The waiter laid the change on the table.

"Finally 'A.' said he had to go to Thirty-first and Indiana and fix up a case for several of the 'brothers' who had robbed a man and got caught. He left with the other detective. Then I told Detective B. to lay his hat on a chair beside him. He did this and I swept up the pile of money from the table and put it in his (B.'s) hat.

"After dumping the money in the detective's hat I handed the hat containing the money over to one of our two investigators, Moss. Moss took it and handed the hat containing the money to the detective. The detective (B.) took the hat and held it in his hand a few minutes.

" 'Well, it's about time we split up,' was suggested.

" 'All right, I'll see you boys later,' said Detective B.

" 'When we see you again we will have some information about those stolen sealskins,' I said. 'Just as soon as we learn where they are stored we'll put you next.'

" 'All right, and we'll split fifty-fifty.' Detective B. said.

"Then we bought a cigar at the counter and he went out.

"We reported to the office of Fletcher Dobyns, attorney for the Crime Commission, and told him of the circumstances by which we gave the two detectives the $34.50.

"We discussed further plans with Mr. Dobyns, Mr. McKeag, and Ald. Merriam. We left Mr. Dobyns' office and walked toward Madison and Dearborn streets. As we arrived in front of the Tribune Building we saw two detectives talking to a man. The detectives were 'C.' and 'D.' They recognized us as soon as we did them. We hurried past as they turned around and watched us.

" 'There go three con men,' said 'C.' 'Let's trail them.'

"We looked back just as the two detectives started after us. We quickened our steps and turned east on Madison street. Just as we turned the corner we glanced back and saw the detectives hurrying after us.

" 'They're trailing us,' somebody said. 'Let's split up and meet in the saloon next door to the McVicker Theater.'

"We separated and I hurried into a run ahead of the other two men. The detectives broke into a run and caught up to me just as I entered the swinging doors of the barroom.

"One of them caught me by the shoulder and the other one grabbed the other two men.

" 'Thought you guys were going to get out of town,' said Detective C.

" 'How can we get out of town when we haven't any money?' was our reply.

" 'How much have you got?'

" 'Only $40 or $50.'

" 'Isn't that enough to get you out of town?'

" 'Why, that isn't enough to keep us running for one day,' we said, 'we're not pikers. We're out after big dough.'

" 'Didn't the judge tell you to get out of town?'

" 'No, he didn't say anything about it.'

" 'Well, when are you going?'

" 'Whenever we can work long enough to get the coin.'

" 'How long will that take you?'

" 'Well, we could get plenty before night and be out of town if we were let alone for a few hours in this crowd.'

" 'You guys are pretty wise,' said 'C.'

" 'Yes, and they'll never leave town, either,' said 'D.'

" 'Well, you be pretty careful and we'll talk to you later,' said 'C.' 'Give me your address and.we'll get in touch with each other.'

"We told him we were living at the Columbia hotel.

" 'You appear to be right guys, but you ought to turn over a new leaf and live on the square,' said 'C.' 'You'll get by pretty easy for a while, but it will end in the pen in the long run. If you would put your brains to a better use you could make a lot of dough.'

"Then they left us.

"Last Saturday (October 3) we met Detective B. at Foley's place. We talked over the various fields for pickpockets and he told us the best place

was around the busy corner of Sixty-third and Halsted streets. We told him
we wanted to get right with several other people around town because we
were afraid to hang around Foley's all the time.

"'The best place for you fellows to hang around is George Graham's,
5514 State street,' he said.

"'Yes, a lot of people have told us to go out and see him because he
was a right guy, but we've never met George.'

"'Well, I'll drop around there at 4 o'clock today and if you guys will be
out there I'll put you in right with him,' said 'B.'

"We agreed to be out there at the stated time. Then I threw a five dollar
bill to B. and said:

"'Buy a drink with all that money you've got.'

"He called a waiter, ordered a drink with my five dollar bill, and kept the
change.

"'That's about all we've been able to get today,' I said. 'Our whole day's
work only netted us $11.'

"We left Foley's and came downtown. We knew that a number of detectives always loafed about the Berghoff and Al Tearney's saloon on Adams
and State streets. We saw two detectives standing in front of the Berghoff.
Then two more came in and stood beside us and bought a drink.

"A few minutes later a detective came in, took a glass of beer, talked a
few minutes, and then went out front. When we went out he was still
standing there.

"We then went down to Al Tearney's saloon. We noted that a partition
had been built about three feet from the wall, behind which was a secret telephone and a ticker. Frequently patrons of the place went behind the partition and we could hear them talking about the race results. The detectives who
entered this place could hardly help from 'thinking' that a hand book on the
races was being conducted behind that partition.

"We went down to George Graham's saloon at 4 o'clock. We found Detective B. talking to Graham. We were introduced to Graham as 'right guys.'
We ordered drinks and talked with Graham about selling some stolen diamonds.

"'Bring them down here; we'll give you more for them than any one else
will,' he said. 'Bring all you've got, and if I'm not here the bookkeeper will
do the business with you.'

"'Will you fix us if we get nailed?' was asked.

"'Sure thing, and it won't cost you like it did before,' he said. 'I'm in
right, and I'll get you out quick. Just hang around here and I'll take care
of you.'

"'Well, we're going over to Sixty-third and Halsted streets tonight to
make a little dough,' (picking pockets), we told him. 'If we get jammed
we'll call for you.'

"'All right. I'm always on the job when the "brothers" get in trouble,' he
said. 'Just call for me and those dicks over there will know you're right
guys. Then I'll come over and get you out. Now bring those diamonds
around.'

"'Are all these guys around here right?' we asked.

"'Sure, there's a nice bunch that hangs around here,' he said. 'You fellows just breeze around and we'll all be big brothers with you.'

"Then we took Detective B. over to a table and talked 'business' with him.

"'Now we're going to follow your tip and work the street cars and the
crowds over at Sixty-third and Halsted streets,' I said. 'Now we want protection. Who are the right dicks?' (detectives).

"'Well, there's a bunch of right dicks over there (Englewood), but some
of them are wrong,' he said. 'Now, you've got to be careful of the wrong
guys.'

"'Well, what we want you to do is to go over there with us and if some
sucker puts up a holler you've got to step in and stall around with us and
square it up,' I said. 'Now, will you do that?'

"'I'll be over there at 9 o'clock,' he said. 'I can't make it any sooner.'

"That night we mingled with the crowds along the corners and saw a
number of detectives standing around. We met in McLaughlin's and saw
several detectives and pickpockets.

"We saw how easy it would have been to pick the pockets of a dozen
persons in the crowds on the streets and we worked the pickpocket 'racket,'

but did not go so far as to attempt to put our hands in any one's pocket. We worked the 'racket' so as to attract the attention of the detectives.

"After this had continued for 30 minutes we went over to the cafe of Ed Weiss and met Detective B. We had a drink at the bar and talked to 'B.' about the stolen furs. We had learned in the meantime that the stolen furs were stored at a downtown hotel. We told Detective B. and he seemed anxious to get the information. He said he would make sure whether they were stored there before he attempted to arrest the persons whom we had named as implicated in the theft.

"We also told him that we had been unable to make but a few dollars that night because we were afraid that too many detectives were on the corner. We told him we would have a lot of money by Monday.

" 'We really didn't get enough to make a split,' I said. 'But we'll get right before Monday and then we'll talk business. We only got about four——' "

" 'Never mind,' he interrupted; 'I'm not supposed to know anything about how many you got.'

" 'Well, we're much obliged for your trouble in coming down here to help us,' I said, 'but we are out of luck.'

"Then he told us he would meet us the next day and he went out. This ended our experience for that day—October 3."

These two detectives were subsequently discharged by the Civil Servcie Commission upon the testimony presented by investigators of the Crime Committee.

That such collusion between police officials and criminals is a widespread practice there can be no doubt. The testimony of all the investigators converges upon this central point, and coming from so wide a variety of sources, confirmed by the Civil Service Commission and the State's Attorney in so many specific instances, leaves the way open to no other conclusion than the existence of an appalling system of partnership in crime between public officials on the one hand and habitual criminals on the other.

In the course of the investigation, the names of many policemen have been mentioned as involved in corrupt relations with various forms of criminals. One of the examples of this is as follows:

One of our investigators testified that criminals paid compensation to the police. He said: "They usually pay 25 per cent of the money stolen by the pickpockets. In some cases they demand 50. The officer won't take anything in some cases unless he gets $50.00 advance."

He also testified that pickpockets refusing to split with the officer are picked up and locked up in jail:

"One man that I know of was working around Harrison and State streets. I heard the officer make the statement, that if the fellow did not come across, he would not let him work around there; that is, if he did not split with him. This fellow would not split with the officer, so he got out. He is not there now."

8. PROFESSIONAL BONDSMEN, DISREPUTABLE LAWYERS AND FIXERS

A part of the criminal system of Chicago is the activities of certain professional bondsmen. Theoretically, the bondsmen are persons who furnish bonds, pending trial, for appearance of one who otherwise would remain in custody instead of at liberty. Practically under our modern system certain bondsmen have gone far beyond their original function and appear in an altogether different position from that of the individual who casually comes forward as surety for a friend.

In the first place he appears upon the bonds of many different persons and becomes a professional bondsman, who makes the giving of bonds a trade from which he derives either all or a part of his living.

In the next place he appears upon the bonds, not merely of occasional criminals, but of well known professional criminals. In some instances he appears to be the agent of well organized groups of habitual criminals, as, for example, pickpockets. And finally he becomes not merely surety for one charged with crime, but may undertake the broader work of a "fixer." He endeavors not merely to obtain the liberty of the accused pending trial, but to insure his complete immunity from punishment, and his final release.

Our investigators undertook an inquiry into the general duties of professional bondsmen as a part of the general crime system of the city. These observations, while by no means complete, nevertheless show with sufficient fullness and accuracy the outlines and scheme of things as they are now operated.

We took the bond index in the office of the Criminal Court for names of persons appearing on various bonds. When these were obtained we examined the dockets and files in these cases and from these obtained the name of the defendant, the amount of the bond, the date of the bond, co-surety on the bond, and disposition made of the case.

The most striking fact about these cases is that in most instances no conviction is secured. This is well illustrated by the following cases:

No.	Offense	What happened
1.	Confidence game	Stricken off
2.	Confidence game	Not guilty
3.	Assault to murder	Stricken off
4.	Burglary	Died
5.	Larceny	Not guilty
6.	Confidence game	Pending
7.	Larceny	Stricken off
8.	Larceny	....
9.	Confidence game	Stricken off
10.	Confidence game	Paroled
11.	Robbery	Nolle prossed
12.	Receiving stolen property	Dismissed for want of prosecution.
13.	Confidence game	Nolle prossed
14.	Assault to kill	Not guilty
15.	Larceny	Pending
16.	Larceny	One day in the County Jail, $1 and no costs
17.	Confidence game	Nolle prossed
18.	Larceny	Not guilty
19.	Burglary	Stricken off
20.	Robbery	Release on probation
21.	Larceny	Stricken off
22.	Crime against children	....
23.	Rape	Pending
24.	Manslaughter	Stricken off
25.	Assault to rob	Pending
26.	Manslaughter	Not guilty
27.	Larceny	House of Correction
28.	Larceny	....
29.	Larceny	Penitentiary
30.	Larceny	Stricken off
31.	Larceny	Stricken off
32.	Confidence game	Not guilty
33.	Larceny	Pending
34.	Burglary	Pending
35.	Burglary	Pending
36.	Larceny	Stricken off
37.	Confidence game	Not guilty
38.	Larceny	Stricken off
39.	Larceny	One hour in the County Jail
40.	Confidence game	One day in the County Jail
41.	Murder	Not guilty
42.	Embezzlement	Not guilty
43.	Rape	Nolle prossed
44.	Larceny	Six months in the County Jail
45.	Larceny	House of Correction nine months
46.	Assault	....
47.	Robbery	....
48.	Larceny	Nolle prossed
49.	Larceny	Penitentiary
50.	Embezzlement	Nolle prossed
51.	Confidence game	Stricken off
52.	Confidence game	Stricken off
53.	Confidence game	Nolle prossed
54.	Confidence game	Nolle prossed
55.	Burglary	Nolle prossed

No.	Offense	What happened
56.	Indecent liberties	Not guilty
57.	Larceny	Stricken off
58.	Confidence game	Stricken off

These cases, it must be understood, represent only a small part of a great circle. No account is taken of the activity of the professional bondsmen in the Municipal Court on the preliminary hearings and around the police stations. Typical cases have been taken from the Criminal Court only.

The following deductions may easily be drawn from an examination of these facts, and from a study of the activities of professional bondsmen:

First: That in 75 per cent of the cases for which a professional goes bond no conviction is secured.

Second: These bonds are given in many instances, not for occasional criminals, but for more or less notorious and professional criminals, of the type of Eddie Jackson, Louis Gazzollo, and others.

These facts raise a strong presumption that the professional bondsman constitutes an important link in the general system by which immunity from the punishment of crime is obtained in so large a number of cases.

It is recommended that the Municipal Court and the Criminal Court investigate the activities of professional bondsmen, more extensively and directly than it is possible for this Committee to do, with special reference to:

1. The number of times that one particular person appears on the bonds within a period of six months.

2. The character of the charge and the previous record of the defendant.

3. The amount of bond that is already given by the bondsman.

4. The political connections, if any, of the bondsman.

It would further appear that if this bondsman appeared more than once on a bond during a six months' period in a list published at intervals, say of six months, the resulting publicity would serve as a useful check upon the creation of a professional bondsman. The acceptance or rejection of bonds is entirely within the discretion of the court, and consequently the development of the present system may readily be checked if the courts will take decisive action.

In connection with the professional bondsmen, and as another link in the same general crime system, the investigators find a certain type of criminal lawyer. These attorneys, although sworn as officers of the court for the purpose of administering justice, have gone far beyond the bounds described by legal ethics, and are close on the fringe of conspiracy with criminals to frustrate the law. A few illustrations will suffice to show the truth of this. The following report from one of our investigators indicates clearly one angle of this situation. He says:

"After some preliminary work in getting acquainted with pickpockets and their hang-outs, I was instructed to get acquainted with ————, an attorney for pickpockets, and see what I could learn about the methods of pickpockets and their methods from him. He hangs around ————'s saloon, and ————, and ———— saloon, and will get in touch with his clients there. As he was about to go into an office in the ———— Building, I suggested to him that I was doing investigating work and would like to occupy the same office with him. He said if I could throw him any business, such as divorce cases, accident cases, or cases of any kind which I was investigating, and I would answer the telephone and help keep in communication with him, with the various hang-outs of crooks he was doing business with, that he would not charge me any office rent. He gave me a list of the various saloons that were used as hang-outs and their telephone numbers, and he told me if he was not in court or outside that he could be reached in some of these places. I often called up at these places and I frequently answered the telephone calls sent from these various places. At different times, well known crooks called up from these various places and they left messages with me for Mr. ———— and left messages with me for criminals. His method of business is almost entirely through telephone calls, and he is being called up from these hang-outs and he is constantly calling them up, and he sacrifices all other kinds of business to handle these telephone calls and business that comes through them. The crooks whom he represents are, of course, the kind who are not part of the police system and who have not split up with the police, and so escape arrest. In other words, they are all crooks who get arrested. These crooks, whenever they start to work, leave word at the hang-outs where they will be, and the arrangment is that they are to call up every half hour. If they fail to call up, the hang-out knows they are in trouble and at once calls up Mr. ———— and informs him that a particular crook or bunch of crooks are at work in a certain district and they probably have been arrested. If it is in the day time ———— at once goes to the Detective Bureau or police station in that district. He very often takes a writ of habeas corpus with him, and sometimes he is at the station ten or fifteen minutes ahead of the crooks. The first thing that he does is to attempt to bluff the police, to tell them they have no case, and unless they turn the man loose or book him at once that he will get him out on a writ. The bluff usually works. If the police have not a definite charge to book the prisoner on they will turn him loose, or if they have a charge they will book him right away. When they refuse to book him or turn him loose, he then comes back with the writ of habeas corpus. I have known him to get out as many as five men on writs of habeas corpus in one day. After he gets them booked, he provides them with bondsmen. He has four regular bondsmen that I know of. After the crook is gotten out on bond ———— works with the various hang-outs in an effort to get the case fixed up, to call off the police, or procure witnesses, or influence prosecutors or courts, in any manner that they can secure the release of the criminal. He also takes as many continuations as possible, making all kinds of excuses in order to wear out the witnesses. He goes around to these hang-outs and spends a great deal of time there, drinks, gambles, and gives a commission to the bartender on the business which he gets."

Another illustration was found in connection with the three investigators who posed as confidence men. In this instance our investigators, after the arrest of the presumed confidence men, secured the services of ————, whose name appears as a professional bondsman, and who was reported as an all-around fixer. ———— at once communicated with an attorney named ————. After stating the facts to him regarding the arrest of the con men, he told our investigator that he would see the arresting officer that night, that he would go down and talk to Halpin and see if he could get them booked. He said it was possible to get the men out without being booked, but "it would cost a lot of money." He then went to Halpin and had the men booked. He secured their release on the following day. When asked how this was brought about so readily, he said, "We have a working arrangement and things run along smooth. We do not have any trouble; they give us very little trouble that way."

When some anxiety was expressed by the investigator as to what would happen to the fellow investigators when brought before the judge, the attorney said: "Now, I am a lawyer. What do you think I am doing here?" He further said, after the release of the investigators: "They will be all right now for ten or fifteen days." . . . "We want you to understand that when we say we guarantee protection, we do not mean absolute protection, but it means as long as things are running along right."

He further advised the investigators when released to get a room with ————, the fixer, and "slip him the jack regularly," that is to say, give him money regularly.

9. THE PROSECUTION OF CRIME

One of the most striking facts in the criminal statistics of Chicago is the large number of persons who are discharged. On felony charges, there is only one chance in five of a man ever getting to the Criminal Court for trial, and only one chance in thirty of going to the penitentiary or reformatory.

In quasi criminal cases, numbering in 1913, 93,711, 41 per cent were convicted. This may be due to unnecessary arrests by the police, or to defects in the prosecuting machinery which may be attributed either to the technicalities of the law or the inadequacy of the prosecution.

It has not been possible for this Committee to undertake a thoroughgoing investigation of the workings either of the prosecuting machinery of the courts or of the criminal law. It is desirable that this be done and for that purpose the appointment of a special commission by the Chief Justice of the Municipal Court and Presiding Judge of the Criminal Court is needed to make a thoroughgoing study of criminal law and practice in the several court and prepare recommendations for the next session of the Legislature.

In the course of the hearings before the commission, important testimony was presented regarding the City Prosecutor's office. Chief Gleason, himself, complained of the inefficiency of this office and of their lack of co-operation with the police. He said:

CHIEF GLEASON: I have seen prosecutors who never open their mouths unless they wanted to get a fellow off.

* * * *

THE CHAIRMAN: What do you do when you find prosecutors who "never open their mouths" except to let a man go?

CHIEF GLEASON: What do I do?

THE CHAIRMAN: Yes.

CHIEF GLEASON: Well, they talk a little more now than they used to.

* * * *

THE CHAIRMAN: Did you report that to the Prosecuting Attorney?

CHIEF GLEASON: No, sir.

THE CHAIRMAN: You did not take any action?

CHIEF GLEASON: No, sir.

This startling testimony on the part of the Chief of the Police was corroborated by Chief Justice Olson, particularly regarding the Assistant State's Attorney. He said:

"It was an accident that they ever manned those courts in the first place. The Criminal Court had jurisdiction of misdemeanors That was before our court came into existence. They were all taken over to the Criminal Court and indicted by the Grand Jury. Now, under the old system these cases were carefully looked after, brought before the Grand Jury and carefully prepared for trial Then our court got to be looked upon as a court to dispose of a lot of old junk for the violation of ordinances, and nobody would come near it. These men were not sent to our court; then I went to the State's Attorney's office and he said he would see about it."

Continuing the Judge said, of the Assistant State's Attorneys:

"It takes at least four years to make a good trial lawyer out of a fairly good lawyer, after he is appointed State's Attorney. Another thing, their tenure of office is, in many cases, too short."

Continuing, he said:

"The city fights its battles with raw recruits who will make good lawyers. Some of them are very good, although they are not there long enough to get experience. I know that a man is much more dangerous as a State's Attorney to the defendants if he has had four years' experience than one who has had six months."

Neither the City Prosecutor's office nor the State's Attorney's office is placed under the protection of the merit system. In both of them the appointments are made on a political basis, and consequently change as administrations change. The effect of this upon the work of both the City Prosecutor's office and the State's Attorney's office is bad. It frequently results in the dismissal of a man from office at the very time when he has become most efficient, and supplanting him with a man who, however well qualified as a general practitioner, does not understand the intricacies of criminal law. The consequence is that during a considerable part of the time both criminal and quasi criminal cases are in the hands of green and inexperienced men. However great their natural endowments or their legal ability, they are evidently at a disadvantage in dealing with skilled attorneys for the defense who have been for many years familiar with all the ins and outs of our complicated criminal procedure. Under our political system, furthermore, many prosecutors will be appointed as reward for party service rather than because of superior qualifications for the particular place they seek. Such a result is almost inevitable under a system of political appointments and is just as characteristic of one party as of another.

As a practical remedy for this situation, it is suggested that the merit system be applied as far as possible to the office of the City Prosecutor and to the office of State's Attorney. If it is not deemed practicable to apply this method to the higher positions in these offices there is nothing to prevent its abuse in regard to investigators and minor prosecutors. The pay-roll of the State's Attorney's is $148.381.48 and of the City Prosecutor's office is $52,042.32. A considerable portion of this pay-roll can and should be placed under the protection of the merit system. In this way, positions will be filled by those who are competent, and when the competent men are found, they will be retained and promoted on the basis of service rendered. This can be accomplished in the case of the City Prosecutor's office by means of a city ordinance, and in the case of State's Attorney's office by amendment of the state law; or in both cases there is nothing to prevent the adoption of a voluntary system of Civil Service. The aid of the Bar Association could be invoked in order to guarantee the impartiality of any examinations held.

It has not been possible in this report to inquire into the practical workings of the courts. However, much testimony, incidentally, has been given before the committee by judges and by others familiar with the workings of the court. It is recommended that the commission above suggested should be appointed for the purpose of studying the practical methods of the police and criminal courts and of the criminal law, and making a report upon that subject.

In the course of the inquiry, attention was directed to the fact that in several cases in which there are defendants who do not speak English, great difficulty was experienced in securing proper interpreters. Judge Uhlir testified that in one instance he had detected a man misinterpreting the Bohemian language, which the Judge understood. Other evidence was presented to the same effect, and it was clear that more adequate provision should be made to secure proper interpretation of statements of those who do not understand the English language.

Under these circumstances, it is possible that a serious wrong may be done a defendant because of his inability to express himself clearly, or on the other hand, that a crooked interpreter may secure the release of a really guilty person. For this purpose, it is recommended that a bureau of interpreters be organized for use in stations where most needed.

Speaking of certain interpreters and fixers who hung around the courts, Judge Uhlir said:

"These men hang around there for the purpose of making a dollar or two and they interpret in these cases and have an interest one way or another or on both sides. They do not interpret right. They started that before me, before they discovered that I understood them, and I would drive them away from the court room because I knew they were trying to 'put something over' on the Judge."

THE CHAIRMAN: "They were misinterpreting?"

JUDGE UHLIR: "Yes. They were a nuisance around the court. These people have no money to employ a lawyer and they get some one to translate the story to the Judge, and these men are there for that particular purpose. I think we ought to have an official interpreter who would be attached to the court, a man of good reputation who could translate properly and be honest."

Judge Newcomer also said in response to the following question:

THE CHAIRMAN: "Did you ever discover any interpreter misinterpreting?"

JUDGE NEWCOMER: "Not only that, but I have held interpreters to the North Side, three of them. I have fined half a dozen and ordered a number of them to keep out of my courtroom."

Miss Grace Abbott, Director of The Immigrants' Protective League, urged before the committee the importance of supplying certain stations with interpreters. "The present system," says the Director of the League, "results in a miscarriage of justice which injures not only the individual concerned, but often leads an entire colony to lose respect for our courts and to conclude that there is one system of law for the Americans and another for the immigrants." A number of distressing cases were cited by Miss Abbott in support of the need of interpreters.

There are some points which obviously should be covered in an inquiry into the working of the courts.

1. A practical plan for securing a consolidated court in place of a number of different courts.

2. The importance of a non-partisan method of selecting judges.

3. The importance of eliminating political influence from the selection and activity of the courts.

Bibliography

Aschaffenburg, Gustav, "Das Verbrechen und seine Bekämpfung." First edition, Berlin, 1903, 2nd edition, 1906. English edition, "Crime and Its Repression." Boston: Little, Brown & Co., 1913. pp. 331.

Atcherley, Major L. W., "M. O." (Modus Operandi) in Criminal Investigation and Detection." West Riding of Yorkshire, 1913.

Boies, H. M., "The Science of Penology." New York: Putnam, 1901. pp. 459.

Breckinridge and Abbott, "The Delinquent Child and the Home." New York: Charities Publication Committee, 1912. pp. 355.

Brockway, Z. R., "The Reformatory System in the United States. 1900.

Brockway, Z. R., "Fifty Years of Prison Service." New York: Charities Publication Committee, 1912.

Conti, Ugo, "Comments on the American Prison System." Journal of Criminal Law and Criminology. July, 1911. p. 207.

Conyngton, Mary, "Relation Between Occupation and Criminality of Women." Vol. XV of Report of Women and Child Wage Earners in the United States. Washington: Government Printing Office.

Devon, J., "The Criminal and the Community." London: Lane, 1912. pp. 348.

Ellis, Havelock, "The Criminal." Third edition, London: Scott Co., 1907. pp. 419.

Fenton, Frances, "The Influence of Newspaper Presentation Upon the Growth of Crime." Thesis. University of Chicago Press, 1911. pp. 96.

Flexner, Abraham, "Prostitution in Europe." New York, 1914.

Flexner and Baldwin, "Juvenile Courts and Probation." New York: Century, 1914.

Folsom, Chas. F., "Studies of Criminal Responsibility. The Case of Jesse Pomeroy." Privately printed, 1909.

Fosdick, Raymond, "European Police Systems." New York, 1915.

Fuld, Leonhard F., "Police Administration." New York, 1910.

Garolafo, R., "Criminology." English edition, Boston: Little, Brown & Co., 1914. pp. 478.

Goring, Charles, "The English Convict, a Statistical Study." London: Wyman & Sons, 1913. pp. 440

Gross, Hans., "Criminal Psychology." English Translation. Boston: Little Brown & Co., 1911. pp. 514.

Gulick and Ayers, "Medical Inspection of Schools." Chapter XII. Retardation and Physical Defects. New York: Charities Publication Committee, 1908.

Hall, Stanley, "Adolescence." Two vols., pp 589 and 784. New York: Appleton, 1904.

Hayford, Leslie, "Immigration and Crime." Report of the Immigration Commission. Washington: Government Printing Office, 1911. pp. 449.

Healy, William, "The Individual Delinquent." Boston, 1914.

Healy, William, Vide "American Institute of Criminal Law," etc.

Healy, William, Pathological Liars, Accusers and Swindlers." To appear later.

Henderson, Charles R. New York: Vol. I, "Prison Reform and Criminal Law." Vol. II, "Penal and Reformatory Institutions." Charities Publication Committee, 1910.

Hopkins, Tighe, "Wards of the State." New York: Little, Brown & Co., 1913.

Holmes, Arthur, "Conservation of the Child." Philadelphia: Lippincott, 1912. pp. 342.

Holmes, Arthur, "Can Impacted Teeth Cause Delinquency?" Psychological Clinic. March, 1910. pp. 19.

Holmes, Thomas, "London Police Courts." Nelson & Sons, 1900. pp. 384.

Ives, George A., "A History of Penal Methods." London: Stanley, Paul & Co., 1914.

Jones, Robert, "Dementia in Relation to Responsibility" (and discussion). Journal of Mental Science, July, 1912.

CPSIA information can be obtained
at www.ICGtesting.com
Printed in the USA
BVHW090443191219
567066BV00005B/711/P

9 781314 756852